A great cook starts with
the best recipes.

100 RECIPES

ALSO BY THE EDITORS AT AMERICA'S TEST KITCHEN

The Complete Vegetarian Cookbook
The Complete Cooking for Two Cookbook
The New Family Cookbook
The America's Test Kitchen Cooking School Cookbook
The Cook's Illustrated Meat Book
The Cook's Illustrated Baking Book
The Cook's Illustrated Cookbook
The Science of Good Cooking
The America's Test Kitchen Menu Cookbook
The America's Test Kitchen Quick Family Cookbook
The America's Test Kitchen Healthy Family Cookbook
The America's Test Kitchen Family Baking Book

THE AMERICA'S TEST KITCHEN LIBRARY SERIES

The How Can It Be Gluten-Free Cookbook Volume 2
The How Can It Be Gluten-Free Cookbook
The Best Mexican Recipes
The Make-Ahead Cook
Healthy Slow Cooker Revolution
Slow Cooker Revolution Volume 2: The Easy-Prep Edition
Slow Cooker Revolution
The 6-Ingredient Solution
Pressure Cooker Perfection
Comfort Food Makeovers
The America's Test Kitchen D.I.Y. Cookbook
Pasta Revolution
Simple Weeknight Favorites
The Best Simple Recipes

THE TV COMPANION SERIES

The Complete Cook's Country TV Show Cookbook
The Complete America's Test Kitchen TV Show Cookbook 2001–2016
America's Test Kitchen: The TV Companion Cookbook (2009 and 2011–2015 Editions)

AMERICA'S TEST KITCHEN ANNUALS

The Best of America's Test Kitchen (2007–2016 Editions)
Cooking for Two (2010–2013 Editions)
Light & Healthy (2010–2012 Editions)

THE COOK'S COUNTRY SERIES

Cook's Country Eats Local
From Our Grandmothers' Kitchens
Cook's Country Blue Ribbon Desserts
Cook's Country Best Potluck Recipes
Cook's Country Best Lost Suppers
Cook's Country Best Grilling Recipes
The Cook's Country Cookbook
America's Best Lost Recipes

THE BEST RECIPE SERIES

The New Best Recipe
More Best Recipes
The Best One-Dish Suppers
Soups, Stews & Chilis
The Best Skillet Recipes
The Best Slow & Easy Recipes
The Best Chicken Recipes
The Best International Recipe
The Best Make-Ahead Recipe
The Best 30-Minute Recipe
The Best Light Recipe
The Cook's Illustrated Guide to Grilling and Barbecue
Best American Side Dishes
Cover & Bake
Steaks, Chops, Roasts & Ribs
Italian Classics
American Classics

FOR A FULL LISTING OF ALL OUR BOOKS

CooksIllustrated.com
AmericasTestKitchen.com

PRAISE FOR OTHER AMERICA'S TEST KITCHEN TITLES

"Some 2,500 photos walk readers through 600 painstakingly tested recipes, leaving little room for error."
ASSOCIATED PRESS ON *THE AMERICA'S TEST KITCHEN COOKING SCHOOL COOKBOOK*

"Ideal as a reference for the bookshelf . . . will be turned to time and again for definitive instruction on just about any food-related matter."
PUBLISHERS WEEKLY ON *THE SCIENCE OF GOOD COOKING*

"A one-volume kitchen seminar, addressing in one smart chapter after another the sometimes surprising whys behind a cook's best practices. . . . You get the myth, the theory, the science, and the proof, all rigorously interrogated as only America's Test Kitchen can do."
NPR ON *THE SCIENCE OF GOOD COOKING*

"Carnivores with an obsession for perfection will likely have found their new bible in this comprehensive collection."
PUBLISHERS WEEKLY (STARRED REVIEW) ON *THE COOK'S ILLUSTRATED MEAT BOOK*

"This encyclopedia of meat cookery would feel completely overwhelming if it weren't so meticulously organized and artfully designed. This is Cook's Illustrated at its finest."
THE KITCHN ON *THE COOK'S ILLUSTRATED MEAT BOOK*

"This book is a comprehensive, no-nonsense guide . . . a well-thought-out, clearly explained primer for every aspect of home baking."
THE WALL STREET JOURNAL ON *THE COOK'S ILLUSTRATED BAKING BOOK*

"The sum total of exhaustive experimentation . . . anyone interested in gluten-free cookery simply shouldn't be without it."
NIGELLA LAWSON ON *THE HOW CAN IT BE GLUTEN-FREE COOKBOOK*

"Even ultra-experienced gluten-free cooks and bakers will learn something from this thoroughly researched, thoughtfully presented volume."
PUBLISHERS WEEKLY ON *THE HOW CAN IT BE GLUTEN-FREE COOKBOOK*

"The 21st-century *Fannie Farmer Cookbook* or *The Joy of Cooking*. If you had to have one cookbook and that's all you could have, this one would do it."
CBS SAN FRANCISCO ON *THE NEW FAMILY COOKBOOK*

"This book upgrades slow cooking for discriminating, 21st-century palates—that is indeed revolutionary."
THE DALLAS MORNING NEWS ON *SLOW COOKER REVOLUTION*

"One bag, 3 meals? Get the biggest bang for your buck."
FOX NEWS ON *THE MAKE-AHEAD COOK*

"The go-to gift book for newlyweds, small families, or empty nesters."
ORLANDO SENTINEL ON *THE COMPLETE COOKING FOR TWO COOKBOOK*

"Buy this gem for the foodie in your family, and spend the extra money to get yourself a copy too."
THE MISSOURIAN ON *THE BEST OF AMERICA'S TEST KITCHEN 2015*

"The perfect kitchen home companion . . . The practical side of things is very much on display . . . cook-friendly and kitchen-oriented, illuminating the process of preparing food instead of mystifying it."
THE WALL STREET JOURNAL ON *THE COOK'S ILLUSTRATED COOKBOOK*

"If this were the only cookbook you owned, you would cook well, be everyone's favorite host, have a well-run kitchen, and eat happily every day."
THECITYCOOK.COM ON *THE AMERICA'S TEST KITCHEN MENU COOKBOOK*

"This comprehensive collection of 800-plus family and global favorites helps put healthy eating in an everyday context, from meatloaf to Indian curry with chicken."
COOKING LIGHT ON *THE AMERICA'S TEST KITCHEN HEALTHY FAMILY COOKBOOK*

"There are pasta books . . . and then there's this pasta book. Flip your carbohydrate dreams upside down and strain them through this sieve of revolutionary, creative, and also traditional recipes."
SAN FRANCISCO BOOK REVIEW ON *PASTA REVOLUTION*

"These dishes taste as luxurious as their full-fat siblings. Even desserts are terrific."
PUBLISHERS WEEKLY ON *THE BEST LIGHT RECIPE*

"Further proof that practice makes perfect, if not transcendent. . . . If an intermediate cook follows the directions exactly, the results will be better than takeout or Mom's."
THE NEW YORK TIMES ON *THE NEW BEST RECIPE*

"The entire book is stuffed with recipes that will blow your dinner-table audience away like leaves from a sidewalk in November."
SAN FRANCISCO BOOK REVIEW ON *THE COMPLETE COOK'S COUNTRY TV SHOW COOKBOOK*

"Rely on this doorstopper for explicit and comprehensive takes on recipes from basic to sophisticated."
TOLEDO BLADE ON *THE COMPLETE AMERICA'S TEST KITCHEN TV SHOW COOKBOOK*

100
RECIPES

THE ABSOLUTE BEST WAYS TO MAKE THE TRUE ESSENTIALS

THE EDITORS AT AMERICA'S TEST KITCHEN

PHOTOGRAPHY: CARL TREMBLAY   FOOD STYLING: MARIE PIRAINO

BROOKLINE, MASSACHUSETTS

Contents

The Absolute Essentials
CLASSIC RECIPES THAT REALLY MATTER

The Surprising Essentials
INNOVATIVE RECIPES YOU DIDN'T KNOW YOU NEEDED

The Global Essentials
EXCITING RECIPES THAT BRING THE WORLD TO YOUR KITCHEN

Welcome to America's Test Kitchen

This book has been tested, written, and edited by the folks at America's Test Kitchen, a very real 2,500-square-foot kitchen located just outside of Boston. It is the home of *Cook's Illustrated* magazine and *Cook's Country* magazine and is the Monday-through-Friday destination for more than four dozen test cooks, editors, food scientists, tasters, and cookware specialists. Our mission is to test recipes over and over again until we understand how and why they work and until we arrive at the "best" version.

We start the process of testing a recipe with a complete lack of preconceptions, which means that we accept no claim, no theory, no technique, and no recipe at face value. We simply assemble as many variations as possible, test a half-dozen of the most promising, and taste the results blind. We then construct our own hybrid recipe and continue to test it, varying ingredients, techniques, and cooking times until we reach a consensus. The result, we hope, is the best version of a particular recipe, but we realize that only you can be the final judge of our success (or failure). As we like to say in the test kitchen, "We make the mistakes, so you don't have to."

All of this would not be possible without a belief that good cooking, much like good music, is indeed based on a foundation of objective technique. Some people like spicy foods and others don't, but there is a right way to sauté, there is a best way to cook a pot roast, and there are measurable scientific principles involved in producing perfectly beaten, stable egg whites. This is our ultimate goal: to investigate the fundamental principles of cooking so that you become a better cook. It is as simple as that.

If you're curious to see what goes on behind the scenes at America's Test Kitchen, check out our daily blog, The Feed, at AmericasTestKitchenFeed.com, which features kitchen snapshots, exclusive recipes, video tips, and much more. You can watch us work (in our actual test kitchen) by tuning in to *America's Test Kitchen* (AmericasTestKitchen.com) or *Cook's Country from America's Test Kitchen* (CooksCountryTV.com) on public television. Tune in to *America's Test Kitchen Radio* (ATKradio.com) on public radio to listen to insights, tips, and techniques that illuminate the truth about real home cooking. Want to hone your cooking skills or finally learn how to bake—from an America's Test Kitchen test cook? Enroll in a cooking class at our online cooking school at OnlineCookingSchool.com. And find information about subscribing to *Cook's Illustrated* magazine at CooksIllustrated.com or *Cook's Country* magazine at CooksCountry.com. Both magazines are published every other month. However you choose to visit us, we welcome you into our kitchen, where you can stand by our side as we test our way to the best recipes in America.

FACEBOOK.COM/AMERICASTESTKITCHEN

TWITTER.COM/TESTKITCHEN

YOUTUBE.COM/AMERICASTESTKITCHEN

INSTAGRAM.COM/TESTKITCHEN

PINTEREST.COM/TESTKITCHEN

AMERICASTESTKITCHEN.TUMBLR.COM

GOOGLE.COM/+AMERICASTESTKITCHEN

Preface

I grew up spending summers in Vermont and learned to cook from Marie Briggs, the town baker. She could make a roast, baked potatoes, gravy, a few vegetables, and a whole array of fabulous baked goods from anadama bread to molasses cookies, from apple pie to baking powder biscuits. After she passed, I was given her recipes. The surprising thing is that she didn't have that many—just 50 to 75 index cards.

After many decades of home cooking, I have come to the same conclusion that Marie did, that cooking is based on a handful of fundamental principles and building block recipes that teach you most of what you need to know: a stew, a braise, how to steam, a few quick breads, a sauté, a yellow cake, a simple soup, etc. Once you understand how to make a stew, you can make almost any stew.

The problem is that you want these building block recipes to represent the very best way of doing something. There are a thousand ways to roast a chicken, but only a few really good methods, the recipes that are foolproof and turn out the best results. And if you want to cook carrots or grill burgers, you want to know that someone has tested every possible method of cooking those foods so that you have the very best approach at your fingertips.

This is where America's Test Kitchen can be valuable. We really do test a recipe 30 times, 40 times, even 50 up to 100 times. This doesn't mean that we have the only way of preparing a particular recipe but we do have the most foolproof method, the one that you can count on the first time, every time. If we are a tiny bit lucky, we come across game changers, new techniques that make a particular recipe that much better or dependable than other approaches, whether it is to add grated apple to blueberry pie filling (the pectin acts as a natural thickener) or to start steaks and roasts in a low oven to turbo-age the meat using the action of enzymes that break down the protein for more flavor and better texture.

This list of 100 recipes not only covers the bases in terms of what skills and techniques ought to be at the fingertips of a good home cook, it's also a list of our greatest hits—recipes where we think that the test kitchen has added real value and has explored new territory. Put simply, these are the recipes that changed how each of us here at the test kitchen cook at home.

So we can argue about whether a Spanish beef stew should be on the list but the notion of not browning beef for a stew, cooking it with the top off in the oven, and then using a ground-almond thickener, a *picada*, was revelatory for us. We became better cooks and learned techniques that we applied to other recipes.

Here's how I would use this book: Pick the 10 recipes that you are most likely to make time and time again. Make them until you don't need to look at the recipe instructions (nobody remembers ingredients lists!). Now you have become a real cook—you can cook without a recipe and you understand the core principles. Then take another 10 recipes...

If you can cook 20 of the recipes in this book without referring to the instructions then you are now a serious cook and more accomplished than 99 percent of your friends and neighbors. It's really that simple.

And that's all you need to know.

Enjoy!

CHRISTOPHER KIMBALL
Founder and Editor,
Cook's Illustrated and *Cook's Country*
Host, *America's Test Kitchen* and
Cook's Country from America's Test Kitchen

Introduction

The simplicity of a list is awfully appealing. Knowing the 10 best books of the year does make it easier to navigate the bookstore. And if you're lucky enough to find just one new book that you love, then the list has served you well. The same thing is true of lists that cover movies and restaurants.

Among all the lists that people make, we think recipe lists are especially valuable. When coupled with reliable recipes, a thoughtful list will actually make you a better cook. (Of course, this assumes you do more than read the list.) Let us explain why we think a recipe list can be a tool for self-improvement.

Why Lists Matter

If your mother, grandmother, or great grandmother was an accomplished cook, she likely had a very limited repertoire. If her family was lucky, she made several dozen dishes really well. Those dishes were identical (or nearly identical) to the ones made by her mother. In fact, she probably learned these dishes at her mother's side.

So why does this matter? The fact that your grandmother had a manageable list of recipes is one reason—perhaps the main reason—she became a good cook. Repetition and practice are keys to success in the kitchen. A good cook will learn from his or her mistakes and then make a dish better the next time. Make the same dish 10 or 20 times and you're likely to master it. Make the same dish 50 times and it becomes second nature.

In this age of information overload, recipes are a particularly notable example of excess. Google the word "recipe" and you get nearly 50 million results—and that's just in English. AllRecipes.com, the largest recipe website in the United States, has more than 50,000 recipes in its search engine. An inquiry for roast chicken yields 737 results on this website, while someone looking for mashed potatoes will find 1,001 options. And these numbers keep increasing!

A good recipe list can cut through all this clutter. You don't need a thousand brownie recipes, you just need one great one. And if you dedicate yourself to mastering a short list of recipes, you can dramatically improve your cooking skills and your confidence.

The good news is that you don't have to make all 100 recipes in this book. Start with a handful and make them until you understand how each one works in your hands and in your kitchen. Even if you only master 20 recipes in this book you will have earned the right to call yourself an accomplished cook.

The Making of Our List

In addition to its educational function, a recipe list tells us something about our culture—about where we come from as a people and where we are going. We recognize that this is the controversial part of this project—actually picking those recipes that belong and excluding those that don't.

We don't expect you to agree with every recipe on our list. You might think half of them have no place in your kitchen. That's fine. We welcome the conversation. We feel less strongly about the particular recipes on this list—even within our test kitchen we can make arguments for including recipes not in this book—than we do about the act of making, and using, a list.

So how did we create this list? We considered three factors—utility, inventiveness, and diversity. Some recipes are just so useful we couldn't imagine leaving them out. Scrambled eggs, spaghetti with garlic and oil, and roasted broccoli fit the bill. Other recipes highlight our test kitchen at its best—recipes where our work has forced a reevaluation of how a classic dish is prepared. Slow-roasted beef, poached chicken, and pie dough fall into this group. Finally, our nation is changing and our collective taste is becoming more varied and adventurous. And once esoteric ingredients are now available everywhere. It's an incredibly exciting time to cook. We think recipes like pho, Italian almond cake, and vegetable curry all make sense in the 21st-century American home kitchen.

So, let's get started. Whether you're a novice cook looking to improve skills and confidence or a seasoned cook looking for new challenges, mastering a short list of new recipes will help you achieve your goal. Our advice is to flag five recipes in this book and make them each five times over the next three or four months. Select your own top five, or use the fun lists on the following pages to get you thinking.

The List of Lists

Top 5 Recipes for the Reluctant Cook

Bulletproof and nearly impossible to mess up

- SMASHED POTATOES (PAGE 38)
- MAPLE-GLAZED PORK ROAST (PAGE 76)
- FRENCH CHICKEN IN A POT (PAGE 135)
- PASTA CAPRESE (PAGE 180)
- CREAMLESS CREAMY TOMATO SOUP (PAGE 194)

Top 5 Recipes for the Tired Cook

Go-to dishes that get dinner on the table with a minimum of fuss

- WEEKNIGHT ROAST CHICKEN (PAGE 60)
- CRISPY PAN-FRIED PORK CHOPS (PAGE 74)
- PAN-SEARED SHRIMP (PAGE 82)
- SPAGHETTI WITH PECORINO ROMANO AND PEPPER (PAGE 168)
- SKILLET MEATY LASAGNA (PAGE 176)

Top 5 Recipes for the Serious Cook

Cool dishes that announce your food cred

- JUICY PUB-STYLE BURGERS (PAGE 102)
- GRILLED BLACKENED RED SNAPPER (PAGE 148)
- INDONESIAN-STYLE FRIED RICE (PAGE 247)
- PORK LO MEIN (PAGE 298)
- VIETNAMESE BEEF PHO (PAGE 304)

Top 5 Recipes to Make with Kids

Easy enough for children to master and eventually make on their own

- PERFECT SCRAMBLED EGGS (PAGE 8)
- FOOLPROOF VINAIGRETTE (PAGE 18)
- CLASSIC MACARONI AND CHEESE (PAGE 36)
- BLUEBERRY PANCAKES (PAGE 54)
- CHEWY BROWNIES (PAGE 120)

Top 5 Recipes to Teach Your Teenagers

Easy to execute, even in a cramped dorm or studio apartment

- PERFECT FRIED EGGS (PAGE 11)
- PASTA WITH GARLIC AND OIL (AGLIO E OLIO) (PAGE 22)
- STIR-FRIED BEEF AND BROCCOLI WITH OYSTER SAUCE (PAGE 64)
- CRISP ROASTED POTATOES (PAGE 42)
- QUINOA PILAF WITH HERBS AND LEMON (PAGE 212)

Top 5 Recipes for Two

Easily scaled down and perfect for date night

- GROWN-UP GRILLED CHEESE SANDWICHES (PAGE 51)
- POACHED SALMON WITH HERB AND CAPER VINAIGRETTE (PAGE 145)
- CHEESE SOUFFLÉ (PAGE 188)
- GRILLED ARGENTINE STEAKS WITH CHIMICHURRI SAUCE (PAGE 310)
- PORK SCHNITZEL (PAGE 314)

Top 5 Recipes You Can Make Without a Trip to the Supermarket

What to make from pantry staples and a bare fridge

- FLUFFY OMELET (PAGE 14)
- QUICK TOMATO SAUCE (PAGE 28)
- RICE PILAF (PAGE 45)
- ALMOST HANDS-FREE RISOTTO WITH PARMESAN (PAGE 254)
- ULTIMATE BANANA BREAD (PAGE 224)

Top 5 Recipes for the Budget-Minded Cook

Cheap ingredients can deliver luxe flavor

- SLOW-ROASTED BEEF (PAGE 158)
- GRILLED STEAK WITH NEW MEXICAN CHILE RUB (PAGE 150)
- SLOW-ROASTED PORK SHOULDER WITH PEACH SAUCE (PAGE 161)
- MOROCCAN CHICKEN WITH OLIVES AND LEMON (PAGE 276)
- TORTILLA SOUP (PAGE 291)

Top 5 Recipes for the Health-Minded Cook

"Good for you" doesn't have to be boring or bland

- PAN-SEARED CHICKEN BREASTS (PAGE 57)
- CRUNCHY OVEN-FRIED FISH (PAGE 80)
- PERFECT POACHED CHICKEN BREASTS (PAGE 132)
- GRILLED GLAZED PORK TENDERLOIN ROAST (PAGE 164)
- GRILLED THAI BEEF SALAD (PAGE 302)

Top 5 Recipes for the Traditional Cook

Familiar recipes made even better

- CLASSIC BASIL PESTO (PAGE 25)
- PAN-SEARED THICK-CUT STRIP STEAKS (PAGE 70)
- CLASSIC CHICKEN NOODLE SOUP (PAGE 94)
- MODERN BEEF BURGUNDY (PAGE 154)
- CHOCOLATE POTS DE CRÈME (PAGE 334)

Top 5 Recipes for the Novice Baker

Dead-simple stuff for cooks who don't bake much
- DROP BISCUITS (PAGE 111)
- ALL-PURPOSE CORNBREAD (PAGE 114)
- ULTIMATE CHOCOLATE CHIP COOKIES (PAGE 117)
- ALMOST NO-KNEAD BREAD (PAGE 220)
- SKILLET APPLE PIE (PAGE 227)

Top 5 Recipes for the Accomplished Baker

When you're ready to tackle a project
- BLUEBERRY PIE (PAGE 126)
- FLUFFY YELLOW LAYER CAKE WITH CHOCOLATE FROSTING (PAGE 230)
- ROSEMARY FOCACCIA (PAGE 324)
- BRITISH-STYLE CURRANT SCONES (PAGE 321)
- ITALIAN ALMOND CAKE (PAGE 328)

Top 5 Recipes for Vegetarians

Hearty mains everyone will enjoy
- SPRING VEGETABLE PASTA (PAGE 170)
- FARMHOUSE VEGETABLE AND BARLEY SOUP (PAGE 198)
- CREAMY PARMESAN POLENTA (PAGE 216)
- RICE AND LENTILS WITH CRISPY ONIONS (MUJADDARA) (PAGE 244)
- INDIAN CURRY WITH POTATOES, CAULIFLOWER, PEAS, AND CHICKPEAS (PAGE 266)

Top 5 Recipes That Will Change Your Mind

See common vegetables in a whole new light
- ROASTED BROCCOLI (PAGE 48)
- CREAMY CAULIFLOWER SOUP (PAGE 192)
- BRAISED RED POTATOES WITH LEMON AND CHIVES (PAGE 204)
- SLOW-COOKED WHOLE CARROTS (PAGE 210)
- MEXICAN-STYLE GRILLED CORN (PAGE 262)

Top 5 Recipes for Anyone Bored with Chicken

Shake up plain old chicken with these big flavors
- PERUVIAN ROAST CHICKEN WITH GARLIC AND LIME (PAGE 273)
- TANDOORI CHICKEN (PAGE 279)
- FILIPINO CHICKEN ADOBO (PAGE 282)
- THAI-STYLE CHICKEN WITH BASIL (PAGE 285)
- GRILLED CHICKEN SOUVLAKI (PAGE 288)

Top 5 Recipes for a Lazy Sunday Afternoon

When you want to hang around the kitchen all day
- CLASSIC SPAGHETTI AND MEATBALLS FOR A CROWD (PAGE 32)
- CLASSIC POT ROAST (PAGE 86)
- BEST CHICKEN STEW (PAGE 142)
- HEARTY TUSCAN BEAN STEW (PAGE 270)
- SPICY MEXICAN SHREDDED PORK (TINGA) TOSTADAS (PAGE 318)

Top 5 Recipes to Make for the Holidays

When getting the classics right really matters
- ROAST BEEF TENDERLOIN (PAGE 66)
- BRAISED TURKEY WITH GRAVY (PAGE 105)
- GLAZED SPIRAL-SLICED HAM (PAGE 108)
- MASHED SWEET POTATOES (PAGE 206)
- GLAZED BUTTER COOKIES (PAGE 123)

Top 5 Recipes for a Potluck

Portable and popular—and they won't break the bank
- SWEET AND TANGY BARBECUED CHICKEN (PAGE 90)
- BAKED MANICOTTI (PAGE 174)
- FRENCH POTATO SALAD WITH MUSTARD AND HERBS (PAGE 183)
- BEST VEGETARIAN CHILI (PAGE 200)
- ENCHILADAS VERDES (PAGE 294)

Top 5 Recipes for a Casual Party

Crowd pleasers that start the celebration
- ULTIMATE BEEF CHILI (PAGE 98)
- BARBECUED PULLED CHICKEN (PAGE 138)
- CUBAN-STYLE BLACK BEANS AND RICE (PAGE 240)
- GRILLED FISH TACOS (PAGE 260)
- CHOCOLATE CUPCAKES WITH GANACHE FILLING (PAGE 234)

Top 5 Recipes for an Elegant Dinner Party

Sophisticated fare for Saturday night
- PAELLA (PAGE 250)
- SALAD WITH HERBED BAKED GOAT CHEESE (PAGE 186)
- PORK AND CABBAGE POTSTICKERS (PAGE 256)
- CATALAN-STYLE BEEF STEW WITH MUSHROOMS (PAGE 308)
- PERFECT LATIN FLAN (PAGE 330)

The Absolute Essentials

CLASSIC RECIPES THAT REALLY MATTER

1 Scrambled Eggs

THE FASTEST WAY TO MAKE A MEAL

Nothing cooks as quickly—and tastes so satisfying—as an egg. A proper dish of scrambled eggs should tumble out of the skillet into soft, creamy curds. But great scrambled eggs require finesse. In fact, scrambled eggs might just be the easiest dish everyone gets wrong. The first mistake is assuming that nature knows best.

Just because an egg contains a set ratio of whites to yolks doesn't mean you should follow suit. Whites are rich in proteins (which help turn liquid eggs into a semisolid when cooked) as well as water, while yolks provide the fat and the flavor. We found that adding a couple extra yolks not only enriches the egg flavor, but also helps stave off overcooking, because the extra fat and emulsifiers in the yolks raise the coagulation temperature. For the same reason, we prefer half-and-half instead of the usual milk. More fat means less chance of overcooking the eggs—and richer flavor.

The right technique is just as important. Most novice cooks use too much heat and the eggs turn out tough and watery. Excess heat actually wrings moisture out of the eggs (much like a sponge), leaving tough curds in a sea of unappealing liquid.

That said, a blast of heat is essential to convert some of the moisture in the eggs to steam. (It's the steam that makes scrambled eggs fluffy.) We recommend starting the eggs over medium-high heat and then turning the heat to low. If working on an electric stovetop, use a second burner (heated on low) to create scrambled eggs that will be a revelation, even to seasoned cooks.

WHY THIS RECIPE WORKS

Crack Cleanly
There's nothing worse than bits of shell in the finished dish. Don't crack eggs on the rim of a bowl. A flat surface, such as the counter, ensures the cleanest break.

Scramble Thoroughly But Gently
Many cooks mistakenly think that "scrambled" refers to the cooking method. In fact, the eggs are scrambled (to combine the whites and yolks) before they go into the pan. Don't bother with a whisk or mixer, which will overbeat the eggs; a fork is the simplest and best tool for the job.

Small Nonstick Pan + Butter
You could make scrambled eggs in a conventional pan (cooks did for many centuries), but nonstick makes it so much easier. A well-seasoned cast-iron pan can work and is the best alternative if you don't use nonstick. For eight eggs, we use a 10-inch pan—crowding the eggs in the pan traps steam and ensures fluffy results. Use an 8-inch pan when cooking four eggs (or less). Whatever the pan material or size, don't bother making scrambled eggs unless you're willing to use butter.

The Right Fold
Despite what you might think, the eggs shouldn't be stirred constantly while they cook. Instead, fold them with a rubber spatula into a tidy (and high) pile that traps steam. More steam means more volume. So, for light, tender eggs, be gentle and use a rubber spatula.

Overbeating will make the eggs tough so combine the yolks and whites with a fork. A nonstick pan guarantees an easy release but you still need butter for flavor.

Perfect Scrambled Eggs

SERVES 4

It's important to follow visual cues, as skillet thickness will have an effect on cooking times. If using an electric stovetop, heat a second burner on low and slide the pan to the cooler burner for the final cooking time over low heat.

8 large eggs plus 2 large yolks	¼ teaspoon pepper
¼ cup half-and-half	1 tablespoon unsalted butter, chilled
Salt	

1. Adjust oven rack to middle position and heat oven to 200 degrees. Place 4 heat-proof plates on rack.

2. Beat eggs and yolks, half-and-half, ¼ teaspoon salt, and pepper with fork until thoroughly combined and mixture is pure yellow; do not overbeat.

3. Melt butter in 10-inch nonstick skillet over medium-high heat (butter should not brown), swirling pan to coat. Add egg mixture and, using heat-resistant rubber spatula, constantly and firmly scrape along bottom and sides of skillet until eggs begin to clump and spatula leaves trail on bottom of skillet, 1½ to 2½ minutes. Reduce heat to low and gently but constantly fold eggs until clumped and slightly wet, 30 to 60 seconds. Immediately transfer eggs to warmed plates and season with salt to taste. Serve immediately.

PERFECT SCRAMBLED EGGS FOR TWO

Use 4 large eggs plus 1 large yolk, 2 tablespoons half-and-half, ⅛ teaspoon salt, ⅛ teaspoon pepper, and ½ tablespoon butter. Cook eggs in 8-inch skillet for 45 to 75 seconds over medium-high heat and then 30 to 60 seconds over low heat.

PERFECT SCRAMBLED EGGS FOR ONE

Use 2 large eggs plus 1 large yolk, 1 tablespoon half-and-half, pinch salt, pinch pepper, and ¼ tablespoon butter. Cook eggs in 8-inch skillet for 30 to 60 seconds over medium-high heat and then 30 to 60 seconds over low heat.

SMOKED SALMON SCRAMBLED EGGS WITH CHIVE BUTTER

Mash 3 tablespoons softened unsalted butter with 3 tablespoons minced fresh chives. Toast 4 (1-inch-thick) slices rustic white bread, then spread with 2 tablespoons chive butter. Cook eggs as directed, first melting remaining chive butter in pan. Immediately spoon eggs on top of buttered toasts, top with 3 ounces smoked salmon, and serve. Garnish with extra chives if desired.

RECIPE DETAILS

Timeline

- 5 minutes (including prep)

Essential Tools

- 10-inch nonstick skillet
- Fork
- Heat-resistant rubber spatula

Substitutions & Variations

- If using extra-large eggs, reduce the number of whole eggs to seven.
- If using jumbo eggs, reduce the number of whole eggs to six.
- If you don't have half-and-half, substitute 2 tablespoons plus 2 teaspoons milk plus 4 teaspoons heavy cream.
- Most electric stovetops do not react quickly enough for the change in heat level (from medium-high to low) as directed in the recipe; instead, preheat a second burner on low and slide the skillet onto the cooler burner at the appropriate time.
- If you like, dress up these eggs by folding in 2 tablespoons minced fresh parsley, chives, basil, or cilantro, or 1 tablespoon minced fresh dill or tarragon, after reducing the heat to low.
- Use the recipe with smoked salmon as a template for turning scrambled eggs into a hearty meal. Replace salmon with sautéed mushrooms, caramelized onions, sautéed peppers, crisp bacon, or browned sausage rounds.

2 Fried Eggs

THE SECOND FASTEST WAY TO MAKE A MEAL

As far as we're concerned, a fried egg should be fried. That's how it's done at the best diners: sunny-side up and crisp on the underside and edges, with a tender opaque white and a perfectly runny yolk.

Maybe it's the lack of a hot, slick commercial griddle or a short-order cook's expertise, but most eggs fried at home fall short in one of two ways: The first likely problem is undercooked whites—specifically, a slippery transparent ring of white surrounding the yolk. The second common flaw is an overcooked yolk—often it is fluid on top but cooked solid on the underside.

These faults are due to a predicament that plagues most egg cookery: Yolks and whites set at different temperatures. This means that yolks, which start to solidify at 158 degrees, are inevitably overcooked by the time the whites set up at 180 degrees. The goal when frying eggs—to have the yolks less set than the whites—would seem impossible, except for the fact that diner cooks regularly succeed.

There are two basic approaches for tackling an egg's disparate doneness temperatures: Cook low and slow, or cook hot and fast. The former calls for breaking the eggs into a warm, greased skillet over low heat and letting the whites gradually firm up, hoping that very little heat actually reaches the yolks. Even if it works, this method produces no browning.

The opposite method blasts the eggs with the goal of getting them out of the pan before the yolks have time to set up. Clearly, strong heat is necessary to achieve any crispness, but how can you manage this process when there are multiple eggs in the pan, each demanding rapid-fire attention? Our solution combines both methods for perfect results.

WHY THIS RECIPE WORKS

Bowls Ensure a Consistent Start
Many home cooks crack the eggs directly in the pan. Not only can bits of shell end up in the pan, but this process takes a minute or so, which means the first egg is racing ahead of the last egg. Cracking four eggs into two small bowls, and then simultaneously pouring the eggs into the pan from either side, ensures that all the eggs start and finish at the same time. And you can fish out any bits of shell before the cooking begins.

Preheat the Pan Over Low Heat
Hot spots are a particular problem with the hot and fast cooking method. Letting the pan heat for 5 minutes over low before turning the heat up ensures that the entire pan is evenly heated. A nonstick pan is a must when cooking eggs, and a large pan (at least 12 inches in diameter) provides ample room to fry four eggs.

Use Oil and Butter
Adding a little vegetable oil to the pan helps the cook gauge the temperature. Once the heat is raised to medium-high the oil should quickly shimmer, indicating the pan is hot enough to fry the eggs. At this point, we add a pat of butter—the milk proteins help brown the edges of the eggs. Don't add the butter at the outset, with the oil, or it might burn. Once the butter melts, the eggs can be slid into the pan.

Cover It Up, Finish Off the Heat
Adding a lid to the skillet traps heat and steam so the eggs cook from above as well as below, which helps the whites to firm up before the yolks overcook. Moving the pan off the heat after 1 minute of covered cooking allows the whites to finish cooking—gently—while keeping the yolks liquid.

Dividing the eggs into small bowls is the first step to perfect cooking. And don't forget the lid, which traps heat and prevents slippery whites.

Perfect Fried Eggs

SERVES 2

When checking for doneness, lift the lid just a crack to prevent loss of steam should the eggs need further cooking. When cooked, the thin layer of white surrounding the yolk will turn opaque. If desired, serve with Oven-Fried Bacon (page 54).

2 teaspoons vegetable oil

4 large eggs

Salt and pepper

2 teaspoons unsalted butter, cut into 4 pieces and chilled

1. Heat oil in 12- or 14-inch nonstick skillet over low heat for 5 minutes. Meanwhile, crack 2 eggs into small bowl and season with salt and pepper. Repeat with remaining 2 eggs and second small bowl.

2. Increase heat to medium-high and heat until oil is shimmering. Add butter to skillet and quickly swirl to coat pan. Working quickly, pour 1 bowl of eggs in 1 side of pan and second bowl of eggs in other side. Cover and cook for 1 minute. Remove skillet from burner and let stand, covered, 15 to 45 seconds for runny yolks (white around edge of yolk will be barely opaque), 45 to 60 seconds for soft but set yolks, and about 2 minutes for medium-set yolks. Slide eggs onto plates and serve.

SPAGHETTI WITH FRIED EGGS AND BREAD CRUMBS   SERVES 4

Be sure to cook the eggs just before serving, so that the yolks will still be runny and help create the sauce. Rather than using vegetable oil and butter, fry the eggs in 4 teaspoons olive oil.

2 slices hearty white sandwich bread, torn into quarters

½ cup extra-virgin olive oil

Salt and pepper

4 garlic cloves, minced

1 pound spaghetti

1 ounce Parmesan cheese, grated (½ cup), plus extra for serving

1 recipe Perfect Fried Eggs

1. Adjust oven rack to middle position and heat oven to 375 degrees. Pulse bread in food processor to coarse crumbs, about 10 pulses. Toss crumbs with 2 tablespoons oil, season with salt and pepper, and spread over rimmed baking sheet. Bake, stirring often, until golden, 8 to 10 minutes.

2. Cook 3 tablespoons oil, garlic, and ¼ teaspoon salt in 12- or 14-inch nonstick skillet over low heat, stirring constantly, until garlic foams and is sticky and straw-colored, 8 to 10 minutes; transfer to bowl.

3. Meanwhile, bring 4 quarts water to boil in large pot. Add pasta and 1 tablespoon salt and cook, stirring often, until al dente. Reserve 1 cup cooking water, then drain pasta and return it to pot. Add Parmesan, remaining 3 tablespoons oil, garlic mixture, and ½ cup reserved pasta cooking water and toss to combine.

4. During final 5 minutes of pasta cooking time, wipe now-empty skillet clean with paper towels and place over low heat for 5 minutes. Fry eggs as directed, making sure yolks are still runny.

5. Season pasta with salt and pepper to taste, and add more reserved cooking water as needed to adjust consistency. Top individual portions with bread crumbs and fried egg and serve, passing extra Parmesan separately.

RECIPE DETAILS

Timeline

• 10 minutes (including prep)

Essential Tools

• 12- or 14-inch nonstick skillet with lid
• 2 small bowls
• Plastic spatula/turner

Substitutions & Variations

• To cook two eggs, use an 8- or 9-inch nonstick skillet and halve the amounts of oil and butter.

• You can use this method with extra-large or jumbo eggs without altering the timing.

• In addition to serving fried eggs over pasta, you can use them to turn salad greens (spinach is especially nice) into a light meal. As with the pasta, the runny yolk helps to moisten the greens.

• For the ultimate breakfast sandwich, fry the eggs in rendered bacon fat or sausage grease. Cook the meat first, drain off all but 1 tablespoon of fat, and then fry the eggs as directed in the same pan. Once the eggs are cooked to your liking, top each egg with the bacon or sausage and a single slice of American cheese. Replace the lid and continue to let stand (the pan is still off the heat) just until the cheese begins to melt. Sandwich the egg-meat-cheese combo in a toasted and buttered English muffin, along with baby spinach and/or a thin slice of tomato, and serve immediately.

3 Omelet

A SECRET INGREDIENT CREATES AN OMELET FOR TWO THAT'S LIGHT, NOT HEAVY

A single omelet is the perfect meal for two. Too bad almost everyone makes this dish incorrectly. To avoid the hassle of making two omelets in sequence, many cooks make a single super-size omelet with too many eggs and too much filling. This "more is better" approach loses the qualities that make omelets so appealing in the first place—their sophistication and their delicacy.

These mega-omelets also fail on a technical level. With so much stuff in the pan, the exterior becomes tough and over-browned while you wait—and wait—for the interior to cook through. If you try to prevent excessive browning, you're pretty much guaranteed a seriously runny (OK, raw) center.

Luckily, there is a solution to this dilemma—one that yields an omelet big enough for two that's still light. The fluffy omelet is made with whipped eggs to achieve an impressive height that's not just about appearance. The interior is airy, almost like a soufflé.

Many recipes call for whipping whole eggs but we find that whipping the whites is a better approach. Whipping the whites creates maximum volume so the omelet is extra tall and fluffy. And since the eggs are separated, we can add fat (in the form of butter) to the yolks for increased tenderness and flavor. (Since fat prevents a foam from forming you can't do this when whipping whole eggs.)

Another appeal of this approach is the nearly hands-off cooking. Once everything is added, the hot pan goes into the oven. The all-around heat encourages maximum puff and cooks the center through. And because the heat is coming from all directions, there's no risk of the bottom overcooking.

WHY THIS RECIPE WORKS

A Little Acid Helps the Whites
Whipped egg whites are mostly air and quickly revert to their natural liquid state. Cream of tartar—a dry acid used in many baking recipes, such as angel food cake—delays the formation of the foam, which ends up creating a stronger network of egg proteins surrounding the air bubbles in the foam. In short, the acid makes for a more stable egg foam and a lighter omelet. What is cream of tartar? It's actually the white powder that forms on the inside of wine barrels. No need to know a winemaker. Cream of tartar is sold in the spice aisle of the supermarket.

Fold, Don't Beat
Once the eggs are whipped, the yolks (first enriched with melted butter and seasoned with a little salt) are folded in. Use a rubber spatula—not a stand mixer—for this part of the recipe. You want the egg mixture to be uniform but you also don't want to beat all the air out of the whipped whites.

Spread Evenly
The eggs for a regular omelet are simply poured into the hot pan. In this recipe, the egg mixture is quite stiff so keep that rubber spatula handy and spread the eggs to ensure even coverage.

Fill Early
Many recipes fill the nearly finished omelet and then fold it in half. But this method means the filling never really warms through or meshes with the eggs. Filling the omelet at the outset (right after the eggs are added to the pan) means that every bite contains cheese and vegetables and the whole thing is piping hot.

An unlikely ingredient creates a stable foam when whipping egg whites. This fluffy omelet is filled before it goes into the oven—so just fold, divide, and serve.

Fluffy Omelet

SERVES 2

The pan used to cook the filling can be wiped clean and used to cook the omelet.

4 large eggs, separated
1 tablespoon unsalted butter, melted, plus 1 tablespoon unsalted butter
¼ teaspoon salt
¼ teaspoon cream of tartar
1 recipe filling (recipes follow)
1 ounce Parmesan cheese, grated (½ cup)

1. Adjust oven rack to middle position and heat oven to 375 degrees. Whisk egg yolks, melted butter, and salt together in bowl. Place egg whites in bowl of stand mixer and sprinkle cream of tartar over surface. Fit stand mixer with whisk and whip egg whites on medium-low speed until foamy, 2 to 2½ minutes. Increase speed to medium-high and whip until stiff peaks just start to form, 2 to 3 minutes. Using rubber spatula, fold egg yolk mixture into egg whites until no white streaks remain.

2. Heat remaining 1 tablespoon butter in 12-inch ovensafe nonstick skillet over medium-high heat, swirling to coat bottom of pan. When butter foams, quickly add egg mixture, spreading into even layer with spatula. Remove pan from heat and gently sprinkle filling and Parmesan evenly over top of omelet. Transfer to oven and cook until center of omelet springs back when lightly pressed, 4½ minutes for slightly wet omelet and 5 minutes for dry omelet.

3. Run spatula around edges of omelet to loosen, shaking gently to release. Slide omelet onto cutting board and let stand for 30 seconds. Using spatula, fold omelet in half. Cut omelet in half crosswise and serve immediately.

ASPARAGUS AND SMOKED SALMON FILLING MAKES ¾ CUP

1 teaspoon olive oil
1 shallot, sliced thin
5 ounces asparagus, trimmed and cut on bias into ¼-inch lengths
Salt and pepper
1 ounce smoked salmon, chopped
½ teaspoon lemon juice

Heat oil in 12-inch nonstick skillet over medium-high heat until shimmering. Add shallot and cook until softened and starting to brown, about 2 minutes. Add asparagus, pinch salt, and pepper to taste, and cook, stirring frequently, until crisp-tender, 5 to 7 minutes. Transfer asparagus mixture to bowl and stir in salmon and lemon juice.

MUSHROOM FILLING MAKES ¾ CUP

1 teaspoon olive oil
1 shallot, sliced thin
4 ounces white or cremini mushrooms, trimmed and chopped
Salt and pepper
1 teaspoon balsamic vinegar

Heat oil in 12-inch nonstick skillet over medium-high heat until shimmering. Add shallot and cook until softened, about 2 minutes. Add mushrooms and ⅛ teaspoon

RECIPE DETAILS

Timeline

• 15 minutes to preheat oven and make filling
• 5 minutes to whip egg whites and combine with yolks, butter, and salt
• 5 minutes to heat skillet and layer ingredients into pan
• 5 minutes to bake omelet

Essential Tools

• 12-inch ovensafe nonstick skillet
• Electric mixer (preferably stand mixer)
• Rubber spatula

Substitutions & Variations

• A teaspoon of distilled white vinegar or lemon juice can be used in place of the cream of tartar.
• A handheld mixer or a whisk can be used in place of a stand mixer, although the timing will be different.
• Other grated or shredded cheeses can be used in place of the Parmesan; choose something potent so a little goes a long way. Good choices include Pecorino, fontina, Gruyère, and sharp cheddar.
• The filling recipes have been specifically designed for this omelet. That said, you can use one of the filling recipes as a template for available ingredients. Vegetables and meats should be precooked to drive off excess moisture and fat and chopped small so they don't tear the omelet. And don't overstuff the omelet—¾ cup of filling is plenty.

salt and season with pepper to taste. Cook until liquid has evaporated and mushrooms begin to brown, 6 to 8 minutes. Transfer mixture to bowl and stir in vinegar.

ARTICHOKE AND BACON FILLING MAKES ¾ CUP

2 slices bacon, cut into ¼-inch pieces
1 shallot, sliced thin
5 ounces frozen artichoke hearts, thawed, patted dry, and chopped

Salt and pepper
½ teaspoon lemon juice

Cook bacon in 12-inch nonstick skillet over medium-high heat until crisp, 3 to 6 minutes. Transfer bacon to paper towel–lined plate. Pour off all but 1 teaspoon fat from skillet. Add shallot and cook until softened, about 2 minutes. Add artichokes, ⅛ teaspoon salt, and pepper to taste. Cook, stirring frequently, until beginning to brown, 6 to 8 minutes. Transfer artichoke mixture to bowl and stir in bacon and lemon juice.

A Better Way to Whip Egg Whites

The first step to accomplishing this task is separating the whites cleanly from the yolks. This is best done when the eggs are cold because the yolks are more taut and less likely to break. Even a speck of yolk can interfere with the whites' ability to create a stable foam, so we employ a special method for separating the whites that allows the cook to discard an egg if the yolk breaks.

1. For cleanest break (and fewest bits of shell), crack side of egg against flat surface, rather than edge of counter or side of mixing bowl.

2. Use 3-bowl method to separate eggs. Separate egg over first bowl, letting white fall into bowl. Transfer yolk to second bowl. If white has no traces of yolk, pour it into third bowl. Repeat process with each egg.

3. Whip egg whites and pinch cream of tartar on medium-low speed until foamy. (A slow start creates more volume and acidic cream of tartar promotes stability.)

4. Increase speed to medium-high and continue beating, gradually adding sugar in sweet recipes. Continue to whip whites to soft peaks (whites will droop slightly from end of whisk) or stiff peaks (whites will stand tall from end of whisk). If whites begin to look curdled or separated, you have gone too far and must start over.

4 Vinaigrette

REAL COOKS DON'T USE BOTTLED DRESSING

A vinaigrette is the simplest of the great French sauces to prepare. That doesn't mean it's easy, though. Despite the fact that there are only two main ingredients, turning oil and vinegar into a dressing that transforms unadorned greens into a finished, well-balanced salad is often hit or miss for most cooks.

The best vinaigrettes do their job quietly, complementing the greens without dominating them or engaging in combat. But all too often vinaigrettes can seem harsh and bristling in one bite, only to be dull and oily in the next. That's because oil and vinegar, like oil and water, naturally repel each other and getting a stable emulsion requires more than just the right whisking technique.

Given the challenges here, it's no wonder that many cooks turn to bottled dressings, which rely on a laundry list of preservatives and stabilizers to keep the oil and vinegar emulsified. Yes, bottled dressings are consistent (no worries about vinegary bites followed by oily bites) but they are also consistently bad. Many contain loads of sugar (yuck!) and dried herbs. Salad should taste fresh, not stale, and that means you must (and we really mean it) make your own dressing.

Enough browbeating. Once you master the basic technique (and use our secret stabilizing ingredient that keeps the vinegar and oil together long enough to dress and serve the salad), making vinaigrette will become second nature—something you can do without consulting a recipe and something you can vary almost endlessly. It's just two ingredients, plus seasonings, after all.

WHY THIS RECIPE WORKS

Get the Ratio Right
Modern recipes often call for 4 parts oil and 1 part vinegar. We find this formula yields a bland, greasy dressing. It turns out that slack attention to mixing (modern recipes tend to favor the dump-and-stir or dump-and-shake method) has bumped up the oil-to-vinegar ratio to mitigate the effects of an improperly emulsified dressing. The 3:1 ratio found in classic French cookbooks is correct.

Whisk Slowly, and Don't Shake
Vinaigrette relies on the principle of emulsification—the combination of two ingredients that don't ordinarily mix, in this case oil and vinegar. In kitchen tests, we found that two common methods—shaking ingredients together in a jar or dumping the vinegar and oil into a bowl and whisking them together—both produce harsh results. In contrast, the classic technique (slowly whisking the oil into the vinegar) yields an emulsified dressing that tastes smoother, at least at the outset.

Double Up on Emulsifiers
Even a well-made vinaigrette, made by slowly whisking in the oil, will quickly taste harsh. That's because vinegar is 95 percent water and the vinegar and oil separate after just a few minutes. To make vinaigrette more stable, some recipes call for mustard, which contains polysaccharides (complex sugars) that bond the oil and vinegar molecules together. But the emulsifier in mustard isn't terribly strong so you have to use too much mustard for our taste. Supplementing a small amount of mustard with a dollop of mayonnaise keeps the dressing emulsified for 90 minutes. The lecithin in the egg yolks is the magic compound that bonds the vinegar and oil molecules together.

Add Seasonings to Vinegar
Salt won't dissolve in oil, so for even seasoning add the salt (and other seasonings and the emulsifiers) to the vinegar and then start whisking in the oil. Herbs can be added to the finished dressing.

Use a whisk (rather than a fork) to produce a stable dressing that won't separate.

Foolproof Vinaigrette

MAKES ABOUT ¼ CUP

You can use red wine, white wine, or champagne vinegar here; however, it is important to use high-quality ingredients. Use about 2 tablespoons of this dressing per 4 cups greens, serving two.

1 tablespoon wine vinegar	½ teaspoon Dijon mustard
1½ teaspoons minced shallot	Salt and pepper
½ teaspoon regular or light mayonnaise	3 tablespoons extra-virgin olive oil

1. Combine vinegar, shallot, mayonnaise, mustard, ⅛ teaspoon salt, and pepper to taste in small bowl. Whisk until mixture is milky in appearance and no lumps of mayonnaise remain.

2. Place oil in small measuring cup so that it is easy to pour. Whisking constantly, very slowly drizzle oil into vinegar mixture. If pools of oil gather on surface as you whisk, stop addition of oil and whisk mixture well to combine, then resume whisking in oil in slow stream. Vinaigrette should be glossy and lightly thickened, with no pools of oil on its surface. (Vinaigrette can be refrigerated for up to 2 weeks. Rewhisk before using.)

LEMON VINAIGRETTE

Substitute fresh lemon juice for vinegar, omit shallot, and add ¼ teaspoon finely grated lemon zest and pinch of sugar along with salt and pepper.

BALSAMIC-MUSTARD VINAIGRETTE

Substitute balsamic vinegar for wine vinegar, increase mustard to 2 teaspoons, and add ½ teaspoon chopped fresh thyme along with salt and pepper.

WALNUT VINAIGRETTE

Substitute 1½ tablespoons roasted walnut oil and 1½ tablespoons regular olive oil for extra-virgin olive oil.

HERB VINAIGRETTE

Add 1 tablespoon minced fresh parsley or chives and ½ teaspoon minced fresh thyme, tarragon, marjoram, or oregano to vinaigrette just before using.

RECIPE DETAILS

Timeline

- 5 minutes (including prep)

Essential Tools

- Whisk
- Liquid measuring cup for pouring oil
- Small bowl

Substitutions & Variations

- This recipe is only as good as the ingredients that go into it. Extra-virgin olive oil is a must. Don't bother with bland substitutes like vegetable oil.
- The master recipe (as well as the walnut and herb variations) works with nearly any type of greens. The lemon vinaigrette is especially designed for mild greens and the balsamic dressing is best with assertive greens.
- The recipe can be doubled or tripled; just make sure to use a larger bowl.
- For a hint of garlic flavor, rub the inside of the salad bowl with a clove of garlic before adding the lettuce.
- Grated orange or lime zest can be used instead of lemon zest. Lime juice works on its own as the sole acid in the recipe; orange juice needs a stronger partner— a shot of sherry vinegar is nice.
- Spices can be used in place of herbs but you will need far less. A pinch of curry powder goes a long way. Seeds (poppy or sesame) are another option for finishing the dressing.

A Better Way to Dress a Salad

Most cooks, even good ones, don't do a very good job when it comes to dressing a salad. There are two key things you must get right—cleaning (especially drying) the greens and coating the greens evenly but lightly. Many a salad suffers from soggy, over-dressed greens. A salad spinner is essential.

1. Fill salad spinner bowl with cool water, add greens, and gently swish them around. Let grit settle to bottom of bowl, then lift greens out and drain water. Repeat until greens no longer release any dirt.

2. Dry greens, stopping several times to dump out excess moisture.

3. Blot greens dry on paper towels. (Even the best salad spinner won't remove all the water.) To refrigerate greens for several days, roll them in paper towels and slip towels inside large plastic bag.

4. Tear greens into bite-size pieces when ready to make salad. You need 2 cups of greens per serving. Place greens in wide bowl with plenty of room for tossing.

5. Rewhisk dressing if made in advance and then drizzle small amount over greens. Figure on 1 tablespoon of dressing per serving of greens but add less than this amount to start.

6. Toss greens with tongs or 2 large forks or spoons, taste, and add more dressing if needed. (Until greens have been well tossed it's impossible to judge whether they need more dressing. You can always add more, but there's no fix for an overdressed salad.)

5 Spaghetti with Garlic and Oil

BECAUSE YOU ALWAYS HAVE THE INGREDIENTS ON HAND

Pasta with garlic and oil looks guileless. It reads as "tangle of spaghetti flecked with parsley." Its aroma and flavor, however, shout garlic in every register. Few dishes require so little work and deliver so much satisfaction. It's the favorite late night meal of Italians and tired cooks everywhere who want maximum pleasure with minimal investment of time and effort.

At first, you might wonder why anyone would need a written recipe for this dish. But garlic is tricky business. Use too little and the pasta is starchy and bland and the olive oil dominates. This dish demands a lot of garlic—there's not much else to it. But all that garlic (we use a whopping 12 cloves) can be overpowering if you don't handle it carefully. Both the preparation and cooking of the garlic will determine the success (or failure) of this dish.

The rest of the dish is quite easy. Good extra-virgin olive oil is a must, as is some heat (we like red pepper flakes but black pepper is fine, too). The parsley is mostly for show. Yes, it adds a subtle herbaceous quality, but if you close your eyes you probably won't miss the parsley if you don't have any on hand. We like a squirt of lemon juice—the acidity balances the richness of the oil and heightens the other flavors.

If you're not already in the habit of reserving some cooking water before draining the pasta, this recipe will teach you the value of this practice. Without cooking water, the spaghetti will be dry. (And there's already a lot of olive oil in the dish so adding more will make things greasy.) Keep a liquid measuring cup in your colander as a handy reminder to save some starchy liquid before pouring the rest down the drain.

WHY THIS RECIPE WORKS

A Fine Mince Is Essential

Finely mincing the garlic ensures that its flavor permeates the dish. Mincing really matters. Even medium-size pieces will become very harsh, and the larger the garlic the more likely it will brown—a big no-no when making this dish. If you're the kind of cook who chops rather than minces garlic, you should use a garlic press rather than a chef's knife to handle this task for this recipe. A good press is effortless to use and ensures a smooth, fine consistency.

Cook Very Slowly

The secret to creating complex garlic flavor is to sauté it very slowly over low heat for 10 minutes. Gentle heat tempers the aggressive notes and develops the sweet flavor compounds that make garlic so alluring. The garlic should turn straw-colored when you're done. To reduce the risk of scorching the garlic, start it in cold oil and then watch the pan carefully. If the garlic starts to bubble vigorously, the heat

is too high. If at any point you notice the garlic is cooking too quickly, slide the pan off the burner. Do not let the garlic brown, as that will make it taste acrid and harsh.

Finish with Fresh Garlic

While two-thirds of the garlic is cooked slowly until sweet and fragrant, we find that a little heat from raw garlic makes this dish even better. We stir a bit more minced garlic into the cooked garlic. The residual heat in the pan mellows this second batch of garlic just a bit to create a variety of complex flavors from the star ingredient.

Split the Oil, Too

We cook the garlic in half the olive oil and then use the other half to cool down the garlic mixture and stop the cooking process. Because this second addition of oil is just barely heated, the final dish retains the fruity, peppery flavor notes of the oil. Good olive oil is a must here.

Patience and low heat transform garlic into the easiest-ever pasta sauce.

Pasta with Garlic and Oil (Aglio e Olio)

SERVES 4

It pays to use high-quality extra-virgin olive oil in this dish. See page 30 for tips on mincing garlic.

6 tablespoons extra-virgin olive oil	¾ teaspoon red pepper flakes
12 garlic cloves, minced	1 pound spaghetti
Salt	1 ounce Parmesan cheese,
3 tablespoons minced fresh parsley	grated (½ cup)
2 teaspoons lemon juice	

1. Heat 3 tablespoons oil, two-thirds of garlic, and ½ teaspoon salt in 10-inch non-stick skillet over low heat. Cook, stirring constantly, until garlic foams and is sticky and straw-colored, about 10 minutes. Off heat, add parsley, lemon juice, pepper flakes, remaining 3 tablespoons oil, and remaining garlic.

2. Meanwhile, bring 4 quarts water to boil in large pot. Add pasta and 1 tablespoon salt and cook, stirring often, until al dente. Reserve ½ cup cooking water, then drain pasta and return it to pot.

3. Stir 2 tablespoons reserved cooking water into garlic mixture. Add garlic mixture to pot and toss to combine, adding remaining reserved cooking water as needed. Season with salt to taste, and serve immediately, passing Parmesan separately.

SPAGHETTI WITH GARLIC, OLIVE OIL, AND ARTICHOKES

To thaw the artichokes quickly, microwave them in a covered bowl for about 3 minutes.

Transfer cooked garlic mixture to bowl before combining with other ingredients at end of step 1. Heat 2 teaspoons more extra-virgin olive oil in now-empty skillet over medium-high heat until shimmering. Add 9 ounces frozen artichoke hearts, thawed and patted dry, and ⅛ teaspoon salt and cook until artichokes are lightly browned and tender, 4 to 6 minutes. Add cooked artichokes to pasta with garlic mixture.

RECIPE DETAILS

Timeline

• 10 minutes to prep ingredients (start by bringing pasta water to boil)
• 10 minutes to cook garlic and pasta (do this simultaneously)

Essential Tools

• Garlic press (for ease and consistency)
• 10-inch nonstick skillet (the master recipe can be prepared in a conventional pan)
• Dutch oven or stockpot (at least 6 quarts)
• Liquid measuring cup to reserve some pasta cooking water

Substitutions & Variations

• If you don't like red pepper flakes, use a little black pepper instead.
• The parsley can be omitted or replaced with another minced fresh herb—cilantro, basil, tarragon, chives, mint, thyme, or even oregano. Use far less of the stronger herbs—a few teaspoons of oregano or thyme is sufficient.
• The cheese can be omitted, or use Pecorino if you prefer a stronger punch. A shower of toasted bread crumbs (panko, please) can be used in place of the cheese.
• As for additions, it's best to keep it simple. A handful of chopped green and/or black olives can be added to the cooked garlic mixture. A few slivered sun-dried tomatoes or a spoonful of capers are other good options.
• A few minced anchovies can be added to the pan with the garlic during the last minute or two of cooking time to ramp up the meaty notes. The dish won't taste fishy, but it will seem more savory.

6 Pesto

THIS NO-COOK SAUCE DOES MORE THAN COAT PASTA

I t's hard to imagine American cooking before the pesto invasion of the 1970s. Today pesto is not just a pasta sauce. It's a sandwich spread (way better than mayonnaise), pizza topping, garnish for soup, and sauce for fish, chicken, and steamed veggies. It seems like any plain dish benefits from a dollop of this potent green sauce. Unfortunately, most Americans are missing out on pesto's true beauty—its bold, fresh flavors—because they are buying rather than making it. Yes, we're talking about the pesto you buy in the refrigerated aisle, too.

You might think that making pesto is simply a matter of throwing basil, garlic, and cheese, along with nuts and olive oil, into a food processor, but you would be wrong. Pesto at its best is a smooth sauce infused with bright basil flavor and undertones of mellowed garlic and cheese. The nuts add richness and creaminess. The truth is that turning out a great pesto requires some finesse and technique and, yes, a recipe.

The biggest problem with most pesto recipes is an abundance of raw garlic flavor that bullies the basil, turning the sauce harsh and bitter. But if you don't use enough garlic, the sauce lacks oomph.

The basil and nuts have the opposite problem. In Italy, you can smell good pesto before you taste it—and it's the basil, not the garlic, that hits your nose first. Likewise, the flavor of the pine nuts should be present. In many store-bought versions there's no hint of nuttiness.

Our recipe relies on some unusual techniques to dial back the garlic flavor and ramp up the basil and nuts. The rest is easy. Use good Parmesan and good olive oil. Remember, this is a no-cook sauce so you can taste every ingredient.

WHY THIS RECIPE WORKS

Toast the Garlic
Toasting is a guaranteed way to control the garlic flavor; you bring out its sweetness while tempering its bite. To do this, leave the peel on the garlic and cook the whole cloves in a dry skillet until spotty brown. Once the garlic cools, remove the skin to reveal cloves that have been lightly cooked. It's like oven-roasted garlic, only faster. Chop the garlic before it goes into the food processor to ensure that there are no stray chunks in the finished sauce.

Toast the Nuts, Too
Toasting nuts brings out their aromatic oils, contributing to a stronger, more complex flavor and aroma. Do this while you wait for the toasted garlic to cool. Watch the pan closely—pine nuts will go from toasted to scorched rather quickly.

Bruise the Herbs
Bruising the basil (i.e., placing the leaves in a zipper-lock bag and beating them up with a meat pounder) releases the full range of herbal and anise flavor notes in a way that the chopping action of the food processor alone cannot accomplish.

Add Parsley to Keep the Pesto Green
A little parsley adds some complexity, but its main job is to keep pesto green and fresh-looking.

Use Extra-Virgin Olive Oil
In uncooked sauces like pesto, you can really taste the oil. Therefore, this isn't the place to skimp. Use high-quality extra-virgin olive oil. There are a lot of strong flavors in pesto, so use a fruity oil rather than a peppery oil, if you have a choice.

Just because pesto is a raw sauce doesn't mean you don't have to handle the ingredients with care—nuts should be toasted and herbs should be bruised.

Classic Basil Pesto

MAKES ¾ CUP

When adding pesto to cooked pasta it is important to include 3 or 4 tablespoons of the pasta cooking water for proper consistency and even distribution. The hot cooking water also softens the flavors of the sauce and highlights the creaminess of the nuts. This recipe makes enough to sauce 1 pound of cooked pasta.

3 garlic cloves, unpeeled	7 tablespoons extra-virgin olive oil
¼ cup pine nuts	Salt and pepper
2 cups fresh basil leaves	¼ cup finely grated Parmesan cheese
2 tablespoons fresh parsley leaves (optional)	

1. Toast garlic in 8-inch skillet over medium heat, shaking pan occasionally, until softened and spotty brown, about 8 minutes; when cool enough to handle, remove and discard skins and chop coarsely. While garlic cools, toast pine nuts in now-empty skillet over medium heat, stirring often, until golden and fragrant, 4 to 5 minutes.

2. Place basil and parsley, if using, in 1-gallon zipper-lock bag. Pound bag with flat side of meat pounder or rolling pin until all leaves are bruised.

3. Process oil, ½ teaspoon salt, garlic, pine nuts, and herbs in food processor until smooth, about 1 minute, scraping down bowl as needed. Transfer mixture to small bowl, stir in Parmesan, and season with salt and pepper to taste. (Pesto can be refrigerated for up to 3 days or frozen for up to 3 months. Press plastic wrap to surface or top with thin layer of oil.)

TOASTED NUT AND PARSLEY PESTO

Parsley makes a delicious substitute for basil, with pecans standing up to its heartier flavor better than pine nuts. You can substitute walnuts, blanched almonds, skinned hazelnuts, or any combination thereof for the pecans.

Substitute 1 cup pecans for pine nuts and ¼ cup fresh parsley leaves for basil, adding parsley directly to processor in step 3.

ARUGULA AND RICOTTA PESTO

Part-skim ricotta can be substituted here; do not use nonfat ricotta or the pesto will be dry and gummy.

Substitute 1 cup baby arugula and 1 cup fresh parsley leaves for basil and pound as directed in step 2. Reduce Parmesan to 2 tablespoons and stir in ⅓ cup whole-milk ricotta cheese.

RECIPE DETAILS

Timeline

• 8 minutes to toast garlic (also prep and bruise basil)

• 5 minutes to toast pine nuts (also grate cheese and chop garlic)

• 2 minutes to make sauce

Essential Tools

• 8-inch skillet

• Zipper-lock bag for bruising herbs

• Food processor

Substitutions & Variations

• You can use an equal amount of toasted chopped almonds or walnuts, but the flavor and texture of the pesto will be different. Almonds are relatively sweet but are fairly hard, so they give the pesto a coarse, granular texture. Walnuts are softer but still fairly meaty in texture and flavor and become very creamy when processed.

• You can double or triple this recipe.

• For sharper flavor, substitute an equal amount of finely grated Pecorino Romano cheese for the Parmesan.

• A food processor does the best job of pureeing ingredients, especially in recipes without much liquid (like this one). A blender, however, will work, especially if you're vigilant about scraping down the sides.

• To make a low-fat version of this sauce, ditch the nuts and then increase the amounts of garlic to four cloves, basil to 3 cups, and Parmesan to ½ cup and add 1 chopped shallot. Reduce the oil to 2 tablespoons and add ¼ cup part-skim ricotta cheese to guarantee the same emulsified texture as classic pesto.

7 Tomato Sauce

IT TAKES JUST 20 MINUTES TO OUTDO JARRED SAUCE

Contrary to what many people think, making a great tomato sauce needn't take hours. In fact, long cooking time is the enemy here, robbing the tomatoes of their freshness. Along with a handful of key partners, canned tomatoes can be transformed into a superior sauce in the time it takes to boil pasta.

Canned tomatoes, packed at the peak of ripeness, consistently taste better than the flavorless supermarket tomatoes you find most times of the year. But they do have one problem. Canned tomatoes contain the preservative citric acid, which throws off the delicate balance between sweetness and acidity found in fresh tomatoes. When using canned tomatoes to make a sauce, the job of the cook is to add back some sweet notes.

Sugar is an obvious place to start but any more than ¼ teaspoon is too much. You need subtler sources of sweetness—compounds that taste more like the natural sugars in fresh tomatoes. We tried a variety of options before settling on onions. When cooked long enough, their flavor changes from pungent to sweet. Onions actually contain long chains of fructose molecules and as the onions break down these chains are broken, allowing the natural sugars in the onions to dominate. At the same time, the volatile compounds that make raw onions so harsh are cooking off.

Slowly cooking the onions for a quick tomato sauce doesn't make much sense so we developed a method for preparing and cooking the onion that shortcuts this process to just 5 minutes.

While not as simple as opening a jar (nothing is), this sauce is a revelation. Make it a few times and you will want to commit it to memory. It's that good.

WHY THIS RECIPE WORKS

Pick the Right Can
Crushed tomatoes are our top choice for a quick sauce because they already have been pureed. Brands that list tomatoes, rather than tomato puree, as the first ingredient will have a fresher flavor. We particularly like Tuttorosso and Muir Glen crushed tomatoes.

Grate, Don't Chop
Grated onion pulp browns faster than chopped onion. The large holes of a box grater are the perfect tool for grating a peeled onion. Use a medium onion, which will easily produce the necessary amount of grated onion while still leaving a sizeable chunk in your hand (thus keeping your fingers and knuckles safe).

Butter to Start
Most tomato sauces start with olive oil. But since the flavor compounds in good olive oil are extremely volatile, even the best extra-virgin oil doesn't add much flavor when used this way. You might as well start with vegetable oil. We took another path. Sautéing the onion in butter does the best job of enhancing the flavor of the tomatoes. That's because the butter speeds the browning of the onion and contributes its own browned milk solids, ramping up the sweet notes in the sauce. The butter also adds a layer of richness.

A Brief Simmer
Simmering a simple sauce for more than 20 minutes actually dulls its flavor. You want to simmer the sauce just long enough to thicken it to the correct consistency—a process that takes just 10 minutes when you start with crushed tomatoes.

A Fresh and Fragrant Finish
Swirling in aromatic fresh basil right before serving adds bright grassy notes and makes up for the lost fragrance of fresh tomatoes. Using olive oil to finish the sauce is the best way to capture its flavor.

Great sauce requires a little sugar and a lot of fresh basil.

Quick Tomato Sauce

MAKES ABOUT 3 CUPS; ENOUGH FOR 1 POUND OF PASTA

Grate the onion on the large holes of a box grater.

2 tablespoons unsalted butter	1 (28-ounce) can crushed tomatoes
¼ cup grated onion	¼ teaspoon sugar
Salt and pepper	2 tablespoons coarsely chopped fresh
¼ teaspoon dried oregano	basil leaves
2 garlic cloves, minced	1 tablespoon extra-virgin olive oil

Melt butter in medium saucepan over medium heat. Add onion, ½ teaspoon salt, and oregano; cook, stirring occasionally, until liquid has evaporated and onion is golden brown, about 5 minutes. Add garlic and cook until fragrant, about 30 seconds. Stir in tomatoes and sugar; increase heat to high and bring to simmer. Lower heat to medium-low and simmer until thickened slightly, about 10 minutes. Off heat, stir in basil and oil; season with salt and pepper to taste. Serve.

SPICY QUICK TOMATO SAUCE
Add 1 teaspoon red pepper flakes with garlic.

CREAMY QUICK TOMATO SAUCE
Add ¾ cup heavy cream to finished sauce and simmer until thickened, about 3 minutes.

ZESTY QUICK TOMATO SAUCE
Add 8 minced anchovy fillets with garlic. Add ½ cup pitted and chopped olives and 3 tablespoons rinsed capers with basil.

RECIPE DETAILS

Timeline

- 5 minutes to prep ingredients
- 5 minutes to cook onion and garlic
- 10 minutes to cook tomatoes and finish sauce

Essential Tools

- Box grater for grating onion
- Can opener
- Medium saucepan
- Chef's knife

Substitutions & Variations

- If you don't have crushed tomatoes, you can substitute one 28-ounce can of whole or diced tomatoes processed with their juice in a food processor until smooth.
- This recipe can be doubled if you use a large saucepan. Note that the simmering time might be slightly longer.

A Better Way to Cook Dried Pasta

Never has so much bunk been written about something so simple. Oil in the water? Throwing pasta against the fridge? Rinsing pasta? Not only do these "tricks" not work, they distract many cooks from the things that do. Here's what you need to know to cook pasta correctly.

1. Bring 4 quarts of water to boil in Dutch oven or large pot (at least 6 quarts). (Pasta leaches starch as it cooks and abundant water dilutes the starch and reduces the risk that the noodles will stick together.)

2. Add 1 tablespoon salt to boiling water. (Most of the salt will go down the drain. And forget about adding oil to the pot. It creates a slick surface on the water but won't keep the pasta from sticking. However, it will end up on the drained pasta and prevent the sauce from adhering properly.)

3. Add pasta and stir constantly for about 1 minute. Stir every minute during first half of cooking process, when noodles are most likely to stick.

4. Several minutes before you think pasta will be done, start tasting. (Forget about the times on the box.) When pasta tastes just shy of al dente, it's done. (Residual heat will continue to soften the noodles so it's best to undercook them ever so slightly.)

5. Reserve cooking water (½ cup or amount specified in recipe) and then drain pasta. Don't rinse pasta and don't shake it bone-dry. (A little moisture on the pasta will help spread the sauce.) Use reserved cooking water if you need to loosen sauce further.

6. Return drained pasta to now-empty pot and toss with sauce. (Saucing in the pot gives you room to toss for even coverage and keeps everything hot.)

8 Spaghetti and Meatballs

THE BEST DISH TO FEED A CROWD THAT INCLUDES KIDS

Making this dish for a crowd can try anyone's patience. Who wants to spend all day at the stove? By rethinking this dish, we found a way to deliver incredibly tender, rich-tasting meatballs in flavorful, full-bodied tomato gravy, all with an hour of hands-on work. And this recipe feeds 12 people.

The meatballs are the hardest part of the equation since they can turn out bland and crumbly. Choosing the right meats is critical, as is the right mix of flavor boosters. But what's most surprising about the ingredient list in our recipe are the two distinctly non-Italian binders—powdered gelatin as well as a panade of panko (Japanese bread crumbs) and buttermilk.

Frying meatballs in batches takes forever and makes a mess. We bypass the frying pan and turn to the oven. When cooked on wire racks the meatballs brown evenly and they don't need to be turned. You can roast a lot of meatballs at once—40 to be exact—in just 30 minutes.

There's one downside to roasting the meatballs—no pan drippings to flavor the sauce. So we drop the roasted meatballs into the simple marinara sauce and braise them in the oven for an hour. With time, the rich flavor of the browned meat infiltrates the sauce. This technique won't work with a regular marinara sauce—the meatballs absorb too much of the liquid around them and the sauce overreduces. Using a mix of crushed tomatoes and tomato juice (the stuff you drink) averts this problem. A sauce that looks much too watery at the outset will cook down to the perfect consistency.

This certainly isn't your grandmother's meatballs and marinara. The cook might actually have time to get out of the kitchen and join the table.

WHY THIS RECIPE WORKS

Mix the Meats
We first tried making meatballs with beef alone, using 85 percent lean ground beef (anything less fatty produces a dry, bland meatball). However, we found that replacing some of the beef with ground pork (we like a 2:1 ratio best) makes for a markedly richer, meatier taste.

Build Flavor
Chopping up some prosciutto, which is packed with glutamates that enhance savory flavor, and mixing it in with the meat is an easy way to add another dimension of meatiness. A generous amount of Parmesan adds more glutamates.

Pick Panko
Meatballs are traditionally bound with a panade—fresh bread crumbs soaked in milk. We find that panko—the super crunchy Japanese bread crumbs—do a better job of holding in the meats' juices and keeping the meatballs from getting tough. (And panko is certainly more convenient than making homemade bread crumbs.) Replacing the usual milk with buttermilk adds another layer of extra flavor.

Add Gelatin
Gelatin-rich veal is a common ingredient in Italian meatballs. While the veal adds suppleness, it can be hard to find in American markets. And if you do, there's another problem—it's usually ground very fine, which makes the meatballs dense and heavy. If you want gelatin, why not go right to the source? Powdered gelatin moistened with a little water does the trick at far less expense and hassle.

Grate the Onion
Grating the onion for the sauce on the large holes of a box grater (a trick we use for our Quick Tomato Sauce on page 28) helps it to cook quickly and flavor the sauce. It also means there are no crunchy bits of onion in the finished sauce.

Gelatin (yes, the stuff in Jell-O) and three eggs keep meatballs nice and tender.

Classic Spaghetti and Meatballs for a Crowd

SERVES 12

Once cooked, the sauce and the meatballs can be cooled and refrigerated for up to two days. To reheat, drizzle ½ cup water over the sauce, without stirring, and reheat on the lower-middle rack of a 325-degree oven for 1 hour.

MEATBALLS

2¼ cups panko bread crumbs

1½ cups buttermilk

1½ teaspoons unflavored gelatin

3 tablespoons water

2 pounds 85 percent lean ground beef

1 pound ground pork

6 ounces thinly sliced prosciutto, chopped fine

3 large eggs

3 ounces Parmesan cheese, grated (1½ cups), plus extra for serving

6 tablespoons minced fresh parsley

3 garlic cloves, minced

1½ teaspoons salt

½ teaspoon pepper

SAUCE

3 tablespoons extra-virgin olive oil

1 large onion, grated

6 garlic cloves, minced

1 teaspoon dried oregano

½ teaspoon red pepper flakes

3 (28-ounce) cans crushed tomatoes

6 cups tomato juice

6 tablespoons dry white wine

Salt and pepper

½ cup minced fresh basil

3 tablespoons minced fresh parsley

Sugar

3 pounds spaghetti

1. *For the Meatballs:* Adjust oven racks to upper-middle and lower-middle positions and heat oven to 450 degrees. Line 2 rimmed baking sheets with aluminum foil. Set wire racks in sheets and spray wire racks with vegetable oil spray.

2. Combine panko and buttermilk in large bowl and let sit, mashing occasionally with fork, until smooth paste forms, about 10 minutes. Meanwhile, sprinkle gelatin over water in bowl and let sit until gelatin softens, about 5 minutes.

3. Mix beef, pork, prosciutto, eggs, Parmesan, parsley, garlic, salt, pepper, and gelatin mixture into panko mixture using your hands. Pinch off and roll mixture into 2-inch meatballs (about 40 meatballs total) and arrange on prepared wire racks. Bake until well browned, about 30 minutes, switching and rotating sheets halfway through baking.

4. *For the Sauce:* While meatballs bake, heat oil in Dutch oven over medium heat until shimmering. Add onion and cook until softened and lightly browned, 5 to 7 minutes. Stir in garlic, oregano, and pepper flakes and cook until fragrant, about 30 seconds. Stir in tomatoes, tomato juice, wine, 1½ teaspoons salt, and ¼ teaspoon pepper; bring to simmer; and cook until thickened slightly, about 15 minutes.

RECIPE DETAILS

Timeline

• 30 minutes to prep ingredients and make panade

• 35 minutes to assemble and bake meatballs (make sauce while meatballs are in oven)

• 1 hour to simmer meatballs in sauce (cook pasta when meatballs are nearly done)

Essential Tools

• 2 rimmed baking sheets

• 2 wire racks

• 6-quart Dutch oven with lid

• Box grater (Use the large holes to prep the onion and the small holes for the cheese.)

• 12-quart stockpot

Substitutions & Variations

• You can substitute 1 cup plain yogurt thinned with ½ cup milk for the buttermilk.

• You can cook the spaghetti in two pots if you don't have a pot that's large enough to cook all of the pasta together.

5. Remove meatballs from oven and reduce oven temperature to 300 degrees. Gently nestle meatballs into sauce. Cover, transfer to oven, and cook until meatballs are firm and sauce has thickened, about 1 hour.

6. Meanwhile, bring 10 quarts water to boil in 12-quart pot. Add pasta and 2 table-spoons salt and cook, stirring often, until al dente. Reserve ½ cup cooking water, then drain pasta and return it to pot.

7. Gently stir basil and parsley into sauce and season with sugar, salt, and pepper to taste. Add 2 cups sauce (without meatballs) to pasta and toss to combine. Add reserved cooking water as needed to adjust consistency. Serve, topping individual portions with more tomato sauce and several meatballs and passing extra Parmesan separately.

A Better Way to Mince Garlic

We have a theory about why some people don't like garlic. They aren't mincing it fine enough and as a result their food is peppered with large nuggets of overpowering garlic. Chopped garlic is also much more likely to burn and turn acrid. Using a garlic press is the easiest way to ensure that you get a fine, uniform mince. If you're not using a garlic press, here's what you need to know.

1. Trim off root end of clove, then crush clove gently between side of chef's knife and cutting board to loosen papery skin. Skin should fall away from garlic.

2. Using two-handed chopping motion, run knife over garlic repeatedly to mince it. Keep one hand on top of blade and make sure to rock blade back and forth as you move it across pile of garlic.

3. Mincing garlic to a smooth paste is a good idea in many recipes (such as sauces or dressings). Sprinkle salt, preferably kosher, over chopped garlic. Coarse grains of salt help break down garlic faster.

4. Continue to mince garlic and alternate with scraping motion. Turn knife on its side and scrape blade back and forth over garlic to form sticky, smooth paste.

9 Macaroni and Cheese

REAL CHEESE MAKES THIS DISH GOOD ENOUGH FOR EVERYONE

Mac and cheese certainly appeals to kids. But who needs processed stuff from a box when you can easily make great homemade macaroni and cheese that appeals to grown-ups too? This family favorite needs to hit the middle ground, boasting tender pasta in a smooth, creamy sauce with great cheese flavor, plain and simple.

There are plenty of mac and cheese recipes out there and they can vex the home cook with their options: Base the sauce on a custard or a roux, bake in the oven or cook on the stovetop, top with toasted bread crumbs or nothing? World-class family-style macaroni and cheese doesn't require fancy cheeses or a fussy, overly rich sauce made with eggs and cream. Instead the base can be a simple white sauce thickened with butter and flour and enriched with lots of cheese.

A pound of cheese is the perfect amount for a pound of pasta. The cheese affects the taste as well as the texture and combining two types works best: sharp cheddar for flavor and Monterey Jack for creaminess. Since fat does separate from the cheeses when they're melted, all that cheese needs some kind of binder to stabilize it; we opt for flour.

It's difficult to get the timing right for macaroni and cheese baked in the oven. Either the pasta is overcooked or it needs more time, and the sauce ends up breaking from being overbaked. It's easier to cook the pasta on the stovetop and thus easier not to ruin the cheese sauce, too.

In the end, a dual method using the stovetop and the broiler provides the way to perfectly cooked macaroni and cheese with a toasty crown of buttery fresh bread crumbs.

WHY THIS RECIPE WORKS

Bind It Up

Most macaroni and cheese recipes use either eggs or starch to stabilize the sauce. Eggs are great, and we've used them on occasion ourselves, but you need to add evaporated milk to prevent the eggs from curdling and the end result is very, very rich. For everyday mac and cheese, we think the flour route (through the use of a béchamel) is better.

Create a Roux

Béchamel is a white sauce made by cooking flour and butter to create a light roux. We use 5 tablespoons of butter and 6 tablespoons of flour (pretty close to a 1:1 ratio), along with a bit of powdered mustard and cayenne (optional). Milk (any kind) is gradually whisked in, and the béchamel is cooked until it thickens.

Forget About "Grown-Up" Cheeses

We tried Parmesan, Gruyère, and some aged cheddars, but were not pleased with their grainy texture and potent flavor. We prefer sharp cheddar for flavor and Monterey Jack for creaminess.

Cook Until Just Past al Dente

The trick is to cook the pasta just past al dente before adding it to the sauce. If cooked less, the pasta releases starch into the sauce and makes it gritty. If cooked until very tender, the noodles won't absorb the sauce. Boiled until just past al dente, however, the noodles retain structure to stand up to the heat of the sauce for a few minutes without turning mushy, and the cheese can fill every nook and cranny.

Get the "Baked" Look

Scrape the pasta and sauce into a baking dish and top with fresh buttered bread crumbs. The broiler will concentrate the heat right on the bread crumbs, turning them a deep, golden brown. This only takes a few minutes—just enough for the crumbs to sink into the cheese sauce and seem baked right in.

A flour-and-butter roux is the base for a stable sauce that coats boiled pasta.

Classic Macaroni and Cheese

SERVES 6 TO 8

We found that it's crucial to cook the pasta until just past the al dente stage so that it doesn't turn mushy as it sits in the sauce. Whole, low-fat, and skim milk all work well in this recipe. If desired, offer celery salt or hot sauce for sprinkling at the table.

6 slices hearty white sandwich bread, torn into quarters	1½ teaspoons dry mustard
5 tablespoons unsalted butter, plus 3 tablespoons cut into 6 pieces and chilled	¼ teaspoon cayenne pepper (optional)
	5 cups milk
1 pound elbow macaroni	8 ounces Monterey Jack cheese, shredded (2 cups)
Salt	8 ounces sharp cheddar cheese, shredded (2 cups)
6 tablespoons all-purpose flour	

1. Pulse bread and 3 tablespoons chilled butter in food processor to coarse crumbs, about 10 pulses; set aside.

2. Adjust oven rack 8 inches from broiler element and heat broiler. Bring 4 quarts water to boil in large pot. Add macaroni and 1 tablespoon salt and cook, stirring often, until tender; drain macaroni.

3. Melt remaining 5 tablespoons butter in now-empty pot over medium-high heat. Add flour, mustard, cayenne, if using, and 1 teaspoon salt and cook, whisking constantly, until mixture becomes fragrant and deepens in color, about 1 minute. Gradually whisk in milk; bring mixture to boil, whisking constantly. Reduce heat to medium and simmer, whisking occasionally, until thickened, about 5 minutes. Off heat, slowly whisk in Monterey Jack and cheddar until completely melted. Add macaroni to sauce and cook over medium-low heat, stirring constantly, until mixture is steaming and heated through, about 6 minutes.

4. Transfer mixture to 13 by 9-inch broiler-safe baking dish and sprinkle with bread-crumb mixture. Broil until topping is deep golden brown, 3 to 5 minutes. Let casserole cool for 5 minutes before serving.

CLASSIC MACARONI AND CHEESE WITH HAM AND PEAS
Add 8 ounces deli ham sliced ¼ inch thick and cut into 1-inch pieces, and 1 cup frozen peas to cheese sauce along with macaroni.

CLASSIC MACARONI AND CHEESE WITH KIELBASA AND MUSTARD
Add 1 finely chopped onion to melted butter in step 3 and cook until softened and lightly browned, 5 to 7 minutes. Add flour to onion and continue with recipe, reducing salt in sauce to ½ teaspoon. Add 8 ounces kielbasa, quartered lengthwise and sliced ½ inch thick, and 4 teaspoons whole-grain Dijon mustard to cheese sauce along with macaroni.

RECIPE DETAILS

Timeline
• 10 minutes to prepare bread-crumb topping and grate cheeses (also bring water to boil)
• 10 minutes to cook pasta
• 20 minutes to make sauce and cook with pasta
• 5 minutes to add topping and broil

Essential Tools
• Food processor to make bread crumbs
• Whisk to cook roux and stir in cheeses
• Broiler-safe baking dish (Tempered glass can't go under the broiler, so choose ceramic or metal.)

Substitutions & Variations
• Do not use preshredded cheeses—they are usually quite bland. Also, these cheeses are coated with various starches to extend shelf life and prevent clumping. These starches make it harder for preshredded cheeses to melt smoothly and can negatively impact this dish.
• The recipe may be halved and baked in an 8-inch square broiler-safe baking dish.

10 Mashed Potatoes

THE EASIEST WAY TO COOK EVERYONE'S FAVORITE SIDE

Smooth and fluffy mashed potatoes have their place on the dinner table. But let's face it: They require some finesse to get just right (you must pull out the ricer) and a lot of last-minute attention. And they just aren't complete without a flavor partner (pass the gravy or spoon on the pan sauce).

Smashed potatoes are their much simpler cousin and our first choice for a regular weeknight meal. Unlike smooth classic mashed potatoes, their coarse texture is rustic and chunky (so they are meant to be "imperfect") and they're often highly seasoned so they can stand on their own without adornment. In our opinion, that makes smashed potatoes the perfect no-fuss side dish.

Potatoes consist mainly of starch and moisture. Low-starch, high-moisture red potatoes are the best choice for smashing since their firm, waxy structure holds up under pressure. Plus their thin red skins are pleasantly tender (no need to peel) and provide flecks of color in the mash.

For the best chunky texture, we smash cooked whole potatoes with a rubber spatula or the back of a wooden spoon; both work better than a potato masher or fork. If the potatoes are cooked just right, they easily split their skins and burst apart. Giving the potatoes a few minutes to dry out ensures the skins aren't too slippery, making the job even easier.

To pack our spuds with plenty of richness and flavor, we knew butter would be essential, but what about a secondary dairy element? Skipping over heavy cream, half-and-half, and milk—more at home in a refined mash—we landed on cream cheese, which pulls double duty here, giving our potatoes not just body, but a luscious tang as well.

WHY THIS RECIPE WORKS

Cook Whole Red Potatoes
When the goal is a rustic, chunky smash, red potatoes are best. We cook these potatoes whole. Cut into chunks, they absorb too much water and the result is a soggy texture and washed-out potato flavor. Additions to the cooking water like salt and a bay leaf (and, for a variation, garlic) penetrate their thin skin easily to flavor the potatoes.

Smash Gently
Potato mashers and forks are too tough on these potatoes. A rubber spatula or wooden spoon breaks them up without reducing them to a smooth puree.

Enrich with Cream Cheese
We liked the idea of tangy sour cream as the dairy element but weren't wild about the texture of the finished dish—the potatoes needed more body. In the end, we had the best results with cream cheese. It adds plenty of tang and a creamy lushness to the potatoes. A little butter is necessary to add richness, and mixing the butter and cream cheese together before adding them to the potatoes reduces the chance of overworking the potatoes and making them gluey.

Reserve Cooking Water
As we often do with pasta, we reserve some of the seasoned cooking water to adjust the consistency of the smash. It keeps the finished dish from being too dry. The water reinforces the salty flavor but doesn't dull the tang as cream or milk would.

Cooking whole potatoes takes a bit longer but yields a more flavorful mash. And reserve some of the salty, starchy cooking water to moisten the mash.

Smashed Potatoes

SERVES 4 TO 6

Potatoes that are 2 inches in diameter are ideal. Try to purchase potatoes of equal size with their skins intact. If only larger potatoes are available, increase the cooking time by about 10 minutes.

2 pounds small red potatoes, unpeeled	4 tablespoons unsalted butter, melted
Salt and pepper	3 tablespoons chopped fresh chives
1 bay leaf	(optional)
4 ounces cream cheese,	
room temperature	

1. Place potatoes in large saucepan and cover with 1 inch cold water. Add 1 teaspoon salt and bay leaf. Bring to boil over high heat, then reduce heat to medium-low and simmer gently until paring knife can be inserted into potatoes with no resistance, 35 to 45 minutes. Reserve ½ cup cooking water, then drain potatoes. Return potatoes to pot, discard bay leaf, and let potatoes sit in pot, uncovered, until surfaces are dry, about 5 minutes.

2. While potatoes dry, whisk cream cheese and melted butter in medium bowl until smooth and fully incorporated. Add ¼ cup of reserved cooking water, chives, if using, ½ teaspoon pepper, and ½ teaspoon salt. Using rubber spatula or back of wooden spoon, smash potatoes just enough to break skins. Fold in cream cheese mixture until most of liquid has been absorbed and chunks of potatoes remain. Add more cooking water as needed, 1 tablespoon at a time, until potatoes are slightly looser than desired (potatoes will thicken slightly with sitting). Season with salt and pepper to taste; serve immediately.

GARLIC-ROSEMARY SMASHED POTATOES

Add 2 peeled garlic cloves to potatoes in saucepan along with salt and bay leaf in step 1. Melt 4 tablespoons unsalted butter in 8-inch skillet over medium heat. Add ½ teaspoon chopped fresh rosemary and 1 minced garlic clove and cook until just fragrant, about 30 seconds; substitute butter-garlic mixture for melted butter, adding cooked garlic cloves to cream cheese along with butter-garlic mixture. Omit chives.

SMASHED POTATOES WITH BACON AND PARSLEY

Cook 6 slices bacon, cut lengthwise in half then crosswise into ¼-inch pieces, in 10-inch skillet over medium heat until crisp, 5 to 7 minutes. Using slotted spoon, transfer bacon to paper towel–lined plate; reserve 1 tablespoon fat. Substitute bacon fat for 1 tablespoon melted butter, 2 tablespoons chopped fresh parsley for chives, and reduce salt added to cream cheese mixture to ¼ teaspoon. Sprinkle potatoes with cooked bacon before serving.

RECIPE DETAILS

Timeline

- 5 minutes to prep ingredients (cream cheese will soften while potatoes cook)
- 40 minutes to cook potatoes
- 6 minutes to drain and dry potatoes (whisk other ingredients together while waiting)
- 4 minutes to smash and finish potatoes

Essential Tools

- Large saucepan (about 4 quarts)
- Paring knife (best way to judge when potatoes are done)
- Rubber spatula or wooden spoon (something heavy enough to smash potatoes)

Substitutions & Variations

- Small white potatoes can be used instead of red, but the dish won't be as colorful.
- Low-fat cream cheese (usually labeled neufchatel) can be used in this recipe.
- We like chives but another fresh herb can be used in its place (parsley would be nice).
- The recipe can be doubled. You will need a Dutch oven or stockpot instead of the specified saucepan. Depending on pot size, the cooking time will increase by 5 to 10 minutes.

11 Roasted Potatoes

AS GOOD AS FRIES—AND A WHOLE LOT EASIER

When done right, roasted potatoes deliver the best of both worlds—creamy bites of potato covered in a crunchy crust. Sound familiar? In our opinion, truly great roasted potatoes should be every bit as enticing as French fries, minus the mess of frying. So why do so many recipes fail?

When roasting potatoes, most cooks simply cut the potatoes into chunks, toss them with oil on a sheet pan (often one that is too small so that the potatoes clump and cook unevenly), and then place the pan in a hot oven. While somewhat serviceable, this method often results in tough, leathery exteriors and mealy centers. Our unique roasting method starts on the stovetop and delivers optimal crunch along with a richly creamy interior.

We tested different potatoes and found that Yukon Golds performed best. Unlike red potatoes (which contain plenty of moisture but not much starch) or russets (which contain very little moisture but plenty of starch), Yukon Golds contain moderate levels of both moisture and starch, which makes them ideally suited to producing roasted potatoes that are crisp on the outside (from the starch) but still creamy in the middle (from the moisture).

If you think roasted potatoes can't be as addictive as fries, you need to think again. Or, at the very least, you need to try this recipe before deciding for sure.

WHY THIS RECIPE WORKS

Get the Pan Hot
Preheating an empty baking sheet is a great way to jump-start browning when roasting potatoes as well as other vegetables. Make sure to use a heavy-duty pan (lighter pans will buckle) with rims (about 1 inch tall) to keep the spuds in place.

Ovals, Not Chunks
Most cooks simply cut potatoes into large chunks when making roasted potatoes. But with so many sides, you need to flip the pieces several times for optimal browning. Thick rounds (about ½ inch is ideal) ensure maximum contact with the hot baking sheet and translate to just one flip during the roasting time. Keep the skins on so the slices remain intact.

Simmer Gently
As counterintuitive as it may seem, cooking the potatoes first in water actually makes them more crisp. The water quickly hydrates starch granules in the potatoes, causing them to swell and eventually burst. These burst granules release amylose (a type of starch), which is the substance that browns in the oven. Don't boil the potatoes—a gentle simmer will hydrate the starch granules without causing structural damage.

Toss Roughly
Tossing the parcooked potato slices with olive oil and salt (the tiny crystals rough up the potatoes) encourages the release of more starch, and more surface starch translates to more browning in the oven.

Flip Carefully
You've worked hard to develop a crisp exterior so the last thing you want is to tear the potato slices as you flip them. Wait until the bottoms are golden brown before starting the flipping. We recommend that you slide a very thin metal spatula (an offset spatula is perfect) under each slice and then flip it with a pair of tongs. If the potatoes are sticking, slide the pan back in the oven and try again in 5 minutes.

Vigorous tossing and gentle turning are key to roasted potatoes that crunch.

Crisp Roasted Potatoes

SERVES 4 TO 6

The potatoes should be just undercooked when they are removed from the boiling water.

2½ pounds Yukon Gold potatoes, unpeeled, cut into ½-inch-thick slices

Salt and pepper

5 tablespoons olive oil

1. Adjust oven rack to lowest position, place rimmed baking sheet on rack, and heat oven to 450 degrees. Place potatoes and 1 tablespoon salt in Dutch oven, then cover with 1 inch cold water. Bring to boil over high heat, then reduce heat and gently simmer until exteriors of potatoes have softened but centers offer resistance when poked with paring knife, about 5 minutes. Drain potatoes well and transfer to large bowl.

2. Drizzle potatoes with 2 tablespoons oil and sprinkle with ½ teaspoon salt; using rubber spatula, toss to combine. Repeat with 2 tablespoons oil and ½ teaspoon salt and continue to toss until exteriors of potato slices are coated with starchy paste, 1 to 2 minutes.

3. Working quickly, remove baking sheet from oven and drizzle remaining 1 tablespoon oil over surface. Carefully transfer potatoes to sheet and spread into even layer (place end pieces skin side up). Bake until bottoms of potatoes are golden brown and crisp, 15 to 25 minutes, rotating sheet after 10 minutes.

4. Remove sheet from oven and, using metal spatula and tongs, loosen potatoes from pan and carefully flip each slice. Continue to roast until second side is golden and crisp, 10 to 20 minutes longer, rotating sheet as needed to ensure potatoes brown evenly. Season with salt and pepper to taste, and serve immediately.

RECIPE DETAILS

Timeline

- 10 minutes to prep potatoes (start by preheating baking sheet in oven)
- 10 minutes to parcook, oil, and season potatoes
- 35 minutes to roast potatoes (mostly hands-off except for rotating baking sheet and flipping potatoes once)

Essential Tools

- Heavy-duty rimmed baking sheet (heavy duty so it won't buckle in oven)
- Dutch oven or other large pot
- Rubber spatula for tossing potatoes
- Colander
- Thin metal spatula, preferably offset (A thin blade minimizes the risk of ripping the crisp exterior when turning the potatoes.)
- Tongs (use in conjunction with spatula)

Substitutions & Variations

- Yukon Gold potatoes offer the best balance of creamy interiors and crisp exteriors. You can use russet potatoes in this recipe, but the interiors won't be quite as creamy. Don't use red potatoes—they don't have enough starch to develop a truly crisp exterior.
- Because of the high oven heat, we don't recommend flavoring the potatoes with anything other than salt before they go into the oven—garlic, herbs, and spices will simply burn.
- You can toss the finished potatoes with a little grated lemon zest, a dash of cayenne, or a shower of fresh parsley—but honestly we're just as happy finishing the potatoes with some good salt (preferably flaky Maldon) and fresh black pepper.

12 Rice Pilaf

THE ABSOLUTE BEST (AND EASIEST) WAY TO COOK RICE

Cooking rice is easy, but cooking rice well isn't. Many cooks who can turn out a decent pie or stew claim they can't cook rice at all. It scorches. It's mushy. The rice is sticky when they want it fluffy. Convenience products, like converted or instant rice, are supposed to take some of the guesswork out of the process, but their texture and flavor makes them poor options.

If you struggle to make good rice, it's probably not you but the recipe. The standard formula on many rice packages is wrong (too much water) and doesn't take advantage of a simple trick—used around the world—to tame the starchiness in rice. Sautéing the rice in a little fat gelatinizes the starches so the rice cooks up firmer and less sticky. Sounds complicated? It's not. It's how you make rice pilaf.

Pilaf should be light and fluffy so you want to use long-grain rice. Long-grain white rice is neutral in flavor, providing a backdrop for other foods. Basmati, with its buttery flavor and sweet aroma, can be an even better choice. A naturally occurring flavor compound gives basmati rice a popcorn-like taste. Sautéing regular long-grain rice in butter creates a similar effect.

Some pilaf recipes call for soaking the rice overnight. But that just complicates what should be a simple preparation. The key thing is to wash away the starch on the exterior of the rice. If you place the rice in a bowl and cover it with water, you can see this starch—it turns the water cloudy. If left in place, this starchy residue will make rice heavy and gummy. Swishing the grains (and changing the water four or five times, or until the water remains clear) is an almost effortless step that ensures a perfect pilaf with light, separate grains.

WHY THIS RECIPE WORKS

Use Less Water
The conventional ratio of 2 parts water to 1 part rice makes rice sticky and soft. The right ratio is 3 parts water to 2 parts rice, which also takes into account the effects of rinsing the rice before cooking.

Sauté the Rice First
Sautéing the rice in a little butter develops the nutty notes in the rice and helps the individual grains to maintain their integrity. This step also gives you the chance to sauté an onion (or another aromatic ingredient to flavor the rice) first.

Use the Lowest Possible Heat
Once the rice looks translucent around the edges, add the water and salt. Bringing the water to a boil before it goes into the pot with the rice speeds the cooking process and gives you a chance to dissolve the salt. Once the water is back to a boil (which will happen very quickly), turn the heat to the lowest setting and cover the pot. If the lowest setting on your stove isn't very low, consider investing in a flame tamer—an inexpensive metal disk that sits on top of the burner (gas or electric) and delivers more even (and more gentle) heat to the pan.

Keep the Lid On
The steam in the pot is cooking the rice and if you keep opening the pot it won't cook properly. At the 16-minute mark, check the rice. In the unlikely event that it's not ready, quickly put the lid back in place and cook the rice for another few minutes.

Steam Off the Heat
After simmering in all that water, the rice will be a bit heavy. To lighten it up, slide a folded dish towel under the lid and let the pot sit off the heat for 10 to 15 minutes. The towel absorbs some of the moisture/steam in the pot and helps produce rice that is tender and fluffy. Just fluff with a fork (to separate the grains) and serve.

A quick sauté and last-minute steam produce fluffy rice with separate grains.

Rice Pilaf

SERVES 4

You will need a saucepan with a tight-fitting lid for this recipe.

1½	cups basmati or long-grain white rice	3	tablespoons unsalted butter
1½	teaspoons salt	1	small onion, chopped fine
	Pinch pepper		

1. Place rice in bowl and add enough water to cover by 2 inches; using your hands, gently swish grains to release excess starch. Carefully pour off water, leaving rice in bowl. Repeat 4 to 5 times, until water runs almost clear. Drain rice in fine-mesh strainer, place over bowl, and set aside.

2. Bring 2¼ cups water to boil, covered, in small saucepan over medium-high heat. Add salt and pepper and cover to keep hot. Meanwhile, melt butter in large saucepan over medium heat. Add onion and cook until softened but not browned, about 4 minutes. Add rice and stir to coat grains with butter; cook until edges of grains begin to turn translucent, about 3 minutes. Stir hot seasoned water into rice. Return to boil, then reduce heat to low, cover, and simmer until all liquid has been absorbed, 16 to 18 minutes. Off heat, remove lid and place dish towel folded in half over saucepan; replace lid. Let stand for 10 minutes. Fluff rice with fork and serve.

RICE PILAF WITH CURRANTS AND PINE NUTS

Add 2 minced garlic cloves, ½ teaspoon ground turmeric, and ¼ teaspoon ground cinnamon to softened onion and cook until fragrant, about 30 seconds. When rice is off heat, before covering saucepan with towel, sprinkle ¼ cup currants over top of rice (do not mix in). When fluffing rice with fork, toss in ¼ cup toasted pine nuts.

INDIAN-SPICED RICE PILAF WITH DATES AND PARSLEY

Add 2 minced garlic cloves, 1 tablespoon grated fresh ginger, ¼ teaspoon ground cinnamon, and ¼ teaspoon ground cardamom to softened onion and cook until fragrant, about 30 seconds. When fluffing rice with fork, toss in ½ cup chopped dates and 3 tablespoons minced fresh parsley.

RECIPE DETAILS

Timeline

• 10 minutes to prep ingredients and rinse rice (bring water to boil at same time)
• 8 minutes to sauté onion and toast rice
• 16 minutes to cook rice (hands-off)
• 10 minutes to let rice steam off heat (hands-off)

Essential Tools

• Fine-mesh strainer for draining rinsed rice
• Large saucepan with lid
• Clean dish towel for absorbing moisture as rice stands off heat

Substitutions & Variations

• Although regular long-grain rice is fine in this recipe, it's even better with basmati rice.
• Olive oil can be substituted for the butter.
• If using a nonstick pan, feel free to use less butter—a tablespoon or two will be plenty.
• If you prefer, the onion can be omitted. Or use a minced shallot or two instead.
• If you want to add spices and other aromatics (garlic, ginger, or fresh chiles), cook them before the rice goes into the pot.
• Add dried fruits, toasted nuts, minced fresh herbs, or grated citrus zest when fluffing rice. One exception: If you want to soften really tough dried fruits (like currants or dried cranberries), add them to the pot when moving it off heat and placing the towel under the lid.

13 Roasted Broccoli

THE RIGHT RECIPE CAN MAKE ANY VEGETABLE APPEALING

The history of vegetable cookery in the United States is mostly a history of failure. Until fairly recently, vegetables were routinely overcooked, oversauced, and underseasoned. It's no wonder so many people claim not to like them.

The root of the problem, at least in our opinion, has been the reliance on boiling and steaming. In theory, these old-fashioned methods are fine, as long as you keep an eye on the clock, but they certainly don't make vegetables taste better. They just make them softer. And if you miss the mark, even by just a minute or two, many vegetables turn stinky and limp.

The best thing you can do for most vegetables, including broccoli, is to choose a better cooking method. Forget about moist heat and roast your veggies instead. In addition to softening woody textures, a hot oven caramelizes natural sugars and drives off excess moisture, thus concentrating flavors. When roasted, broccoli actually becomes sweet and its texture can range from crisp to creamy—all in the same bite.

Now, at first glance, broccoli might not look like the best candidate for roasting. Its awkward shape, tough stems, and shrubby florets might seem ill-suited for cooking via high, dry heat. But with some simple knife work, broccoli is as easy to roast as asparagus, green beans, Brussels sprouts, carrots, turnips, eggplant, squash, parsnips, shallots, artichokes....You get the idea. You really can roast almost any vegetable.

WHY THIS RECIPE WORKS

Preheat the Sheet
Preheating the baking sheet means the broccoli starts to sear as soon as it hits the hot pan. This cuts down the cooking time so the delicate florets don't have time to burn. (They will crisp a bit, though.)

Cut Big Wedges
Given its disparate parts, broccoli is tricky to roast so how it's prepped is absolutely key. Cutting the crown into uniform wedges creates flat surfaces for maximum contact with the hot baking sheet. Cut the stalk at the juncture of the stems and florets and then cut the crown into four or six wedges. Larger wedges (rather than small florets) can spend more time in the oven and this promotes more browning, as does flat sides.

Don't Toss the Best Part
Do not throw the stalk away. Instead, trim away its tough outer peel to reveal the lighter colored flesh below. A sturdy vegetable peeler will glide over the bumps on the stalk and make this process easy. Once peeled, cut the stalk into planks (remember that flat sides equal more browning). Roasting turns these pieces especially tender, creamy, and sweet. And you end up throwing away a lot less broccoli during the prep process.

Oil and Sugar
Tossing the broccoli with olive oil helps it brown. But since broccoli doesn't have a lot of natural sugars it needs help to caramelize. Seasoning with a little sugar facilitates the browning process. You won't taste the sugar but you will notice more roasted, caramelized notes in the broccoli.

Save the Lemon for the Table
A little acidity balances the sweetness of the broccoli. But wait to add lemon juice—if added during the cooking process it will dull the brilliant green color.

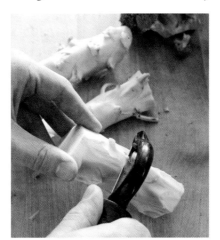 

Reinvent lowly broccoli by peeling the stalks and adding a pinch of sugar.

Roasted Broccoli

SERVES 4

Make sure to trim away the outer peel from the broccoli stalks as directed; otherwise, it will turn tough when cooked.

1¾	**pounds broccoli**
3	**tablespoons extra-virgin olive oil**
	Salt and pepper
½	**teaspoon sugar**
	Lemon wedges

1. Adjust oven rack to lowest position, place rimmed baking sheet on rack, and heat oven to 500 degrees. Cut broccoli at juncture of florets and stalks; remove outer peel from stalks. Cut stalks into 2- to 3-inch lengths and each length into ½-inch-thick pieces. Cut crowns into 4 wedges if 3 to 4 inches in diameter or 6 wedges if 4 to 5 inches in diameter. Place broccoli in large bowl; drizzle with oil and toss well until evenly coated. Sprinkle with ½ teaspoon salt, sugar, and pepper to taste, and toss to combine.

2. Working quickly, remove sheet from oven. Carefully transfer broccoli to sheet and spread into even layer, placing flat sides of broccoli pieces down. Return sheet to oven and roast until stalks are well browned and tender and florets are lightly browned, 9 to 11 minutes. Transfer to platter and serve immediately with lemon wedges.

ROASTED BROCCOLI WITH GARLIC

Stir 3 minced garlic cloves into oil before drizzling it over prepared broccoli in step 1.

ROASTED BROCCOLI WITH SHALLOTS, FENNEL SEEDS, AND PARMESAN

While broccoli roasts, heat 1 tablespoon extra-virgin olive oil in 8-inch skillet over medium heat until shimmering. Add 3 thinly sliced shallots and cook, stirring frequently, until soft and beginning to turn light golden brown, 5 to 6 minutes. Add 1 teaspoon coarsely chopped fennel seeds and continue to cook until shallots are golden brown, 1 to 2 minutes longer. Off heat, toss roasted broccoli with shallots, sprinkle with 1 ounce shaved Parmesan, and serve immediately.

ROASTED BROCCOLI WITH OLIVES, GARLIC, OREGANO, AND LEMON

Omit pepper when seasoning broccoli in step 1. While broccoli roasts, heat 2 tablespoons extra-virgin olive oil, 5 thinly sliced garlic cloves, and ½ teaspoon red pepper flakes in 8-inch skillet over medium-low heat. Cook, stirring frequently, until garlic is soft and beginning to turn light golden brown, 5 to 7 minutes. Remove from heat and stir in 2 tablespoons finely chopped pitted black olives, 1 teaspoon minced fresh oregano, and 2 teaspoons lemon juice. Toss roasted broccoli with olive mixture and serve immediately.

14 Grilled Cheese

A SIMPLE SANDWICH CAN ALSO BE A GREAT SANDWICH

The first bite of a grilled cheese sandwich is always the best one. The aroma of toasted butter is a familiar prelude to the crunch of crispy bread, which gives way to warm, gooey cheese. But the mystique fades quickly, mainly because the American cheese that is typically used has no taste.

The solution would seem simple enough—just use better cheese. But it's not that simple. Good cheeses are usually aged—that's what makes them taste so potent and delicious. But it's the aging that makes them so tricky to use in grilled cheese.

During the aging process, moisture evaporates and flavor compounds become more concentrated. A young, moist cheese will eventually dry out and become crumbly. Think of the difference between squeaky supermarket cheddar and the good stuff from England that crumbles when you slice it.

Because of their low moisture content, aged cheeses tend to be grainy when they melt. Even worse, they can break and leak fat. The proteins in the cheese (called casein) become weaker with age and simply can't contain the fat. Liquefy an aged cheese and you can see the fat separating out. In a grilled cheese sandwich, already rich with butter, the result is very unappealing.

But we like a good challenge in the test kitchen and have developed a formula for restoring moisture to aged cheeses so they melt well. And we've rethought the process for "grilling" the sandwich, too. With this recipe, every bite of your grilled cheese will be great.

WHY THIS RECIPE WORKS

Take a Cue From Fondue

Fondue is basically just melted cheese and it doesn't break, even when using older cheeses. Could something in this recipe solve the grilled cheese dilemma? Yes and no. Fondue relies on two key ingredients—wine and flour—to stabilize the cheese. The wine (blended into the cheese with the help of a food processor) is a great addition to grilled cheese. The added moisture helps drier, older cheese melt more evenly and it tastes great. The flour, however, is a bust—it makes the sandwich filling starchy.

In with the Young

Cutting an older cheese (which melts poorly) with a younger cheese (which melts well) proved to be a better strategy than flour. Creamy Brie works perfectly for this job. Again, using the food processor ensures that the two cheeses become one—and maximizes the stabilizing power of the Brie. Turning the cheeses (and wine) into a smooth paste also means the filling melts faster and will be nice and gooey when the bread is perfectly toasted.

Ramp Up the Flavor

A little bit of shallot adds savory complexity and depth of flavor to the sandwich without detracting from the cheese. Other options include chives, cornichon, dates, chipotle chile, or olives. Figure on a teaspoon or so (per sandwich) for any add-ins. Anything that tastes good on a cheese board will taste good in grilled cheese sandwiches.

Butter the Bread, Not the Pan

Using a nonstick skillet and buttering just the outside of the slices make the bread toast nicely. Preheating the skillet slowly means no hot spots so the bread will brown evenly, as does turning down the heat level once the pan is hot. Adding a little Dijon to the butter adds a subtle pleasant taste of mustard.

Wine and butter make everything better, including grilled cheese.

Grown-Up Grilled Cheese Sandwiches with Cheddar and Shallot

SERVES 4

To quickly bring the cheddar to room temperature, microwave the pieces until warm, about 30 seconds. The first two sandwiches can be held in a 200-degree oven on a wire rack set in a baking sheet.

7 ounces aged cheddar cheese, cut into 24 equal pieces, room temperature	4 teaspoons minced shallot
2 ounces Brie cheese, rind removed	3 tablespoons unsalted butter, softened
2 tablespoons dry white wine or vermouth	1 teaspoon Dijon mustard
	8 slices hearty white sandwich bread

1. Process cheddar, Brie, and wine in food processor until smooth paste is formed, 20 to 30 seconds. Add shallot and pulse to combine, 3 to 5 pulses. Combine butter and mustard in small bowl.

2. Working on parchment paper–lined counter, spread mustard butter evenly over 1 side of slices of bread. Flip 4 slices of bread over and spread cheese mixture evenly over slices. Top with remaining 4 slices of bread, buttered sides up.

3. Preheat 12-inch nonstick skillet over medium heat for 2 minutes. (Droplets of water should just sizzle when flicked onto pan.) Place 2 sandwiches in skillet; reduce heat to medium-low; and cook until both sides are crispy and golden brown, 6 to 9 minutes per side, moving sandwiches to ensure even browning. Remove sandwiches from skillet and let stand for 2 minutes before serving. Repeat with remaining 2 sandwiches.

GROWN-UP GRILLED CHEESE SANDWICHES WITH ASIAGO AND DATES
Substitute Asiago for cheddar, finely chopped pitted dates for shallot, and oatmeal sandwich bread for white sandwich bread.

GROWN-UP GRILLED CHEESE SANDWICHES WITH COMTÉ AND CORNICHON
Substitute Comté for cheddar, minced cornichon for shallot, and rye sandwich bread for white sandwich bread.

GROWN-UP GRILLED CHEESE SANDWICHES WITH GRUYÈRE AND CHIVES
Substitute Gruyère for cheddar, chives for shallot, and rye sandwich bread for white sandwich bread.

GROWN-UP GRILLED CHEESE SANDWICHES WITH ROBIOLA AND CHIPOTLE
Substitute Robiola for cheddar, ¼ teaspoon minced chipotle chile in adobo sauce for shallot, and oatmeal sandwich bread for white sandwich bread.

RECIPE DETAILS

Timeline

- 10 minutes to assemble sandwiches (preheat pan during final minutes)
- 15 minutes to toast sandwiches (per batch)
- 2 minutes to let cheese set up

Essential Tools

- Food processor to prepare cheese mixture
- 12-inch nonstick skillet

Substitutions & Variations

- Look for a cheddar aged for about one year (avoid cheddar aged for longer; it won't melt well). The same thing holds true for other cheeses used in the variations. Feel free to use your favorite flavorful cheese, making sure to avoid anything aged for more than a year.
- A little Brie is the key to using a more potent aged cheese. If you prefer, an equal amount of Monterey Jack can serve the same purpose. Like Brie, this young cheese melts very well.
- Hearty sandwich bread (with large thick slices) is a must. We like Arnold Country Classics. Other sliced breads (rye, oatmeal) work well, too. Avoid rustic loaves—all those air pockets provide exit routes for the filling. When making grilled cheese, you want bread with a uniform crumb.

15 Pancakes and Bacon

SUNDAY SOMETIMES DEMANDS A REAL BREAKFAST

Breakfast might get a lot of attention in the media, but in most homes it's rarely more than a bowl of cold cereal or an energy bar eaten on the run. And while you might consider a smoothie "a meal in a blender," none of these options is good enough for Sunday morning, when the clock slows down and there's time to make a real meal—one where everyone gathers around the table and eats together.

We understand why people resort to store-bought pie crust, but pancakes from a boxed mix don't make much sense to us. Homemade pancakes require an additional 5 minutes to prepare and the results are so much better. The secret is as simple as a little acid, which jump-starts the leavening reaction and guarantees fluffy hotcakes.

The hard part of this recipe, if there is one, is the cooking process—and that's the case whether you use a homemade batter or a mix. Many cooks struggle to regulate the heat so each batch comes out golden brown. An electric griddle makes this easy. If you're using a non-stick skillet, don't use butter in the pan (it burns). Instead, put vegetable oil in a cold pan and heat the oil and pan together. When the oil is shimmering, use a paper towel to wipe out the oil, leaving just a thin film on the pan. Why do this? You need enough oil to gauge the pan temperature, but pools of oil cause uneven heating, which leads to blotches on your pancakes.

Finally, what are pancakes without a side of bacon? Our oven-fried recipe is so much easier than the traditional stovetop method that you will wonder why you never made bacon this way. Best of all, cooking bacon in the oven means all your attention is on the flapjacks.

WHY THIS RECIPE WORKS

Fake the Buttermilk
There's no need to buy buttermilk to make pancakes with tangy flavor and fluffy texture. Soured milk, made by adding a little lemon juice to regular milk, has a tang similar to buttermilk and makes especially fluffy pancakes.

Two Leaveners Are Better Than One
Both baking soda and baking powder are essential in our pancakes. Baking soda reacts with the acid in the lemon juice and produces carbon dioxide to aerate the pancakes and provide lift. Baking powder reacts to the heat of the pan to release more carbon dioxide. Baking soda also helps the pancakes turn a nice golden-brown color.

A Lumpy Batter Is Best
Mixing the batter until smooth encourages excess gluten to form, which will produce tough, dense pancakes. Mix the batter until the ingredients are just combined. Lumps are okay—in fact they are essential to make pancakes with a light and fluffy texture.

Add Berries to the Pan, Not the Batter
No matter how careful you are, stirring the berries into the batter causes a few to break and produce blue-gray pancakes. Plus, the extra stirring makes for tough pancakes. The best method is simply to ladle some batter onto the hot skillet and then scatter a handful of berries on top.

Bake the Bacon
Cooking bacon on the stovetop requires constant attention and the hot splattering fat makes a greasy mess. The strips need to be turned and flipped in order to cook evenly. Using the oven instead of the frying pan is far easier, less messy, and more consistent. Also, oven frying allows you to cook a lot of bacon at one time—12 slices on a rimmed baking sheet in 10 minutes while you tend to the pancakes.

A lumpy batter is a good sign you haven't overmixed the wet and dry ingredients. And waiting to add the berries prevents the pancakes from turning purple.

Blueberry Pancakes

MAKES SIXTEEN 4-INCH PANCAKES; SERVES 4 TO 6

To make sure frozen blueberries don't bleed, rinse them under cool water in a fine-mesh strainer until the water runs clear, then spread them on a paper towel–lined plate to dry.

2	cups milk	1	large egg
1	tablespoon lemon juice	3	tablespoons unsalted butter, melted and cooled
2	cups (10 ounces) all-purpose flour	1–2	teaspoons vegetable oil
2	tablespoons sugar	5	ounces (1 cup) fresh or frozen blueberries, rinsed and dried
2	teaspoons baking powder		
½	teaspoon baking soda		
½	teaspoon salt		

1. Adjust oven rack to middle position and heat oven to 200 degrees. Set wire rack in rimmed baking sheet and spray with vegetable oil spray; place in oven. Whisk milk and lemon juice together in 4-cup liquid measuring cup; set aside to thicken while preparing other ingredients. Whisk flour, sugar, baking powder, baking soda, and salt together in medium bowl.

2. Add egg and melted butter to milk mixture and whisk until combined. Make well in center of dry ingredients; pour in milk mixture and whisk very gently until just combined (few lumps should remain). Do not overmix.

3. Heat 1 teaspoon oil in 12-inch nonstick skillet over medium heat until shimmering. Using paper towels, carefully wipe out oil, leaving thin film of oil on bottom and sides of pan. Using ¼-cup measure, portion batter into pan in 4 places. Sprinkle 1 tablespoon blueberries over each pancake. Cook pancakes until large bubbles begin to appear, 1½ to 2 minutes. Using thin, wide spatula, flip pancakes and cook until second side is golden brown, 1 to 1½ minutes longer. Serve pancakes immediately or transfer to wire rack in preheated oven. Repeat with remaining batter, using remaining oil as necessary.

LEMON-CORNMEAL BLUEBERRY PANCAKES

Add 2 teaspoons grated lemon zest to milk along with lemon juice and substitute 1½ cups stone-ground yellow cornmeal for 1 cup flour.

OVEN-FRIED BACON   SERVES 4 TO 6

Make bacon then turn down the heat and use oven to keep pancakes warm. This recipe is easy to double for a crowd: Simply double the amount of bacon and use two rimmed baking sheets—be sure to rotate the sheets and switch their oven positions halfway through cooking.

12	slices bacon

Adjust oven rack to middle position and heat oven to 400 degrees. Arrange bacon on rimmed baking sheet. Cook until fat begins to render, 5 to 6 minutes; rotate sheet. Continue cooking until bacon is crisp and brown, 5 to 6 minutes for thin-cut bacon or 8 to 10 minutes for thick-cut bacon. Transfer bacon to paper towel–lined plate, drain, and serve.

RECIPE DETAILS

Timeline

• 10 minutes to preheat oven, mix pancake batter, and heat skillet
• 15 minutes to cook pancakes

Essential Tools

• 12-inch nonstick skillet for cooking pancakes
• Wire rack set in rimmed baking sheet for holding pancakes in oven
• Large rimmed baking sheet (essential to contain rendered bacon fat)

Substitutions & Variations

• An equal amount of distilled white vinegar can be used in place of the lemon juice.
• If you have buttermilk on hand, use 2 cups instead of the milk and lemon juice.
• Omit the blueberries if you like, or use another fruit (sliced as necessary), toasted nuts, or even mini chocolate chips instead.
• The pancakes can be cooked on an electric griddle. Set the griddle temperature to 350 degrees and cook as directed.
• Making and holding the pancake batter for up to 1 hour has no detrimental effect on the pancakes. After 1 hour, however, the batter spreads out too easily, producing thin and floppy cakes.
• To freeze leftover pancakes, cool the pancakes to room temperature, then wrap them individually in plastic wrap and freeze for up to one month. When ready to serve, unwrap and spread them out on a wire rack set on top of a baking sheet, let thaw on the counter for 15 minutes, then reheat in a 350-degree oven until warm, 5 to 8 minutes.

16 Pan-Seared Chicken Breasts

THE SIMPLEST WAY TO PREPARE A MODERN STAPLE

What cook desperate for a quick dinner hasn't thrown four boneless, skinless chicken breasts into a hot pan, keeping fingers crossed for edible results? The fact is, traditional pan searing is a surefire way to ruin this cut. Unlike a split chicken breast, which has the bone and skin to help keep the meat moist and juicy, a boneless, skinless breast is fully exposed to the intensity of the hot pan. Inevitably, it emerges dry at the edges, with an exterior that's leathery and tough. That's a shame because a boneless, skinless chicken breast can be both convenient and delicious.

One way to solve the problem of dry, flavorless chicken breasts is to shorten the cooking time by cutting each breast in half horizontally to yield two cutlets. You can now sauté the cutlets (four at a time) in a hot pan. There are two drawbacks to this method, however: To serve four people you have to cook the cutlets in two batches and you need to butcher what was once a "ready-to-cook" cut. (You can forget about buying store-bought cutlets: The machines that do this mangle the chicken, and the high-quality brands we like don't sell cutlets.)

There has to be a way to take regular boneless, skinless chicken breasts, weighing 6 to 8 ounces each, and cook them without any butchering or batch cooking. We have developed a solution that starts in the oven. When the chicken is nearly up to temperature, it is quickly seared in a hot pan to brown the exterior. And a simple trick from Chinese cookery ensures that the browned exterior comes out crisp.

This recipe seems unlikely, at least when you first read it, but this unusual technique proves that simple food can be great food.

WHY THIS RECIPE WORKS

Poke and Salt
Salting helps the chicken to retain moisture, ensuring it will be juicy and flavorful. To help the salt penetrate the chicken more quickly and maximize a short salting time, poke holes with a fork in the thicker end of the breasts and then sprinkle them with kosher salt. The salt dissolves during baking and acts like a brine, seasoning the chicken and keeping it moist.

Cover and Bake
The chicken is baked at a low temperature in a covered dish to minimize moisture loss. In the enclosed environment, any moisture released by the chicken stays trapped under the foil and keeps the exterior from drying out.

Brush on a Coating
To keep the exterior of the skinless chicken breasts from becoming tough and leathery, they need a light coating. The coating takes the place of chicken skin and protects the meat during searing. We took a cue from a Chinese technique called velveting, where strips of chicken are dipped in a mixture of oil and cornstarch before stir-frying. We adapted this technique to use on a whole breast, preferring the flavor of melted butter to oil and a mix of cornstarch and flour. The protein in the flour dilutes the cornstarch so that it doesn't turn pasty, and the cornstarch keeps the crust from becoming too bready.

Sear Quickly
With the chicken nearly cooked, it needs very little time in the hot pan—just enough time to brown the exterior. Less time in a hot skillet means less moisture loss.

Rest and Sauce
To help retain juices, all cooked chicken should rest before it is served. In the case of this cut, 5 minutes is sufficient. Use this time (and the empty pan) to prepare a simple pan sauce.

A brush-on paste creates a crisp coating that acts like a second skin.

Pan-Seared Chicken Breasts

SERVES 4

For the best results, buy similarly sized chicken breasts. If the breasts have the tenderloin attached, leave it in place and follow the upper range of baking time in step 1. For optimal texture, sear the chicken immediately after removing it from the oven. Serve with a pan sauce (recipe follows), if desired.

4 (6- to 8-ounce) boneless, skinless chicken breasts, trimmed	2 tablespoons unsalted butter, melted
2 teaspoons kosher salt	1 tablespoon all-purpose flour
1 tablespoon vegetable oil	1 teaspoon cornstarch
	½ teaspoon pepper

1. Adjust oven rack to lower-middle position and heat oven to 275 degrees. Using fork, poke thickest half of breasts 5 or 6 times and sprinkle each with ½ teaspoon salt. Transfer breasts, skinned side down, to 13 by 9-inch baking dish and cover tightly with aluminum foil. Bake until breasts register 145 to 150 degrees, 30 to 40 minutes.

2. Remove chicken from oven; transfer, skinned side up, to paper towel–lined plate; and pat dry with paper towels. Heat oil in 12-inch skillet over medium-high heat until just smoking. While skillet is heating, whisk butter, flour, cornstarch, and pepper together in bowl. Lightly brush top of chicken with half of butter mixture. Place chicken in skillet, coated side down, and cook until browned, about 4 minutes. While chicken browns, brush with remaining butter mixture. Flip breasts, reduce heat to medium, and cook until second side is browned and breasts register 160 degrees, 3 to 4 minutes. Transfer breasts to large plate and let rest for 5 minutes before serving.

LEMON AND CHIVE PAN SAUCE MAKES ABOUT ¾ CUP

1 shallot, minced	1 tablespoon minced fresh chives
1 teaspoon all-purpose flour	1 tablespoon unsalted butter, chilled
1 cup chicken broth	Salt and pepper
1 tablespoon lemon juice	

Add shallot to now-empty skillet and cook over medium heat until softened, about 2 minutes. Add flour and cook, stirring constantly, for 30 seconds. Slowly whisk in broth, scraping up any browned bits. Bring to vigorous simmer and cook until reduced to ¾ cup, 3 to 5 minutes. Stir in any accumulated chicken juices; return to simmer and cook for 30 seconds. Off heat, whisk in lemon juice, chives, and butter. Season with salt and pepper to taste. Pour sauce over chicken and serve immediately.

RECIPE DETAILS

Timeline

- 40 minutes to parcook chicken in oven
- 10 minutes to coat chicken and sear in skillet
- 5 minutes to rest chicken (use this time to make pan sauce)

Essential Tools

- Fork to poke chicken
- 13 by 9-inch baking dish
- Aluminum foil to trap steam and juices while chicken cooks
- 12-inch skillet (A conventional pan will create better fond; if not making the pan sauce you can use nonstick.)

Substitutions & Variations

- We prefer kosher salt in this recipe. If using table salt, reduce salt amounts by half.
- Follow the pan sauce recipe to create your own variation. Garlic, onion, or leeks can be used in place of the shallot. Other liquids (wine, broth, juices) can be used to deglaze the pan. Stir in herbs, nuts, citrus zest, dried fruits, vinegars, or other potent ingredients at the end. No matter how you finish the sauce, a tablespoon of cold butter will emulsify everything.
- If you prefer to skip the pan sauce, think about a potent raw sauce, such as pesto, tomato salsa, spicy fruit salsa, or chutney. Just make sure to let the chicken rest for 5 minutes, even when serving it with a sauce you make before cooking the chicken.

17 Roast Chicken

COOKING A WHOLE BIRD CAN BE EASY AND FAST

For most people, "weeknight roast chicken" means a pricey rotisserie bird picked up on the way home from work. But it doesn't have to be this way. The ingredients for this recipe couldn't be simpler: just chicken, salt, and pepper—with fat (oil or butter) as a common fourth—and the cooking method is mostly hands-off. The problem is the prep.

Brining or salting the bird before it hits the oven solves the classic roast poultry predicament: how to keep the lean, delicate breast meat from overcooking by the time the fattier leg quarters come up to temperature. The salt in both methods buffers the meat against overcooking by restructuring its proteins, enabling it to retain more of its natural juices.

While these methods may be the ideal, they are not terribly practical on a weeknight. Even a small chicken requires an hour of roasting time and then time to rest and carve the bird, so adding more up-front work means a very late dinner. Wouldn't it be nice to remove the chicken from its packaging and put it in the oven?

And while we were at it, could we figure out a way to achieve allover crisp skin and even cooking of the meat without flipping the bird (so to speak)? Most modern recipes place the bird in a rack (to promote heat circulation) and then call for several turns. Reliable, yes. Easy, no.

By rethinking everything (oven temperature, vessel for the chicken), we were able to come up with a truly easy recipe. Literally, you put the chicken into the oven and walk away. It's so simple you might have the energy to make a quick sauce. You certainly will have enough free time.

WHY THIS RECIPE WORKS

Rub with Oil and Salt
Since the chicken isn't getting any flavor from brining, it needs lots of salt and pepper. Rubbing the chicken with olive oil helps anchor the seasonings. The oil also helps the skin to crisp. Be sure to pat the chicken dry with paper towels before oiling it. And don't bother rinsing the bird—that's a dangerous practice that spreads bacteria around the sink and it does nothing to improve the flavor of the bird.

Tie the Legs, Tuck the Wings
Tying the legs together makes them cook more evenly and helps to keep the heat in when the oven is off and carryover cooking is happening. It also holds the legs up so that the skin can brown and crisp underneath. Tucking the wing tips back exposes more of the skin covering the breast area so it also will brown and crisp.

Use a Skillet
A skillet makes getting the chicken in and out of the oven easier than using a roasting pan. The juices pool in the skillet's smaller space, slowing their evaporation and leaving more for a pan sauce.

A Preheated Pan = No Turning
Placing the bird breast side up into the preheated skillet sears the thighs, giving them a head start so that they cook in sync with the delicate breast meat. Direct contact with the hot pan would dry out the breast meat too much so there's no need to flip the bird over.

Turn Off the Oven
Turning off the oven when the meat is halfway done allows the chicken to finish cooking very gently (its internal temperature will rise 40 degrees) and slows the evaporation of juices, ensuring moist, tender meat.

Twine holds the legs in place, and an instant-read thermometer determines when it's time to turn off the oven and switch over to cooking via residual heat.

Weeknight Roast Chicken

SERVES 4

Serve with a pan sauce (recipes follow), if desired.

1 tablespoon kosher salt

½ teaspoon pepper

1 (3½- to 4-pound) whole chicken, giblets discarded

1 tablespoon olive oil

1. Adjust oven rack to middle position, place 12-inch ovensafe skillet on rack, and heat oven to 450 degrees. Combine salt and pepper in bowl. Pat chicken dry with paper towels. Rub entire surface with oil. Sprinkle salt mixture evenly over surface of chicken, then rub in mixture with your hands to coat evenly. Tie legs together with kitchen twine and tuck wing tips behind back.

2. Transfer chicken, breast side up, to preheated skillet in oven. Roast chicken until breast registers 120 degrees and thighs register 135 degrees, 25 to 35 minutes. Turn oven off and leave chicken in oven until breast registers 160 degrees and thighs register 175 degrees, 25 to 35 minutes.

3. Transfer chicken to carving board and let rest, uncovered, for 20 minutes. Carve chicken and serve.

TARRAGON-LEMON PAN SAUCE MAKES ABOUT ¾ CUP

1 shallot, minced

1 cup chicken broth

2 teaspoons Dijon mustard

2 tablespoons unsalted butter

2 teaspoons minced fresh tarragon

2 teaspoons lemon juice

Pepper

While chicken rests, remove all but 1 tablespoon fat from skillet (handle will be very hot) using large spoon, leaving any browned bits and jus in skillet. Place skillet over medium-high heat, add shallot, and cook until softened, about 2 minutes. Stir in broth and mustard, scraping up any browned bits. Simmer until reduced to ¾ cup, about 3 minutes. Off heat, whisk in butter, tarragon, and lemon juice. Season with pepper to taste.

THYME–SHERRY VINEGAR PAN SAUCE MAKES ABOUT ¾ CUP

1 shallot, minced

2 garlic cloves, minced

2 teaspoons chopped fresh thyme

1 cup chicken broth

2 teaspoons Dijon mustard

2 tablespoons unsalted butter

2 teaspoons sherry vinegar

Pepper

While chicken rests, remove all but 1 tablespoon fat from skillet (handle will be very hot) using large spoon, leaving any browned bits and jus in skillet. Place skillet over medium-high heat, add shallot, garlic, and thyme; cook until softened, about 2 minutes. Stir in broth and mustard, scraping up any browned bits. Simmer until reduced to ¾ cup, about 3 minutes. Off heat, whisk in butter and vinegar. Season with pepper to taste.

RECIPE DETAILS

Timeline

- 15 minutes to preheat oven
- 1 hour to roast chicken (30 minutes with oven on, 30 with oven off)
- 20 minutes to rest chicken before carving

Essential Tools

- 12-inch ovensafe skillet
- Kitchen twine for legs
- Instant-read thermometer (If you have a high-tech meat thermometer with a cord that snakes out of the oven and attaches to a monitor, use it; that way you can monitor the progress of the bird without opening the oven door and letting the residual heat escape.)

Substitutions & Variations

- We prefer to use a 3½- to 4-pound chicken for this recipe. If roasting a larger bird, increase the time when the oven is on in step 2 to 35 to 40 minutes.
- We prefer kosher salt because it's easy to distribute the large crystals and avoid clumps. That said, you can use table salt if you cut the amount in half.
- Use one of the two pan sauces here or a favorite combination. You need several tablespoons of concentrated sauce to moisten each serving of chicken—plan on ¾ cup in total.

A Better Way to Carve a Roast Chicken

Carving isn't difficult but there is definitely a way to approach it that will yield nice-looking parts and slices of boneless meat that are easy to serve. Before you start, make sure that you've let the chicken rest for 20 minutes. The resting time not only allows the juices to redistribute, it makes carving easier. You can also use this technique for carving a whole roast turkey.

1. Remove twine used to hold legs together. Slice through skin between leg and breast to expose hip joint. (Removing the leg quarters first makes carving the breast easier.)

2. Pull each leg quarter away from carcass and separate joint by gently pressing leg out to side and pushing up on joint. Carefully cut through joint where joint popped out of socket and remove leg quarter.

3. Separate each drumstick from thigh by cutting through joint that connects them. (If you have positioned your knife correctly, it should push easily through the joint. If you're getting a lot of resistance, shift the position of the knife.)

4. Pull wing away from carcass and carefully cut through joint between wing and breast to remove wing.

5. Cut down along 1 side of breastbone, pulling breast meat away from breastbone as you cut. Continue to cut and pry until breast has been removed in 1 piece. (It's much easier to get neat slices if you remove the entire breast half and then slice.)

6. Slice skin and breast crosswise into attractive slices for serving. Repeat on other side of chicken.

18 Stir-Fried Beef and Broccoli

MASTER ONE CLASSIC TO MAKE DOZENS OF STIR-FRIES

Stir-frying is a great way to turn beef, pork, or chicken as well as a handful of vegetables into a complete dinner. It seems so simple. You start with a tender cut (we like flank steak, pork tenderloin, or chicken breasts) and a few well-chosen vegetables (to provide a variety of colors, flavors, and textures). Add seasonings (garlic and ginger are almost always a must) and a quick sauce, and dinner is served, right? Too bad that "fast" dinner is often a watery, bland disappointment.

The problem is that the classic restaurant method—the one described in most recipes—doesn't work in most home kitchens. In restaurants, round-bottomed woks rest in cutouts in the stovetop, and intense flames heat the entire pan. At home, on a flat burner, the results are usually underwhelming, with poor browning and not nearly enough evaporation and concentration of flavors.

Our advice is to skip a wok in favor of a large nonstick skillet. The diameter of a large skillet provides a wide, broad cooking surface that promotes good browning, which translates to great flavor. We like a nonstick pan because it reduces the amount of oil needed. In addition to switching up the pan, you need to cook items sequentially. You can't dump all of your ingredients into the pan all at once and expect good results.

On the following page, we offer a detailed beef and broccoli recipe plus guidelines for creating your own combinations. If you have a protein, one or two vegetables, and some Asian pantry staples on hand, you have the makings of a good stir-fry. All you need is a method designed for your stovetop rather than for a restaurant kitchen.

WHY THIS RECIPE WORKS

Slice the Meat Thin and Marinate
Beef, pork, and chicken must be sliced thin (¼ inch is ideal) and marinated. (Freezing the meat for about 15 minutes will make slicing easier.) Make sure to cut across the grain to maximize tenderness. Salty liquids like soy sauce or fish sauce not only boost meat's savory flavor but also act as a brine, helping the meat retain moisture during cooking. When ready to cook, drain well to remove excess moisture and promote browning.

Use a Heavy Pan
It is essential to use a skillet that heats evenly and that quickly recovers heat each time food is added to it. Flimsy pans need not apply.

Cook in Batches
Adding all the ingredients at once will cause the food to steam rather than sear. Cook the protein in small ½-pound batches and make sure to leave space between individual pieces for even browning. And batch-cook vegetables, too, especially if using vegetables with varying cooking times (such as broccoli and bell pepper).

Stir Infrequently
Nomenclature aside, it's best to stir your stir-fry infrequently. Western-style burners have a relatively low heat output, so stirring food infrequently allows for proper browning.

Don't Add the Aromatics Too Early
Garlic and ginger can scorch if added to the pan too early. Wait until the protein and vegetables are done before adding the aromatics (mixed with 1½ teaspoons of oil to help them cook).

Make a Potent Sauce
Watery sauces will wash away the browning on food. Use small amounts of potent ingredients and add 1 to 2 teaspoons cornstarch so liquids thicken quickly when they hit the pan.

Batch-cooking is the key to a stir-fry that ends well.

Stir-Fried Beef and Broccoli with Oyster Sauce

SERVES 4

To make slicing the flank steak easier, freeze it for 15 minutes. If you prefer, replace the flank steak with an equal amount of sirloin tip steaks or blade steaks. Serve with steamed rice.

SAUCE

- 5 tablespoons oyster sauce
- 2 tablespoons chicken broth
- 1 tablespoon dry sherry
- 1 tablespoon packed light brown sugar
- 1 teaspoon toasted sesame oil
- 1 teaspoon cornstarch

BEEF STIR-FRY

- 1 (1-pound) flank steak, trimmed and sliced thin against grain on slight bias
- 3 tablespoons soy sauce
- 6 garlic cloves, minced
- 1 tablespoon grated fresh ginger
- 3 tablespoons peanut or vegetable oil
- 1¼ pounds broccoli, florets cut into bite-size pieces, stalks peeled and cut ⅛ inch thick on bias
- ⅓ cup water
- 1 small red bell pepper, stemmed, seeded, and cut into ¼-inch pieces
- 3 scallions, sliced ½ inch thick on bias

1. *For the Sauce:* Whisk all ingredients together in small bowl and set aside.

2. *For the Beef Stir-Fry:* Combine beef and soy sauce in medium bowl and toss to coat. Cover with plastic wrap and let marinate for at least 10 minutes or up to 1 hour, stirring once. Meanwhile, combine garlic, ginger, and 1½ teaspoons oil in small bowl.

3. Drain beef and discard liquid. Heat 1½ teaspoons oil in 12-inch nonstick skillet over high heat until just smoking. Add half of beef in single layer, break up clumps, and cook, without stirring, for 1 minute. Stir beef and continue to cook until beef is browned, about 30 seconds. Transfer beef to clean medium bowl. Repeat with 1½ teaspoons oil and remaining beef.

4. Add 1 tablespoon oil to skillet and heat until just smoking. Add broccoli and cook for 30 seconds. Add water to pan, cover, and lower heat to medium. Steam broccoli until crisp-tender, about 2 minutes, then transfer to paper towel–lined plate. Add remaining 1½ teaspoons oil to skillet, increase heat to high, and heat until just smoking. Add bell pepper and cook, stirring frequently, until spotty brown, about 1½ minutes. Clear center of skillet, add garlic mixture, and cook, mashing mixture into pan, until fragrant, 15 to 20 seconds; stir mixture into bell pepper.

5. Return beef and broccoli to skillet and toss to combine. Whisk sauce to recombine, then add to skillet and cook, stirring constantly, until sauce is thickened and evenly distributed, about 30 seconds. Transfer to platter, sprinkle with scallions, and serve.

RECIPE DETAILS

Timeline

- 20 minutes to prep ingredients (start by placing meat in freezer to make slicing it easier)
- 10 minutes to make sauce and marinate meat
- 10 minutes to cook (don't start until everything is prepped and ready to go)

Essential Tools

- 12-inch nonstick skillet with lid
- Chef's knife (very sharp)
- Tongs

Substitutions & Variations

- The technique embedded in this recipe can be used to cook 1 pound of pork tenderloin (cut crosswise into ¼-inch-thick slices, then cut into ¼-inch-thick strips) or boneless, skinless chicken breasts (remove tenderloins and cut across grain into ¼-inch-thick slices). Add 1½ pounds of your favorite vegetables and you have enough food to serve four people as a main course.
- Long-cooking vegetables such as broccoli, carrots, cauliflower, eggplant, and green beans should cook for 3 to 7 minutes (less if you add water and steam them as directed in this recipe).
- Medium-cooking vegetables such as asparagus, bell pepper, bok choy stalks, celery, frozen shelled edamame, mushrooms, napa cabbage, onions, scallion whites, snap peas, and snow peas cook in 1 to 3 minutes.
- Fast-cooking vegetables such as bean sprouts, bok choy greens, frozen peas, scallion greens, tender greens, tomatoes, and water chestnuts cook in 30 to 60 seconds.

19 Beef Tenderloin

THE BEST WAY TO COOK EVERYONE'S FAVORITE FANCY ROAST

Nothing beats the extravagantly buttery texture of beef tenderloin. It's not the most flavorful cut (by a long shot), but that is easily overcome with a rich sauce or other accompaniment (we think a compound butter is best). The challenge is to expertly cook this expensive cut. Tenderloin is very lean and even slight overcooking can compromise its chief asset—its juicy, melt-in-the-mouth texture.

Creating a browned crust is almost as important. The meat itself doesn't have much fat or flavor, and that browned exterior is key to developing the beefy notes. This crust is usually accomplished by a hard sear before the roast goes into the oven and/or a high oven temperature.

Searing in a hot skillet followed by a quick spin in a hot oven can seem to work. The crust will look well browned and the center will be pink (assuming you catch the roast at just the right moment). But there's a serious problem lurking just below that crust. All that heat produces uneven cooking and there's a wide band of gray meat between the crust and center of the roast. You may get the center and the exterior right, but half of each slice is dry.

The ideal slice of tenderloin is well browned around the edges but then evenly cooked—juicy and pink—from the center right to the crust. And the recipe should be goofproof—something even a novice cook could pull off. No one wants to fret about ruining the centerpiece of a special meal.

Good news. You can relax. Our recipe slows things down so overcooking is far less likely. You spent a lot of money on this roast so shouldn't the cooking be easy?

WHY THIS RECIPE WORKS

Buy a Center-Cut Roast
The center-cut tenderloin, also called a Châteaubriand, comes from the middle of the whole tenderloin. The meat sits beneath the spine of the cow and gets no exercise at all, making it exceptionally tender. Adding to its appeal is that it is already trimmed, has a fairly even shape, and fits in a skillet.

Tie It Up
Tying the roast at intervals with kitchen twine makes it more compact and helps give it an even shape, which promotes even cooking.

Salt and Butter at the Outset
To enhance the beef flavor and help it hold on to its juices, salt the roast before cooking. The salt breaks down the surface proteins in the meat, allowing the salt in and drawing flavor deep into the meat. To counteract the leanness of this cut, smear the exterior with softened butter.

Roast in a Low Oven, and Then Sear
We reverse the usual cooking process for tenderloin, roasting it first and then searing it. This eliminates the ring of gray overdone meat usually found under the roast's crust. The roast starts cooking on a wire rack in a fairly cool 300-degree oven, which minimizes the temperature differential between the exterior and interior. Once out of the oven, the surface of the meat is very dry, so it will sear very quickly—before any overcooking of the meat can occur.

Finish with More Butter
Slather the roast with a compound butter as it rests. As the savory butter melts, the heat of the roast unlocks the full flavor and aroma of the ingredients in the butter. You can spoon any melted butter on the carving board over individual slices.

Twine cinches the roast into a uniform shape that cooks evenly, and a double dose of butter builds big flavor.

Roast Beef Tenderloin

SERVES 4 TO 6

Center-cut beef tenderloin roasts are sometimes sold as Châteaubriand. Ask your butcher to prepare a trimmed center-cut Châteaubriand, as this cut is not usually available without special ordering.

1 (2-pound) center-cut beef tenderloin roast, trimmed

2 teaspoons kosher salt

1 teaspoon coarsely ground pepper

2 tablespoons unsalted butter, softened

1 tablespoon vegetable oil

1 recipe flavored butter (recipes follow)

1. Using 12-inch lengths of kitchen twine, tie roast crosswise at 1½-inch intervals. Sprinkle roast evenly with salt, cover loosely with plastic wrap, and let stand at room temperature for 1 hour. Meanwhile, adjust oven rack to middle position and heat oven to 300 degrees.

2. Pat roast dry with paper towels. Sprinkle roast evenly with pepper and spread unsalted butter evenly over surface. Transfer roast to wire rack set in rimmed baking sheet. Roast until meat registers 125 degrees (for medium-rare), 40 to 55 minutes, or 135 degrees (for medium), 55 minutes to 1 hour 10 minutes, flipping roast halfway through cooking.

3. Heat oil in 12-inch skillet over medium-high heat until just smoking. Place roast in skillet and sear until well browned on all sides, 4 to 8 minutes total. Transfer roast to carving board and spread 2 tablespoons flavored butter evenly over top of roast; let rest for 15 minutes. Remove twine and cut roast crosswise into ½-inch-thick slices. Serve, passing remaining flavored butter separately.

SHALLOT AND PARSLEY BUTTER MAKES ABOUT ½ CUP

4 tablespoons unsalted butter, softened

½ shallot, minced

1 tablespoon minced fresh parsley

1 garlic clove, minced

¼ teaspoon salt

¼ teaspoon pepper

Combine all ingredients in bowl.

CHIPOTLE AND GARLIC BUTTER WITH LIME AND CILANTRO MAKES ABOUT ½ CUP

5 tablespoons unsalted butter, softened

1 tablespoon minced canned chipotle chile in adobo sauce plus 1 teaspoon adobo sauce

1 tablespoon minced fresh cilantro

1 garlic clove, minced

1 teaspoon honey

1 teaspoon grated lime zest

½ teaspoon salt

Combine all ingredients in bowl.

RECIPE DETAILS

Timeline

• 1 hour to salt meat
• 40 minutes to 1 hour 10 minutes to roast meat (depending on desired doneness)
• 6 minutes to sear meat on all sides
• 15 minutes to rest meat

Essential Tools

• Kitchen twine to tie roast
• Wire rack set in rimmed baking sheet
• Instant-read thermometer
• 12-inch skillet

Substitutions & Variations

• We prefer kosher salt in this recipe. If using table salt, reduce salt amounts by half.

• If you are cooking for a crowd, this recipe can be doubled to make two roasts. Sear the roasts one after the other, wiping out the pan and adding new oil after searing the first roast. Both pieces of meat can be roasted on the same rack.

• To make a blue cheese and chive butter, crumble 1½ ounces room-temperature mild blue cheese. Combine with 3 tablespoons softened unsalted butter and ⅛ teaspoon salt in medium bowl and mix with stiff rubber spatula until smooth. Fold in 2 tablespoons minced fresh chives.

20 Steak

COOKING STEAK INDOORS DOESN'T HAVE TO BE A MESS

Thick steaks are better than thin ones. At least that's the common thinking when we eat out. But the rules seem to change at home. Most home cooks shy away from anything over an inch thick if the weather or space doesn't permit outdoor cooking.

What can seem like an asset—the time to put a serious crust on those thick steaks—becomes a huge handicap. Unless you have a professional ventilation system, the house will fill with smoke. (Get the stepstool ready to turn off the alarm.) And even if you manage to keep the smoke at bay, the stovetop will be a greasy mess. Worse still, a thick steak won't cook evenly—the meat right under the crust gets so much heat that it becomes gray and dry.

The solution turns out to be quite simple: Treat thick steaks like a roast. That means gently warming the steaks in the oven (as we do with a beef tenderloin roast; see page 66) and then searing them just before serving. Because most of the cooking is quite gentle, the meat is perfectly cooked, even right under the crust.

If you don't believe that the best seared steaks really do start low and slow, just ask any forward-thinking chef. Many top restaurants are cooking steaks via *sous vide*. That is, they are vacuum-sealing steaks in plastic pouches, gently cooking them in a warm water bath held at a constant temperature, and then searing them just before serving. Our method trades the water bath for a cool oven (and requires no vacuum sealer or expensive sous vide machine!), but the principle is the same.

WHY THIS RECIPE WORKS

Size Matters
Be sure to check the thickness of your steak with a stainless-steel kitchen ruler. Steaks that are thinner than specified in our recipe will overcook. To get the right portion size, we cut 1-pound boneless strip steaks (or rib eyes or filets mignons) in half crosswise to create 8-ounce steaks and gently shape them into a uniform thickness.

Rack 'Em Up
When trying to sear a thick steak, it's a problem to start out with a cold piece of meat. It will take a long, long time for the interior to reach 130 degrees. Instead of starting the meat in the pan, we move the steaks straight from the fridge onto a wire rack set into a baking sheet and slowly warm them to 95 degrees (for medium-rare) in a 275-degree oven. The low oven temperature minimizes internal moisture loss and promotes even cooking from edge to center. It also gives the meat's tenderizing enzymes time to work, in effect "aging" the steaks during their stint in the oven.

Finish By Searing—All Over
With the steaks warmed, the searing process goes quickly. And there's less smoke and a lot less splattering because the oven dehydrates the exterior of each steak (it's the water that causes all the mess). While most recipes instruct to sear steaks on both flat sides, we think it maximizes the flavor to sear the steaks on their edges as well. Once the flat sides are browned, use a pair of tongs to hold two steaks at a time to sear their edges.

Rest the Meat, Reuse the Pan
Pan-seared steaks pair well with a pan sauce, relish, or flavored butter, all of which can be made while the steaks rest. If making a pan sauce, you should reuse the same skillet in which the steaks were cooked (the browned bits are key to making a great sauce), but you will need to start with fresh oil.

For steak perfection, start in the oven and then quickly finish in a hot pan.

Pan-Seared Thick-Cut Strip Steaks

SERVES 4

If cooking lean strip steaks (without an external fat cap), add an extra tablespoon of oil to the pan. Serve with a pan sauce or flavored butter (recipes follow), if desired.

2	(1-pound) boneless strip steaks, 1½ to 1¾ inches thick, trimmed		Salt and pepper
		1	tablespoon vegetable oil

1. Adjust oven rack to middle position and heat oven to 275 degrees. Pat steaks dry with paper towels. Cut each steak in half vertically to create four 8-ounce steaks. Season steaks with salt and pepper; gently press sides of steaks until uniform 1½ inches thick. Place steaks on wire rack set in rimmed baking sheet. Cook until meat registers 90 to 95 degrees (for rare to medium-rare), 20 to 25 minutes, or 100 to 105 degrees (for medium), 25 to 30 minutes.

2. Heat oil in 12-inch skillet over high heat until just smoking. Place steaks in skillet and sear until well browned and crusty, about 1½ to 2 minutes, lifting once halfway through cooking to redistribute fat underneath each steak. (Reduce heat if fond begins to burn.) Using tongs, turn steaks and cook until well browned on second side, 2 to 2½ minutes. Transfer all steaks to clean wire rack and reduce heat to medium. Use tongs to stand 2 steaks on their sides. Holding steaks together, return to skillet and sear on all sides until browned, 1½ minutes. Repeat with remaining 2 steaks.

3. Transfer steaks to wire rack and let rest, tented loosely with aluminum foil, for 10 minutes. Arrange steaks on individual plates and spoon sauce, if using, over steaks; serve.

RED WINE–MUSHROOM PAN SAUCE MAKES ABOUT 1 CUP

1	tablespoon vegetable oil	1	tablespoon balsamic vinegar
8	ounces white mushrooms, trimmed and sliced thin	1	teaspoon Dijon mustard
1	small shallot, minced	2	tablespoons unsalted butter, cut into 4 pieces and chilled
1	cup dry red wine	1	teaspoon minced fresh thyme
½	cup chicken broth		Salt and pepper

After transferring steaks to wire rack, pour off fat from skillet. Add oil to now-empty skillet and heat over medium-high heat until just smoking. Add mushrooms and cook, stirring occasionally, until beginning to brown and liquid has evaporated, about 5 minutes. Add shallot and cook, stirring frequently, until beginning to soften, about 1 minute. Increase heat to high; add red wine and broth, scraping up any browned bits. Simmer rapidly until liquid and mushrooms are reduced to 1 cup, about 6 minutes. Add vinegar, mustard, and any juices from resting steaks; cook until thickened, about 1 minute. Off heat, whisk in butter and thyme; season with salt and pepper to taste. Spoon sauce over steaks and serve.

RECIPE DETAILS

Timeline

- 5 minutes to prep steaks
- 20 to 30 minutes to warm steaks in oven (prepare ingredients for any pan sauce or butter during this time)
- 6 minutes to sear steaks
- 10 minutes to rest steaks (and make pan sauce)

Essential Tools

- Wire rack set in rimmed baking sheet plus another clean rack
- Instant-read thermometer (critical to determine when steaks should come out of the oven)
- 12-inch skillet
- Tongs to turn steaks and stand them up as you sear edges

Substitutions & Variations

- Rib-eye steaks or filets mignons of similar thickness can be substituted for the strip steaks.
- If using filets mignons, buying a 2-pound center-cut tenderloin roast and portioning it into four 8-ounce steaks will produce more consistent results than using individual store-cut steaks.
- If using filets mignons, increase the oven time by about 5 minutes and add an extra tablespoon of oil to the pan.
- We prefer kosher salt in this recipe. If using table salt, reduce salt amounts by half.

THAI CHILI BUTTER MAKES ½ CUP

If red curry paste isn't available, increase the Asian chili-garlic sauce to 2½ teaspoons. You can prepare the butter while the steaks are in the oven.

- 4 tablespoons unsalted butter, softened
- 1 tablespoon chopped fresh cilantro
- 2 teaspoons Asian chili-garlic sauce
- 1½ teaspoons thinly sliced scallion, green part only
- ½ teaspoon red curry paste
- 1 small garlic clove, minced
- 2 teaspoons lime juice
- Salt

Beat butter vigorously with spoon until soft and fluffy. Add cilantro, chili-garlic sauce, scallion, red curry paste, and garlic; beat to incorporate. Add lime juice a little at a time, beating vigorously between each addition until fully incorporated. Season with salt to taste. Top each cooked steak with portion of flavored butter and serve.

A Better Way to Make a Pan Sauce

A pan sauce is built on the flavorful browned bits (called fond) that are left sticking to the pan from the searing process. Although the ingredients and amounts change depending on the sauce, the basic steps for any pan sauce are the same.

1. Use traditional skillet to sear meat; fond won't form in nonstick skillet. Once meat is cooked, transfer it to plate to rest. Pour off fat from now-empty skillet and heat fresh oil.

2. Add small amount of minced shallot, garlic, onion, or leek and cook over medium or medium-high heat until softened, 1 to 3 minutes. Browning sliced mushrooms first is a nice option.

3. Add liquid, usually broth and/or wine, use wooden spoon to scrape up browned bits from pan, and simmer rapidly to reduce liquid. (The liquid lets you loosen the fond from the pan bottom; as the liquid simmers, the browned bits dissolve and enrich the sauce with meaty flavor.) Stir in any accumulated juices from resting meat.

4. Remove pan from heat and whisk in chilled unsalted butter, 1 small piece at a time. (Chilled butter helps pull the sauce together and makes it thick and glossy.) Add any fresh herbs or potent ingredients (they don't need any cooking time) and season with salt and pepper. Spoon sauce over meat and serve immediately.

21 Breaded Pork Chops

FORGET THE SHAKE AND THE BAKE

Progress isn't always a good thing. In the old days, when pigs were fatty, pork chops could be pan-seared and served as is. They were loaded with flavor and there was little risk of them drying out. Unfortunately this simple preparation makes no sense with the chops sold in today's supermarkets.

Farmers (OK, food manufacturers and scientists) have engineered the modern pig to be much leaner. In fact, today's pork contains about half as much fat as our grandparents' pork. This change is especially apparent in traditionally lean parts of the pig, like the loin. As a result, the modern pork chop (which typically comes from the loin) doesn't have much flavor (remember fat equals flavor) and it tends to be dry and chewy (fat also lubricates meat and makes it more tender).

For many home cooks, the solution to this dilemma comes in a box. Coating the pork with seasoned bread crumbs adds much-needed flavor and the crisp coating protects against dryness. Or at least that's how the recipe is supposed to work. But packaged breading mixes are marred by stale flavors. And opting for baking rather than pan-frying, as many cooks do, means that the coating is more sandy than crisp.

For a truly great breaded pork chop, we turn off the oven and get out a skillet. As for the coating, we have done some engineering of our own to build a better breading—one that is crisp and light, and stays in place. Best of all, it's simple. Now that's our idea of progress.

WHY THIS RECIPE WORKS

Lose the Bone
To keep these pork chops quick and easy to prepare, choose boneless loin chops instead of bone-in chops. Shallow frying these thin, tender chops takes just a few minutes per side.

Go Light and Crispy and Score
A breaded coating can be just the thing to give lean, bland pork chops a flavor boost—but not when it turns gummy and flakes off the meat. For a light, crisp coating, skip the usual flour and start with cornstarch, which releases sticky starch as it absorbs water and forms an ultracrisp sheath when exposed to heat and fat. Scoring the surface of the chops prior to dredging releases juices and sticky proteins that dampen the cornstarch and help the coating adhere.

Dip in Buttermilk
Instead of the typical egg wash, which puffs up when cooked and contributes to a heavier coating that pulls away from the meat, use buttermilk for the liquid component. It makes a lighter shell that clings nicely to the chops. And the buttermilk contributes a subtle tang, while a dollop of mustard and a little minced garlic perk up its flavor even more.

Cornflakes Plus
With buttermilk as the wash, bread crumbs don't make sense for the final layer. Instead, use cornflakes, which are engineered to retain their crunch in milk. Mixing some cornstarch into the cornflake crumbs makes them even stronger and crispier.

Rest to Solidify the Coating
It is important to let the pork rest after breading and before cooking. Letting the chops sit for 10 minutes before they hit the oil gives the cornstarch more time to wick up moisture and turn into a stickier paste that remains intact during the cooking process.

A scored surface helps the coating cling for maximum crunch.

Crispy Pan-Fried Pork Chops

SERVES 4

We prefer natural to enhanced pork (pork that has been injected with a salt solution to increase moistness and flavor) for this recipe. Don't let the chops drain on the paper towels for longer than 30 seconds per side or the heat will steam the crust and make it soggy.

⅔ cup cornstarch	Salt and pepper
1 cup buttermilk	8 (3- to 4-ounce) boneless pork chops,
2 tablespoons Dijon mustard	½ to ¾ inch thick, trimmed
1 garlic clove, minced	⅔ cup vegetable oil
3 cups cornflakes	Lemon wedges

1. Place ⅓ cup cornstarch in shallow dish. In second shallow dish, whisk buttermilk, mustard, and garlic until combined. Process cornflakes, ½ teaspoon salt, ½ teaspoon pepper, and remaining ⅓ cup cornstarch in food processor until cornflakes are finely ground, about 10 seconds. Transfer cornflake mixture to third shallow dish.

2. Adjust oven rack to middle position and heat oven to 200 degrees. Cut ¹⁄₁₆-inch-deep slits on both sides of chops, spaced ½ inch apart, in crosshatch pattern. Season chops with salt and pepper. Dredge 1 chop in cornstarch; shake off excess. Using tongs, coat with buttermilk mixture; let excess drip off. Coat with cornflake mixture; gently pat off excess. Transfer coated chop to wire rack set in rimmed baking sheet and repeat with remaining chops. Let coated chops stand for 10 minutes.

3. Heat ⅓ cup oil in 12-inch nonstick skillet over medium-high heat until shimmering. Place 4 chops in skillet and cook until golden brown and crisp, 2 to 5 minutes. Carefully flip chops and continue to cook until second side is golden brown, crisp, and chops register 145 degrees, 2 to 5 minutes longer. Transfer chops to paper towel–lined plate and let drain for 30 seconds on each side. Transfer to clean wire rack set in rimmed baking sheet, then transfer to oven to keep warm. Discard oil in skillet and wipe clean with paper towels. Repeat process with remaining oil and pork chops. Serve with lemon wedges.

CRISPY PAN-FRIED PORK CHOPS WITH LATIN SPICE RUB
Combine 1½ teaspoons ground cumin, 1½ teaspoons chili powder, ¾ teaspoon ground coriander, ⅛ teaspoon ground cinnamon, and ⅛ teaspoon red pepper flakes in bowl. Omit pepper; coat chops with spice rub after seasoning with salt in step 2.

CRISPY PAN-FRIED PORK CHOPS WITH THREE-PEPPER RUB
Combine 1½ teaspoons pepper, 1½ teaspoons white pepper, ¾ teaspoon ground coriander, ¾ teaspoon ground cumin, ¼ teaspoon red pepper flakes, and ¼ teaspoon ground cinnamon in bowl. Omit pepper and coat chops with spice rub after seasoning with salt in step 2.

RECIPE DETAILS

Timeline
• 20 minutes to bread chops and let them rest
• 15 minutes to brown chops in 2 batches

Essential Tools
• Paring knife to score surface of chops
• 3 shallow dishes for coating process
• Tongs for dipping chops in buttermilk and for frying
• Wire rack set in rimmed baking sheet
• Paper towels

Substitutions & Variations
• You can substitute ¾ cup store-bought cornflake crumbs for the whole cornflakes. If using crumbs, omit the processing step and mix the crumbs with the cornstarch, salt, and pepper.
• Although we prefer real buttermilk, even in the test kitchen we occasionally find ourselves without it. In a pinch, you can make a buttermilk substitute by mixing 1 cup milk with 1 tablespoon lemon juice or distilled white vinegar.
• Add some hot sauce to the buttermilk mixture to spice things up. Dried herbs (oregano, sage, and thyme work well) can be added to the crumbs.

22 Pork Roast

A SWEET GLAZE CONCEALS THE FLAWS IN A BORING ROAST

A crisp breading is a great way to camouflage the problems associated with today's too-lean, too-bland pork chops (see page 74). But when it comes to a loin roast, cut from the same part of the animal as those chops, a sweet glaze is a better agent for this cover-up operation. The glaze keeps the exterior of the roast from becoming tough and dry. And when the roast is carved, the glaze coats each slice, making every bite tastier and juicier.

Glazed pork roast usually begins on the stovetop, with a quick sear to build flavor. The roast is then transferred to a roasting pan and the glaze (we like maple syrup) is brushed on. The result should be a glistening roast—if only you could get the glaze to stick.

Although we think of maple syrup as being thick and viscous, when heated it becomes quite thin. Even the thickest glaze ends up pooling at the base of the roast and you need to brush it back on. This is slow work, especially if you have to reapply the glaze several times. For quick, even coverage, ditch the brush and use tongs to roll the roast in the glaze. The process is so easy you won't mind repeating it several times.

There is one possible downside here: As the glaze bubbles away in a roasting pan it can burn in spots. Switching to a skillet prevents the glaze from spreading out and keeps more of the roast submerged. (It also makes this a one-pan recipe.) Once the roast is browned, the maple syrup goes into the pan—almost deglazing it and ensuring that the browned bits stuck to the pan contribute their meaty flavor to the glaze. Roasting and turning the pork in the glaze makes covering the whole roast easy and keeps the pork plenty moist.

WHY THIS RECIPE WORKS

Use Natural Pork
Today's pork is very lean, and less fat means less flavor and moisture. The industry addressed this issue by introducing "enhanced pork"—meat injected with a solution of water, salt, and sodium phosphate meant to both season the pork and prevent it from drying out. However, natural pork has a better flavor and if cooked correctly it will stay juicy. When shopping, read labels carefully. If pork has been enhanced its label will have an ingredient list. Natural pork contains just pork and won't have an ingredient list.

Pick the Right Roast
A boneless blade-end loin roast, cut from the tender loin near the pig's shoulder blade, has a lot of flavor and juiciness, which it receives in part from a little deposit of fat that separates the two muscle sections at one end of the roast.

A Tied Roast Cooks Evenly
Straight from the package, most pork loins lie flat in the pan and cook unevenly. Tying the roast ensures that the roast will have an even shape and yield attractive slices. Tied into a neat bundle, the roast fits well into a skillet on the stovetop.

The Glazing Is Easy
Dry pork is a problem, but so usually is the glaze, which is either too thin or overly sweet. The sweetness of maple complements the pork, which has a faint sweetness of its own. Small amounts of spices add subtle heat and dimension to maple syrup and cut its sweetness. Using a nonstick skillet helps to prevent the maple syrup from burning and sticking. Reducing the syrup in the skillet used to sear the pork takes full advantage of the browned bits left in the pan and eliminates the need for an extra pan; cooling the glaze briefly thickens it up quite a bit.

A skillet ensures that the roast really browns and the glaze really sticks.

Maple-Glazed Pork Roast

SERVES 4 TO 6

Note that you should not trim the pork of its thin layer of fat.

½ cup maple syrup, preferably dark	¾ teaspoon salt
⅛ teaspoon ground cinnamon	½ teaspoon pepper
Pinch ground cloves	2 teaspoons vegetable oil
Pinch cayenne pepper	
1 (2½-pound) boneless blade-end pork loin roast, tied at even intervals along length with 5 pieces kitchen twine	

1. Adjust oven rack to middle position and heat oven to 325 degrees. Stir maple syrup, cinnamon, cloves, and cayenne together in measuring cup or bowl; set aside. Pat roast dry with paper towels, then season with salt and pepper.

2. Heat oil in 10-inch ovensafe nonstick skillet over medium-high heat until just smoking. Place roast fat side down in skillet and cook until well browned, about 3 minutes. Using tongs, rotate roast one-quarter turn and cook until well browned, about 2½ minutes; repeat until roast is well browned on all sides. Transfer roast to large plate. Reduce heat to medium and pour off fat from skillet; add maple syrup mixture and cook until fragrant, about 30 seconds (syrup will bubble immediately). Off heat, return roast to skillet; using tongs, roll to coat roast with glaze on all sides.

3. Place skillet in oven and roast until meat registers 140 degrees, 35 to 45 minutes, using tongs to roll and spin roast to coat with glaze twice during roasting time (skillet handle will be hot). Transfer roast to carving board; set skillet aside to cool slightly to thicken glaze, about 5 minutes. Pour glaze over roast and let rest 15 minutes longer. Remove twine, cut roast into ¼-inch-thick slices, and serve.

MAPLE-GLAZED PORK ROAST WITH ROSEMARY
Substitute 2 teaspoons minced fresh rosemary for cinnamon, cloves, and cayenne.

MAPLE-GLAZED PORK ROAST WITH ORANGE ESSENCE
Add 1 tablespoon grated orange zest to maple syrup along with spices.

MAPLE-GLAZED PORK ROAST WITH STAR ANISE
Add 4 star anise pods to maple syrup along with spices.

MAPLE-GLAZED PORK ROAST WITH SMOKED PAPRIKA
Add 2 teaspoons smoked hot paprika to maple syrup along with spices.

RECIPE DETAILS

Timeline

- 15 minutes to tie and sear roast
- 35 to 45 minutes to roast and glaze pork
- 5 minutes to cool and thicken glaze
- 15 minutes to let glazed roast rest

Essential Tools

- Kitchen twine to tie roast
- 10-inch ovensafe nonstick skillet
- Tongs to rotate roast in glaze
- Oven mitts to handle scorching-hot skillet as it comes out of oven

Substitutions & Variations

- Maple syrup is graded based on color. The darker the color, the more flavorful the syrup.
- A nonstick pan will be easier to clean, but this recipe can be tough on delicate nonstick surfaces—make sure to use tongs with nonstick-friendly nylon tips. If using a traditional pan, let the pan cool completely and then bring a cup or two of water to a boil in the pan. The boiling water will loosen the glaze and make cleaning a snap.
- This dish is unapologetically sweet, so we recommend side dishes that take well to the sweetness. Garlicky sautéed greens, braised cabbage, and soft polenta are good choices.

23 Fried Fish

"FRY" THE BREADING, NOT THE FISH

The appeal of fried fish is pretty clear. The crisp coating is a nice foil for the moist, tender fish and the short cooking time ensures that the fish doesn't dry out. There's just one problem—fried fish isn't a "cook-friendly" recipe. The high moisture content in fish guarantees a lot of splattering so the stovetop becomes a mess. And then there's the ventilation issue. Do you really want to wake up the next morning to the stale odor of fried fish?

Moving the operation to the oven is the standard workaround for home cooks. But talk about disappointing. The coating is never all that crisp; in fact, it's often downright soggy. While frying proceeds very quickly and at very high temperatures, in the oven the process is much slower and there's plenty of time for the fish to exude a lot of moisture.

But don't abandon the idea of crunchy fish fillets. There is a fix to this dish—as long as you're willing to rethink the process. First off, you must change the coating. Fried fish is generally dusted with flour or cornmeal and then dropped into hot oil. This approach doesn't work in the oven—flour and cornmeal don't stand a chance against the inevitable onslaught of fish juices.

A bound breading—dusting the fish in flour, followed by a dip in eggs, and then the application of bread crumbs—builds a stronger foundation. And if you want a crunchy coating, then start with really crisp crumbs. You can transform this dish simply by tossing fresh bread crumbs with butter and seasonings and then "frying" (OK, baking) the crumbs on a rimmed baking sheet until golden brown. Pass on the mess, pass on the lingering smell, and pass that tartar sauce.

WHY THIS RECIPE WORKS

Go for Firm and Thick Fillets

For the ultimate contrast between the crust and interior, choose medium-firm cod or haddock fillets. And skip thin pieces—they'll cook through before the crust has time to crisp. To ensure uniform pieces of fish, buy a thick whole fillet and cut it into pieces yourself.

Fresh Crumbs Are Best

Bread-crumb coatings for fish often disappoint, ranging from thin and sandy to soggy and crumbly. Homemade bread crumbs make the best coating; processing fresh crumbs is easy and making them coarse maximizes their crunch. Toasting buttered crumbs before coating the fish ensures that they are brown and crisp when the fish is done. Minced shallot and parsley boost the flavor of the crumbs. A thick crust is a crunchier crust so pack on as many crumbs as possible, pressing down gently on the crumbs to help them adhere the fish.

Thicken the Eggs

Thickening the usual egg wash with flour and mayonnaise helps the coating stay put. The thick batter forms a barrier between the moist fish and the dry bread crumbs, keeping the moisture in the fish and the crumbs from getting soggy. Paprika adds flavor to the batter and the optional prepared horseradish and cayenne will add further zip if used.

Elevate on a Rack

Baking the fillets on a wire rack set inside a baking sheet allows air to circulate underneath, crisping the fish on all sides and preventing the bottom crust from getting soggy. Make sure to coat the rack with vegetable oil spray so the crumbs stick to the fish, not the rack. And use a thin metal spatula to transfer the fish to serving plates—thicker plastic turners (like you might use to flip pancakes) can shear the bottom crust away from the fish.

A flavorful "glue" helps crumbs coat meaty cod fillets.

Crunchy Oven-Fried Fish

SERVES 4

To prevent overcooking, buy fish fillets that are at least 1 inch thick. Make sure you buy refrigerated prepared horseradish, not the shelf-stable kind, which contains preservatives and additives. Serve with Sweet and Tangy Tartar Sauce (recipe follows).

4 slices hearty white sandwich bread, torn into quarters	3 tablespoons mayonnaise
2 tablespoons unsalted butter, melted	2 teaspoons prepared horseradish (optional)
Salt and pepper	½ teaspoon paprika
2 tablespoons minced fresh parsley	¼ teaspoon cayenne pepper (optional)
1 shallot, minced	1¼ pounds skinless cod, haddock, or other thick white fish fillet, 1 to 1½ inches thick, cut into 4 pieces
½ cup plus 1 tablespoon all-purpose flour	Lemon wedges
2 large eggs	

1. Adjust oven rack to middle position and heat oven to 350 degrees. Pulse bread, melted butter, ¼ teaspoon salt, and ¼ teaspoon pepper in food processor to coarse crumbs, about 10 pulses (you should have about 3½ cups crumbs). Transfer to rimmed baking sheet and bake until deep golden brown and dry, about 15 minutes, stirring twice during baking time. Let crumbs cool completely, about 10 minutes. Transfer crumbs to shallow dish and toss with parsley and shallot. Increase oven temperature to 425 degrees.

2. Place ¼ cup flour in second shallow dish. In third shallow dish, whisk together eggs; mayonnaise; horseradish, if using; paprika; cayenne, if using; and ¼ teaspoon pepper until combined. Whisk in remaining ¼ cup plus 1 tablespoon flour until smooth.

3. Set wire rack in rimmed baking sheet and spray with vegetable oil spray. Pat fish dry with paper towels and season with salt and pepper. Dredge 1 fillet in flour and shake off excess. Using tongs, dip fillet in egg mixture, then coat with breadcrumb mixture, pressing gently so that thick layer of crumbs adheres to fillet. Transfer breaded fillet to prepared wire rack. Repeat with remaining 3 fillets.

4. Bake until fish flakes apart when gently prodded with paring knife and registers 140 degrees, 18 to 25 minutes. Using thin spatula, transfer fillets to plates and serve immediately with lemon wedges.

SWEET AND TANGY TARTAR SAUCE MAKES ABOUT 1 CUP

¾ cup mayonnaise	1½ teaspoons distilled white vinegar
2 tablespoons capers, rinsed and minced	½ teaspoon Worcestershire sauce
2 tablespoons sweet pickle relish	½ teaspoon pepper
½ shallot, minced	

Mix all ingredients together in small bowl. Cover and let sit to allow flavors to blend, about 15 minutes. Stir again before serving. (Sauce can be refrigerated for up to 1 week.)

RECIPE DETAILS

Timeline

- 40 minutes to make crumb coating (crumbs can be toasted up to 3 days in advance, cooled, and stored at room temperature in airtight container)
- 30 minutes to coat and bake fish (make tartar sauce while fish is in the oven)

Essential Tools

- Food processor
- 3 shallow dishes for coating process
- Wire rack set in rimmed baking sheet for baking fish
- Instant-read thermometer (best tool for judging when fish is done)
- Thin spatula to transfer fish to serving plates

Substitutions & Variations

- Cod and haddock are the best choices for this recipe but other white fish can be used, including snapper, sea bass, and even halibut. Fillets must be the proper thickness; thin fillets like flounder or sole will overcook by the time the coating crisps up.
- Replace the shallot with a clove or two of minced garlic. A few teaspoons of minced fresh thyme or oregano could take the place of the parsley in the coating.
- Horseradish adds a subtle kick to the fish, as does the cayenne. If you prefer, add a dash of hot sauce to the egg wash.

24 Pan-Seared Shrimp

ONE TECHNIQUE SIMULTANEOUSLY COOKS AND SAUCES SHRIMP

Plump, briny, and sweet—shrimp that are cooked well can be a weeknight treat or impressive enough for company. As for cooking method, pan searing is ideal. Browning enhances the sweet notes in shrimp and deepens flavor overall. The method is so fast that you can cook a generous platter of these crustaceans in less than 5 minutes.

As fast as pan searing is, it seems like there shouldn't be enough time for the shrimp to dry out. But if you wait for the shrimp to brown it can actually toughen first. Seasoning the shrimp with sugar (along with the usual salt and pepper) speeds up the browning process. Don't go overboard—you don't want to taste the sugar. Just ⅛ teaspoon is plenty for 1½ pounds of shrimp. Batch cooking and the smart use of residual heat are also keys to preventing overcooking.

When you're done, the pan will look promising for making a sauce—there should be some browned bits (aka fond), especially if you use a conventional rather than a nonstick skillet. But if you make a traditional pan sauce—sauté aromatics, deglaze with wine or broth, reduce, and then enrich—the shrimp will be cold long before you're done—even if you cover them with foil.

The solution? You need a sauce that cooks with (not after) the shrimp. A concentrated glaze or potent butter added to the pan during the last minute or two of cooking is the answer. By the time the shrimp are cooked, the flavors in the glaze or butter have bloomed and the dish is ready to eat. Dinner can't get easier than that.

WHY THIS RECIPE WORKS

Shell the Shrimp at Home
We find shell-on shrimp to be firmer and sweeter than already peeled shrimp. To peel shrimp, break the shell under the swimming legs, which will come off as the shell is removed.

Remove the Vein
The vein that runs along the back of the shrimp doesn't affect flavor but it doesn't look appetizing. To remove it, use a paring knife or seafood scissors to make a shallow cut along the back of the shrimp to expose the vein. Use the tip of the blade to lift out the vein and discard it by wiping the vein against a paper towel.

Cook in Batches
If the pan is overcrowded, the shrimp will steam instead of sear. It is crucial to arrange the shrimp in a single even layer to allow for the best contact with the pan and so they cook all at once. We find that 1½ pounds of shrimp (enough for four servings) are best cooked in two batches. Since the shrimp cook really fast and are seared on only one side, a smoking-hot pan is essential.

Count on Residual Heat
This recipe makes use of residual heat twice to prevent the shrimp from overcooking. Once the shrimp are seared on the first side, take the pan off the heat and turn them (using tongs). Allow the shrimp to cook for another 30 seconds before transferring them to a bowl. The second batch is cooked the same way—seared on the first side, then taken off the heat and cooked on the second side. When this batch is done, return the first batch and the sauce to the pan and throw the cover on. Letting all of the shrimp sit for another minute or so ensures that both batches of shrimp are warm and ready to eat. The heat also distributes the sauce evenly.

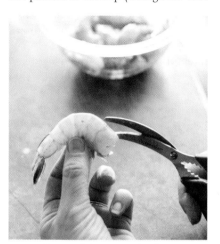 

Yes, peeling and deveining the shrimp is a pain but they cook in a flash.

Pan-Seared Shrimp

SERVES 4

We recommend buying shell-on frozen shrimp. Almost all the "fresh" shrimp sold in super-markets has been frozen and you might as well control the thawing process at home to ensure optimal results. (And forget about peeled shrimp—it loses a lot of flavor and moisture so you're best doing this at home, too.) Simply place the frozen shrimp in a colander under cold running water and let the water run until they are soft enough to peel and devein. If you want to plan ahead, you can thaw frozen shrimp overnight in the refrigerator.

2 **tablespoons vegetable oil**	¼ **teaspoon salt**
1½ **pounds extra-large shrimp (21 to 25**	¼ **teaspoon pepper**
per pound), peeled and deveined	⅛ **teaspoon sugar**

Heat 1 tablespoon oil in 12-inch skillet over high heat until just smoking. Meanwhile, toss shrimp, salt, pepper, and sugar in medium bowl. Add half of shrimp to pan in single layer and cook until spotty brown and edges turn pink, about 1 minute. Off heat, flip each shrimp using tongs and allow shrimp to continue to cook in skillet until all but very center is opaque, about 30 seconds. Transfer shrimp to large plate. Repeat with remaining 1 tablespoon oil and remaining shrimp. After second batch has cooked off heat, return first batch to skillet and toss to combine. Cover skillet and let sit until shrimp are cooked through, 1 to 2 minutes. Serve immediately.

PAN-SEARED SHRIMP WITH GARLIC-LEMON BUTTER

Beat 3 tablespoons softened unsalted butter with fork in small bowl until light and fluffy. Stir in 2 tablespoons chopped fresh parsley, 1 tablespoon lemon juice, 1 minced garlic clove, and ⅛ teaspoon salt until combined. Add butter mixture to skillet when returning first batch of shrimp to skillet. Serve with lemon wedges if desired.

PAN-SEARED SHRIMP WITH GINGER-HOISIN GLAZE

Stir together 2 tablespoons hoisin sauce, 1 tablespoon rice vinegar, 2 teaspoons grated fresh ginger, 2 teaspoons water, 1½ teaspoons soy sauce, and 2 scallions, sliced thin, in small bowl. Substitute ¼ teaspoon red pepper flakes for pepper and add hoisin mixture to skillet when returning first batch of shrimp to skillet.

PAN-SEARED SHRIMP WITH CHIPOTLE-LIME GLAZE

Stir together 2 tablespoons lime juice, 2 tablespoons chopped fresh cilantro, 1½ tea-spoons minced canned chipotle chile in adobo sauce plus 2 teaspoons adobo sauce, and 4 teaspoons packed brown sugar in small bowl. Add chipotle mixture to skillet when returning first batch of shrimp to skillet.

RECIPE DETAILS

Timeline

- 20 minutes to thaw, peel, and devein shrimp
- 5 minutes to cook shrimp in batches and heat with sauce

Essential Tools

- 12-inch skillet with lid (Either a nonstick or a traditional skillet will work for this recipe, but a nonstick will simplify cleanup.)
- Tongs to flip shrimp one at a time

Substitutions & Variations

- We like to use extra-large shrimp in this recipe, 21 to 25 shrimp per pound. Smaller or larger shrimp can be used; just be sure to adjust the cooking time as needed.
- For other sauce ideas, try a few table-spoons of salsa verde, chimichurri, or even barbecue sauce. Or try another type of compound butter, using fresh herbs of your choice, lime or orange juice (add some grated zest if you like) instead of lemon, and a little minced shallot, scallion, or ginger in place of the garlic.

25 Pot Roast

USE THE POWER OF PATIENCE TO TRANSFORM TOUGH CUTS

There are two general approaches to cooking, both equally valid. The first might be described as "buy the best ingredients and don't mess them up." Careful shopping and a willingness to pay top dollar are required. A second class of recipes starts with cheaper ingredients that require more effort and time to prepare.

Grilling a fine steak or searing a piece of locally caught fish falls into the first camp. These ingredients cook quickly, which is one reason why restaurant chefs love them. Pot roast is a perfect example of the second category. Instead, the investment of time (not money) yields big rewards.

Many cuts of beef are well marbled (which means they're streaked with flavorful fat), but they are also loaded with connective tissue (a translucent membrane that surrounds muscle fibers, providing structure and support). Connective tissue makes these cuts very tough to chew. That's why chuck roasts and briskets are so cheap.

However, through prolonged cooking, the main protein in connective tissue, something called collagen, will break down and become gelatin. And while collagen is hard to chew, gelatin has the opposite effect because it can hold 10 times its weight in moisture. (Think of the absorption powers of Jell-O.) A cut that was tough is now tender, almost silky. Slow cooking is the key to this transformation.

A covered pot maintains the proper heat level to facilitate the conversion of collagen to gelatin. The result is a meltingly tender, sliceable roast sauced with a full-bodied gravy made from the other ingredients added to the pot. This is home cooking at its very best.

WHY THIS RECIPE WORKS

Split the Roast in Two

Our preferred cut for pot roast is a chuck-eye roast. This boneless roast contains a good amount of fat, which guarantees good flavor. In fact, this roast has a bit too much fat. Pulling the roast apart at its major seams exposes the hard knobs of fat that never melt away. Having two mini roasts increases the surface area that can brown and also cuts back on the cooking time.

Salt Ahead

Salting the meat before cooking draws moisture out of the meat, forming a shallow brine that migrates back into the meat and flavors it throughout. Although brines usually take hours, salting for just an hour makes a big difference here—especially with the amount of exposed surface area. Along with the beef broth and glutamate-rich tomato paste, salting really brings out the meaty flavors in this cut.

Skimp on the Liquid

Many pot roast recipes submerge the meat in broth and wine. But if you cut back on the liquid, the meat can actually brown in the covered pot (the cooking time is so long that the meat above the surface of the liquid browns and becomes more flavorful). In addition, less liquid translates to a concentrated gravy that requires less work at serving time.

Foil the Pot

To create a tight seal and trap liquid inside, cover the pot first with foil, and then with the lid. The roasts cook in the oven at a low simmer for a good 3½ hours until the meat is very well-done—to the point at which the fat and connective tissue are really melting. The meat becomes so tender that a fork poked into its center nearly disappears.

Keeping other ingredients to a minimum promotes more browning. When the meat is tender, puree the aromatics and liquid to create an easy gravy.

Classic Pot Roast

SERVES 6 TO 8

Chilling the whole cooked pot roast overnight improves its flavor and makes it moister and easier to slice.

1 (3½- to 4-pound) boneless beef chuck-eye roast, pulled apart at seams and trimmed
Kosher salt and pepper
2 tablespoons unsalted butter
2 onions, halved and sliced thin
1 large carrot, peeled and chopped
1 celery rib, chopped
2 garlic cloves, minced
2–3 cups beef broth
¾ cup dry red wine
1 tablespoon tomato paste
1 bay leaf
1 sprig fresh thyme plus ¼ teaspoon chopped
1 tablespoon balsamic vinegar

1. Season pieces of meat with 1 tablespoon salt, place on wire rack set in rimmed baking sheet, and let stand at room temperature for 1 hour.

2. Adjust oven rack to lower-middle position and heat oven to 300 degrees. Melt butter in Dutch oven over medium heat. Add onions and cook, stirring occasionally, until softened and beginning to brown, 8 to 10 minutes. Add carrot and celery; continue to cook, stirring occasionally, for about 5 minutes. Add garlic and cook until fragrant, about 30 seconds. Stir in 1 cup broth, ½ cup wine, tomato paste, bay leaf, and thyme sprig; bring to simmer.

3. Pat meat dry with paper towels and season with pepper. Tie 3 pieces of kitchen twine around each piece of meat to create 2 evenly shaped roasts.

4. Nestle meat on top of vegetables. Cover pot tightly with large piece of aluminum foil and cover with lid; transfer pot to oven. Cook meat until fully tender and fork slips easily in and out of meat, 3½ to 4 hours, turning meat halfway through cooking.

5. Transfer roasts to carving board and tent loosely with foil. Strain liquid through fine-mesh strainer into 4-cup liquid measuring cup. Discard bay leaf and thyme sprig. Transfer vegetables to blender. Let liquid settle for 5 minutes, then skim fat; add broth to bring liquid amount to 3 cups. Add liquid to blender and process until smooth, about 2 minutes. Transfer sauce to medium saucepan and bring to simmer over medium heat.

6. Meanwhile, remove twine from roasts and slice against grain into ½-inch-thick slices. Transfer meat to serving platter. Stir remaining ¼ cup wine, chopped thyme, and vinegar into gravy and season with salt and pepper to taste. Spoon half of gravy over meat. Serve, passing remaining gravy separately.

RECIPE DETAILS

Timeline

• 1¼ hours to trim and salt meat
• 30 minutes to prepare and cook flavor base (do this while salted roasts rest)
• 3½ to 4 hours to cook roasts
• 15 minutes to finish sauce and slice roasts

Essential Tools

• Kitchen twine to tie roasts
• Dutch oven with lid
• Aluminum foil to create tight seal on pot
• Blender to puree cooked vegetables for gravy

Substitutions & Variations

• To make pot roast in advance, follow recipe through step 4, then transfer cooked roasts to large bowl. Strain and defat liquid and add broth to bring liquid amount to 3 cups; transfer liquid and vegetables to bowl with roasts, let cool for 1 hour, cover with plastic wrap, cut vents in plastic with paring knife, and refrigerate up to 2 days. One hour before serving, adjust oven rack to middle position and heat oven to 325 degrees. Slice roasts as directed, place pieces in 13 by 9-inch baking dish, cover tightly with foil, and bake until heated through, about 45 minutes. Process liquid and vegetables in blender, bring gravy to simmer, and finish as directed.
• A top blade roast, also known as chuck roast first cut, blade roast, or top chuck roast, can be used in this recipe. Note that it will take slightly longer to cook. Do not separate this roast into 2 pieces. Do tie top blade with twine before cooking to promote even cooking.

CLASSIC POT ROAST WITH ROOT VEGETABLES

Add 1 pound carrots, peeled and cut into 2-inch pieces; 1 pound parsnips, peeled and cut into 2-inch pieces; and 1½ pounds russet potatoes, peeled and halved lengthwise, each half quartered, to Dutch oven after cooking beef for 3 hours. Continue to cook until meat is fully tender, 30 minutes to 1 hour longer. Transfer large pieces of carrot, parsnip, and potato to serving platter using slotted spoon, cover tightly with aluminum foil, and proceed with recipe as directed.

CLASSIC POT ROAST WITH MUSHROOM AND PRUNE GRAVY

Substitute ½ cup dark beer (porter or stout) for red wine. Add 1 ounce dried porcini mushrooms, rinsed, soaked for 1 hour, and drained, and ½ cup pitted prunes with broth and beer. While roast is resting, sauté 1 pound thinly sliced cremini mushrooms in 2 tablespoons butter until softened and lightly browned and add to finished gravy, along with ¼ cup dark beer instead of balsamic vinegar.

A Better Way to Tie a Roast

Most roasts are unevenly shaped, which leads to uneven cooking. For cylindrical cuts, even out the thickness and make a more uniform shape by tying them with kitchen twine. Butchers often cinch roasts with a single long piece of twine and complicated adjustable loops. We take a much simpler approach (no Boy Scout skills required). If you can tie your shoes, you can tie up a roast.

1. To tie roast, wrap piece of kitchen twine around roast and fasten it with simple double knot. If roast has thinner end, simply fold that end under to create roast of equal thickness from end to end.

2. Use additional pieces of twine to tie roast at even intervals along entire length of roast. Leave about 1½ inches between pieces of twine.

26 Barbecued Chicken

THIS SUMMER CLASSIC DOESN'T HAVE TO LEAD TO DISASTER

For something so common, it's surprising how often this dish is downright awful. Barbecued chicken has many possible pitfalls, including burnt skin, parched meat, meat that is raw at the bone, and a sugary sweet sauce that can be its own abomination. It's the rare grill master who avoids all of these mistakes.

The problem with this recipe is both the technique (or lack thereof) and the bottled sauce slathered on the chicken parts. While a roaring fire is nice in a fireplace, flare-ups are NOT the goal when grilling. Fat dripping down from chicken skin can turn the occasional flame into a towering inferno. The result is a sooty-tasting exterior that fools many inexperienced cooks into thinking the parts are "done." Only the meat is still bloody at the bone. Talk about putting a damper on dinner.

Success with this recipe begins with a more nuanced approach to managing heat levels on the grill (see page 91). It also requires a more sophisticated method for flavoring the chicken. Bottled barbecue sauce is convenient, but it's almost as easy to make something much better with pantry staples. Even more important, you shouldn't marinate chicken parts in any sweet sauce. That just encourages excessive charring. And barbecue sauce doesn't do much to flavor the meat below the skin anyway.

While we don't marinate barbecued chicken, we do salt it. Rubbing the parts with salt (and spices) ensures that the meat is well seasoned—and the salt also helps the meat hold on to its natural juices. For the salt to work its magic, you need to plan ahead, which means you can really enjoy the cookout, especially since you know the results will be so good.

WHY THIS RECIPE WORKS

Give It a Rub
Salting flavors chicken and helps it stay moist, but for chicken that is well seasoned all the way to the bone, we apply a spice rub 6 hours before grilling. The garlic and onion powders work well with the salt, paprika and cayenne add some heat, and brown sugar adds a touch of sweetness and helps with browning.

Build a Two-Level Fire
A modified two-level or half-grill fire creates two cooking zones with dramatically different heat levels (see page 91). One side is intensely hot, and the other side is cooler. This produces perfectly cooked chicken because it browns over the hot side, rendering the fat and crisping the skin, then is moved over the cooler side so it can finish cooking more slowly and gently via indirect heat.

Add a Pan of Water
Placing a disposable aluminum pan opposite the coals and filling it partially with water lowers the temperature inside the grill by about 50 degrees; this ensures that all the chicken pieces cook at a slow, steady rate.

Sharpen the Sauce
Homemade barbecue sauce makes a big difference and is easy to make from everyday ingredients. We smarten the typical ketchup-based sauce with molasses, while cider vinegar, Worcestershire sauce, and Dijon mustard keep the sweetness in check. Grated onion, minced garlic, chili powder, cayenne, and pepper round out the flavors. Grating the onion helps it to break down in the sauce. Also a plus, the sauce can be made up to 1 week ahead.

Hold Off on the Sauce
Waiting to apply the barbecue sauce until after searing prevents the sauce from burning and gives the skin a chance to develop color first. Applying it in stages, rather than all at once, ensures that its bright tanginess isn't lost.

Make homemade BBQ sauce but don't apply it until the chicken is nearly done.

Sweet and Tangy Barbecued Chicken

SERVES 6 TO 8

When browning the chicken over the hotter side of the grill, move it away from any flare-ups.

CHICKEN

- 2 tablespoons packed dark brown sugar
- 4½ teaspoons kosher salt
- 1½ teaspoons onion powder
- 1½ teaspoons garlic powder
- 1½ teaspoons paprika
- ¼ teaspoon cayenne pepper
- 6 pounds bone-in chicken pieces (split breasts and/or leg quarters), trimmed

SAUCE

- 1 cup ketchup
- 5 tablespoons molasses
- 3 tablespoons cider vinegar
- 2 tablespoons Worcestershire sauce
- 2 tablespoons Dijon mustard
- ¼ teaspoon pepper
- 2 tablespoons vegetable oil
- ⅓ cup grated onion
- 1 garlic clove, minced
- 1 teaspoon chili powder
- ¼ teaspoon cayenne pepper

- 1 large disposable aluminum roasting pan (if using charcoal) or 2 disposable aluminum pie plates (if using gas)

1. *For the Chicken:* Combine sugar, salt, onion powder, garlic powder, paprika, and cayenne in bowl. Arrange chicken on rimmed baking sheet and sprinkle both sides evenly with spice rub. Cover with plastic wrap and refrigerate for at least 6 hours or up to 24 hours.

2. *For the Sauce:* Whisk ketchup, molasses, vinegar, Worcestershire, mustard, and pepper together in bowl. Heat oil in medium saucepan over medium heat until shimmering. Add onion and garlic; cook until onion is softened, 2 to 4 minutes. Add chili powder and cayenne and cook until fragrant, about 30 seconds. Whisk in ketchup mixture and bring to boil. Reduce heat to medium-low and simmer gently for 5 minutes. Set aside ⅔ cup sauce to baste chicken and reserve remaining sauce for serving. (Sauce can be refrigerated for up to 1 week.)

3A. *For a Charcoal Grill:* Open bottom vent halfway and place disposable pan filled with 3 cups water on 1 side of grill. Light large chimney starter filled with charcoal briquettes (6 quarts). When top coals are partially covered with ash, pour evenly over other half of grill (opposite disposable pan). Set cooking grate in place, cover, and open lid vent halfway. Heat grill until hot, about 5 minutes.

3B. *For a Gas Grill:* Place 2 disposable pie plates, each filled with 1½ cups water, directly on 1 burner of gas grill (opposite primary burner). Turn all burners to high, cover, and heat grill until hot, about 15 minutes. Turn primary burner to medium-high and turn off other burner(s). (Adjust primary burner as needed to maintain grill temperature of 325 to 350 degrees.)

RECIPE DETAILS

Timeline

- 6 to 24 hours to refrigerate chicken with spice rub
- 15 minutes to make barbecue sauce (can be done days in advance)
- 20 minutes to set up grill
- 1 hour to grill chicken
- 10 minutes to rest chicken before serving

Essential Tools

- Box grater (Use large holes to prep onion.)
- Basting brush
- Instant-read thermometer

Substitutions & Variations

- This recipe can be made with all white meat, all dark meat, or a mix. We strongly suggest that you buy chicken parts individually from a butcher, who can select similar-size pieces that will cook at the same rate. If you buy packaged parts (which come from multiple birds), be prepared to check each piece for doneness and remove them one at a time. Why? In our tests, we have found that the same package of split breasts or leg quarters might contain pieces that vary in size by as much as 100 percent—that is, some pieces are twice the size of others.

- Some leg quarters come with a piece of the backbone still attached. If that's the case, bend the backbone back to pop out the thigh bone and then cut through the joint to sever the backbone from the thigh. Discard the backbone pieces or save them to make stock.

4. Clean and oil cooking grate. Place chicken, skin side down, over hotter part of grill and cook until browned and blistered in spots, 2 to 5 minutes. Flip chicken and cook until second side is browned, 4 to 6 minutes. Move chicken to cooler part and brush both sides with ⅓ cup sauce. Arrange chicken, skin side up, with leg quarters closest to fire and breasts farthest away. Cover (positioning lid vent over chicken if using charcoal) and cook for 25 minutes.

5. Brush both sides of chicken with remaining ⅓ cup sauce and continue to cook, covered, until breasts register 160 degrees and leg quarters register 175 degrees, 25 to 35 minutes longer. Serve, passing reserved sauce separately.

A Better Way to Grill Slow-Cooking Foods

A blazing hot fire isn't really the best for most foods. Foods like bone-in chicken that need to stay on the grill longer require a two-level fire: high heat for browning and lower or indirect heat over which the food can cook through. Here's how to set up a charcoal grill. If using a gas grill, adjust the dials to create different heat levels before the cooking grate has been cleaned and oiled.

1. Use chimney starter to light charcoal and get coals hot. (This simple device easily gets all the charcoal ready at once and there's no need to use lighter fluid, which can impart an off flavor to food.)

2. For half-grill fire with two heat zones, arrange lit coals in even layer over half of grill. If using disposable pan, put it on charcoal grate first and pour coals next to it.

3. Once cooking grate is heated, scrub it clean with grill brush and slick it down with vegetable oil using wad of paper towels and tongs. (The oil helps prevent food—like chicken skin—from sticking.)

4. For foods that require long cooking times, brown on hotter side of grill, then move it to cooler side to finish cooking with indirect heat. Arrange food so that slower-cooking items are closer to fire. (This setup also helps with flare-ups since there is a coal-free area to move food to if necessary.)

27 Chicken Soup

THE ONE-DISH MEAL THAT COMFORTS THE WORLD

In a world with so many regional differences, chicken soup is the great unifier. Most cuisines have a version, as varied as matzoh ball, tortilla, egg drop, and coconut–red curry soup. And while scientists debate its healing powers, there is universal agreement about the power of chicken soup to comfort.

Making chicken soup for someone who's under the weather is a nice way to show you care. But the process is slow. Great chicken soup begins with rich chicken stock and according to most recipes it takes many hours to transfer flavor from the chicken to the water. The standard recipe calls for throwing chicken bones (or parts) into the pot along with a variety of aromatic vegetables and a lot of water. The key, we are told, is to let everything bubble away for hours and hours—and that's just the stock.

While there's no arguing with the results—this approach yields golden stock—is there a faster way to get there? Some sources suggest roasting the chicken first—to intensify its flavor. But to our tastes, the roasted notes overpower the sweet, pure chicken flavor.

Our approach simplifies and improves upon the roasted method. To this end, we discovered that less is more when it comes to other ingredients. Salt is key and an onion adds complexity. But other vegetables compete with the chicken in stock. Save your vegetables for the soup.

Speaking of the soup, once the stock is ready you're almost done. The key is to cook the ingredients in the broth so that every piece of carrot and every bite of noodle becomes infused with chicken flavor. We can't guarantee our soup will cure the common cold, but it will make you feel better.

WHY THIS RECIPE WORKS

Hack the Chicken
Many chicken stock recipes use whole chicken parts. Cutting the parts, except for the breasts, into 2-inch chunks releases more chicken flavor in a shorter amount of time because more surface area of the meat is exposed. It also exposes more bone marrow, which easily seeps into the water and is key for both rich flavor and full body.

Brown and Sweat
Browning the chicken (minus the split breasts)—before adding the water—creates a ton of flavor that would otherwise take hours to eke out. Onions are vital for a flavorful stock so we sauté one before adding the chicken back to the pot. Cooking the browned onion and chicken pieces in a covered pot in their own juices for 20 minutes, a process called sweating, further speeds the release of flavor and shortens the simmering time.

Cook the White Meat in Broth
Once water and bay leaves are added to the pot, the split breasts are simmered in the broth for just 20 minutes. This infuses them with flavor and ensures that the white meat won't overcook. The breast meat is then removed from the pot, shredded, and reserved for the soup.

Skim and Reserve Some Fat
Skimming off the fat is an essential step when making stock. Waiting several minutes after straining allows the fat to rise to the surface where it can be skimmed off with a ladle or wide spoon. Saving some of the chicken fat from skimming and using it to sauté the aromatics for the soup imparts excellent chicken flavor.

Cook the Pasta Right in the Broth
The dried noodles are added uncooked to the soup and simmered in the broth until tender so that they soak up chicken flavor. If boiled in water separately from the soup, the noodles end up mushy and bland.

Every part of the bird—even fat skimmed from the stock—goes into this soup.

Classic Chicken Noodle Soup

SERVES 6 TO 8

Make sure to reserve the chicken breast pieces until step 2; they should not be browned. Be sure to reserve 2 tablespoons of chicken fat for sautéing the aromatics in step 4.

STOCK

- 1 tablespoon vegetable oil
- 1 (4-pound) whole chicken, giblets discarded, breast removed, split, and reserved; remaining chicken cut into 2-inch pieces
- 1 onion, chopped
- 8 cups boiling water
- 2 teaspoons salt
- 2 bay leaves

SOUP

- 1 onion, chopped
- 1 large carrot, peeled and sliced ¼ inch thick
- 1 celery rib, sliced ¼ inch thick
- ½ teaspoon dried thyme
- 3 ounces (2 cups) wide egg noodles
- ¼ cup minced fresh parsley
- Salt and pepper

1. *For the Stock:* Heat oil in Dutch oven over medium-high heat until shimmering. Add half of chicken pieces (reserving breast pieces) and cook until lightly browned, about 5 minutes per side. Transfer to bowl and repeat with remaining chicken pieces; transfer to bowl with first batch. Add onion and cook, stirring frequently, until onion is translucent, 3 to 5 minutes. Return chicken pieces to pot. Reduce heat to low, cover, and cook until chicken releases its juices, about 20 minutes.

2. Increase heat to high; add boiling water, salt, bay leaves, and reserved chicken breast pieces. Reduce heat to medium-low and simmer until flavors have blended, about 20 minutes.

3. Remove breast pieces from pot. When cool enough to handle, remove skin from breasts, then remove meat from bones. Using 2 forks, shred meat into bite-size pieces, discarding skin and bones. Strain stock through fine-mesh strainer; discard solids. Allow liquid to settle, about 5 minutes, then skim off fat; reserve 2 tablespoons. (After skimming stock, shredded chicken, cooled stock, and reserved fat can be refrigerated in separate containers for up to 2 days.)

4. *For the Soup:* Heat reserved chicken fat in Dutch oven over medium-high heat. Add onion, carrot, and celery and cook until softened, about 5 minutes. Add stock and thyme and simmer until vegetables are tender, 10 to 15 minutes.

5. Add noodles and shredded chicken and cook until just tender, 5 to 8 minutes. Stir in parsley, season with salt and pepper to taste, and serve.

CLASSIC CHICKEN SOUP WITH ORZO AND SPRING VEGETABLES

Substitute 1 leek, quartered lengthwise, sliced thin crosswise, and washed thoroughly, for onion and ½ cup orzo for egg noodles. Along with orzo, add 4 ounces trimmed asparagus, cut into 1-inch lengths, and ¼ cup fresh or frozen peas. Substitute 2 tablespoons minced fresh tarragon for parsley.

RECIPE DETAILS

Timeline

- 30 minutes to hack up and brown chicken pieces
- 5 minutes to sauté onion
- 20 minutes to sweat browned chicken and onion
- 20 minutes to simmer stock and cook breast meat
- 10 minutes to strain and defat stock
- 25 minutes to make soup

Essential Tools

- Meat cleaver (best for hacking up chicken parts, but chef's knife or kitchen shears also work)
- Dutch oven (at least 6 quarts) with lid
- Fine-mesh strainer

Substitutions & Variations

- Chicken fat, skimmed from the surface of the stock, is our first choice for sautéing the aromatics in step 4; however, if you prefer not to use chicken fat, vegetable oil can be substituted.
- We don't recommend varying the stock but the soup can be varied with other vegetables and starches:
- Leeks, fennel, bell peppers, zucchini, and mushrooms can be used in place of (or with) the onion, carrot, and celery. Potent ingredients (such as garlic, ginger, or spices) should be added during the final minute of cooking the vegetables.
- Rice or grains (about ½ cup) can take the place of the pasta but cooking times will vary considerably.
- Finish the soup with a variety of fresh herbs, a shower of grated Parmesan, a swirl of pesto, or a spoonful of gremolata (minced parsley, garlic, and lemon zest).

A Better Way to Make Chicken Stock

Nothing compares to the flavor of homemade chicken stock, especially as the base for chicken soup. Using small pieces of chicken and onion as the only vegetable simplifies the process. Browning and sweating the chicken delivers maximum flavor in a minimal amount of time. If you want meat for soup, start with a whole chicken; add the breast (split in two but not hacked) with the boiling water in step 5. When straining the stock, reserve the breast pieces and when cool, shred the meat, discarding the skin and bones.

1. Use meat cleaver or heel of chef's knife to hack 4 pounds chicken legs, backs, and wings into 2-inch pieces.

2. Heat 1 tablespoon vegetable oil in large Dutch oven until just smoking. Lightly brown chicken on all sides (in 2 batches), which helps fond form on bottom of pot. Transfer chicken to large bowl.

3. Add 1 chopped onion to fat left in pot and cook until softened, 3 to 5 minutes. (Only onion is crucial; it adds dimension and complexity.)

4. Return browned chicken pieces to pot, cover, and cook over low heat, stirring occasionally, until chicken has released its juices, about 20 minutes.

5. Add 8 cups boiling water, 2 teaspoons salt, and 2 bay leaves and bring to boil. Cover, reduce heat to gentle simmer, and cook until stock tastes rich and flavorful, about 20 minutes longer. (Bringing the water to a boil while the chicken sweats is another way to save time.)

6. Remove large bones and pour stock through fine-mesh strainer into large liquid measuring cup or other large container. Let stock settle for 5 minutes and use ladle or wide, shallow spoon to remove fat from surface.

28 Chili

THE BIG GAME DESERVES SOMETHING WITH BIG FLAVOR

Chili devotees—especially the serious enthusiasts who compete on the cook-off circuit—are an opinionated, even cheerily belligerent bunch. Each cook will swear that the only chili worth eating is his or her own.

There's broad agreement about how to define this dish—slow-cooked meat redolent of chiles and spices, all bound in an unctuous sauce. But how you get there is a matter of serious debate. The key, any chili master will tell you, lies in the all-powerful "secret ingredients."

These proprietary add-ins fall into five categories: cooking liquids, complexity builders, sweeteners (to balance the heat), meat enhancers, and thickeners. Recipes on the Internet, which is where most serious chili recipes seem to live, include everything from prunes, anchovies, shiitake mushrooms, Marmite, soy sauce, boullion cubes, cinnamon, chocolate, molasses, and peanut butter to beer, red wine, coffee, and cola.

Surprisingly, there's also plenty of debate on the core ingredients. Beef is a must but should it be ground or cubed? (We think the latter.) Pinto beans are controversial (we include them) as are tomatoes (their acidity is key in our opinion). Most sources agree that onion, garlic, and chiles belong, but with so many fresh, dried, and ground chiles available the combinations are nearly endless.

Our version relies on three chiles (two dried, one fresh) and three secret ingredients—molasses, cocoa powder, and cornmeal. Before you claim that your chili is the best, please taste our recipe. If you like our chili, feel free to claim it as your own at the next game day party. Even if your team loses, this chili will make you a winner—at least when it comes to bragging rights.

WHY THIS RECIPE WORKS

Upgrade the Meat
This dish is best with meaty chunks that remain tender even with prolonged cooking. That means choosing a cut with a fair amount of fat—and flavor. Blade steak is a well-marbled shoulder cut that doesn't require much trimming.

Brine the Beans
Soaking beans in salt water before cooking seasons them throughout and helps them remain creamy. And the timing works out perfectly: By the time the beans quick-brine in an hour, the rest of the chili is ready to go.

Seed, Toast, and Puree
For complex chile flavor, grind your own powder. Dried ancho chiles add warm spice and toasting them develops their flavor. De árbol chiles bring the hot spice and fresh jalapeños add grassy heat. Remove their seeds and ribs to control the chile heat. Oregano, cumin, cocoa, and salt round out our homemade chili powder.

Secret Weapons
Several other ingredients work to balance the flavors in this chili. A small amount of cornmeal, ground with the chiles, adds great body to the sauce and the right level of thickness. Unsweetened cocoa powder adds warm deep flavor and complexity—not sweetness—to the chili. The mild sweetness of molasses tempers the heat of the chiles and the acid of the tomatoes.

Simmer in the Oven
Chili starts on the stovetop—you must brown the beef and sauté the onions, garlic, and chiles. To speed up the process, separate these operations—using a skillet to brown the beef and cooking the vegetables in the pot that will be used to make the chili. Deglazing the skillet with beer after the beef is browned loosens the fond so its flavor can be added to the chili. Once everything is in the pot, move it to the oven. The all-around heat of the oven ensures even cooking and means no stirring is necessary.

Great chili starts by salting the beef and making homemade chili powder.

Ultimate Beef Chili

SERVES 6 TO 8

Because much of the chili flavor is held in the fat of this dish, refrain from skimming fat from the surface. Good choices for condiments include diced avocado, finely chopped red onion, chopped cilantro, lime wedges, sour cream, and shredded Monterey Jack or cheddar cheese.

Salt	2½ cups chicken broth
8 ounces (1¼ cups) dried pinto beans, picked over and rinsed	2 onions, cut into ¾-inch pieces
6 dried ancho chiles, stemmed, seeded, and torn into 1-inch pieces	3 small jalapeño chiles, stemmed, seeded, and cut into ½-inch pieces
2–4 dried de árbol chiles, stemmed, seeded, and split in 2 pieces	3 tablespoons vegetable oil
3 tablespoons cornmeal	4 garlic cloves, minced
2 teaspoons dried oregano	1 (14.5-ounce) can diced tomatoes
2 teaspoons ground cumin	2 teaspoons molasses
2 teaspoons unsweetened cocoa powder	3½ pounds blade steak, ¾ inch thick, trimmed and cut into ¾-inch pieces
	1½ cups mild lager, such as Budweiser

1. Combine 3 tablespoons salt, 4 quarts water, and beans in Dutch oven and bring to boil over high heat. Remove pot from heat, cover, and let stand for 1 hour. Drain and rinse well.

2. Adjust oven rack to lower-middle position and heat oven to 300 degrees. Toast anchos in 12-inch skillet over medium-high heat, stirring frequently, until flesh is fragrant, 4 to 6 minutes, reducing heat if chiles begin to smoke. Transfer to food processor and let cool. Do not wash out skillet.

3. Add de árbols, cornmeal, oregano, cumin, cocoa, and ½ teaspoon salt to food processor with toasted anchos; process until finely ground, about 2 minutes. With processor running, slowly add ½ cup broth until smooth paste forms, about 45 seconds, scraping down sides of bowl as necessary. Transfer paste to small bowl. Place onions in now-empty processor and pulse until roughly chopped, about 4 pulses. Add jalapeños and pulse until consistency of chunky salsa, about 4 pulses, scraping down bowl as necessary.

4. Heat 1 tablespoon oil in Dutch oven over medium-high heat. Add onion mixture and cook, stirring occasionally, until moisture has evaporated and vegetables are softened, 7 to 9 minutes. Add garlic and cook until fragrant, about 1 minute. Add chile paste, tomatoes and their juice, and molasses; stir until chile paste is thoroughly combined. Add remaining 2 cups broth and drained beans; bring to boil, then reduce heat to simmer.

5. Meanwhile, heat 1 tablespoon oil in now-empty skillet over medium-high heat until shimmering. Pat beef dry with paper towels and sprinkle with 1 teaspoon salt. Add half of beef and cook until browned on all sides, about 10 minutes. Transfer meat to Dutch oven. Add half of beer to skillet, scraping up any browned bits from bottom

RECIPE DETAILS

Timeline

• 1 hour to quick-brine dried pinto beans (toast chiles, make chile paste, and brown vegetables and beef during this time)
• 1½ to 2 hours to cook chili in oven
• 10 minutes to let chili stand uncovered before serving

Essential Tools

• 2 large pots, one for brining beans and one for making chili (If you have just one large pot, you can transfer the beans and boiling water to a large bowl and cover the bowl with plastic wrap.)
• 12-inch skillet for toasting chiles and browning beef
• Food processor for grinding chile paste

Substitutions & Variations

• Blade steak is also known as top blade steak or flat-iron steak. Be sure to remove the line of gristle that runs lengthwise down the center before cutting steaks into pieces. A 4-pound chuck-eye roast, well trimmed of fat, can be substituted for the steak.
• Dried New Mexican or guajillo chiles make a good substitute for the anchos; each dried de árbol may be replaced with ⅛ teaspoon cayenne pepper.
• If you prefer not to work with any whole dried chiles, the anchos and de árbols can be replaced with ½ cup commercial chili powder and ¼ to ½ teaspoon cayenne pepper, though the texture of the chili will be slightly compromised.

of pan, and bring to simmer. Transfer beer to Dutch oven. Repeat with remaining 1 tablespoon oil, remaining steak, and remaining beer. Stir to combine and return mixture to simmer.

6. Cover pot and transfer to oven. Cook until meat and beans are fully tender, 1½ to 2 hours. Let chili stand, uncovered, for 10 minutes. Stir well, season with salt to taste, and serve. (Chili can be refrigerated up to 3 days.)

A Better Way to Make Chili Powder

Store-bought chili powder is OK, but it can taste dull and give chili a gritty feel (because the stems and seeds are not separated out). Grinding your own powder from freshly toasted dried chiles is easy and makes a big flavor difference. You can toast chiles on the stovetop or the oven.

1. STOVETOP: Snap off and discard stems. Open chiles and brush out seeds. Tear chiles into small pieces.

2. Toast chiles in large skillet (no oil needed) over medium-high heat, stirring occasionally, until fragrant, 4 to 6 minutes. Do not let chiles smoke or burn.

3. OVEN: If you prefer, toast whole chiles on rimmed baking sheet in 350-degree oven until fragrant and puffed, about 6 minutes. When cool, snap off stems, remove seeds, and tear into small pieces.

4. Process chile pieces with other ingredients (such as oregano, cumin, garlic, and salt) in food processor until finely ground, 2 minutes. (Note: If you want to store chili powder, use dry ingredients only and replace garlic with garlic powder.) If you prefer, grind dried chiles alone in spice grinder to make 100 percent pure chile powder.

29 Burgers

GOOD BURGERS BEGIN WITH GOOD BEEF

Making burgers from supermarket ground beef gets dinner on the table in a hurry. But when the goal is a memorably thick, juicy burger full of big beefy flavor—the kind served in the best high-end pubs—the preground stuff is not an option.

Because it's typically purchased in bulk from beef processing plants, supplemented with meat scraps from the local store, and then reground, the flavor and texture vary from package to package. Who knows what cuts are in that ground beef? (You don't want to think about this too much.) Just as important: The beef has literally been ground to a pulp. Why does this matter? Beef that has been ground too fine or too often can't hold on to its natural moisture during the cooking process, which translates to tough, dry burgers.

Grinding meat at home lets you choose the cut so you know the burgers will have big beefy flavor. And because the meat is ground just once, and because the cook rather than an automated machine controls this process, the texture of the ground meat will be coarser and looser. As long as you don't overwork the meat during the shaping process, your minimal effort will translate into the tenderest, juiciest burgers you've ever eaten at home.

Now, we know what you're going to say: It's crazy to spend money on a meat grinder for something as humble as a burger. We agree. That's why we developed a technique that relies on the "grinder" already in your kitchen—a food processor. If you don't own a food processor, we've just given you one more reason to make the investment in this true multitasker.

WHY THIS RECIPE WORKS

The Right Cut
Sirloin steak tips, also sold as flap meat, have a supremely beefy flavor and coarse grainy texture (so the meat doesn't become overly compact when ground). In addition, there's not much gristly sinew to pick out.

Cut into Small Pieces
Cutting the meat into small ½-inch chunks and freezing them until just firm before grinding ensures a relatively coarse grind. Grinding the meat in small batches also reduces the risk of overworking the meat. Lightly shaping the meat into patties gives these pub-size burgers just enough structure to hold their shape in the skillet. Remember: A looser pack translates to a more tender burger.

Add Flavorful Fat
Sirloin tips are pretty lean so adding melted butter to the ground meat ups its richness. The butter solidifies when it hits the cold meat and creates tiny particles of fat throughout the patties, which improves the burgers' flavor and juiciness. Also, the dairy proteins and sugar in the butter boost the browning of the burgers' exterior.

Use Two Cooking Methods
Using a standard skillet-only method for these thick burgers doesn't work. Our combination stove-oven technique produces a great crust and a juicy interior. After an initial sear in a hot skillet, the gentler heat of the oven quickly finishes cooking the burgers and prevents a gray band of overcooked meat from forming beneath the crust.

Transfer to a Cold Baking Sheet
Moving the skillet with the burgers directly to the oven would allow the meat in direct contact with the hot skillet to cook faster than the top half of the burger. Transferring the seared burgers from the hot skillet to a baking sheet, and then to the oven, fixes the problem.

Beef ground at home plus melted butter makes the ultimate pub-style burgers.

Juicy Pub-Style Burgers

SERVES 4

Sirloin steak tips are also sold as flap meat. When stirring the butter and pepper into the ground meat and shaping the patties, take care not to overwork the meat or the burgers will become dense. For the best flavor, season the burgers aggressively just before cooking. Serve with Pub-Style Burger Sauce (at right), if desired.

2 **pounds sirloin steak tips or boneless beef short ribs, trimmed and cut into ½-inch chunks**

4 **tablespoons unsalted butter, melted and cooled slightly**

Salt and pepper

1 **teaspoon vegetable oil**

4 **large hamburger buns, toasted and buttered**

1. Place beef chunks on rimmed baking sheet in single layer. Freeze meat until very firm and starting to harden around edges but still pliable, 15 to 25 minutes.

2. Place one-quarter of meat in food processor and pulse until finely ground into ¹⁄₁₆-inch pieces, about 35 pulses, stopping and redistributing meat around bowl as necessary to ensure beef is evenly ground. Transfer meat to clean baking sheet, over turning workbowl and without directly touching meat. Repeat grinding with remaining 3 batches of meat. Spread meat over sheet and inspect carefully, discarding any long strands of gristle or large chunks of hard meat or fat.

3. Adjust oven rack to middle position and heat oven to 300 degrees. Drizzle melted butter over ground meat and add 1 teaspoon pepper. Gently toss with fork to combine. Divide meat into 4 lightly packed balls. Gently flatten into patties ¾ inch thick and about 4½ inches in diameter. Refrigerate patties until ready to cook. (Patties can be refrigerated for up to 24 hours.)

4. Season 1 side of patties with salt and pepper. Using spatula, flip patties and season other side. Heat oil in 12-inch skillet over high heat until just smoking. Using spatula, transfer burgers to skillet and cook without moving for 2 minutes. Using spatula, flip burgers over and cook for 2 minutes longer. Transfer patties to rimmed baking sheet and bake until burgers register 125 degrees (for medium-rare), 3 to 5 minutes.

5. Transfer burgers to plate and let rest for 5 minutes. Transfer to buns, add desired toppings, and serve.

JUICY PUB-STYLE BURGERS WITH CRISPY SHALLOTS AND BLUE CHEESE

Heat ½ cup vegetable oil and 3 thinly sliced shallots in medium saucepan over high heat; cook, stirring frequently, until shallots are golden, about 8 minutes. Using slotted spoon, transfer shallots to paper towel–lined plate, season with salt, and let drain until crisp, about 5 minutes. (Cooled shallots can be stored at room temperature for up to 3 days.) Top each burger with 1 ounce crumbled blue cheese before transferring to oven. Top with Pub-Style Burger Sauce (at right) and crispy shallots just before serving.

RECIPE DETAILS

Timeline

• 25 minutes to cut up beef and freeze beef chunks
• 15 minutes to grind beef and shape burgers
• 10 minutes to cook burgers
• 5 minutes to rest burgers before serving

Essential Tools

• 2 rimmed baking sheets, one for freezing beef chunks and holding ground beef and one for finishing burgers in oven (You can use one sheet for both tasks if you wash it with hot, soapy water between uses.)
• Food processor for grinding beef chunks
• 12-inch skillet for cooking burgers

Substitutions & Variations

• Top burgers with lettuce, tomato, sliced red onion, and our homemade burger sauce. An ounce of good cheese is enough for each burger. In addition to blue cheese and aged cheddar, try smoked cheddar or Gruyère. No matter the variety, add the cheese to the burgers right before they go into the oven.
• Fancy adds-on can help make this great burger even better. Try crispy shallots (see recipe, left), peppered bacon, caramelized onions, or pan-roasted mushrooms. Add these embellishments when assembling the burgers in the buns.
• Great burgers demand a good sauce. To make our Pub-Style Burger Sauce, whisk together ¾ cup mayonnaise, 2 tablespoons soy sauce, 1 tablespoon packed dark brown sugar, 1 tablespoon Worcestershire sauce, 1 tablespoon minced chives, 1 minced garlic clove, and ¾ teaspoon pepper.

30 Turkey

THE BEST (AND EASIEST) WAY TO TACKLE A HOLIDAY BIRD

The star of the Thanksgiving meal is terribly flawed. Modern mass-produced turkey doesn't have much flavor and even the best gravies can't hide that fact. Turkey is also hard to cook right. Its unwieldy structure (huge breast that easily overcooks and smaller legs that require a long time to become tender) makes preparing this bird a real challenge.

Most cooks roast the holiday bird and hope for the best. However, many early American cookbook authors actually advocated a different method: cooking a whole bird (or its parts) in liquid in a covered pot set over an open fire. Braising, after all, would have been uniquely suited to the tough wild fowl available in Colonial times, as hours of simmering would have broken down the dark meat's chewy connective tissue and turned it meltingly tender.

But braising in the oven (no need to worry about an open fire these days!) is also a terrific way to cook today's lean turkey. Since the temperature in the pan can never rise above the boiling point of water (212 degrees), the method is inherently gentle, minimizing the risk of drying out the breast. On top of that, simmering the bird in broth creates a flavor exchange between the meat and the liquid, giving today's bland turkey a much-needed flavor boost and producing a rich, ready-made gravy.

Yes, you do lose the crisp skin if you braise the bird, but turkey skin is rarely all that crisp and most people don't eat it. In any case, trading crisp skin for supremely tender, juicy meat seems like a good deal. We don't usually think of the Pilgrims as culinary pioneers, but this is one case where adapting an old-fashioned technique solves a very modern problem.

WHY THIS RECIPE WORKS

Parts, Please
Braising parts rather than a whole bird provides extra insurance that the white and the dark meat cook at an even rate. Turkey parts are readily available at the supermarket so no butchering is required. And parts make carving so simple.

Use a Roasting Pan
A roasting pan—rather than an old-fashioned Dutch oven—is the perfect vessel to fit 10 pounds of bone-in turkey parts. A single layer, with every part in contact with the braising liquid, ensures even cooking. A piece of parchment keeps the parts from drying out while foil takes the place of a lid and creates a tight seal.

Brown, Then Braise
Roasting the turkey parts in a 500-degree oven—before turning down the heat and adding the braising liquid—allows them to develop good color and contributes rich, roasted flavor to the broth. The browning stint also helps render some fat.

Building Flavor
Simmering the turkey in chicken broth cut with a little white wine (for acidity and complexity) produces almost-ready gravy. Build in flavor by browning aromatic vegetables (onions, carrots, celery, and garlic) along with earthy porcini mushrooms, and herbs. Simply add these ingredients to the roasting pan at the outset and they will brown along with the turkey. How easy!

Effortless Gravy
Once the turkey is done, the braising liquid left in the pan is ready to become gravy. Start by straining out the solids—and make sure to press out every last drop of flavor. Next, skim fat from the strained liquid. Combine this flavorful turkey fat with flour to make a roux that will thicken the braising liquid. Simmer the gravy until it reaches the proper consistency. By the time the gravy is done, the turkey has rested and is ready to carve.

Start a new tradition: Brine turkey parts before braising them in a covered pan.

Braised Turkey with Gravy

SERVES 10 TO 12

If using self-basting or kosher turkey parts, do not brine in step 1, but do sprinkle with 1½ teaspoons salt.

Salt and pepper	½ ounce dried porcini mushrooms, rinsed
1 cup sugar	6 garlic cloves, crushed and peeled
1 (5- to 7-pound) whole bone-in turkey breast, trimmed	6 sprigs fresh thyme
	6 sprigs fresh parsley
4 pounds turkey drumsticks and thighs, trimmed	2 bay leaves
	4 tablespoons unsalted butter, melted
3 onions, chopped	4 cups chicken broth
3 celery ribs, chopped	1 cup dry white wine
2 carrots, peeled and chopped	3 tablespoons all-purpose flour

1. Dissolve 1 cup salt and sugar in 2 gallons cold water in large container. Submerge turkey pieces in brine, cover, and refrigerate for at least 3 hours or up to 6 hours.

2. Adjust oven rack to lower-middle position and heat oven to 500 degrees. Remove turkey from brine and pat dry with paper towels. Toss onions, celery, carrots, mushrooms, garlic, thyme sprigs, parsley sprigs, bay leaves, and 2 tablespoons melted butter together in large roasting pan; arrange in even layer. Brush turkey pieces with remaining 2 tablespoons melted butter and season with pepper. Place turkey pieces, skin side up, on vegetables, leaving at least ¼ inch between pieces. Roast until skin is lightly browned, about 20 minutes.

3. Remove pan from oven and reduce temperature to 325 degrees. Pour broth and wine around turkey pieces (liquid should come about three-quarters up drumsticks and thighs). Place 16 by 12-inch piece of parchment paper over turkey pieces. Cover pan tightly with aluminum foil. Return covered pan to oven and cook until breast registers 160 degrees and thighs register 175 degrees, 1¾ to 2¼ hours. Transfer turkey to carving board, tent loosely with foil, and let rest for 20 minutes.

4. Strain vegetables and liquid from roasting pan through fine-mesh strainer set in large bowl; discard solids. Pour liquid into fat separator and let settle for 5 minutes. Reserve 3 tablespoons fat and 3 cups braising liquid (set aside any remaining braising liquid for another use).

5. Heat reserved fat in medium saucepan over medium-high heat. Add flour and cook, stirring constantly, until flour is dark golden brown and fragrant, about 5 minutes. Whisk in reserved braising liquid and bring to boil. Reduce heat to medium-low and simmer, stirring occasionally, until gravy is thick and reduced to 2 cups, 15 to 20 minutes. Remove gravy from heat and season with salt and pepper to taste.

6. Carve turkey and serve, passing gravy separately.

RECIPE DETAILS

Timeline

- 3 to 6 hours to brine turkey
- 40 minutes to prep vegetables and brown turkey and veggies
- 1¾ to 2¼ hours to braise turkey
- 20 minutes to rest turkey (and start gravy)
- 10 minutes to carve turkey (and finish gravy)

Essential Tools

- Large container to hold turkey and brine
- Large roasting pan
- Parchment paper and aluminum foil to seal roasting pan
- Fine-mesh strainer to strain braising liquid
- Medium saucepan to make gravy

Substitutions & Variations

- Instead of drumsticks and thighs, you can use two whole leg quarters, 1½ to 2 pounds each.
- The recipe will also work with a turkey breast alone; in step 1, reduce the salt and sugar to ½ cup each and the water to 4 quarts.

31 Ham

NOTHING ELSE FEEDS A BIG CROWD AND REQUIRES SO LITTLE WORK

A spiral-sliced bone-in half ham easily feeds a dozen people with plenty of leftovers. If you put a lot of sides on the table and aren't concerned about sandwiches the next day, then that one ham can feed 20 people. That's a lot of food from something that requires so little effort.

A ham seems much easier to prepare than other holiday centerpieces like turkey or prime rib. You just throw the ham in the oven, slather on some glaze, and wait. However, this simple method fails many cooks. The ham is dried-out and leathery—think salty jerky. The mistake? Spiral-sliced hams are cured and fully cooked, so they don't need to be cooked a second time. A reheat is sufficient.

So what's the secret to ham that's moist and flavorful? Gently warm the ham, taking care at every stage to minimize moisture loss. As you might imagine, slow and low is the way to go. And don't overcook the ham. Heating the ham causes moisture loss. Once the ham is warm, it's done.

Now how are you supposed to caramelize the sticky glaze in a slow and low oven? Wait to apply the glaze until the ham has almost reached the desired serving temperature, then paint on the glaze and 10 minutes is enough. And, please, don't use the glaze packet that comes with many hams. It's way too sweet and full of preservatives (and tastes like it, too). Make your own glaze from pantry staples. It takes just 5 minutes and given how little effort it takes to cook a ham, it seems like the least you could do.

WHY THIS RECIPE WORKS

Choose the Right Ham
Bone-in hams with natural juices are the least processed of all the options at the supermarket and offer the best flavor. While "water added" ham might sound juicier, these hams taste awful and shed all that extra water in the oven. Bone-in half hams are available in two distinct cuts. If the labeling is unclear, it is easy to identify them by their shape: A shank ham has a tapered, more pointed end opposite the flat cut side of the ham, whereas the sirloin (or butt) end is rounded. We prefer the shank ham because there are fewer bones to work around. Whether you buy a shank or sirloin ham, make sure it's spiral-sliced to facilitate carving.

A Warm Bath
A big ham, cold from the refrigerator, can take hours to heat through in the oven, by which time the meat becomes very dry. This drying is especially noticeable around the outer edges of the ham. Soaking the packaged ham in warm water for 90 minutes raises its internal temperature to 60 degrees and cuts the total roasting time by over an hour.

Bake in a Bag
Roasting the ham in a plastic oven bag traps heat and reduces cooking time. Less cooking time means less loss of juices so the finished ham is especially moist.

Warm Is Good
While fresh ham should reach an internal temperature of 160 degrees, a cured ham only needs to reach an internal temperature of 110 to 120 degrees. You're reheating rather than cooking the ham.

Know When to Glaze
It's best to apply the glaze toward the end of cooking and quickly caramelize it so the ham won't dry out. Then glaze again once the ham comes out of the oven and rests. As a bonus, you can make a serving sauce with the remaining glaze and the drippings in the oven bag.

A bath gently warms the ham while an oven bag reduces the cooking time.

Glazed Spiral-Sliced Ham

SERVES 12 TO 14, WITH LEFTOVERS

We prefer a tapered shank ham but a rounded sirloin ham will work in this recipe. If there is a tear or hole in the ham's inner covering, wrap it in several layers of plastic wrap before soaking it in hot water. Cut slits in the oven bag so it does not burst.

1 **(7- to 10-pound) spiral-sliced bone-in half ham**	1 **large plastic oven bag**
	1 **recipe glaze (recipes follow)**

1. Leaving ham's inner plastic or foil covering intact, place ham in large container and cover with hot tap water; set aside for 45 minutes. Drain and cover again with hot tap water; set aside for another 45 minutes.

2. Adjust oven rack to lowest position and heat oven to 250 degrees. Unwrap ham; discard plastic disk covering bone. Place ham in oven bag. Gather top of bag tightly so bag fits snugly around ham, tie bag, and trim excess plastic. Set ham cut side down in large roasting pan and cut 4 slits in top of bag with paring knife.

3. Bake ham until center registers 100 degrees, 1 to 1½ hours (about 10 minutes per pound).

4. Remove ham from oven and increase oven temperature to 350 degrees. Cut open oven bag and roll back sides to expose ham. Brush ham with one-third of glaze and return to oven until glaze becomes sticky, about 10 minutes (if glaze is too thick to brush, return to heat to loosen).

5. Remove ham from oven, transfer to carving board, and brush entire ham with one-third of glaze. Tent ham loosely with aluminum foil and let rest for 15 minutes. While ham rests, add 4 to 6 tablespoons ham juices to remaining one-third of glaze and cook over medium heat until thick but fluid sauce forms. Carve and serve ham, passing sauce separately.

MAPLE-ORANGE GLAZE MAKES 1 CUP

¾ **cup maple syrup**	1 **tablespoon Dijon mustard**
½ **cup orange marmalade**	1 **teaspoon pepper**
2 **tablespoons unsalted butter**	¼ **teaspoon ground cinnamon**

Combine all ingredients in small saucepan. Cook over medium heat, stirring occasionally, until mixture is thick, syrupy, and reduced to 1 cup, 5 to 10 minutes; set aside.

APPLE-GINGER GLAZE MAKES 1½ CUPS

1 **cup packed dark brown sugar**	1 **tablespoon grated fresh ginger**
¾ **cup apple jelly**	**Pinch ground cloves**
3 **tablespoons apple butter**	

Combine all ingredients in small saucepan. Cook over medium heat, stirring occasionally, until sugar dissolves and mixture is thick, syrupy, and reduced to 1½ cups, 5 to 10 minutes; set aside.

32 Biscuits

RELIABLE BISCUITS START WITH CLUMPY BUTTERMILK (REALLY)

Making biscuits is a study in simplicity and speed. A half-dozen staple ingredients quickly mixed together and popped into the oven emerge minutes later as hot, buttery biscuits. Because biscuits are leavened chemically rather than with yeast, they can be on the table fast—really fast.

Perhaps this speed is why most cooks are willing to tolerate less than perfect results. Many bakers talk about having the "touch," indicating that some people can work the fat into the flour just right. But what about the rest of us, with our too-warm or too-cold hands? A food processor makes cutting the butter and/or shortening into the dry ingredients easier, but it doesn't make it any more reliable than more old-fashioned methods such as your fingertips, two knives, or a pastry blender.

And even if you get this step right, there's the rolling and stamping process. If you work the dough too much, the biscuits are tough. If you twist rather than punch out the dough rounds, the biscuits don't rise. And forget about the biscuits you make from the scraps—they are guaranteed to be squatter than the rest.

There is one style that guarantees simplicity—the humble drop biscuit. The butter is melted so mixing the ingredients together is easy and the shaping is idiot-proof. There's only one problem—cold chunks of butter guarantee a light, tender biscuit and many drop biscuits are heavy and gummy. But if you add cold milk to the hot melted butter—you create lumps in the melted butter that end up functioning much like cold chunks of butter in the traditional recipe. This simple step makes superior drop biscuits that are utterly foolproof.

WHY THIS RECIPE WORKS

Pick Buttermilk
Using buttermilk instead of milk provides rich, buttery tang in such a basic biscuit recipe. It also allows us to add baking soda (along with baking powder). The baking soda reacts with the acid in the buttermilk and gives the biscuits a crispier, browner exterior and fluffier middle. Adding baking soda also eliminates the metallic taste that occurs when just baking powder is used.

The Power of Steam
More liquid in the dough (a full cup of buttermilk) translates into more steam created in the hot oven. This steam acts as a powerful leavener, which, in conjunction with the chemical leaveners, lightens the texture of the biscuits. The tender, fluffy interior is the perfect contrast to the craggy, golden-brown exterior.

Keep It Clumpy
Usually, properly combining melted butter with buttermilk (or any liquid) requires that both ingredients be at just the right temperature; if they aren't, the melted butter clumps in the cold buttermilk. This may look like a mistake (and in recipes like fine-textured cake it is), but it actually mimics the process of cutting cold butter into flour and is the secret to this recipe. The result is a surprisingly better biscuit, slightly higher and with better texture. That's because the lumps of butter turn to steam in the oven and help create more rise.

Scoop, Drop, and Bake
A greased ¼-cup measure is the perfect tool to easily scoop up biscuit dough and drop it onto a parchment-lined baking sheet. Baking the biscuits in a very hot oven is the key to a quick rise and good dark brown crust. The biscuits end up with very crisp tops that can withstand a final brush of melted butter.

This clumpy mess looks like a mistake but it's actually the secret to these oh-so-easy scoop-and-bake biscuits.

Drop Biscuits

MAKES 12 BISCUITS

You will need about 2 tablespoons melted butter for brushing the tops of the biscuits.

2 cups (10 ounces) all-purpose flour
2 teaspoons baking powder
½ teaspoon baking soda
1 teaspoon sugar

¾ teaspoon salt
1 cup buttermilk, chilled
8 tablespoons unsalted butter, melted and still warm, plus extra for serving

1. Adjust oven rack to middle position and heat oven to 475 degrees. Line rimmed baking sheet with parchment paper.

2. Whisk flour, baking powder, baking soda, sugar, and salt together in large bowl. In separate bowl, stir chilled buttermilk and melted butter together until butter forms small clumps. Stir buttermilk mixture into flour mixture until just incorporated and dough pulls away from sides of bowl.

3. Using greased ¼-cup measure, scoop out and drop 12 mounds of dough onto prepared sheet, spaced about 1½ inches apart (scant ¼ cup per mound). Bake until tops are golden brown and crisp, 12 to 14 minutes, rotating sheet halfway through baking.

4. Brush baked biscuits with extra melted butter to taste, transfer to wire rack, and let cool slightly. Serve warm.

CHEDDAR DROP BISCUITS
Whisk ¼ teaspoon dry mustard and ⅛ teaspoon cayenne pepper into flour mixture, then stir in 1 cup shredded cheddar cheese, breaking up any clumps, until coated with flour.

TARRAGON-GRUYÈRE DROP BISCUITS
Stir 1 cup shredded Gruyère cheese and 1 tablespoon minced fresh tarragon into flour mixture, breaking up any clumps, until coated with flour.

BASIL-PARMESAN DROP BISCUITS
Stir 1 cup grated Parmesan cheese and 2 tablespoons chopped fresh basil into flour mixture, breaking up any clumps, until coated with flour.

RECIPE DETAILS

Timeline

• 25 minutes to mix and bake biscuits (preheat oven, too)
• 5 minutes to brush biscuits with melted butter and cool before serving

Essential Tools

• ¼-cup dry measure to scoop out biscuit dough
• Parchment paper
• Rimmed baking sheet
• Pastry brush for brushing baked biscuit tops with melted butter

Substitutions & Variations

• If buttermilk is unavailable, substitute ¾ cup plain whole-milk or low-fat yogurt thinned with ¼ cup milk.
• To refresh day-old biscuits, heat them in a 300-degree oven for 10 minutes.
• In addition to the variations listed at left, feel free to use other herbs (chives, rosemary, thyme, and sage work especially well). Use no more than a teaspoon or two of stronger herbs like rosemary and sage. One teaspoon of coarsely ground black pepper is another good stir-in as is ¼ cup thinly sliced scallions. Crisp bits of fried bacon (6 slices, cut in half lengthwise and then crosswise into ¼-inch strips) can also be folded into the dry ingredients.

33 Cornbread

CAN A MODERN INNOVATION CREATE A RECIPE THAT PLEASES THE WHOLE COUNTRY?

Deeply rooted in American history, cornbread has been around long enough to take on a distinctly different character depending on where it is made. In the South, cornbread is a decidedly savory skillet bread served with everything from a pot of greens to barbecue. It's often quite squat and has a pleasantly crumbly texture. In the North, cornbread is more cake than bread and has a light and fluffy crumb. And Northern cornbread is generously sweetened.

Despite these regional variations in texture and appearance, cornbread has one constant: It lacks convincing corn flavor. Southern versions, with more cornmeal than flour, are certainly more corn-y than Northern recipes that usually reverse the ratio of these two key ingredients. But even Southern recipes with little or no flour taste more like cornmeal than corn. If we could create a truly corny cornbread would regional partisans come together over one great bread?

The solution would seem obvious—just stir in some fresh corn kernels. But nubby bits of corn bake up tough and chewy and don't impart much flavor. Our recipe starts with convenient frozen corn and then purees it with the liquid elements, in effect creating "corn milk" to moisten the batter. This simple change is a revelation. Our cornbread tastes like fresh corn and it's sweet but not sugary.

Many cooks don't own a cast-iron skillet so we developed a recipe that relies on a baking dish but still yields a browned crust. As for the crumb, we decided to build a recipe with a fluffy but not cakey texture. And we add enough sweetener to reinforce the sweet corn flavor without pushing cornbread into the dessert category. It's hard to make a classic recipe that pleases everyone, but you can try.

WHY THIS RECIPE WORKS

Choose the Right Cornmeal
Cornmeal comes in a variety of textures. For consistent results, we recommend using widely available Quaker yellow cornmeal. This isn't the most flavorful option at the supermarket but that's OK since it's not the primary source of corn flavor. Perhaps just as important, Quaker is ground fine. Coarse cornmeal can give cornbread an unappealing gritty texture. A ratio of 3 parts flour to 2 parts cornmeal ensures a fluffy texture.

The Cold Secret
Corn kernels are the key to big corn flavor. While fresh corn is best, frozen is nearly as good—and a lot easier to use. Pureeing the thawed kernels in a food processor releases their full flavor while breaking down the tough, chewy kernels. We prefer the tang of buttermilk to regular milk in this recipe. (You can add lemon juice to regular milk to make a close approximation.)

Sugar and Soda
White granulated sugar makes good cornbread but using brown sugar instead adds mellow molasses flavor without too much sweetness and accentuates the corn flavor. Using a little baking soda with the baking powder makes for a fluffy but not too cakey crumb, plus the baking soda helps promote browning.

Streaks of Butter
Gently folding melted butter into the assembled batter leaves subtle streaks of unmixed butter that rise to the surface and create a more deeply browned top crust and stronger butter flavor.

Use a Hot Oven
In lieu of a hot skillet, a baking dish can yield a thick crust, especially if you use a glass pan (the glass heats quickly and conducts heat better than metal). Baking the bread at a higher than conventional temperature produces a crust that is crunchy and full of buttery, toasted corn flavor.

Starting this recipe in a food processor guarantees big corn flavor.

All-Purpose Cornbread

SERVES 6

Before preparing the baking dish or any of the other ingredients, measure out the frozen kernels and let them stand at room temperature until needed. This recipe was developed with Quaker yellow cornmeal; a stone-ground whole-grain cornmeal will work but will yield a drier and less tender cornbread.

1½ cups (7½ ounces) all-purpose flour
1 cup (5 ounces) cornmeal
2 teaspoons baking powder
¼ teaspoon baking soda
¾ teaspoon salt
¼ cup packed (1¾ ounces) light brown sugar

¾ cup frozen corn, thawed
1 cup buttermilk
2 large eggs
8 tablespoons unsalted butter, melted and cooled

1. Adjust oven rack to middle position and heat oven to 400 degrees. Spray 8-inch square baking dish with vegetable oil spray. Whisk flour, cornmeal, baking powder, baking soda, and salt in medium bowl until combined; set aside.

2. In food processor or blender, process brown sugar, corn kernels, and buttermilk until combined, about 5 seconds. Add eggs and process until well combined (corn lumps will remain), about 5 seconds longer.

3. Using rubber spatula, make well in center of dry ingredients; pour wet ingredients into well. Begin folding dry ingredients into wet, giving mixture only a few turns to barely combine. Add melted butter and continue folding until dry ingredients are just moistened. Pour batter into prepared baking dish and smooth surface with rubber spatula.

4. Bake until cornbread is deep golden brown and toothpick inserted in center comes out clean, 25 to 35 minutes. Let cool on wire rack for 10 minutes, then invert onto wire rack, and turn right side up and let cool until warm, about 10 minutes longer, and serve. (Leftover cornbread can be wrapped in aluminum foil and reheated in a 350-degree oven for 10 to 15 minutes.)

BLUEBERRY BREAKFAST CORNBREAD
Reduce salt to ½ teaspoon. Reduce buttermilk to ¾ cup and add ¼ cup maple syrup to food processor along with buttermilk in step 2. Add 1 cup fresh or frozen blueberries with melted butter in step 3. Sprinkle 2 tablespoons granulated sugar over batter in baking dish just before baking.

SPICY JALAPEÑO-CHEDDAR CORNBREAD
Reduce salt to ½ teaspoon. Add ⅜ teaspoon cayenne pepper, 1 finely chopped jalapeño chile, and ½ cup shredded cheddar cheese to flour mixture and toss well to combine. Reduce brown sugar to 2 tablespoons and sprinkle ½ cup shredded cheddar cheese over batter in dish just before baking.

RECIPE DETAILS

Timeline
- 15 minutes to mix batter
- 30 minutes to bake cornbread
- 20 minutes to cool (in and out of pan)

Essential Tools
- 8-inch baking dish (We prefer a glass baking dish because it yields a nice golden-brown crust, but a metal baking pan will also work.)

Substitutions & Variations
- When corn is in season, fresh cooked kernels can be substituted for the frozen corn.
- If necessary, the buttermilk can be replaced with a mixture of 1 cup whole or low-fat milk and 1 tablespoon lemon juice or distilled white vinegar.
- Delicious on its own, cornbread is even better with Whipped Honey Butter. Beat 8 tablespoons room-temperature unsalted butter in stand mixer fitted with whisk attachment at medium speed until smooth, about 30 seconds. Add 1 tablespoon honey and pinch salt and mix until combined, about 15 seconds. Increase speed to high and whip until very light and fluffy, about 2 minutes, scraping down bowl as needed.

34 Chocolate Chip Cookies

IT'S TIME TO MOVE BEYOND THE BACK OF THE BAG

Figuring out the origins of a particular recipe is a murky business. You can find plenty of convincing-sounding "histories" on the web and in books, but most are pure fiction. However, that's not the case for chocolate chip cookies, which trace their history back to a single recipe.

In the 1930s, Ruth Wakefield, owner of the Toll House Inn in Whitman, Massachusetts, cut up a bar of Nestlé semisweet chocolate and mixed it into her batter for Butter Drop Do cookies. Soon newspapers around New England were printing her recipe for chocolate chip cookies, and sales of Nestlé semisweet chocolate bars soared. In what might just qualify as the worst deal of the century, Nestlé offered Wakefield a lifetime supply of chocolate for the rights to what's now the world's most famous cookie recipe. By 1939, Nestlé began selling packages of small pieces of chocolate, named Toll House morsels, and the rest is history.

The Toll House cookie's cakey texture and buttery flavor certainly have their appeal. But is it really the best that a chocolate chip cookie can be?

A truly great version would offer real complexity, with deep notes of toffee and butterscotch to balance the sweetness. And rather than a uniform texture, our ideal would be moist and chewy in the middle yet crisp and caramelized around the edges.

By rethinking everything—including the chips—we think we have developed the ultimate version. Best of all, our recipe skips the time-consuming step of waiting for the butter to soften on the counter so you can satisfy a cookie craving even faster.

WHY THIS RECIPE WORKS

The Sugar Ratio
The Toll House recipe calls for equal amounts of white sugar and light brown sugar. White sugar lends crispness, while brown sugar enhances chewiness. We get the best results by using dark brown for its deeper full flavor and by using a bit more brown sugar than white.

Brown the Butter
Creaming the butter and sugar creates a cakey texture in Toll House cookies. Using melted butter makes all cookies, including this one, chewier. That's because the water in the melted butter promotes gluten development in the flour. Browning (rather than just melting) the butter develops complex flavor to balance the sweetness in the cookie. As butter browns, it takes on the flavor and aroma of toasted nuts. Browning burns off moisture, so brown only a portion of the butter.

Whisk and Wait
After stirring together the butter, sugars, and egg and yolk, wait. After 10 minutes (and three rounds of whisking and resting), the sugars will have dissolved and the mixture will turn thick and shiny. Sugar that is dissolved in liquid before baking caramelizes more easily in the oven, creating finished cookies with more complex toffee-like flavor.

Use More Dough
Bigger cookies mean chewier centers. We use 3 tablespoons of dough versus the rounded tablespoon called for in the Toll House recipe. This also promotes a satisfying contrast in textures between the center and the crisp edges.

Don't Overbake
Bake the cookies just until golden brown and set around the edges, but still soft in the center; they continue to firm up as they cool on the baking sheet.

Browned butter and dark brown sugar build flavor in our oversized cookies.

Ultimate Chocolate Chip Cookies

MAKES ABOUT 16 LARGE COOKIES

Use fresh, moist brown sugar, as hardened brown sugar will make the cookies too dry.

1¾ cups (8¾ ounces) all-purpose flour
½ teaspoon baking soda
14 tablespoons unsalted butter
¾ cup packed (5¼ ounces) dark brown sugar
½ cup (3½ ounces) granulated sugar
1 teaspoon salt

2 teaspoons vanilla extract
1 large egg plus 1 large yolk
1¼ cups (7½ ounces) semisweet or bittersweet chocolate chips or chunks
¾ cup pecans or walnuts, toasted and chopped (optional)

1. Adjust oven rack to middle position and heat oven to 375 degrees. Line 2 baking sheets with parchment paper. Whisk flour and baking soda together in medium bowl; set aside.

2. Melt 10 tablespoons butter in 10-inch skillet over medium-high heat. Continue cooking, swirling pan constantly, until butter is dark golden brown and has nutty aroma, 1 to 3 minutes. Transfer browned butter to large heatproof bowl. Add remaining 4 tablespoons butter and stir until completely melted.

3. Add brown sugar, granulated sugar, salt, and vanilla to melted butter; whisk until fully incorporated. Add egg and yolk; whisk until mixture is smooth with no sugar lumps remaining, about 30 seconds. Let mixture stand for 3 minutes, then whisk for 30 seconds. Repeat process of resting and whisking 2 more times until mixture is thick, smooth, and shiny. Using rubber spatula, stir in flour mixture until just combined, about 1 minute. Stir in chocolate chips and nuts, if using. Give dough final stir to ensure that no flour pockets remain and ingredients are evenly distributed.

4. Working with 3 tablespoons of dough at a time, roll into balls and space 2 inches apart on prepared sheets.

5. Bake 1 sheet at a time until cookies are golden brown and still puffy and edges have begun to set but centers are still soft, 10 to 14 minutes, rotating sheet halfway through baking. Transfer sheet to wire rack; let cookies cool to room temperature.

RECIPE DETAILS

Timeline

• 5 minutes to melt and brown butter
• 10 minutes to whisk and rest butter and sugar mixture
• 5 minutes to stir in dry ingredients and shape dough balls
• 25 minutes to bake 2 batches of cookies

Essential Tools

• 10-inch skillet with traditional finish (Avoid using a nonstick skillet to brown the butter; the dark color of the nonstick coating makes it difficult to gauge when the butter is sufficiently browned.)
• Whisk
• 2 baking sheets
• Parchment paper (so much better than greasing baking sheets)

Substitutions & Variations

• This recipe works with light brown sugar, but the cookies will be less full-flavored.
• We think bittersweet chocolate chips are best (Ghirardelli 60 Percent Cacao Bittersweet Chips are the test kitchen's favorite) but this recipe works with semisweet, milk, or even white chocolate chips.
• The nuts are optional but toasting them is not. (Toasting ensures a crisp texture and brings out their flavor.) You can toast nuts in a dry 10-inch skillet set over medium heat or on a small rimmed baking sheet in a 350-degree oven. Make sure to stir the nuts (especially if you're working on the stovetop) and stop as soon as the nuts are fragrant. This will take less than 5 minutes on the stovetop and less than 10 minutes in the oven.

35 Brownies

THE ULTIMATE BROWNIE RECIPE STEALS A SECRET FROM BOX MIXES

There's a reason why box-mix brownies are so popular. You might think it's because they are convenient. While that's certainly the marketing pitch, in truth, mixes aren't all that much faster than homemade since you still need to add water, eggs, and oil. Homemade brownies take 10 minutes of hands-on work so let's not kid ourselves that using a mix is saving much time.

We think the real reason why box-mix brownies dominate bake sales and potlucks is because people really like them. Most of us overlook their prefab, slightly "manufactured" flavor. (Yes, you can almost taste the chemicals.) What keeps box mix brownies in business is their uniquely chewy texture and shiny, crackly top.

Depending on the amounts of chocolate and flour in the recipe, homemade brownies are either fudgy or cakey. But they are rarely chewy. Food manufacturers have developed something called the "shortening system" (a very specific ratio of saturated to unsaturated fats) that gives their brownies an irresistible chewy texture. The powdered mix contains the saturated fat (in the form of partially hydrogenated oils) and the liquid vegetable oil (added by the cook) supplies the unsaturated fat.

Manufacturers prioritize shelf life over flavor, which is why butter is not part of the mix. However, could we supplement the butter in homemade brownies with just the right amount of vegetable oil to create our own version of the shortening system? We got out our calculators and began a two-month testing odyssey in search of the ultimate brownie that combined excellent flavor with real chew. Talk about good chemistry!

WHY THIS RECIPE WORKS

Adjusting Fat Ratios

Homemade brownies are generally made with butter so they contain a lot of saturated fat. But box mixes contain just 1 part saturated fat for 3 parts unsaturated fat. For truly chewy brownies, mix a small amount of butter (for flavor) with a hefty amount of oil.

Chocolate Times Three Plus Espresso

Using unsweetened Dutch-processed cocoa powder provides a jolt of pure chocolate flavor, and because cocoa powder contains very little fat it doesn't interfere with the ratio of saturated to unsaturated fats. Ounce for ounce, cocoa powder has more cocoa solids—and thus more chocolate flavor—than any other type of chocolate. Blooming the cocoa in boiling water brings out its flavor and adding espresso powder reinforces that chocolate flavor. Melting a small amount of finely chopped unsweetened chocolate in this boiling water adds another layer of chocolate oomph. And for a final punch of chocolate flavor, we stir bittersweet chocolate chunks into the batter. During baking, the chocolate melts into gooey, bittersweet pockets throughout the chewy bars.

Extra Egg Yolks

Emulsifiers can help prevent fats from separating and leaking out during baking. Lecithin, a substance that occurs naturally in egg yolks, is just such an emulsifier. The simple addition of two extra egg yolks, along with two whole eggs, holds our brownie batter together and prevents the brownies from being greasy.

Surface Details

Granulated sugar, which contains less moisture than either brown sugar or corn syrup, is key to brownies with a crackly top. And because white sugar is pure sucrose, it forms a smooth, glass-like surface that reflects light and creates a shiny crust. In contrast, brownies made with other sweeteners have a dull, matte finish.

Boiling water blooms flavor in cocoa and forms the base of our brownie batter.

Chewy Brownies

MAKES 24 BROWNIES

For an accurate measurement of boiling water, bring a full kettle of water to a boil, then measure out the desired amount. For the chewiest texture, it is important to let the brownies cool thoroughly before cutting.

⅓ cup (1 ounce) Dutch-processed cocoa powder

1½ teaspoons instant espresso powder (optional)

½ cup plus 2 tablespoons boiling water

2 ounces unsweetened chocolate, chopped fine

½ cup plus 2 tablespoons vegetable oil

4 tablespoons unsalted butter, melted

2 large eggs plus 2 large yolks

2 teaspoons vanilla extract

2½ cups (17½ ounces) sugar

1¾ cups (8¾ ounces) all-purpose flour

¾ teaspoon salt

6 ounces bittersweet chocolate, cut into ½-inch pieces

1. Adjust oven rack to lowest position and heat oven to 350 degrees. Make foil sling for 13 by 9-inch baking pan by folding 2 long sheets of aluminum foil; first sheet should be 13 inches wide and second sheet should be 9 inches wide. Lay sheets of foil in pan perpendicular to one another, with extra foil hanging over edges of pan. Push foil into corners and up sides of pan, smoothing foil flush to pan. Grease foil and set pan aside.

2. Whisk cocoa, espresso powder, if using, and boiling water together in large bowl until smooth. Add unsweetened chocolate and whisk until chocolate is melted. Whisk in oil and melted butter. (Mixture may look curdled.) Add eggs and yolks and vanilla and continue to whisk until smooth and homogeneous. Whisk in sugar until fully incorporated. Whisk together flour and salt in small bowl and then mix into batter with rubber spatula until combined. Fold in bittersweet chocolate pieces.

3. Transfer batter to prepared pan; spread batter into corners of pan and smooth surface. Bake until toothpick inserted in center of brownies comes out with few moist crumbs attached, 30 to 35 minutes, rotating pan halfway through baking. Transfer pan to wire rack and let cool for 1½ hours.

4. Remove brownies from pan using foil. Return brownies to wire rack and let cool completely, about 1 hour. Cut brownies into 2-inch squares and serve. (Brownies can be stored at room temperature for up to 3 days.)

RECIPE DETAILS

Timeline

• 20 minutes to assemble brownies
• 30 minutes to bake brownies
• 1½ hours to cool brownies in pan
• 1 hour to cool brownies out of pan

Essential Tools

• 13 by 9-inch baking pan (If using a glass dish, let the brownies cool in the pan for 10 minutes, then remove them promptly; otherwise, the superior heat retention of glass can cause brownies left in the pan to overbake.)
• Aluminum foil to make sling
• Toothpick or wooden skewer to test brownies for doneness (Once you overbake brownies, there is no going back.)

Substitutions & Variations

• Use high-quality chocolate in this recipe. Hershey's is our top-rated unsweetened chocolate and Ghirardelli is our top-rated bittersweet chocolate.
• If you like nuts, toast them until fragrant before stirring them into the batter. This step not only improves their flavor but also ensures that they won't become soggy. One cup of toasted (and chopped) pecans or walnuts is the right amount for this recipe.

36 Holiday Cookies

FOOLPROOF THE DOUGH SO YOU CAN FOCUS ON DECORATING

Baking holiday cookies should be a fun endeavor, but instead it's often an exercise in frustration. The dough clings to the rolling pin, causing rips and tears. If you avoid this pitfall, you then have to worry that the cutout pieces of dough will glue themselves to the counter. Finally, you hold your breath while the cookies bake, hoping that those pretty shapes will hold their crisp edges in the oven. No wonder so many people turn to tubes of prefab cookie dough.

Classic holiday cookies—the kind you cut out and decorate—are butter cookies. Their texture should be thin and crisp and their rich, all-butter flavor should boast just a hint of sweetness. And while good butter cookies are tender and light, they must be sturdy enough to survive the glazing and decorating process.

This recipe poses a culinary catch-22. Butter is the ingredient that makes the cookies worth eating, but it's also what makes the dough so challenging to handle. Most recipes load up on the flour to make the dough less tacky, but the baked cookies are tough and dry. The other approach is to regulate the temperature of the dough—chilling it at every stage to keep the butter firm.

The latter approach is more promising but it's still not sufficient. As we uncovered in the test kitchen, you need to adopt an unconventional mixing method. And you need the help of a secret ingredient that adds richness without making the dough sticky or hard to handle. Relax, we've got you covered. The holidays will be fun this year now that you have a cookie recipe that is cause for celebration.

WHY THIS RECIPE WORKS

Use Superfine Sugar
Regular granulated sugar makes cookies with a flaky texture and some large holes. In contrast, superfine sugar yields crisp, compact cookies with a fine, even crumb that is preferable for a cookie that will be glazed. There's no leavener in these cookies (so no puffing up in the oven) and no eggs (which would make them moist and chewy).

Reverse-Cream
Instead of the traditional creaming method, which relies on aerating the butter with the sugar, we use the reverse-creaming method which calls for beating the butter into the flour and sugar. Less air in the batter means fewer bubbles in the baked cookies. The cookies bake up flat, sturdy, and crisp—perfect for glazing.

A Little Cream Cheese
We use just enough butter for rich flavor and tenderness. More butter just makes the dough sticky and hard to handle.

We found that adding cream cheese, which is softer than butter when chilled, makes the dough particularly easy to work with. And it adds a nice flavor.

Roll, Then Chill
To prevent the dough from sticking to the counter—and to the rolling pin—roll it between two large pieces of parchment. Cold, stiff dough cuts more cleanly than soft dough, so the dough is chilled after rolling. Sliding the bottom piece of parchment onto a baking sheet keeps the dough flat while chilling.

Minimize Scraps
Cut shapes close together, starting from the outside and working your way to the middle to use as much dough as possible. While you can reroll this dough once, you want to reduce scraps; if you overwork the dough, too much gluten will develop and the cookies will be tough. Make sure to chill the dough scraps again before rolling them out a second time.

Invest in parchment and a sharp cutter before baking holiday cookies.

Glazed Butter Cookies

MAKES ABOUT 38 COOKIES

If desired, the cookies can be finished with sprinkles or other decorations immediately after glazing.

COOKIES

2½ cups (12½ ounces) all-purpose flour
¾ cup (5¼ ounces) superfine sugar
¼ teaspoon salt
16 tablespoons unsalted butter, cut into 16 pieces and softened

2 tablespoons cream cheese, room temperature
2 teaspoons vanilla extract

GLAZE

1 tablespoon cream cheese, room temperature

3 tablespoons milk
1½ cups (6 ounces) confectioners' sugar

1. *For the Cookies:* Using stand mixer fitted with paddle, mix flour, sugar, and salt at low speed until combined, about 5 seconds. With mixer running on low, add butter 1 piece at a time; continue to mix until mixture looks crumbly and slightly wet, 1 to 2 minutes longer. Beat in cream cheese and vanilla until dough just begins to form large clumps, about 30 seconds.

2. Knead dough by hand in bowl, 2 or 3 turns, until it forms large, cohesive mass. Transfer dough to counter and divide it into 2 even pieces. Press each piece into 4-inch disk, wrap disks in plastic wrap, and refrigerate until dough is firm but malleable, about 30 minutes. (Dough can be refrigerated for up to 3 days or frozen up to 2 weeks; defrost in refrigerator before using.)

3. Adjust oven rack to middle position and heat oven to 375 degrees. Line 2 rimmed baking sheets with parchment paper. Working with 1 piece of dough at a time, roll ⅛ inch thick between 2 large sheets of parchment paper; slide rolled dough, still on parchment, onto baking sheets and refrigerate until firm, about 10 minutes.

4. Working with 1 sheet of dough at a time, peel parchment from 1 side of dough and cut into desired shapes using cookie cutters; space cookies 1½ inches apart on prepared sheets. Bake 1 sheet at a time until cookies are light golden brown, about 10 minutes, rotating sheet halfway through baking. (Dough scraps can be patted together, chilled, and rerolled once.) Let cookies cool on sheet for 3 minutes; transfer cookies to wire rack and let cool to room temperature.

5. *For the Glaze:* Whisk cream cheese and 2 tablespoons milk together in medium bowl until combined and no lumps remain. Add sugar and whisk until smooth, adding remaining 1 tablespoon milk as needed until glaze is thin enough to spread easily. Using back of spoon, drizzle or spread scant teaspoon of glaze onto each cooled cookie. Allow glazed cookies to dry at least 30 minutes before serving.

RECIPE DETAILS

Timeline

- 15 minutes to make cookie dough (soften butter first)
- 30 minutes to chill cookie dough
- 20 minutes to roll, chill, and cut out dough
- 40 minutes to bake and cool cookies
- 40 minutes to glaze cookies and let glaze dry

Essential Tools

- Stand mixer
- Parchment paper for rolling out dough and lining rimmed baking sheets
- Cookie cutter(s) with sharp edges

Substitutions & Variations

- If you cannot find superfine sugar, process granulated sugar in a food processor for 30 seconds.
- The glazed cookies are great as is, but you can dress them up in a number of ways:
- Place decorations in the glaze while it is still soft; once the glaze dries, it will act like glue. In addition to the usual decorating options, consider cinnamon candies, crushed peppermint candies, gum drops, or mini chocolate morsels.
- Apply dots of a different color glaze and then drag a toothpick through them to create a variety of patterns and designs.
- Once the glaze has been applied, sprinkle it with colored sugar. Colored sugar is easy to make at home. Place ½ cup granulated sugar in bowl. Add about 5 drops of food coloring and mix thoroughly. To ensure even color, push sugar through fine-mesh strainer. Spread sugar in shallow dish and let it dry completely. Excess sugar can be brushed or gently shaken off when glaze is dry.

37 Blueberry Pie

ADD VODKA AND ANYONE CAN MAKE A PERFECT PIE

Pie crust seems so simple: Mix together flour, salt, and sugar, cut in some fat, add ice water just until the dough sticks together, roll it out, and bake. What could go wrong in something with so few elements? Well, a lot.

The dough is almost always too crumbly to roll out successfully. And the results are seemingly random: The recipe that gave you a perfect crust last month results in a tough-as-nails crust when followed this week. Is it too much to expect that the dough will roll out easily and bake up both tender and flaky, every time?

Butter contributes great flavor but it also contains water, which encourages gluten development in the flour. And too much gluten translates into toughness. For a crust that's flavorful and tender, cut the butter with some shortening, a pure fat that doesn't contain water. Processing some of the flour with all of the fat further limits gluten development. The fat coats the flour and prevents this portion of the flour from absorbing water.

Many recipes skimp on ice water, fearing that too much water will cause excess gluten development. But then the dough is too dry. Vodka moistens the dough just as well as water but there's no need to be stingy because alcohol doesn't trigger gluten development. Replacing some of the ice water with chilled vodka lets you add more total liquid so the dough is easy to handle. But there's less total gluten in the alcohol-spiked dough so it still bakes up tender.

Now that you've got the "hard part" done, filling and baking a pie is easy. Blueberries require no peeling, pitting, or hulling. The challenge is to create a filling that's not too stiff, yet not too fluid.

WHY THIS RECIPE WORKS

The Right Thickener
Blueberries have a lot of juice that can prevent a pie from slicing neatly. The trick is to use a minimum of thickener—too much and the fruit filling is rubbery. Flour and cornstarch yield a pasty, starchy filling and mute fresh fruit flavor so we prefer to use tapioca to thicken berry pies. To make sure the tapioca doesn't add any telltale "pearls" in the finished pie, turn it to a fine powder using a spice grinder.

Pectin Power
Pectin is a gentle thickener that occurs naturally in many fruit. It's the thing that helps jam to set. Unfortunately, blueberries are low in natural pectin. Commercial pectin in the form of a liquid or powder won't work in a pie filling—this stuff needs a lot of sugar to work. The solution? An apple. Apples have a lot of natural pectin. One peeled and grated Granny Smith apple, along with a modest amount of tapioca, provides enough thickening power to set the pie beautifully.

Cook Half the Berries
Cooking and mashing half of the berries reduces their liquid, concentrates their flavor, and releases what little pectin they have. Folding in the remaining berries creates a satisfying combination of intensely flavored cooked fruit and bright-tasting fresh fruit.

Make Holes, Not Lattice
A lattice top is a great way to vent the steam from the berries—a must if you want a crisp crust. But weaving strips of sticky pie dough is a messy business. For a no-fuss top crust that accomplishes the same thing, use a small biscuit or cookie cutter to cut out holes in the dough round before it goes on top of the filling.

Let It Cool
If you want neat slices of pie, it must cool. The filling will continue to set as the pie cools down to room temperature—a process that will take 4 hours.

Use heat, muscle power, and natural pectin from an apple to help set the filling.

Blueberry Pie

SERVES 8

Use the large holes of a box grater to shred the apple. Grind the tapioca to a powder in a spice grinder or mini food processor.

1 recipe Foolproof Double-Crust Pie Dough (recipe follows)

30 ounces (6 cups) blueberries

1 Granny Smith apple, peeled, cored, and shredded

¾ cup (5¼ ounces) sugar

2 tablespoons instant tapioca, ground

2 teaspoons grated lemon zest plus 2 teaspoons juice

Pinch salt

2 tablespoons unsalted butter, cut into ¼-inch pieces

1 large egg white, lightly beaten

1. Roll 1 disk of dough into 12-inch circle on lightly floured counter. Loosely roll dough around rolling pin and gently unroll it onto 9-inch pie plate, letting excess dough hang over edge. Ease dough into plate by gently lifting edge of dough with your hand while pressing into plate bottom with your other hand. Leave any dough that overhangs plate in place. Wrap dough-lined pie plate loosely in plastic wrap and refrigerate until dough is firm, about 30 minutes.

2. Roll other disk of dough into 12-inch circle on lightly floured counter. Using 1¼-inch round cookie cutter, cut round from center of dough. Cut 6 more rounds from dough, 1½ inches from edge of center hole and equally spaced around center hole. Transfer dough to parchment paper–lined baking sheet; cover with plastic and refrigerate for 30 minutes.

3. Place 3 cups berries in medium saucepan and set over medium heat. Using potato masher, mash berries several times to release juices. Continue to cook, stirring often and mashing occasionally, until about half of berries have broken down and mixture is thickened and reduced to 1½ cups, about 8 minutes; let cool slightly.

4. Adjust oven rack to lowest position and heat oven to 400 degrees.

5. Place shredded apple in clean dish towel and wring dry. Transfer apple to large bowl and stir in cooked berries, remaining 3 cups uncooked berries, sugar, tapioca, lemon zest and juice, and salt until combined. Spread mixture in dough-lined pie plate and scatter butter over top.

6. Loosely roll remaining dough round around rolling pin and gently unroll it onto filling. Trim overhang of both crusts to ½ inch beyond lip of pie plate. Pinch edges of top and bottom crusts firmly together. Tuck overhang under itself; folded edge should be flush with edge of pie plate. Crimp dough evenly around edge of pie using your fingers. Brush surface with egg white.

7. Place pie on rimmed baking sheet and bake until crust is light golden brown, about 25 minutes. Reduce oven temperature to 350 degrees, rotate sheet, and continue to bake until juices are bubbling and crust is deep golden brown, 35 to 50 minutes longer. Let pie cool on wire rack to room temperature, about 4 hours. Serve.

RECIPE DETAILS

Timeline

- 2 hours to make, roll out, and chill pie dough
- 30 minutes to make filling and assemble pie (can be started while dough chills)
- 1 to 1¼ hours to bake pie
- 4 hours to cool pie before serving

Essential Tools

- Food processor to make pie dough
- Rolling pin
- 9-inch pie plate (preferably glass, which makes it easy to see when bottom crust has browned sufficiently)
- 1¼-inch biscuit or cookie cutter to punch holes in top crust
- Spice grinder to grind tapioca
- Box grater to shred apple
- Potato masher to mash berries

Substitutions & Variations

- This recipe was developed using fresh blueberries, but unthawed frozen berries will work as well. In step 3, cook half the frozen berries over medium-high heat, without mashing, until reduced to 1¼ cups, 12 to 15 minutes.
- If you like to serve warm pie, let it cool fully (so the filling sets), then briefly warm the pie in the oven before slicing. But don't overdo it! Leave the pie in a 350-degree oven for 10 minutes—just long enough to warm the pie without causing the filling to loosen.

FOOLPROOF DOUBLE-CRUST PIE DOUGH

MAKES ENOUGH FOR ONE 9-INCH PIE

Vodka is essential to the tender texture of this crust and imparts no flavor—do not substitute water. This dough is moister than most standard pie doughs and will require lots of flour to roll out (up to ¼ cup). A food processor is essential for making this dough—it cannot be made by hand.

2½ cups (12½ ounces) all-purpose flour

2 tablespoons sugar

1 teaspoon salt

12 tablespoons unsalted butter, cut into ¼-inch pieces and chilled

8 tablespoons vegetable shortening, cut into 4 pieces and chilled

¼ cup vodka, chilled

¼ cup ice water

1. Process 1½ cups flour, sugar, and salt in food processor until combined, about 5 seconds. Scatter butter and shortening over top and continue to process until incorporated and mixture begins to form uneven clumps with no remaining floury bits, about 15 seconds.

2. Scrape down bowl and redistribute dough evenly around processor blade. Sprinkle remaining 1 cup flour over dough and pulse until mixture has broken up into pieces and is evenly distributed around bowl, 4 to 6 pulses.

3. Transfer mixture to large bowl. Sprinkle vodka and ice water over mixture. Stir and press dough together, using stiff rubber spatula, until dough sticks together.

4. Divide dough into 2 even pieces. Turn each piece of dough onto sheet of plastic wrap and flatten each into 4-inch disk. Wrap each piece tightly in plastic and refrigerate for 1 hour. Before rolling out dough, let it sit on counter to soften slightly, about 10 minutes. (Dough can be wrapped tightly in plastic and refrigerated for up to 2 days or frozen for up to 1 month. If frozen, let dough thaw completely on counter before rolling it out.)

A Better Way to Roll Out Pie Dough

Even if you successfully make the dough, you still need to turn that thick slab into a thin (and even) circle. This is where pie making goes wrong for many people. The dough sticks to the counter or rolls out into a lopsided oval. Sticking is easy to avoid—just generously flour the counter. As for rolling the perfect circle, it's all about using a light touch and rotating the dough as you roll.

1. Lay dough on floured counter and sprinkle lightly with flour. Place rolling pin in center of dough with ends at 9 o'clock and 3 o'clock and roll dough outward from center to edges, applying even, gentle pressure.

2. Use bench scraper to lift and turn dough 90 degrees. Roll outward again from center, keeping hands at 9 and 3 positions. Lightly flour underneath dough to prevent sticking. Repeat rolling and turning steps (keeping hands at 9 and 3) until dough forms 12-inch circle. Don't roll back and forth in same spot without turning dough.

The Surprising Essentials

INNOVATIVE RECIPES YOU DIDN'T KNOW YOU NEEDED

38 Poached Chicken

A FRESH APPROACH REINVIGORATES AN OLD-FASHIONED METHOD

Hardly anyone poaches chicken anymore. Most renditions are a real snooze, one step up from bland institutional fare. But poaching does have one potential advantage over other ways to prepare boneless, skinless chicken breasts: It should, in theory, be foolproof.

Grilling, broiling, and sautéing are high-wire acts, each with a substantial risk of producing a very dry, very stringy end result. Because these cooking methods require so much dry heat (and because chicken breasts have so little fat), there's not much room for error—the chicken goes from perfectly cooked to overcooked in seconds.

Gentle poaching is more forgiving. The poaching liquid never gets all that hot so the chicken is exposed to very little heat. If only poached chicken wasn't so boring.

Our first decision was to throw out the poaching liquid once the chicken was cooked. Most classic recipes use a small amount of poaching liquid, with the idea that the liquid can be reduced to a sauce. Unfortunately, it's a lot of work to eke out flavor from the poaching liquid and the sauce often isn't very tasty. It's easier to make a separate vinaigrette, salsa, or creamy yogurt sauce while the chicken poaches.

Since the poaching liquid is no longer destined to become a sauce, you can season the liquid very aggressively, with a lot of salt and soy sauce (to enhance the meaty, savory notes in the chicken). Coupled with a unique poaching method designed to prevent overcooking, the chicken emerges moist and perfectly seasoned. When paired with a bold sauce, this poached chicken is no longer a relic—it's a revelation.

WHY THIS RECIPE WORKS

Prop Up the Chicken
When food rests on the bottom of a pot of water, the side touching the metal will cook more quickly because of its proximity to the burner. Elevating the chicken breasts in a steamer basket ensures that they will be surrounded by water and all sides will cook at the same rate.

Add Flavor Boosters
Most flavorings in a cooking liquid can't migrate very far into meat. We add a few that can—soy sauce, salt, sugar, and garlic. (The flavor compounds in most herbs and spices are oil-soluble but those in garlic are soluble in water, which is why garlic works in this recipe but herbs and spices don't.) Don't use less salt or soy sauce than the recipe directs—most of it goes down the drain with the water.

Brine, Then Poach
Use the well-seasoned poaching liquid to brine the chicken before turning on the heat. Thirty minutes is sufficient for the salt and soy sauce to penetrate deep into the chicken, ensuring that it will be well seasoned and tender. (The salt changes the structure of the muscle fibers and prevents moisture loss during cooking.) Finally, because the chicken loses its chill during the 30-minute brining time, it needs less exposure to the heat to come up to the desired final serving temperature so there's less risk of overcooking it.

Finish Gently
Bringing the cooking liquid to 175 degrees, turning off the heat, covering the pot, and cooking the chicken via residual heat is foolproof and hands-off. It's impossible to cook the chicken beyond the desired internal temperature of 160 degrees because the pot is moved off the heat and the temperature of the water is dropping as the temperature of the chicken slowly climbs. Make sure to use the full 4 quarts of water to ensure plenty of reserve heat.

Poach the chicken breasts in a steamer basket and then sauce them with a fresh tomato vinaigrette.

Perfect Poached Chicken Breasts

SERVES 4

Serve with a vinaigrette or sauce (recipes follow).

4 (6- to 8-ounce) boneless, skinless chicken breasts, trimmed	¼ cup salt
	2 tablespoons sugar
½ cup soy sauce	6 garlic cloves, smashed and peeled

1. Cover chicken breasts with plastic wrap and pound thick ends gently with meat pounder until ¾ inch thick. Whisk 4 quarts water, soy sauce, salt, sugar, and garlic in Dutch oven until salt and sugar are dissolved. Arrange breasts, skinned side up, in steamer basket, making sure not to overlap them. Submerge steamer basket in brine and let sit at room temperature for 30 minutes.

2. Heat pot over medium heat, stirring liquid occasionally to even out hot spots, until water registers 175 degrees, 15 to 20 minutes. Turn off heat, cover pot, remove from burner, and let stand until meat registers 160 degrees, 17 to 22 minutes.

3. Transfer breasts to cutting board, cover tightly with aluminum foil, and let rest for 5 minutes. Slice each breast on bias into ¼-inch-thick slices, transfer to serving platter or individual plates, and serve.

WARM TOMATO-GINGER VINAIGRETTE MAKES ABOUT 2 CUPS
Parsley may be substituted for the cilantro.

¼ cup extra-virgin olive oil	12 ounces cherry tomatoes, halved
1 shallot, minced	Salt and pepper
1½ teaspoons grated fresh ginger	1 tablespoon red wine vinegar
⅛ teaspoon ground cumin	1 teaspoon packed light brown sugar
⅛ teaspoon ground fennel	2 tablespoons chopped fresh cilantro

Heat 2 tablespoons oil in 10-inch nonstick skillet over medium heat until shimmering. Add shallot, ginger, cumin, and fennel and cook until fragrant, about 15 seconds. Stir in tomatoes and ¼ teaspoon salt and cook, stirring frequently, until tomatoes have softened, 3 to 5 minutes. Off heat, stir in vinegar and sugar and season with salt and pepper to taste; cover to keep warm. Stir in cilantro and remaining 2 tablespoons oil just before serving.

PARSLEY SAUCE WITH CORNICHONS AND CAPERS
MAKES ABOUT 1¼ CUPS

6 tablespoons minced cornichons plus 1 teaspoon brine	¼ cup capers, rinsed and chopped coarse
¾ cup minced fresh parsley	¼ teaspoon pepper
½ cup extra-virgin olive oil	Pinch salt
2 scallions, minced	

Mix all ingredients together in bowl.

RECIPE DETAILS

Timeline

- 5 minutes to prep chicken and brine
- 30 minutes to brine chicken (completely hands-off)
- 35 minutes to poach chicken (make sauce while chicken cooks)
- 7 minutes to rest and slice chicken

Essential Tools

- Meat pounder (You can use a heavy small skillet in a pinch.)
- Dutch oven (or other large pot)
- Steamer basket
- Instant-read thermometer

Substitutions & Variations

- The cooking times in this recipe are designed to work with standard size chicken breasts that weigh 6 to 8 ounces. Don't use this method with thin cutlets (they usually weigh just 3 or 4 ounces) or breasts that weigh more than 8 ounces (they might not cook through in the allotted time).
- You can use this method to cook chicken for any salad, dressing the chicken as the salad recipe directs.
- If you like, serve the chicken with another potent sauce. Good choices include pureed sauces (like pesto), warm vinaigrettes, juicy salsas (with fruit or tomatoes), or creamy yogurt-based sauces.
- To cook just two chicken breasts, use 2 quarts of water and cut brine ingredients in half. Use medium-low heat (not medium) and reduce off-heat cooking time to 12 to 17 minutes.

39 Chicken in a Pot

A COVERED POT IS A SURPRISINGLY GOOD PLACE TO ROAST A BIRD

Led by their presidential candidate, Herbert Hoover, Republicans promised to put "a chicken in every pot and a car in every garage" during the campaign of 1928. The stock market crash a year later and the ensuing decade of economic hardship forever made Americans skeptical about claims surrounding chickens and pots. That's a shame because we are missing out on one of the best dishes in the French repertoire, *poulet en cocotte*.

Despite what you might first think, poulet en cocotte isn't a braise or a stew. No, the whole bird is roasted in a heavy covered pot with no added liquid. And unlike so many dishes from France, this one is simple. There might be an aromatic vegetable or two as well as a sprig of fresh herb in the pot, but that's it. The idea is to capture the natural juices exuded by the bird—the juices that evaporate when an open roasting pan is used—and produce meat that is unbelievable tender and succulent and very, very flavorful.

A warning here: This recipe isn't for cooks (or diners) who prize crisp skin above all else. The skin renders and is certainly pleasant enough to eat, but this recipe doesn't employ enough heat to make it crisp. But that's fine by us. We think it makes more sense to choose a low-temperature cooking method that prioritizes the meat instead. Heck, many people don't even eat the skin anymore.

One final selling point: As the bird cooks, it creates an intense jus—think essence of chicken—that becomes a fuss-free sauce. Simplicity and perfection—those are two campaign promises we can all get behind.

WHY THIS RECIPE WORKS

Brown First
When chicken is browned, it's often to crisp the skin. However, in this recipe, the chicken is browned on the stovetop to build fond on the bottom of the pot. This fond deepens the flavor of the jus that will be served with the chicken. The back side of the chicken browns for a few extra minutes because dark meat takes longer to cook. Caramelizing the small amount of onion, celery, and garlic in the pot wicks away their moisture and adds both rich color and flavor.

Cover with Foil
Placing a sheet of aluminum foil over the pot before covering it with the lid creates the tightest possible seal and prevents any steam from escaping. Every drop of chicken flavor remains in the pot.

Cook Low and Slow
A chicken cooked in a covered pot with no added liquid is essentially a "dry" braise. The juices are drawn from the chicken into the pot where they create moist heat, so that the meat cooks gently, in effect braising in its own juices. Cooking at a really low temperature, 250 degrees, helps to retain moisture and intensifies the flavors of the meat; many of juices that come out of the chicken go right back into it. The rest are trapped in the pot and become the sauce.

Cook Breast Up
Arranging the chicken breast side up allows the dark meat to rest on the bottom of the pot, where heat transfer is best; combined with its extra browning time, this enables the dark meat to cook faster than the white meat, so that both reach the proper temperature at the same time.

Rest and Strain
To maximize moisture retention, it is important to let the chicken rest before carving. While it rests, strain the concentrated liquid from the pot to yield a smooth and intensely flavored jus.

"Pot-roasted" chicken begins on the stovetop and ends under a foil tent on a carving board.

French Chicken in a Pot

SERVES 4

If you choose not to serve the skin with the chicken, simply remove it before carving. The amount of jus will vary depending on the size of the chicken; season it with about ¼ teaspoon lemon juice for every ¼ cup.

1 (4½- to 5-pound) whole chicken, giblets discarded	1 small celery rib, chopped
Salt and pepper	6 garlic cloves, peeled
1 tablespoon olive oil	1 bay leaf
1 small onion, chopped	1 sprig fresh rosemary (optional)
	½–1 teaspoon lemon juice

1. Adjust oven rack to lowest position and heat oven to 250 degrees. Pat chicken dry with paper towels, tuck wings behind back, and season with salt and pepper. Heat oil in Dutch oven over medium heat until just smoking. Add chicken breast side down and scatter onion, celery, garlic, bay leaf, and rosemary sprig, if using, around chicken. Cook until breast is lightly browned, about 5 minutes. Using wooden spoon inserted into cavity of chicken, flip chicken breast side up and cook until chicken and vegetables are well browned, 6 to 8 minutes.

2. Off heat, place large sheet of aluminum foil over pot and cover tightly with lid. Transfer pot to oven and cook chicken until breast registers 160 degrees and thighs register 175 degrees, 1 hour 20 minutes to 1 hour 50 minutes.

3. Transfer chicken to carving board, tent loosely with foil, and let rest for 20 minutes. Meanwhile, strain chicken juices from pot through fine-mesh strainer into fat separator, pressing on solids to extract liquid; discard solids. Let juices settle for 5 minutes, then pour into small saucepan and set over low heat. Carve chicken, adding any accumulated juices to saucepan. Season sauce with lemon juice, salt, and pepper to taste. Serve chicken, passing sauce separately.

RECIPE DETAILS

Timeline

- 15 minutes to prep and brown chicken on stovetop
- 80 minutes to 110 minutes to cook chicken in oven
- 25 minutes to rest and carve chicken (use this time to prepare sauce)

Essential Tools

- Dutch oven (at least 6 quarts) with lid
- Wooden spoon to flip chicken as it browns
- Aluminum foil to cover pot under lid

Substitutions & Variations

- A slightly smaller or larger chicken can be used (provided the bird still fits in your pot). Although you don't need to change the amounts of the other ingredients, the cooking time will likely fall outside the range listed in the recipe.
- As long as you don't put too much stuff in the pot, you can try this technique with other flavorings, including herbs, citrus zest, or shallots. Some simple ideas:
- For a stronger garlic flavor, increase the number of cloves to twelve.
- Replace the rosemary with two thyme sprigs.
- Replace the celery and rosemary with 4 ounces diced shiitake mushrooms and 1 tablespoon grated fresh ginger. Finish the pan sauce with rice wine vinegar and soy sauce to taste.

40 Pulled Chicken

AS GOOD AS PULLED PORK AND SO MUCH EASIER

Smoky, spicy pulled pork bathed in a tangy tomato-based barbecue sauce might just be one of the best things you can eat, which is why people from all over the country (in truth, all over the world) trek to the barbecue belt.

And though pulled pork appears unfussy—the shredded pork is usually piled onto squishy hamburger buns and served on paper plates with pickle chips and coleslaw—this dish takes a lot of skill and time to execute. It's an all-day project (the pork must smoke for 8 to 12 hours) best left to seasoned pit masters.

We have a more practical alternative for the home cook that is almost as appealing and far less work—chicken. Now, we know many of you are rolling your eyes as you read this claim. How can pulled chicken even come close to pulled pork? First off, the spice, smoke, and sauce are pretty much the same. As for the meat, we tend to think of chicken as bland, and the white meat certainly is. But barbecued leg quarters are a revelation.

As with pork shoulder, leg quarters are loaded with flavorful fat as well as collagen, which converts to gelatin during the cooking process and gives the pulled meat its silky texture. Indirect heat is key to slowing things down so the chicken has enough time to absorb plenty of smoke. And it's important to cook the chicken past the usual stopping point, until the meat is fall-off-the-bone tender. In effect, "overcooking" maximizes the conversion of collagen to gelatin—so the pulled chicken is really tender.

We will still travel to the Carolinas and Kansas City for great pulled pork, but we think pulled chicken is the most practical option at home. Try this recipe once and see if you don't agree.

WHY THIS RECIPE WORKS

A Leg Up
Whole chicken legs (thighs and drumsticks attached) are our top choice for this recipe. They are inexpensive, the dark meat is nearly impossible to overcook, and they have a rich, meaty flavor that stands up to smoke and barbecue sauce.

Light the Right Fire
A double-banked charcoal fire divides the lit coals into two steep piles on opposite sides of the grill, leaving the center free of coals. The chicken is placed in the center of the grill and receives a steady, even level of indirect heat from both sides. A disposable pan placed in the center catches drips and prevents flare-ups. A wood chip packet placed on either pile of charcoal will generate a significant amount of smoke (see page 139 for more details).

"Overcook" the Chicken
Chicken must always be cooked thoroughly. Technically dark meat is "done" when the internal temperature reaches 170 degrees, but we keep on cooking the leg quarters to 185 degrees—the point at which the meat is falling off the bone. The intermuscular fat (as well as the skin, which is rendering and basting the chicken during grilling) keeps the meat plenty moist and tender.

Make Your Own Sauce
Homemade barbecue sauce is easy to make from pantry ingredients and isn't overpoweringly sweet or smoke-flavored like store-bought. Pureeing onion and water to make "onion juice" gets onion flavor into the sauce without any distracting bits of onion to mar the texture.

Pulse and Shred
Shredding pulled chicken with forks yields attractive strips, but the meat doesn't hold together very well on the bun. To fix this problem, pulse half of the chicken in a food processor to create smaller pieces that absorb sauce better and bind the larger pulled chicken pieces.

Dark meat chicken is a surprisingly good vehicle for smoky barbecue flavors.

Barbecued Pulled Chicken

SERVES 6 TO 8

Chicken leg quarters consist of drumsticks attached to thighs; often also attached are back-bone sections that must be trimmed away. Serve the pulled chicken on hamburger rolls or sandwich bread, with pickles and coleslaw.

CHICKEN

2	cups wood chips, soaked in water for 15 minutes and drained	8	(14-ounce) chicken leg quarters, trimmed
1	(16 by 12-inch) disposable aluminum roasting pan (if using charcoal)		Salt and pepper

SAUCE

1	large onion, peeled and quartered	3	tablespoons Dijon mustard
¼	cup water	½	teaspoon pepper
1½	cups ketchup	1	tablespoon vegetable oil
1½	cups apple cider	1½	tablespoons chili powder
¼	cup molasses	2	garlic cloves, minced
¼	cup cider vinegar	½	teaspoon cayenne pepper
3	tablespoons Worcestershire sauce		Hot sauce

1. *For the Chicken:* Using large piece of heavy-duty aluminum foil, wrap soaked chips in foil packet and cut several vent holes in top.

2A. *For a Charcoal Grill:* Open bottom vent halfway and place roasting pan in center of grill. Light large chimney starter three-quarters filled with charcoal briquettes (4½ quarts). When top coals are partially covered with ash, pour into 2 even piles on either side of roasting pan. Place wood chip packet on 1 pile of coals. Set cooking grate in place, cover, and open lid vent halfway. Heat grill until hot and wood chips are smoking, about 5 minutes.

2B. *For a Gas Grill:* Place wood chip packet directly on primary burner. Turn all burners to high, cover, and heat grill until hot and wood chips are smoking, about 15 minutes. Turn off all burners except primary burner. (Adjust burner as needed during cooking to maintain grill temperature between 300 and 350 degrees.)

3. Clean and oil cooking grate. Pat chicken dry with paper towels and season with salt and pepper. Place chicken skin side up in single layer on center of grill (over roasting pan if using charcoal), or on cooler side of grill (if using gas). Cover (position lid vent over meat if using charcoal) and cook until chicken registers 185 degrees, 1 to 1½ hours, rotating chicken pieces halfway through cooking. Transfer chicken to carving board, tent loosely with foil, and let rest until cool enough to handle.

4. *For the Sauce:* Meanwhile, process onion and water in food processor until mixture resembles slush, about 30 seconds. Pass through fine-mesh strainer into liquid measuring cup, pressing on solids with rubber spatula (you should have ¾ cup strained onion juice). Discard solids in strainer.

5. Whisk onion juice, ketchup, cider, molasses, 3 tablespoons vinegar, Worcestershire, mustard, and pepper together in bowl. Heat oil in large saucepan over medium heat until shimmering. Stir in chili powder, garlic, and cayenne and cook until fragrant,

RECIPE DETAILS

Timeline

• 20 to 25 minutes to soak chips and set up fire
• 1 to 1½ hours to cook chicken (make barbecue sauce while chicken is cooking)
• 30 minutes to rest, pull, and sauce chicken

Essential Tools

• Disposable roasting pan (if using charcoal)
• Heavy-duty aluminum foil to make wood chip packet
• Wood chips

Substitutions & Variations

• Two medium wood chunks, soaked in water for 1 hour, can be substituted for the wood chip packet on a charcoal grill.
• To make this recipe for a crowd, arrange the chicken quarters in a slotted rib rack or roasting rack. Depending on the rack, you should be able to stand up a dozen or so leg quarters. Make sure to position the rack over the disposable pan. The cooking time might be slightly longer if the leg quarters are squeezed tightly together.
• To make serving easier, the pulled chicken can be held in a 250-degree oven for up to 1 hour. Once the chicken and sauce have been combined and heated through, transfer the mixture to a 13 by 9-inch glass or ceramic baking dish, cover with foil, and keep warm in the oven.

about 30 seconds. Stir in ketchup mixture, bring to simmer, and cook over medium-low heat until slightly thickened, about 15 minutes (you should have about 4 cups of sauce). Transfer 2 cups sauce to serving bowl; leave remaining sauce in saucepan.

6. *To Serve:* Remove and discard skin from chicken legs. Using your fingers, pull meat off bones, separating larger pieces (which should fall off bones easily) from smaller, drier pieces into 2 equal piles.

7. Pulse smaller chicken pieces in food processor until just coarsely chopped, 3 to 4 pulses, stirring chicken with rubber spatula after each pulse. Add chopped chicken to sauce in saucepan. Using your fingers or 2 forks, pull larger chicken pieces into long shreds and add to saucepan. Stir in remaining 1 tablespoon vinegar, cover, and heat chicken over medium-low heat, stirring occasionally, until heated through, about 10 minutes. Add hot sauce to taste, and serve, passing remaining sauce separately.

A Better Way to Add Smoke Flavor

Real barbecue requires the addition of smoke flavor. (Without smoke, you're just grilling.) Many cooks rely on wood chips sold in hardware stores. Unfortunately, these chips burn up very quickly—releasing a blast of smoke rather than the slow, steady smoke that imparts real barbecue flavor. Here's how to get maximum smoke flavor from wood chips.

1. Place wood chips in bowl and cover with water. Soak for 15 minutes. We prefer hickory chips. If you prefer wood chunks (with pieces about the size of a lime), soak them for 1 hour.

2. Wrap soaked and drained chips in large piece of heavy-duty aluminum foil. (The combination of soaking and the foil will slow down the rate at which the chips burn.) Use paring knife to cut several slits in packet so smoke can escape. Use 2 cups of chips in 1 single packet and add second packet for additional smoke flavor.

3. If using gas grill, lift up cooking grate and place packet on primary burner (burner that will remain on during cooking time). Light and heat grill as directed. (Note that wood chunks cannot be used on a gas grill.)

4. If using a charcoal grill, arrange lit coals as directed in recipe and then place packet with wood chips onto coals. (If using chunks, don't bother with foil; simply nestle soaked chunks into lit charcoal.) Position lid vents over food to draw smoke into maximum contact with food.

41 Chicken Stew

YES, A STEW MADE WITH CHICKEN CAN BE GOOD

Despite what you might think, chicken (not beef) is king in the United States. Just look at the stats. Forty years ago, per capita beef consumption reached an all-time high of 95 pounds. That number now stands at 54 pounds, and falling. During the same period, per capita chicken consumption doubled to more than 80 pounds.

Whatever the reasons (cost, health, convenience), Americans are eating a lot more chicken. We fry it, roast it, and grill it. We turn it into soups, salads, and casseroles. But there's one thing we don't do with chicken—stew it. That still remains beef's domain. But isn't it possible to make a similar dish with chicken, one with succulent chunks of meat, tender vegetables, and a truly robust gravy?

It turns out the gravy is the real challenge when making chicken stew. Beef is practically made for stewing. Chuck roast (cut from the shoulder) can be simmered for hours until fall-apart tender, all the while remaining juicy. This treatment is made possible by the meat's network of connective tissue, which slowly converts to lubricating gelatin during cooking. This turns the beef tender while the gravy is infused with rich beefiness and body—a culinary win-win.

Today's chicken is butchered very young so even its thighs and drumsticks have little time to develop much connective tissue. As a result, you can't simmer chicken, even dark meat, for hours and hours. That means you need a different way to build flavor in the gravy. Our recipe employs a novel approach—one that will convince even meat lovers that stewing is a great way to cook chicken.

WHY THIS RECIPE WORKS

Winging It
Chicken wings are relatively inexpensive and they have a decent amount of collagen. Browning a pound of halved wings and then cooking them in the stew (they are discarded before serving) adds rich body when the collagen converts to gelatin, and a lot of meaty flavor to the gravy. As for the chunks of stew meat, fattier dark meat in the form of boneless, skinless chicken thighs can withstand a relatively long cooking time and is therefore the best choice.

Big Flavor Boosters
A few strips of bacon, crisped in the pot before browning the wings, lend porky depth and just a hint of smoke. And while they may sound like strange additions to chicken stew, soy sauce and anchovy paste, ingredients rich in glutamates, are meaty and savory flavor enhancers that ensure this stew is not bland or boring.

Build a Great Gravy
A full-flavored gravy starts with the rendered fat from the bacon and the chicken wings. It is used to sauté the aromatics, thyme, and anchovy paste until a rich dark fond forms on the bottom of the pan. Then some chicken broth, white wine, and soy sauce are added to loosen the fond and boiled down until the liquid fully evaporates, leaving concentrated flavor as the base for the gravy.

Ring of Fond
Most stews are cooked in the oven with the lid on. In this recipe, the pot is uncovered so that some of the liquid can evaporate, thus concentrating flavors in the gravy. Leaving the lid off also browns the surface of the stew and leads to the development of fond on the sides of the Dutch oven. To take advantage of this flavor-packed substance, we deglaze the sides by wetting them with a bit of gravy and scraping it into the stew.

Browned bacon and collagen-rich wings are two keys to a memorable chicken stew.

Best Chicken Stew

SERVES 6 TO 8

Use small red potatoes measuring 1½ inches in diameter.

2	pounds boneless, skinless chicken thighs, halved crosswise and trimmed	1	cup dry white wine, plus extra for seasoning
	Kosher salt and pepper	1	tablespoon soy sauce
3	slices bacon, chopped	3	tablespoons unsalted butter, cut into 3 pieces
1	pound chicken wings, halved at joint	⅓	cup all-purpose flour
1	onion, chopped fine	1	pound small red potatoes, unpeeled, quartered
1	celery rib, minced		
2	garlic cloves, minced	4	carrots, peeled and cut into ½-inch pieces
2	teaspoons anchovy paste		
1	teaspoon minced fresh thyme	2	tablespoons chopped fresh parsley
5	cups chicken broth		

1. Adjust oven rack to lower middle position and heat oven to 325 degrees. Arrange chicken thighs on baking sheet and lightly season both sides with salt and pepper; cover with plastic wrap and set aside.

2. Cook bacon in large Dutch oven over medium-low heat, stirring occasionally, until fat renders and bacon browns, 6 to 8 minutes. Using slotted spoon, transfer bacon to medium bowl. Add chicken wings to pot, increase heat to medium, and cook until well browned on both sides, 10 to 12 minutes; transfer wings to bowl with bacon.

3. Add onion, celery, garlic, anchovy paste, and thyme to fat in pot; cook, stirring occasionally, until dark fond forms on pan bottom, 2 to 4 minutes. Increase heat to high; stir in 1 cup broth, wine, and soy sauce, scraping up any browned bits; and bring to boil. Cook, stirring occasionally, until liquid evaporates and vegetables begin to sizzle again, 12 to 15 minutes. Add butter and stir to melt; sprinkle flour over vegetables and stir to combine. Gradually whisk in remaining 4 cups broth until smooth. Stir in potatoes, carrots, and wings and bacon; bring to simmer. Transfer to oven and cook, uncovered, for 30 minutes, stirring once halfway through cooking.

4. Remove pot from oven. Use wooden spoon to draw gravy up sides of pot and scrape browned fond into stew. Place over high heat, add thighs, and bring to simmer. Return pot to oven, uncovered, and continue to cook, stirring occasionally, until chicken offers no resistance when poked with fork and vegetables are tender, about 45 minutes longer. (Stew can be refrigerated for up to 2 days.)

5. Discard wings and season stew with up to 2 tablespoons extra wine. Season with salt and pepper to taste, sprinkle with parsley, and serve.

RECIPE DETAILS

Timeline

- 45 minutes to build flavor base on stovetop (hands-on)
- 30 minutes to build flavor base in oven (hands-off)
- 5 minutes to scrape fond and add chicken thighs
- 45 minutes to simmer chicken thighs in oven (hands-off)

Essential Tools

- Dutch oven (at least 6 quarts)
- Wooden spoon for scraping fond

Substitutions & Variations

- Mashed anchovy fillets (rinsed and dried before mashing) can be used instead of anchovy paste.

42 Poached Salmon

A FORGIVING WAY TO COOK A NEARLY FOOLPROOF FISH

Salmon has become America's favorite fish because it's relatively cheap and easy to cook (all that fat makes it hard to mess things up). Poaching would seem like the ideal way to prepare salmon. It's fast and there's no splattering oil or strong odors to permeate the house. And because it relies on gentle moist heat, poaching should highlight salmon's irresistibly supple, velvety texture.

But the classic French technique for poaching fish makes no sense at home. In restaurants, an entire side of salmon (weighing several pounds) is poached in a highly flavorful broth called a court bouillon. The poached fish is removed from the broth and served with a separately prepared sauce. The broth can be saved to poach fish the next day.

At home, this approach is plain crazy. No one wants to spend time building flavor in a broth that is never served. And very few people want to poach an entire side of salmon. We reinvented this recipe so that the poaching liquid becomes a sauce for four servings of fish.

Our recipe starts out with 1 cup of liquid, not quarts of broth. Besides being practical, we think this method produces superior results. Poaching in a pot of broth causes flavor to leach out of the fish. (That's why the court bouillon must be so fortified—it has to add something back to the fish.) Our shallow-poach method relies on a fraction of the typical liquid so flavor loss is minimized.

But with so little liquid in the pan how do you prevent the fish from cooking unevenly? A clever use of lemon slices along with a hefty portion of wine ensures that the top and bottom of the fish cook at the same rate. Talk about American ingenuity.

WHY THIS RECIPE WORKS

Buy One Fillet
Although it is easiest to cook individual servings of fish, it's preferable to buy a single piece of salmon fillet and then cut those pieces yourself. If the pieces come from the same side of fish, they will be the same thickness and that means they will cook at the same rate.

A Lift from Lemons
To keep the bottom of the fillets from overcooking due to direct contact with the skillet, we place them on top of a single layer of lemon slices for insulation. (The acidity of the lemon also helps balances the richness of the salmon.) Scattering minced shallot and parsley and tarragon stems over the slices adds more flavor to the cooking liquid.

Wine and Steam
Because the salmon isn't totally submerged as it cooks, it relies on steam to deliver heat. But water at a subsimmer (necessary to keep the fish from falling apart) doesn't generate much steam. The solution? Cut the water with some wine. The alcohol lowers the boiling temperature of the water; the higher the concentration of alcohol, the more vapor will be produced as the liquid is heated. More steam ensures that the portion of each fillet that is above the liquid cooks just as quickly as the fish that is submerged, even at temperatures below a simmer. And the wine improves the flavor of the poaching liquid, too.

Turn Liquid into Sauce
While the resting cooked salmon drains and firms up, reduce the poaching liquid to 2 tablespoons. This concentrates its flavor and provides the perfect foundation for making just the right amount of sauce to serve with the salmon. Straining the reduced liquid (which is used as the "vinegar") and adding it to some olive oil, chopped capers, parsley, tarragon, and honey creates an easy light and fresh vinaigrette-style sauce.

A bed of lemon slices and herb stems shields the salmon from the hot pan and adds flavor.

Poached Salmon with Herb and Caper Vinaigrette

SERVES 4

This recipe will yield salmon fillets cooked to medium-rare.

2	lemons
2	tablespoons chopped fresh parsley, stems reserved
2	tablespoons chopped fresh tarragon, stems reserved
1	large shallot, minced
½	cup dry white wine
½	cup water

1	(1¾- to 2-pound) skinless salmon fillet, about 1½ inches thick
2	tablespoons capers, rinsed and chopped
2	tablespoons extra-virgin olive oil
1	tablespoon honey
	Salt and pepper

1. Line plate with paper towels. Cut top and bottom off 1 lemon, then cut into eight to ten ¼-inch-thick slices. Cut remaining lemon into 8 wedges and set aside. Arrange lemon slices in single layer across bottom of 12-inch skillet. Scatter herb stems and 2 tablespoons shallot evenly over lemon slices. Add wine and water to skillet.

2. Use sharp knife to remove any whitish fat from belly of salmon and cut fillet into 4 equal pieces. Place salmon fillets in skillet, skinned side down, on top of lemon slices. Set pan over high heat and bring liquid to simmer. Reduce heat to low, cover, and cook until center of fillets is still translucent when checked with tip of paring knife, or until fillets register 125 degrees (for medium-rare), 11 to 16 minutes. Remove pan from heat and, using spatula, carefully transfer salmon and lemon slices to prepared plate and tent loosely with aluminum foil.

3. Return pan to high heat and simmer cooking liquid until slightly thickened and reduced to 2 tablespoons, 4 to 5 minutes. Meanwhile, combine capers, oil, honey, chopped parsley and tarragon, and remaining shallot in medium bowl. Strain reduced cooking liquid through fine-mesh strainer into bowl with herb mixture, pressing on solids to extract as much liquid as possible. Whisk to combine and season with salt and pepper to taste.

4. Using spatula, carefully lift and tilt salmon fillets to remove lemon slices. Place salmon on serving platter or individual plates and spoon vinaigrette over top. Season with salt and pepper to taste. Serve, passing lemon wedges separately.

POACHED SALMON WITH DILL AND SOUR CREAM SAUCE

Substitute 8 to 12 dill stems for parsley and tarragon stems and omit capers, honey, and olive oil. Strain cooking liquid through fine-mesh strainer into medium bowl; discard solids. Return strained liquid to skillet; whisk in 1 tablespoon Dijon mustard and remaining 2 tablespoons shallot. Simmer over high heat until slightly thickened and reduced to 2 tablespoons, 4 to 5 minutes. Whisk in 2 tablespoons sour cream and juice from 1 reserved lemon wedge; simmer 1 minute. Remove from heat; whisk in 2 tablespoons minced fresh dill fronds. Season with salt and pepper to taste. Continue with recipe from step 4, spooning sauce over salmon before serving.

RECIPE DETAILS

Timeline

- 10 minutes to prep ingredients
- 20 minutes to cook salmon and make sauce

Essential Tools

- 12-inch skillet with lid
- Instant-read thermometer to gauge doneness of fish
- Thin, wide spatula to transfer fish
- Fine-mesh strainer to strain reduced cooking liquid

Substitutions & Variations

- To ensure uniform pieces of salmon that cook at the same rate, buy a whole center-cut fillet and cut it into four pieces. If a skinless whole fillet is unavailable, remove the skin yourself or follow the recipe as directed with skin-on fillets, adding 3 to 4 minutes to the cooking time in step 2. Once rested, gently slide a thin, wide spatula between the flesh and skin and use the fingers of your free hand to help separate the skin. It should peel off easily and in one piece.

43 Blackened Fish

A CAJUN CLASSIC TRAVELS OUTSIDE TO CLEAR THE SMOKE

Ever since Paul Prudhomme popularized his signature dish of blackened redfish in the 1980s, blackened anything has become popular in restaurants far from Cajun country. And with good reason. When done right, the dark brown, crusty, sweet-smoky, toasted exterior provides a rich contrast to the moist, mild-flavored fish inside.

This dish is traditionally prepared in a white-hot cast-iron skillet and requires a lot of butter, both to rub on the fish before it's dredged in the spices and to grease the pan. As with most restaurant dishes, you don't want to know how much fat is used. Prudhomme's original recipe called for 6 tablespoons of butter per serving. (His more recent versions have slimmed down considerably.)

But there's an even bigger problem with this recipe—it generates so much smoke that Prudhomme quips in one of his books that the preparation of this dish will set off not only your smoke alarm, but your neighbor's alarm as well. To keep the fire department at bay, we suggest moving this dish to the grill. No need to worry if your kitchen ventilation system is up to snuff. And making this dish on a grill rather than in a hot pan means no butter is needed during the cooking process. (We still use butter in the application of the spice coating.)

But grilling fish is tricky business and a buttery spice coating makes it even more likely to stick. It's fine if the smoke stays outdoors, but you do want the grilled fish to make it back into the kitchen. Slashing and chilling the fish and oiling the cooking grate make this recipe grill-friendly, so the only alarm ringing will be the one in your head from all those Cajun spices.

WHY THIS RECIPE WORKS

Here's the Rub

Mixing your own blackening rub delivers superior results. Our recipe uses garlic powder and onion powder so there are no bits of the fresh stuff to burn on the grill. Coriander, which can take the heat, gives a fragrant floral aroma. Three kinds of pepper (cayenne, black, and white) add a range of heat levels.

Bloom in Butter

Raw spices will burn on the grill, but sautéing them in melted butter releases additional flavors and turns them several shades darker (bright red to dark, rusty brown). After the spice mixture cools, break apart the large clumps and coat the fish on both sides. By the time the fish cooks through, the spices are blackened.

Slash the Skin

Skin-on fillets will buckle when grilled because the skin shrinks back, pulling the flesh along with it. And curled fillets won't cook evenly. Slashing the skin prevents it from contracting more quickly than the flesh. Score the skin at 1-inch intervals, making sure not to cut too deep into the flesh.

Catch and Release

To keep the fish from sticking to the grill, you have to take some preventive measures. First, chill the fish. At room temperature, the fillets become floppy and will stick more readily. Second, heat the grill, scrape the grill grate clean with a brush, and wipe it with oil-dipped paper towels at least five times, until the grate is black and glossy. To cook, place the fish diagonal to the grill grate with skin side facing down. To flip, slide one spatula underneath the fillet to lift, while using another to help support the fish as it's flipped. When used in tandem, these measures take the fear out of grilling fish.

Cooking spices in butter creates a rub with big flavor and superior sticking power.

Grilled Blackened Red Snapper

SERVES 4

Keep the fish refrigerated until ready to grill. Serve the fish with lemon wedges or a classic Creole Rémoulade (recipe follows).

2 tablespoons paprika

2 teaspoons onion powder

2 teaspoons garlic powder

¾ teaspoon ground coriander

¾ teaspoon salt

¼ teaspoon pepper

¼ teaspoon cayenne pepper

¼ teaspoon white pepper

3 tablespoons unsalted butter

4 (6- to 8-ounce) red snapper fillets, ¾ inch thick

1. Combine paprika, onion powder, garlic powder, coriander, salt, pepper, cayenne, and white pepper in bowl. Melt butter in 10-inch skillet over medium heat. Stir in spice mixture and cook, stirring frequently, until fragrant and spices turn dark rust color, 2 to 3 minutes. Transfer mixture to pie plate and let cool to room temperature. Use fork to break up any large clumps.

2A. *For a Charcoal Grill:* Open bottom vent completely. Light large chimney starter two-thirds filled with charcoal briquettes (4 quarts). When top coals are partially covered with ash, pour evenly over half of grill. Set cooking grate in place, cover, and open lid vent completely. Heat grill until hot, about 5 minutes.

2B. *For a Gas Grill:* Turn all burners to high, cover, and heat grill until hot, about 15 minutes.

3. Clean cooking grate, then repeatedly brush grate with well-oiled paper towels until black and glossy, 5 to 10 times.

4. Meanwhile, pat fillets dry with paper towels. Using sharp knife, make shallow diagonal slashes every inch along skin side of fish, being careful not to cut into flesh. Place fillets skin side up on large plate. Using your fingers, rub spice mixture in thin, even layer on top and sides of fish. Flip fillets over and repeat on other side (you should use all of spice mixture).

5. Place fish skin side down on grill (hotter side if using charcoal) with fillets diagonal to grate. Cook until skin is very dark brown and crisp, 3 to 5 minutes. Carefully flip fish and continue to cook until dark brown and beginning to flake and center is opaque but still moist, about 5 minutes longer. Serve.

RÉMOULADE MAKES ABOUT ½ CUP

½ cup mayonnaise

1½ teaspoons sweet pickle relish

1 teaspoon hot sauce

1 teaspoon lemon juice

1 teaspoon minced fresh parsley

½ teaspoon capers, rinsed

½ teaspoon Dijon mustard

1 small garlic clove, minced

Salt and pepper

Pulse all ingredients in food processor until well combined but not smooth, about 10 pulses. Season with salt and pepper to taste. Transfer to serving bowl. (Sauce can be refrigerated for up to 3 days.)

Timeline

• 10 minutes to prepare spice rub (let it cool while grill is heating)

• 20 minutes to heat grill and prepare fish

• 10 minutes to grill fish

Essential Tools

• 10-inch skillet to make spice rub

• Sharp paring knife to slash fish

• Tongs for holding paper towels used to oil cooking grate

• Thin metal spatula to flip fish, plus second wide spatula to support fish while flipping

Substitutions & Variations

• Striped bass, halibut, or grouper can be substituted for the snapper; if the fillets are thicker or thinner, they will have slightly different cooking times.

• If you prefer, serve the fish with a bright, fruit-based salsa. We particularly like a mix of pineapple, cucumber, shallot, chile, ginger, mint, and lime juice, but other combinations such as mango-jícama or peach–red bell pepper are equally good.

44 Grilled Steak

A CHEAP STEAK CAN BE A GREAT STEAK, WITH SOME HELP

It's easy enough to grill an expensive steak. With their tender texture and big-time beef flavor, pricey cuts like rib eyes and T-bones need little more than salt and pepper to make them taste great. After paying $15 or even $20 per pound, the cooking should be easy, right?

But try this minimalist approach on cheaper cuts from the sirloin and the round and you end up with chewy, dry steaks. And the flavors often veer toward liver-y and gamy. It's probably these flavor challenges that inspire cooks to apply spice rubs to these inexpensive steaks. But this approach often fails; because cheap steaks exude little fat to bond with the spices, the rub falls off.

So what's the key to grilling steaks on a budget? First off, you must shop carefully. We think boneless shell sirloin steaks, which retail for about $6 per pound in most supermarkets, are the best of the cheap choices. Although shell sirloin steak isn't as beefy as premium cuts, it doesn't have the liver-y notes that ruin other budget options.

At home, your first task is to amp up the beef flavor. Salting meat is the easiest way to make any cut taste better. And if you let the salt penetrate—a process that takes an hour with a relatively thin steak—it can really work wonders. Adding flavor boosters to the salt is even better.

Next, use the salting time to make a really good rub. That means starting with dried chiles and whole spices and toasting them to unlock their full potential. And that sticking problem? It's easily solved with a knife and a spritz of oil. Yes, it takes some finesse to cook a cheap steak well, but think of all the money in your pocket.

WHY THIS RECIPE WORKS

A Salty Glutamate Wet Rub

Most flavor compounds in spices are oil-soluble rather than water-soluble, so they can't penetrate below the surface of the meat. Other than salt, the only flavor compounds that can travel deep into meat are glutamates. Two of the most potent sources of glutamates are tomato paste and fish sauce. A wet paste made from these two pantry items plus kosher salt gives the steaks a noticeably richer, beefier flavor. Onion powder and garlic powder are also added to this paste—their water-soluble compounds are potent enough (especially in concentrated dry form) to flavor the exterior of the steak.

A Spicy Dry Rub

Dried herbs and other delicate spices can lose their flavor in the intense heat of the grill, but potent spices containing capsaicin, such as chiles, peppers, and paprika, fare well. Toasting and then grinding dried chiles and whole spices leads to a more substantial crust with complex flavor. Adding some sugar to the mix helps the crust to caramelize.

Score the Meat for Sticking Power

Cutting shallow slits in a crosshatch pattern into the steak helps the salt paste and spice rub adhere to the meat and penetrate more deeply. The slits increase the surface area for the initial wet rub to get into the meat and the crosshatches give the dry spice rub something to hold on to.

Oil the Grate and the Rub

Since the steaks are thin, you need a superhot fire to get a good crust. Slicking down the grill grate with oil helps protect against sticking. Eliminate the raw spice flavors of the rub by lightly misting the steaks with vegetable oil; this allows the spices to bloom and release their flavor right on the grill. The vegetable oil spray also helps the rub cling to the steaks, not the grill, for a crisp, crunchy crust.

Steaks are smeared with a savory paste followed by a mix of toasted chiles and spices.

Grilled Steak with New Mexican Chile Rub

SERVES 6 TO 8

Shell sirloin steak is also known as round-bone steak or New York sirloin steak. Spraying the rubbed steaks with oil helps the spices bloom, preventing a raw flavor.

STEAK

- 2 teaspoons tomato paste
- 2 teaspoons fish sauce
- 1½ teaspoons kosher salt
- ½ teaspoon onion powder
- ½ teaspoon garlic powder
- 2 (1½- to 1¾-pound) boneless shell sirloin steaks, 1 to 1¼ inches thick, trimmed

SPICE RUB

- 2 dried New Mexican chiles, stemmed, seeded, and torn into ½-inch pieces
- 4 teaspoons cumin seeds
- 4 teaspoons coriander seeds
- ½ teaspoon red pepper flakes
- ½ teaspoon black peppercorns
- 1 tablespoon sugar
- 1 tablespoon paprika
- ¼ teaspoon ground cloves
- Vegetable oil spray

1. *For the Steak:* Combine tomato paste, fish sauce, salt, onion powder, and garlic powder in bowl. Pat steaks dry with paper towels. With sharp knife, cut 1/16-inch-deep slits on both sides of steaks, spaced ½ inch apart, in crosshatch pattern. Rub salt mixture evenly on both sides of steaks. Place steaks on wire rack set in rimmed baking sheet; let stand at room temperature for at least 1 hour. After 30 minutes, prepare grill.

2. *For the Spice Rub:* Toast chiles, cumin, coriander, pepper flakes, and peppercorns in 10-inch skillet over medium-low heat, stirring frequently, until just beginning to smoke, 3 to 4 minutes. Transfer to plate to cool, about 5 minutes. Grind spices in spice grinder or in mortar with pestle until coarsely ground. Transfer spices to bowl and stir in sugar, paprika, and cloves.

3A. *For a Charcoal Grill:* Open bottom vent completely. Light large chimney starter mounded with charcoal briquettes (7 quarts). When top coals are partially covered with ash, pour two-thirds evenly over grill, then pour remaining coals over half of grill. Set cooking grate in place, cover, and open lid vent completely. Heat grill until hot, about 5 minutes.

3B. *For a Gas Grill:* Turn all burners to high, cover, and heat grill until hot, about 15 minutes. Leave primary burner on high and turn other burner(s) to medium.

4. Clean and oil cooking grate. Sprinkle half of spice rub evenly over 1 side of steaks and press to adhere until spice rub is fully moistened. Lightly spray rubbed side of steak with oil spray, about 3 seconds. Flip steaks and repeat process of sprinkling with spice rub and coating with oil spray on second side.

5. Place steaks over hotter part of grill and cook until browned and charred on both sides and center registers 125 degrees (for medium-rare) or 130 degrees (for medium), 3 to 4 minutes per side. If steaks have not reached desired temperature, move to cooler side of grill and continue to cook. Transfer steaks to clean wire rack set in rimmed baking sheet, tent loosely with aluminum foil, and let rest for 10 minutes. Slice meat thin against grain and serve.

RECIPE DETAILS

Timeline

- 5 minutes to prepare salt mixture and coat steaks
- 1 hour to rest salted steaks (also prepare spice rub and set up grill)
- 10 minutes to coat steaks with spice rub and grill them
- 10 minutes to rest steaks before serving

Essential Tools

- Wire rack set in rimmed baking sheet for holding steak
- 10-inch skillet for toasting chiles and spices
- Spice grinder or mortar and pestle

Substitutions & Variations

- Chile-based rubs work especially well with this technique. Here are two other variations you can use with this steak recipe:
- Ancho Chile–Coffee Rub: Substitute 1 dried ancho chile for New Mexican chiles, 2 teaspoons ground coffee for paprika, and 1 teaspoon unsweetened cocoa powder for ground cloves.
- Spicy Chipotle Chile Rub: Substitute 2 dried chipotle chiles for New Mexican chiles, 1 teaspoon dried oregano for paprika, and ½ teaspoon ground cinnamon for ground cloves.

45 Beef Burgundy

STREAMLINE THIS FRENCH CLASSIC BY MOVING IT TO THE OVEN

Julia Child once wrote that *boeuf bourguignon* "is the best beef stew known to man." We can't argue with that. This hearty braise is the ultimate example of how rich, savory, and satisfying beef stew can be.

Unfortunately, beef Burgundy is a real pain to make. Most recipes, Child's included, come with a serious time commitment: at least 40 minutes of browning bacon lardons and batch-searing beef, in addition to the lengthy braising time. Then there's the "garnish"—not a quick embellishment, but rather an integral part of the dish that requires the cook to sauté pearl onions and button mushrooms in a separate pan.

In an effort to make this recipe more hands-off (by definition a braise will never be quick), we move the entire operation to the oven. The onion and mushroom garnish roasts on one rack while the braise cooks on another. Browning the lardons in the oven requires no stirring. We build the sauce in the same pan by whisking in flour, broth, and wine. We then add the aromatic vegetables, herbs, and finally chunks of stew meat.

Now what about browning the meat, you ask? We typically think of browning as a high-heat operation that occurs on the stovetop. But given sufficient time (and there's plenty of unattended braising time) browning can occur in a cooler environment—like an oven—as long as the beef is exposed to the air. Switching from a lidded Dutch oven (the usual vessel for a braise) to an open roasting pan accomplishes this. With the beef arranged on top of the vegetables and other solid ingredients, it can brown quite a lot—and all the while you can do something else. We think even Julia would approve.

WHY THIS RECIPE WORKS

Flavor Development

Cooking stew in the oven is a game changer in terms of time and ease, but it's important to eke out flavor at every turn. Salting the roast (well-marbled chuck eye is your best choice) seasons the meat and helps it retain moisture during cooking. And don't throw out those scraps when cutting the meat into chunks—brown them with salt pork (the best choice for lardons). The payoff? A meaty flavor boost at no extra cost.

No Bones, No Problem

Homemade beef broth is a nonstarter in our streamlined stew. Commercial beef broth is the next best option, but it needs a little help on the flavor front from umami enhancers like porcini mushrooms, tomato paste, and anchovy paste. As for the broth's body, stirring in a little powdered gelatin mimics the rich consistency of homemade beef stock made with gelatin-rich beef bones.

Giving Props

With a roasting pan of rendered salt pork and beef scraps, the rest of the operation is all about assembly, layer by layer—vegetables first, then beef. After adding flour (to thicken the stew) and deglazing the pan with the doctored broth, we prop up the beef with a bed of aromatics (onions, carrots, garlic, porcini mushrooms, and herbs) so the chunks of meat poking above the liquid brown nicely and the surrounding liquid simmers and gains complexity.

Finish Bright, Not Flat

This stew is called Burgundy for a reason. A full bottle delivers full flavor—but after all that braising, it's also a bit flat. Popping the cork on another just to splash some in at the end of cooking is downright extravagant. A more economical solution is to hold back part of the bottle until the final reduction of the sauce, for a noticeably brighter, but not boozy, finish.

Building beef Burgundy in a roasting pan eliminates much of the hands-on work.

Modern Beef Burgundy

SERVES 6 TO 8

If the pearl onions have a papery outer coating, remove it by rinsing them in warm water and gently squeezing individual onions between your fingertips. To save time, salt the meat and let it stand while you prep the remaining ingredients. Serve with mashed potatoes or buttered noodles.

1 (4-pound) boneless beef chuck-eye roast, trimmed and cut into 1½- to 2-inch pieces, scraps reserved
Salt and pepper
6 ounces salt pork, cut into ¼-inch pieces
3 tablespoons unsalted butter
1 pound cremini mushrooms, trimmed, halved if medium or quartered if large
1½ cups frozen pearl onions, thawed
1 tablespoon sugar
⅓ cup all-purpose flour
4 cups beef broth
1 (750-ml) bottle red Burgundy or Pinot Noir

5 teaspoons unflavored gelatin
1 tablespoon tomato paste
1 teaspoon anchovy paste
2 onions, chopped coarse
2 carrots, peeled and cut into 2-inch lengths
1 garlic head, cloves separated, unpeeled, and smashed
½ ounce dried porcini mushrooms, rinsed
10 sprigs fresh parsley, plus 3 tablespoons minced
6 sprigs fresh thyme
2 bay leaves
½ teaspoon black peppercorns

1. Toss beef and 1½ teaspoons salt together in bowl and let stand at room temperature for 30 minutes.

2. Adjust oven racks to lower-middle and lowest positions and heat oven to 500 degrees. Place salt pork, 2 tablespoons butter, and beef scraps in large roasting pan. Roast on upper rack until well browned and fat has rendered, 15 to 20 minutes.

3. While salt pork and beef scraps roast, toss cremini mushrooms, pearl onions, sugar, and remaining 1 tablespoon butter together on rimmed baking sheet. Roast on lower rack, stirring occasionally, until moisture released by mushrooms evaporates and vegetables are lightly glazed, 15 to 20 minutes. Transfer vegetables to large bowl, cover, and refrigerate.

4. Remove roasting pan from oven and reduce temperature to 325 degrees. Sprinkle flour over rendered fat and whisk until no dry flour remains. Whisk in broth, 2 cups wine, gelatin, tomato paste, and anchovy paste until combined. Add onions, carrots, garlic, porcini mushrooms, parsley sprigs, thyme sprigs, bay leaves, and peppercorns to pan. Arrange beef in single layer on top of vegetables. Add water as needed to come three-quarters up side of beef (beef should not be submerged). Return roasting pan to oven and cook until meat is tender, 3 to 3½ hours, stirring after 1½ hours and adding water to keep meat at least half-submerged.

RECIPE DETAILS

Timeline

- 30 minutes to salt beef (hands-off)
- 20 minutes to roast salt pork and beef scraps (roast mushrooms and onions at same time)
- 3½ hours to braise stew (mostly hands-off)
- 30 minutes to strain liquid and reduce sauce

Essential Tools

- Large roasting pan for making stew
- Rimmed baking sheet for roasting mushroom and onion garnish
- Fine-mesh strainer
- Dutch oven for finishing stew

Substitutions & Variations

- Blade steak (also known as flat-iron steak) can be used in this recipe. Make sure to trim the line of gristle that runs through the center of each steak as well as all external fat around each steak. While blade steak will yield slightly thinner pieces after trimming, it should still be cut into 1½-inch pieces. Note that the cooking time might be a bit shorter.
- Two minced anchovy fillets can be used in place of the anchovy paste.
- A red Burgundy (from France, of course) is the classic choice, but any Pinot Noir (including something from California or Oregon) will work just fine. Do buy something that is good enough to drink on its own, but don't splurge—nuances in a really expensive wine will be lost in this dish.

5. Using slotted spoon, transfer beef to bowl with cremini mushrooms and pearl onions; cover and set aside. Strain braising liquid through fine-mesh strainer set over large bowl, pressing on solids to extract as much liquid as possible; discard solids. Stir in remaining wine and let cooking liquid settle, 10 minutes. Using wide, shallow spoon, skim fat from surface and discard.

6. Transfer liquid to Dutch oven and bring mixture to boil over medium-high heat. Simmer briskly, stirring occasionally, until sauce is thickened to consistency of heavy cream, 15 to 20 minutes. Reduce heat to medium-low, stir in beef and mushroom-onion mixture, cover, and cook until just heated through, 5 to 8 minutes. Season with salt and pepper to taste. Stir in minced parsley and serve. (Stew can be refrigerated for up to 3 days.)

A Better Way to Buy Stew Meat

Prepackaged beef stew meat is convenient but not very good. In most markets, the pieces are much too small and they are unevenly butchered—so small pieces overcook by the time larger ones are done. Even more problematic is the meat itself. Sometimes it comes from the desired chuck but often packages contain scraps from all over the animal, many of which are not very flavorful. Instead, buy a single cut.

1. With your hands, pull apart roast at its major seams, delineated by lines of fat. Cut away all exposed fat. (For beef stew, start with a chuck-eye roast. For pork stew, buy a Boston butt or picnic shoulder.)

2. Cut meat into large chunks, usually 1½ to 2 inches. (We think bigger chunks make a better stew. They also are less likely to overcook.) Trim any hard knobs of white fat as you work. (Don't bother trimming soft, thin lines of fat—they will melt during the stewing process and lubricate the meat.)

46 Roast Beef

A TWO-DAY RECIPE MAKES A TOUGH CUT AMAZINGLY TENDER

For special occasions, nothing beats beef tenderloin (see page 66). The Sunday roast, however, is generally more humble. But the cooking goal for both is the same: a tender roast with beefy flavor.

Among the low-cost options, we think the eye-round roast is best. Slice it thin for serving, and it's fairly tender. But can you make it really tender? And can you amp up its mild flavor?

Butchers dry-age meat in climate-controlled refrigerators for up to a month to improve tenderness and flavor. If you've been lucky enough to eat great beef—the kind with a buttery texture and nutty flavor—it likely was aged this way.

Evaporation during the aging process contributes to a stronger meat flavor. But most of the positive effects of dry aging stem from the activity of naturally occurring enzymes in the meat, which are breaking down muscle fibers and creating new flavor compounds. Now, dry-aging a roast for a month at home isn't practical. But is there a way to accelerate this process? In a word, salt.

Salting an eye-round roast for 24 hours weakens the muscle fibers so the enzymes don't have to work as hard. And letting the roast hang out in the fridge for a day also maximizes the flavor boost from the salt.

But the real magic occurs in the oven. That's because the enzymatic reaction speeds up as the roast heats, but then abruptly shuts off when the temperature of the meat reaches 122 degrees. The trick is to stretch the cooking time. In a hot oven, a 4-pound roast will be done in less than an hour. But if you turn the heat way down, you can double, even triple, the cooking time. Good things really do come to cooks who wait.

WHY THIS RECIPE WORKS

Choose Wisely from Low-Cost Cuts
Not all bargain cuts have the potential to taste like a million bucks. Eye-round roast possesses good flavor, relative tenderness, and a uniform shape, which means even cooking and good looks when sliced into juicy slabs.

Aging in Record Time
When meat is dry-aged, naturally occurring enzymes are breaking down muscle fibers and making the meat tender. These enzymes also encourage the formation of new amino acid compounds, and that translates to a meatier flavor. Salting the roast for a full 24 hours gives it the most time to penetrate deep into the meat and season the roast evenly (though as few as 18 hours is effective). The salt dissolves some of the proteins, too, making it easier for the enzymes to break them down.

Sear, Then Elevate
A quick sear in a hot skillet develops a flavorful crust on the meat and is an essential first step in this recipe. Rather than placing the roast directly in a roasting pan, elevate the roast on a rack set in a rimmed baking sheet. The rack allows the oven heat to circulate evenly around the meat and prevents the bottom crust from steaming in the oven.

Slow Down to the Finish
Slow-roasting isn't just about cooking in a cool oven—it's about carryover cooking, too. The enzymes in the meat that break down its connective tissues, essentially acting as a meat tenderizer, work faster as the temperature of the meat rises—but just until 122 degrees. This means starting the oven at 225 degrees and then shutting off the oven to finish cooking the roast—in this case, once the roast reaches 115 degrees. The roast will take another 30 to 50 minutes to climb from 115 to a final temperature of 130 degrees for medium-rare, yielding exceptionally tender, rosy meat all the way through—not just in the center.

Salting tenderizes a tough cut, while cooking by temperature not time guarantees rosy results.

Slow-Roasted Beef

SERVES 6 TO 8

We don't recommend cooking this roast past medium. Open the oven door as little as possible and remove the roast from the oven while taking its temperature. If the roast has not reached the desired temperature in the time specified in step 3, heat the oven to 225 degrees for 5 minutes, shut it off, and continue to cook the roast to the desired temperature. Slice the roast as thin as possible and serve with Horseradish Cream Sauce (recipe follows), if desired.

1 **(3½- to 4½-pound) boneless eye-round roast, trimmed**	2 **teaspoons plus 1 tablespoon vegetable oil**
4 **teaspoons kosher salt**	2 **teaspoons pepper**

1. Season all sides of roast evenly with salt. Wrap with plastic wrap and refrigerate 18 to 24 hours.

2. Adjust oven rack to middle position and heat oven to 225 degrees. Pat roast dry with paper towels; rub with 2 teaspoons oil and season all sides evenly with pepper. Heat remaining 1 tablespoon oil in 12-inch skillet over medium-high heat until just smoking. Sear roast until browned on all sides, about 12 minutes. Transfer roast to wire rack set in rimmed baking sheet. Roast until meat registers 115 degrees (for medium-rare), 1¼ to 1¾ hours, or 125 degrees (for medium), 1¾ to 2¼ hours.

3. Turn oven off; leave roast in oven, without opening door, until meat registers 130 degrees (for medium-rare) or 140 degrees (for medium), 30 to 50 minutes longer. Transfer roast to carving board and let rest for 15 minutes. Slice meat as thin as possible and serve.

HORSERADISH CREAM SAUCE MAKES ABOUT 1 CUP

½ **cup heavy cream**	1 **teaspoon salt**
½ **cup prepared horseradish**	⅛ **teaspoon pepper**

Whisk cream in bowl until thickened but not yet holding soft peaks, 1 to 2 minutes. Gently fold in horseradish, salt, and pepper. Transfer to serving bowl and refrigerate at least 30 minutes or up to 1 hour before serving.

RECIPE DETAILS

Timeline

- 18 to 24 hours to salt roast (hands-off)
- 15 minutes to season and sear roast
- 1¾ to 3 hours to roast (will vary based on size of roast and desired doneness)
- 15 minutes to rest meat

Essential Tools

- 12-inch skillet for searing roast
- Wire rack set in rimmed baking sheet for roasting beef
- Instant-read thermometer or meat probe thermometer (A meat-probe thermometer is left in the meat as it cooks, transmitting readings to a digital console, avoiding the need to continually open the oven to check on a roast's temperature with an instant-read thermometer. It's the best choice for this recipe.)

Substitutions & Variations

- You can use this technique to cook a smaller or larger roast. For a 2½- to 3½-pound roast, reduce the amount of salt to 1 tablespoon and pepper to 1½ teaspoons. For a 4½- to 6-pound roast, cut it in half crosswise before cooking to create two smaller roasts.

47 Roast Pork

AN UNLIKELY ROAST REQUIRES TIME BUT LITTLE EFFORT

I t's been almost 30 years since the National Pork Producers Council launched a campaign to persuade poultry-loving Americans to eat more pig—specifically the lean "other white meat" between the pig's shoulder and leg, known as the loin. This promotion coincided with the introduction of slimmer pigs. Ever since, consumers have been flocking to butcher cases to buy up the center-cut loin and then heading home to try everything under the sun to improve the almost-fat-free meat's bland flavor and stringy chew.

News flash: Pork is not white meat. And that's a good thing. Also, pork is supposed to have some fat. And that's a really good thing. To experience the glories of old-fashioned roast pork, you have to buy a cut with some fat—and some flavor.

Our favorite choice for roasting is the pork butt. This shoulder roast packs plenty of intramuscular fat that melts and bastes the meat during cooking. It also boasts a thick fat cap that renders to a bronze, baconlike crust. And it's cheap—$15 buys a roast that can feed a crowd.

Now, there's just one problem. You need to forget everything you know about roasting pork, starting with the desired internal temperature. A loin is best cooked to 145 degrees. But a shoulder roast is the same cut used to make pulled pork, so it must cook well past well-done in order to render the fat and convert the collagen to gelatin. But don't worry; roasting (unlike barbecuing) is dead simple. All you need is some patience as the enticing aroma of pork fills the kitchen for hours. Your wait will be rewarded with the best roast pork of your life.

WHY THIS RECIPE WORKS

Use Bone-In Pork Butt
We prefer bone-in for two reasons: First, the bone acts as an insulator against heat. This means that the meat surrounding it stays cooler and the roast cooks at a slower, gentler pace. Second, bones have a large percentage of the meat's connective tissue attached to them, which eventually breaks down to gelatin and helps the roast retain moisture.

Here's the Rub
Using a salt rub on meat is a common technique to improve flavor and texture. Salt penetrates deep beneath the surface of a tough roast, seasoning it throughout and helping to break down its proteins. But for our pork roast, we wanted an exceptionally crisp crust. In Chinese barbecue, the pork is heavily seasoned with equal parts salt and sugar to encourage an ultracrisp crust that veers toward candied bacon. Following suit, we rub our roast with a mixture of salt and brown sugar (scoring the fat cap first to help the rub stick and encourage the fat to render) and then let it rest overnight.

Go Slow
Cooking the pork slowly (at 325 degrees for 5 to 6 hours) pushes the meat well beyond its "done" mark into the 190-degree range. In lean cuts, this would result in an incredibly dry piece of meat. But because there is so much collagen and fat in this roast, the high internal temperature encourages intramuscular fat to melt, collagen to break down and tenderize the meat, and the fat cap to render and crisp.

V-Rack to the Rescue
If you cook the pork directly in the pan, the dark layer of drippings burn (thanks to its high sugar content). A V-rack and a quart of water poured into the bottom of the pan prevent this problem. Because the roast is perched higher up, its fat drips down and mixes with the water to create a significant amount of flavorful jus.

Five hours in the oven transforms a salt and brown sugar rub into a crackling-like crust.

Slow-Roasted Pork Shoulder with Peach Sauce

SERVES 8 TO 12

Add more water to the roasting pan as necessary during the last hours of cooking to prevent the fond from burning. Serve the pork with the accompanying peach sauce or with cherry sauce (recipe follows).

PORK ROAST

- 1 (6- to 8-pound) bone-in pork butt roast
- ⅓ cup kosher salt
- ⅓ cup packed light brown sugar
- Pepper

PEACH SAUCE

- 10 ounces frozen peaches, cut into 1-inch chunks, or 2 fresh peaches, peeled, pitted, and cut into ½-inch wedges
- 2 cups dry white wine
- ½ cup granulated sugar
- ¼ cup plus 1 tablespoon unseasoned rice vinegar
- 2 sprigs fresh thyme
- 1 tablespoon whole-grain mustard

1. *For the Pork Roast:* Using sharp knife, cut slits 1 inch apart in crosshatch pattern in fat cap of roast, being careful not to cut into meat. Combine salt and sugar in bowl. Rub salt mixture over entire pork shoulder and into slits. Wrap roast tightly in double layer of plastic wrap, place on rimmed baking sheet, and refrigerate for 12 to 24 hours.

2. Adjust oven rack to lowest position and heat oven to 325 degrees. Unwrap roast and brush any excess salt mixture from surface. Season roast with pepper. Set V-rack in large roasting pan, spray with vegetable oil spray, and place roast on rack. Add 1 quart water to roasting pan.

3. Cook roast, basting twice during cooking, until meat is extremely tender and roast near (but not touching) bone registers 190 degrees, 5 to 6 hours. Transfer roast to carving board and let rest, tented loosely with aluminum foil, for 1 hour. Transfer liquid in roasting pan to fat separator and let stand for 5 minutes. Pour off ¼ cup jus and set aside; discard fat and reserve remaining jus for another use.

4. *For the Peach Sauce:* Bring peaches, wine, sugar, ¼ cup vinegar, ¼ cup defatted jus, and thyme sprigs to simmer in small saucepan; cook, stirring occasionally, until reduced to 2 cups, about 30 minutes. Stir in mustard and remaining 1 tablespoon vinegar. Remove thyme sprigs, cover, and keep warm.

5. Using sharp paring knife, cut around inverted T-shaped bone until it can be pulled free from roast (use clean dish towel to grasp bone). Using serrated knife, slice roast. Serve, passing sauce separately.

SLOW-ROASTED PORK SHOULDER WITH CHERRY SAUCE

Substitute 10 ounces fresh or frozen pitted cherries for peaches, red wine for white wine, and red wine vinegar for rice vinegar, and add ¼ cup ruby port along with defatted jus. Increase granulated sugar to ¾ cup, omit thyme sprigs and mustard, and reduce mixture to 1½ cups.

RECIPE DETAILS

Timeline

- 12 to 24 hours to score and salt roast
- 5 to 6 hours to roast pork
- 1 hour to rest roast (prepare sauce while roast is resting)

Essential Tools

- Sharp paring knife to score roast and remove bone
- Rimmed baking sheet to hold roast in fridge
- Roasting pan with V-rack to roast pork
- Fat separator

Substitutions & Variations

- Pork butt roast is also called Boston shoulder, pork butt, or Boston-style butt. Do not confuse this cut with arm shoulder or picnic shoulder roast.
- Like most pork roasts, this one works well with a sweet sauce. To balance the richness of this cut, we especially like the acidity of fruit-based sauces or chutneys.

48 Grilled Pork Tenderloin

DOUBLE UP TO MAKE THIS SKINNY CUT EASIER TO COOK WELL

Pork tenderloin is wonderfully tender and versatile, it doesn't require much prep, and it's relatively inexpensive. But alas, this cut also comes with some challenges. Because tenderloin is incredibly lean, it's highly susceptible to drying out during cooking. Then there's the ungainly tapered shape: By the time the large end hits a perfect medium (140 degrees), the skinnier tail is guaranteed to be overcooked.

Grilling might seem like the best way to cook pork tenderloin. The tender, mild-tasting meat would benefit from the creation of a crisp crust and the infusion of grill flavor. But with all that grill heat, how do you avoid turning tenderloin into shoe leather?

The biggest challenge with this roast is its size and shape. Tenderloins are very skinny, which means they cook very quickly. But what if we could fashion two tenderloins into a single thick roast? If we aligned the fat end on one roast with the skinny end on the other roast, we'd be able to produce one big roast with uniform thickness. (Picture two shoes together in a box, with the thick end of one nestled against the thin end of the other.)

With some twine, it was easy to tie two roasts together. And, as we hoped, this bigger roast cooked much more evenly and spent more time on the grill, helping to create a really nice crust. The roast also absorbed more grill flavor. But everything fell apart—quite literally—on the carving board. For this idea to work, we'd have to get two roasts to cook—and eat—like a single thick piece of meat. Sounds like we need a magician's wand, but the actual solution relies on a dinner fork and some basic meat science.

WHY THIS RECIPE WORKS

Brine First
It's important to brine pork tenderloin, especially if it's going to withstand the dry, hot fire of the grill and still remain juicy. An hour in salt water offers plenty of protection.

The Glue That Binds
Trying to get meat to stick together sounds unorthodox, but it's something that happens naturally all the time, at least with ground meat. Any time meat is damaged (such as during grinding, slicing, or even pounding), sticky proteins are released. The gluey texture of these proteins makes it possible to form a cohesive burger from nothing but ground beef. Before tying together the two pork tenderloins in this recipe, scrape the length of each roast with a fork to release those sticky proteins. When the tied roasts are cooked, these proteins bond and create a single roast that says together, even when the twine is removed after grilling.

Low Heat First, Then High
Grilling pork tenderloin directly over a hot fire the entire time results in a well-browned exterior—but a thick band of dry, overcooked meat below its surface. A better approach is to start the tenderloin over low heat followed by searing over high heat. The initial stint on the cooler side of the grill allows the meat's surface to warm and dry, which makes for fast, efficient browning (and therefore safeguards against overcooking) when it moves to the hotter part of the grate.

Glazed and Infused
Adding glutamate-rich ingredients such as mirin, hoisin, or fish sauce to a glaze significantly enhances the savory, meaty flavor of the pork. Adding the glaze to the tenderloins over high heat allows the glaze to char and caramelize, further enhancing the rich, flavorful crust. Reserved glaze makes an ideal accompaniment at the table.

Scraping releases sticky proteins that help glue two tenderloins into a single large roast.

Grilled Glazed Pork Tenderloin Roast

SERVES 6

Since brining is a key step in having the two tenderloins stick together, we don't recommend using enhanced pork in this recipe.

2 (1-pound) pork tenderloins, trimmed	Vegetable oil
Salt and pepper	1 recipe glaze (recipes follow)

1. Lay tenderloins on cutting board, flat side (side opposite where silverskin was) up. Holding thick end of 1 tenderloin with paper towels and using dinner fork, scrape flat side lengthwise from end to end 5 times, until surface is completely covered with shallow grooves. Repeat with second tenderloin. Dissolve 3 tablespoons salt in 1½ quarts cold water in large container. Submerge tenderloins in brine and let stand at room temperature for 1 hour.

2. Remove tenderloins from brine and pat completely dry with paper towels. Lay 1 tenderloin, scraped side up, on cutting board and lay second tenderloin, scraped side down, on top so that thick end of 1 tenderloin matches up with thin end of other. Spray five 14-inch lengths of kitchen twine thoroughly with vegetable oil spray; evenly space twine underneath tenderloins and tie. Brush roast with oil and season with pepper. Transfer ⅓ cup glaze to bowl for grilling; reserve remaining glaze for serving.

3A. *For a Charcoal Grill:* Open bottom vent completely. Light large chimney starter filled with charcoal briquettes (6 quarts). When top coals are partially covered with ash, pour into steeply banked pile against side of grill. Set cooking grate in place, cover, and open lid vent completely. Heat grill until hot, about 5 minutes.

3B. *For a Gas Grill:* Turn all burners to high, cover, and heat grill until hot, about 15 minutes. Leave primary burner on high and turn off other burner(s).

4. Clean and oil cooking grate. Place roast on cooler side of grill, cover, and cook until meat registers 115 degrees, 22 to 28 minutes, flipping and rotating halfway through cooking.

5. Slide roast to hotter part of grill and cook until lightly browned on all sides, 4 to 6 minutes. Brush top of roast with about 1 tablespoon glaze and grill, glaze side down, until glaze begins to char, 2 to 3 minutes; repeat glazing and grilling with remaining 3 sides of roast, until meat registers 140 degrees.

6. Transfer roast to carving board, tent loosely with aluminum foil, and let rest for 10 minutes. Carefully remove twine and slice roast into ½-inch-thick slices. Serve with reserved glaze.

RECIPE DETAILS

Timeline

- 1 hour and 10 minutes to prepare and brine tenderloins (make glaze and set up grill while pork brines)
- 5 minutes to tie up tenderloins
- 40 minutes to grill and glaze roast
- 10 minutes to rest roast

Essentials Tools

- Large container for brining
- Kitchen twine
- Long-handled tongs
- Instant-read thermometer

Substitutions & Variations

- A sticky, savory glaze turns grilled pork tenderloin into something special. We offer three options, each built around an ingredient that enhances the meaty flavor of the pork—miso, soy sauce, and fish sauce. Create your own glazes, making sure to use one of these ingredients. Other keys to creating a good glaze—add something sweet as well as something acidic. Make sure to heat glazes to dissolve sugars and/or bloom aromatics like garlic, ginger, or spices. Finally, a thick glaze clings to the meat so keep liquids to a minimum.

MISO GLAZE MAKES ABOUT ¾ CUP

3 **tablespoons sake**	2 **teaspoons Dijon mustard**
3 **tablespoons mirin**	1 **teaspoon rice vinegar**
⅓ **cup white miso paste**	¼ **teaspoon grated fresh ginger**
¼ **cup sugar**	¼ **teaspoon toasted sesame oil**

Bring sake and mirin to boil in small saucepan over medium heat. Whisk in miso and sugar until smooth, about 30 seconds. Remove pan from heat and continue to whisk until sugar is dissolved, about 1 minute. Whisk in mustard, vinegar, ginger, and oil until smooth.

SWEET AND SPICY HOISIN GLAZE MAKES ABOUT ¾ CUP

1 **teaspoon vegetable oil**	½ **cup hoisin sauce**
3 **garlic cloves, minced**	2 **tablespoons soy sauce**
1 **teaspoon grated fresh ginger**	1 **tablespoon rice vinegar**
½ **teaspoon red pepper flakes**	

Heat oil in small saucepan over medium heat until shimmering. Add garlic, ginger, and pepper flakes; cook until fragrant, about 30 seconds. Whisk in hoisin and soy sauce until smooth. Remove pan from heat and stir in vinegar.

SATAY GLAZE MAKES ABOUT ¾ CUP

1 **teaspoon vegetable oil**	¼ **cup packed dark brown sugar**
1 **tablespoon red curry paste**	2 **tablespoons peanut butter**
2 **garlic cloves, minced**	1 **tablespoon lime juice**
½ **teaspoon grated fresh ginger**	2½ **teaspoons fish sauce**
½ **cup canned coconut milk**	

Heat oil in small saucepan over medium heat until shimmering. Add curry paste, garlic, and ginger; cook, stirring constantly, until fragrant, about 1 minute. Whisk in coconut milk and sugar and bring to simmer. Whisk in peanut butter until smooth. Remove pan from heat and whisk in lime juice and fish sauce.

49 Spaghetti with Pecorino and Pepper

MAC AND CHEESE FOR GROWN-UPS—THANK YOU, ITALY

We love macaroni and cheese, but even the best versions don't really put the marquee ingredients in the spotlight. The milky sauce (our recipe on page 36 starts with 5 cups of milk) is the true star of American-style macaroni and cheese.

Perhaps that's why the Roman specialty *pasta alla cacio e pepe* is such a revelation. Like the best Italian cooking, this dish is a study in minimalism—all you taste is spaghetti and Pecorino cheese, with a strong punch of freshly ground pepper in the background. This dish reminds us that sometimes less truly is more.

In Rome, cacio e pepe is a late night favorite because it's so fast and so satisfying. You don't even dirty a second saucepan or skillet because the cooked pasta is tossed directly with sauce ingredients.

But with something so simple there's no room for error, and this dish can be a disappointment. Instead of producing pasta tossed in a silky smooth sauce, sometimes the cheese doesn't melt, and instead clumps into unappealing strings that stick to the tongs. But the solution to this problem can be found in the pasta pot—literally.

Along with the cheese, the pasta cooking water is the main ingredient in the sauce. It turns out that upping the starch content of this water is the key to creating a smooth sauce. That means cooking the pasta in far less water than usual. Yes, you need to stir the pasta vigilantly to prevent it from sticking. But in addition to producing a super-starchy base for the cheese sauce, using less water cuts the waiting time for the pot to boil so you can enjoy this grown-up pasta with cheese that much sooner.

WHY THIS RECIPE WORKS

Start with Good Cheese
Imported Pecorino Romano is a hard, aged sheep's milk cheese with a distinctively pungent, salty flavor that bears almost no resemblance to domestic cheeses simply labeled "Romano." These wan stand-ins are made with cow's milk and lack the punch of the real deal.

Pay Attention to Starch
Even when finely grated, cheese can still clump. Starch helps. In a hard lump of Pecorino, the fat, protein, and water (the three main components of cheese) are locked into position by the solid structure of the cheese. But when the cheese is heated, the proteins can fuse together. The starch from the semolina-infused pasta water, however, coats the cheese and prevents the proteins from sticking. Make sure to use the correct amount of water for your pasta: 2 quarts of water for a pound of pasta, rather than the usual 4 quarts. This volume will yield the optimal concentration of starch in the liquid.

Cream Helps, Too
Starch on its own can't completely prevent the cheese from clumping. But there is another factor that affects how proteins and fat interact: emulsifiers. Milk, cream, and fresh cheeses have special molecules called lipoproteins that can associate with both fat and protein, acting as a sort of liaison between the two and keeping them from separating. But as cheese ages, the lipoproteins break down, losing their emulsifying power. No wonder Pecorino Romano, aged for at least eight months, forms clumps. How to get an infusion of lipoproteins? Add milk or cream. When we replace the traditional butter with the same amount of cream, the cheese forms a light, perfectly smooth sauce that coats the spaghetti.

Finish with More Cheese
For this dish, you can't have too much of a good thing, so pass coarsely grated cheese at the table—the contrast of creamy pasta and pungent shards of cheese is a delight.

Starchy water from cooking the pasta turns grated cheese into a creamy sauce.

Spaghetti with Pecorino Romano and Pepper

SERVES 4 TO 6

High-quality ingredients are essential in this dish; most importantly, imported Pecorino Romano. Do not adjust the amount of water for cooking the pasta; the amount used is critical to the success of the recipe. Make sure to stir the pasta frequently while cooking so that it doesn't stick to the pot. Draining the pasta water into the serving bowl warms the bowl and helps keep the dish hot until it is served. Letting the dish rest briefly before serving allows the flavors to develop and the sauce to thicken.

6	ounces Pecorino Romano cheese, 4 ounces grated fine (2 cups) and 2 ounces grated coarse (1 cup)	1½	teaspoons salt
1	pound spaghetti	2	tablespoons heavy cream
		2	teaspoons extra-virgin olive oil
		1½	teaspoons pepper

1. Place finely grated Pecorino in medium bowl. Set colander in large bowl.

2. Bring 2 quarts water to boil in large pot. Add pasta and salt and cook, stirring often, until al dente. Drain pasta into prepared colander, reserving cooking water. Pour 1½ cups cooking water into 2-cup liquid measuring cup and discard remainder. Return drained pasta to now-empty bowl.

3. Slowly whisk 1 cup reserved cooking water into finely grated Pecorino until smooth, then whisk in heavy cream, oil, and pepper. Gradually pour cheese mixture over pasta and toss to combine. Let pasta rest for 1 to 2 minutes, tossing frequently and adding remaining cooking water as needed to adjust consistency. Serve, passing coarsely grated Pecorino separately.

RECIPE DETAILS

Timeline

- 10 minutes to grate cheese and heat water
- 10 minutes to cook pasta
- 2 to 3 minutes to sauce pasta

Essential Tools

- Box grater (Use the small holes to grate cheese fine and the large holes to grate cheese coarse.)
- 2-cup liquid measuring cup for reserving pasta water
- Whisk

Substitutions & Variations

- For a slightly less rich dish, substitute half-and-half for the heavy cream.
- If you prefer to grind the cheese fine in a food processor, cut the Pecorino into 2-inch pieces and process until finely ground, about 45 seconds. You will still need to grate the remaining cheese by hand—a food processor doesn't do "coarse."

50 Pasta Primavera

TREATING PASTA LIKE RICE SIMPLIFIES EVERYTHING

You'd never guess that pasta primavera, a pseudo-Italian dish that appears on virtually every chain restaurant menu, has its roots at New York's Le Cirque restaurant, a temple of French haute cuisine. Now, you're probably thinking that something has been lost in translation since this dish was invented in the 1970s. Well, yes and no.

The typical strip mall reproduction—a random jumble of produce tossed with noodles in a heavy, flavor-deadening cream sauce—tastes nothing like spring. But the original Le Cirque recipe isn't all that inspiring either, despite taking 2 hours to prepare and dirtying five pans.

There are two main problems with this recipe, no matter its pedigree—the vegetable selection and the cooking method. Most recipes include tomatoes and broccoli, and zucchini and mushrooms are almost as common. None of these vegetables is at its best in spring. And the cooking method for the green vegetables—to blanch each one separately—doesn't help. Talk about bland.

A smarter approach is to pick vegetables that show up at markets at roughly the same time—leeks and asparagus—and then add peas. (Since fresh peas are rarely good, stick with frozen.) And to make the vegetables shine, use vegetable broth—not cream and butter—to build the backbone of the sauce.

Finally, ditch the multiple pans and turn this into a one-pot recipe where the pasta cooks in the sauce, much like risotto. The flavor of the vegetables is infused into every bite. Best of all, cooking pasta like risotto releases the starches in the noodles and creates a creamy sauce, all without adding a drop of cream or butter. Now that sounds like spring. Talk about taking a good idea and making it better.

WHY THIS RECIPE WORKS

Growing Vegetable Flavor
Chicken broth is typically used as the base of the sauce in primavera, but is it really the best choice? To build multiple levels of vegetable flavor, vegetable broth makes a lot more sense in this dish. To intensify the broth's flavor, save the trimmings from the leeks and asparagus to simmer in the store-bought broth. Peas and garlic punch up the flavor too.

Blanching Is Boring
Blanching each vegetable separately isn't just tedious—it's a poor way to cook the vegetables for this dish because much of the flavor goes down the drain. Instead, sauté the vegetables to concentrate their flavor. And this way, you can punch up their flavor further by adding garlic and red pepper flakes to the pan.

Cook the Pasta Like Rice
Tossing boiled pasta and sautéed vegetables with fortified broth, butter, and cream (the latter two for richness and body) delivers an OK dish. But for extraordinary flavor in every bite, rethink the pasta-cooking method. In risotto, rice is cooked in broth and swells into tender, flavorful grains. Pasta can be cooked this way too—starting by toasting it just as you would with rice before adding white wine (to brighten the sauce) and the broth. Once the liquid is absorbed, the pasta is coated with a light but lustrous, creamy sauce, bursting with vegetable flavor. Even better, this method negates the need for cream and butter, which can dull the vegetable flavor.

A Bright, Flavorful Finish
Sure, grated cheese is a fine finish for this dish, but a potent mix of chopped fresh mint, chives, and grated lemon zest (similar to a *gremolata*—an Italian condiment used to brighten dishes) will really make this pasta pop. Stir a portion into the hot pasta and serve the rest at the table along with grated Parmesan.

Cook pasta in vegetable broth and then finish with mint, chives, and lemon zest.

Spring Vegetable Pasta

SERVES 4 TO 6

Campanelle is our pasta of choice in this dish, but farfalle and penne are acceptable substitutes.

1½ pounds leeks, white and light green parts halved lengthwise, sliced ½ inch thick, and washed thoroughly; 3 cups coarsely chopped dark green parts, washed thoroughly

1 pound asparagus, tough ends trimmed, chopped coarse, and reserved; spears cut on bias into ½-inch lengths

2 cups frozen peas, thawed

4 garlic cloves, minced

4 cups vegetable broth

1 cup water

2 tablespoons minced fresh mint

2 tablespoons minced fresh chives

½ teaspoon grated lemon zest plus 2 tablespoons juice

6 tablespoons extra-virgin olive oil
Salt and pepper

¼ teaspoon red pepper flakes

1 pound campanelle

1 cup dry white wine

1 ounce Parmesan cheese, grated (½ cup), plus extra for serving

1. Bring leek greens, asparagus trimmings, 1 cup peas, half of garlic, broth, and water to simmer in large saucepan. Reduce heat to medium-low and simmer gently for 10 minutes. While broth simmers, combine mint, chives, and lemon zest in bowl; set aside.

2. Strain broth through fine-mesh strainer into large liquid measuring cup, pressing on solids to extract as much liquid as possible (you should have 5 cups broth; add water as needed to measure 5 cups). Discard solids and return broth to saucepan. Cover and keep warm.

3. Heat 2 tablespoons oil in Dutch oven over medium heat until shimmering. Add leeks and pinch salt and cook, covered, stirring occasionally, until leeks begin to brown, about 5 minutes. Add asparagus and cook until asparagus is crisp-tender, 4 to 6 minutes. Add pepper flakes and remaining garlic and cook until fragrant, about 30 seconds. Add remaining 1 cup peas and continue to cook 1 minute longer. Transfer vegetables to plate and set aside. Wipe out pot.

4. Heat remaining ¼ cup oil in now-empty pot over medium heat until shimmering. Add pasta and cook, stirring often, until just beginning to brown, about 5 minutes. Add wine and cook, stirring constantly, until absorbed, about 2 minutes.

5. When wine is fully absorbed, add warm broth and bring to boil. Cook, stirring frequently, until most of liquid is absorbed and pasta is al dente, 8 to 10 minutes. Off heat, stir in half of herb mixture, vegetables, lemon juice, and Parmesan. Season with salt and pepper to taste, and serve immediately, passing additional Parmesan and remaining herb mixture separately.

RECIPE DETAILS

Timeline

- 30 minutes to make broth (combine herbs and zest while broth simmers)
- 15 minutes to sauté vegetables (can be done while broth simmers)
- 8 minutes to toast pasta and cook off wine
- 10 minutes to cook pasta in broth and combine with other ingredients

Essential Tools

- Large saucepan to simmer broth
- Dutch oven to saute vegetables and cook pasta
- Rasp grater for lemon zest and Parmesan

Substitutions & Variations

- Good vegetable broth is key in this recipe. The test kitchen's favorite brands are Orrington Farms Vegan Chicken Flavored Broth Base (a powder you rehydrate as needed) and Swanson Certified Organic Vegetable Broth.
- You can vary the herbs if you like. Replace the mint with basil or tarragon and try thyme instead the chives. Even plain old parsley can be used in a pinch.
- If you can find fava beans, they make a nice addition to this dish. Replace the 1 cup of peas used in step 3 with an equal amount of freshly cooked and peeled fava beans. (Use the remaining 1 cup peas in step 1; it's a waste of expensive favas to use them in the broth.)

51 Manicotti

A SURPRISING NOODLE MAKES THIS DISH SO MUCH EASIER

We have a love/hate relationship with manicotti. Well-made versions of this Italian-American classic—pasta tubes stuffed with a rich ricotta filling and blanketed with tomato sauce—are true comfort food. So what's not to love? How about putting it all together?

For such a straightforward collection of ingredients (after all, manicotti is just pasta, cheese, and sauce), the directions found in most cookbooks are surprisingly fussy. Blanching, shocking, draining, and stuffing slippery pasta tubes requires a lot of patience and time. And who wants to wrestle with a pastry bag to make a family dinner?

Some historical research prompted us to devise an unorthodox method for simplifying this dish. Traditional recipes call for homemade crespelle (thin, crêpe-like pancakes) or rectangular sheets of fresh pasta. In either case, the filling is spread over the flat wrappers and the sheets are then rolled up into neat bundles. Since the filling isn't piped, there's no need for the dreaded pastry bag. Now, making crêpes or fresh pasta isn't convenient, but this research triggered a very good idea. Could we use another flat pasta sold in every supermarket—namely no-boil lasagna noodles—in their place?

The answer, we found, was yes. Soaking the noodles in boiling water for 5 minutes softens them just enough so they are pliable enough to roll around the filling. And hydrating the lasagna noodles in the baking dish that will eventually hold the filled manicotti means there are no extra pots of water, bowls of ice water, or colanders. When paired with a quick sauce, this humble family favorite is now easy to enjoy—and easy to prepare.

WHY THIS RECIPE WORKS

A Separate Soak

Briefly soaking the lasagna noodles in boiling water makes them pliable enough to roll. But the noodles can easily stick together. Use the tip of a paring knife to separate the noodles as they soak. And don't leave the noodles in the dish past the 5-minute mark or they'll become mushy. Transfer the soaked noodles to a clean dish towel to dry off excess moisture that might otherwise dilute the cheese filling.

A Better Filling

It's a given that ricotta makes the best base for the filling. Mozzarella (for both gooey richness and its binding properties) and Parmesan (for sharp, salty tang) round out the mild ricotta. However, mozzarella doesn't bind the filling sufficiently. Two eggs thicken it nicely. Fresh parsley and basil balance the dairy richness.

A Smooth Sauce in a Hurry

A fairly smooth tomato sauce is the best option for smothering the filled and rolled manicotti. Rather than slow-cooking the sauce to break down the tomatoes, we simply chop the canned diced tomatoes in a food processor before adding them to a pan with olive oil, garlic, and red pepper flakes. The sauce takes just 15 minutes to reach the perfect consistency. And we punch up the finished sauce with chopped basil for a hit of freshness.

Cover and Bake

To ensure fully cooked noodles, it's important to make sure the manicotti are thoroughly covered with the sauce. Covering the dish with foil also helps cook through the noodles since it traps the steam to create a moist cooking environment. A toasty crust of cheese is a must-have finishing touch and easy to do during the last few minutes of cooking. Sprinkling the manicotti with Parmesan and running the dish under the broiler does the job in about 5 minutes.

No-boil lasagna noodles are novel wrappers for an egg-enriched cheese and herb filling.

Baked Manicotti

SERVES 6 TO 8

Some brands contain only 12 no-boil noodles per package so buy two. If your baking dish is not broiler-safe (and glass dishes are not), brown the manicotti at 500 degrees for 10 minutes.

TOMATO SAUCE

- 2 (28-ounce) cans diced tomatoes
- 2 tablespoons extra-virgin olive oil
- 3 garlic cloves, minced
- ½ teaspoon red pepper flakes (optional)
- Salt
- 2 tablespoons chopped fresh basil

CHEESE FILLING

- 24 ounces (3 cups) part-skim ricotta cheese
- 8 ounces mozzarella cheese, shredded (2 cups)
- 4 ounces Parmesan cheese, grated (2 cups)
- 2 large eggs
- 2 tablespoons chopped fresh parsley
- 2 tablespoons chopped fresh basil
- ¾ teaspoon salt
- ½ teaspoon pepper

- 16 no-boil lasagna noodles

1. *For the Tomato Sauce:* Pulse 1 can tomatoes with their juice in food processor until coarsely chopped, 3 or 4 pulses; transfer to bowl. Repeat with remaining can tomatoes.

2. Heat oil, garlic, and pepper flakes, if using, in large saucepan over medium heat. Cook, stirring often, until garlic turns golden but not brown, about 3 minutes. Stir in chopped tomatoes and ½ teaspoon salt, bring to simmer, and cook until thickened slightly, about 15 minutes. Stir in basil and season with salt to taste.

3. *For the Cheese Filling:* Combine ricotta, mozzarella, 1 cup Parmesan, eggs, parsley, basil, salt, and pepper in bowl.

4. Adjust oven rack to middle position and heat oven to 375 degrees. Pour 2 inches boiling water into 13 by 9-inch broiler-safe baking dish. Slip noodles into water, one at a time, and soak until pliable, about 5 minutes, separating noodles with tip of sharp knife to prevent sticking. Remove noodles from water and place in single layer on clean dish towels; discard water and dry dish.

5. Spread 1½ cups sauce evenly over bottom of dish. Using spoon, spread ¼ cup cheese mixture evenly onto bottom three-quarters of each noodle (with short side facing you), leaving top quarter of noodle exposed. Roll into tube shape and arrange in dish seam side down. Top evenly with remaining sauce, making certain that pasta is completely covered. (Assembled manicotti can be covered with sheet of parchment paper, wrapped in aluminum foil, and refrigerated for up to 3 days or frozen for up to 1 month. If frozen, thaw manicotti in refrigerator for 1 to 2 days. To bake, remove parchment, replace foil, and increase baking time to 1 to 1¼ hours.)

6. Cover dish tightly with foil and bake until bubbling, about 40 minutes, rotating dish halfway through baking. Remove dish from oven and remove foil. Adjust oven rack 6 inches from broiler element and heat broiler. Sprinkle manicotti evenly with remaining 1 cup Parmesan. Broil until cheese is spotty brown, 4 to 6 minutes. Let manicotti cool for 15 minutes before serving.

RECIPE DETAILS

Timeline

- 25 minutes to make tomato sauce (prepare filling while sauce is simmering)
- 10 minutes to soak noodles and assemble dish
- 50 minutes to bake, then broil, manicotti
- 15 minutes to rest before serving (the cheese filling will firm up)

Essential Tools

- Food processor to puree tomatoes
- 13 by 9-inch broiler-safe baking dish (ceramic is best)
- Aluminum foil to trap steam and soften noodles

Substitutions & Variations

- It's easy enough to vary this recipe:
- Sausage: Cook 1 pound hot or sweet Italian sausage, casings removed, in 2 tablespoons olive oil in large saucepan over medium-high heat, breaking sausage into ½-inch pieces with wooden spoon, until no longer pink, about 6 minutes. Omit olive oil in sauce and cook remaining sauce ingredients in saucepan with sausage.
- Prosciutto: Reduce salt in cheese filling to ½ teaspoon and arrange 1 thin slice prosciutto on each noodle before topping with cheese mixture.
- Spinach: Add one 10-ounce package frozen chopped spinach, thawed, squeezed dry, and chopped fine, and pinch ground nutmeg to cheese filling. Increase salt in filling to 1 teaspoon.
- Puttanesca: Cook 3 rinsed and minced anchovy fillets with oil, garlic, and pepper flakes. Add ¼ cup pitted kalamata olives, quartered, and 2 tablespoons rinsed capers to cheese filling.

52 Lasagna

EVERYTHING YOU LOVE, MINUS THE COMPLICATED CONSTRUCTION

Lasagna is eminently popular, served at potlucks, church suppers, and kitchen tables. But in most homes lasagna is weekend food, prepared only when time permits. You need to make the sauce, grate the cheeses, and then layer ingredients into the baking dish. The advent of no-boil noodles has eliminated the tedious steps of cooking, draining, and shocking the pasta, but the process still takes at least 90 minutes once you factor in the baking time.

However, if you are willing to live without the layered construction, you can make lasagna in a skillet in half the time. Because the pasta cooks in the same pan used to make the sauce, the "baking" time is just 20 minutes. On the stovetop, the heat transfer is superefficient and the lid traps heat and cooks the noodles very quickly. Best of all, cleanup is a breeze since there are no other pots to wash.

To our surprise, this recipe is better with old-fashioned curly-edged pasta (the kind used by your mother) than newfangled no-boil noodles. The latter become mushy in this preparation. And reducing the simmering time even further (yes, we tried this) doesn't give the sauce time to thicken properly.

But there's another unexpected benefit to using curly-edged noodles. Because these dry noodles are typically boiled, they are designed to soak up liquid. Rather than absorbing water, these noodles soak up tons of flavor from the sauce and actually taste better than noodles baked in a conventional lasagna. Just another good reason to trade in your baking dish for a skillet.

WHY THIS RECIPE WORKS

Three Meats Are Better Than One
After sautéing onion and garlic, brown the meat in the pan to develop its flavor. Meatloaf mix (a blend of ground beef, pork, and veal) contributes deep, meaty flavor to the dish and requires no extra work.

Pasta Break
Naturally, you can't fit full sheets of lasagna noodles in a skillet, but you can break them up into fork-friendly pieces. No-boil lasagna noodles don't work well here—regular, curly-edged noodles are thicker so they'll absorb (and capture) more flavor from the meaty tomato sauce.

Make It Saucy
Canned diced tomatoes and tomato sauce, thinned with water, provide ample liquid to cook our noodles and they thicken to just the right consistency after simmering. The richness of the seasoned browned meat simmering in the sauce also gives it long-cooked flavor in very little time. Don't worry if everything seems too watery at first—the dried noodles will absorb much of the liquid. Remember to use a skillet with a tight-fitting lid for tender noodles and a perfectly thickened sauce.

Wait on the Ricotta
Parmesan is stirred into the cooked noodles to add salty, nutty flavor, but when it comes to cheese in lasagna, ricotta is the star of the show. Too bad it often turns out dry and grainy. That's because this naturally low-fat cheese easily dries out in the oven. Things are even worse in a lidded skillet—the agitation of the bubbling sauce will break the ricotta into tiny, unappealing curds. For creamy pockets of cheese, remove the skillet from the heat and drop big spoonfuls of ricotta over the cooked noodles. Quickly cover the pan and let it sit just long enough to warm up the ricotta. A handful of chopped basil sprinkled over the skillet lasagna provides a bright, fresh finishing touch.

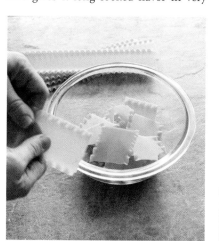

Making lasagna in a skillet means breaking some rules—and some noodles.

Skillet Meaty Lasagna

SERVES 4 TO 6

Do not use no-boil noodles in this recipe. If the curly-edged noodles are especially dry and prone to shattering, you may need to add extra water to the skillet while the pasta cooks.

1	(28-ounce) can diced tomatoes	10	curly-edged lasagna noodles, broken into 2-inch lengths
	Water		
1	tablespoon olive oil	1	(8-ounce) can tomato sauce
1	onion, chopped fine	1	ounce Parmesan cheese, grated (½ cup), plus 2 tablespoons, grated
	Salt and pepper		
3	garlic cloves, minced	8	ounces (1 cup) whole-milk ricotta cheese
⅛	teaspoon red pepper flakes		
1	pound meatloaf mix	3	tablespoons chopped fresh basil

1. Place tomatoes and their juice in 4-cup liquid measuring cup. Add water until mixture measures 4 cups.

2. Heat oil in 12-inch nonstick skillet over medium heat until shimmering. Add onion and ½ teaspoon salt and cook until onion begins to brown, about 5 minutes. Stir in garlic and pepper flakes and cook until fragrant, about 30 seconds. Add meatloaf mix and cook, breaking up meat into small pieces with wooden spoon, until it is no longer pink, about 4 minutes.

3. Scatter noodles over meat but don't stir. Pour tomato mixture and tomato sauce over noodles, cover, and bring to simmer. Reduce heat to medium-low and simmer, stirring occasionally, until noodles are tender, about 20 minutes.

4. Off heat, stir in ½ cup Parmesan and season with salt and pepper to taste. Dollop heaping tablespoons of ricotta over top, cover, and let sit for 5 minutes. Sprinkle with basil and remaining 2 tablespoons Parmesan. Serve.

SKILLET LASAGNA WITH SAUSAGE AND RED BELL PEPPER

Substitute 1 pound Italian sausage, casings removed, for meatloaf mix. Add 1 chopped red bell pepper to skillet with onion.

RECIPE DETAILS

Timeline

- 10 minutes to prepare ingredients
- 10 minutes to sauté ingredients
- 20 minutes to cook noodles (mostly hands-off)
- 5 minutes to finish dish

Essential Tools

- 12-inch nonstick skillet with tight-fitting lid

Substitutions & Variations

- If meatloaf mix is not available, use 8 ounces each ground pork and 85 percent lean ground beef.
- You can substitute part-skim ricotta in this recipe, but do not use nonfat ricotta, which has a very dry texture and bland flavor.
- To make this dish spicy, increase the amount of pepper flakes to 1 teaspoon.

53 Pasta with Fresh Tomatoes

THE BEST DISH TO MAKE WITH PERFECT SUMMER INGREDIENTS

Legend has it that the popular Caprese trio of garden tomatoes, fresh mozzarella, and basil leaves was introduced in the 1950s at Trattoria Da Vincenzo, a beachside restaurant on the Italian island of Capri. According to creator Margherita Cosentino, the red, white, and green salad of local produce and cheese allowed ladies to "have a nice lunch while still fitting into their bikinis."

Swimsuit season or not, the combination became so popular that chefs everywhere took to mixing it with hot pasta, minced garlic, and extra-virgin olive oil for an entrée that captures the flavors of summer. This light pasta dish also requires very little effort, which probably explains its popularity in home kitchens.

But the fresh mozzarella used in Italian restaurants is not the same as the fresh cheese packed in water and sold at American supermarkets. Most good restaurants use handmade cheese, made either with cow's milk or the milk of Italian water buffalo. It turns out the type of milk doesn't really affect this dish—but the way the cheese is kneaded does.

When this dish is made with handmade cheese, the mozzarella softens beautifully into pillowy chunks that play nicely with the tomatoes and hot pasta. But the fresh mozzarella packed in tubs of water and sold in American supermarkets is kneaded by machine. And when this cheese is tossed with hot pasta it clumps together into a tough, rubbery ball. Since buying handmade mozzarella isn't always an option, we needed to figure out a way to keep supermarket fresh mozzarella from balling up into an unappealing tangle. Luckily, the solution to this American problem doesn't destroy the simplicity of this Italian summer classic.

WHY THIS RECIPE WORKS

All Mozzarella Is Not Created Equal

The fresh mozzarella packed in water and sold in American supermarkets has a long shelf life, often several months. That's because it's kneaded by machines to facilitate production and it also has less water, fat, and whey than handmade cheese. This kneading process also changes the structure of the protein network in the cheese, which causes it to turn tough and ropy when melted. But because supermarket cheese is so much more convenient, we were convinced we had to find a way to make it work in this pasta dish.

The Quick Chill

It turns out that the proteins in fresh mozzarella begin to melt at about 130 degrees. As the temperature climbs past 130 degrees, the proteins clump together. Slowing down the melting process is an easy fix. Place the cheese in the freezer for about 10 minutes to chill the cheese enough so that once it's combined with the pasta, it doesn't overheat and push past that 130-degree mark and instead slowly melts into creamy pockets.

Marinate the Tomatoes

To capture the flavors of summer, this sauce is marinated rather than cooked. Be sure to start with good extra-virgin olive oil (the kind that tastes fruity and peppery) and add lemon juice, garlic, shallot, salt, and few grinds of pepper to produce a well-seasoned sauce. Marinate the tomatoes while the pasta cooks; avoid marinating the tomatoes further ahead—after 45 minutes the tomatoes will turn mealy.

Sauce and Wait

This pasta isn't meant to be served piping hot—remember that it's a summertime dish. After combining the pasta with the tomato sauce and mozzarella, let it sit for about 5 minutes so that the pasta can absorb some of the sauce. A sprinkling of chopped fresh basil adds another layer of summery flavor.

Pasta Caprese requires just a handful of ingredients, but each one must be perfectly prepared.

Pasta Caprese

SERVES 4

This dish will be very warm, not hot. The success of this recipe depends on high-quality ingredients, including ripe, in-season tomatoes and a fruity olive oil. Don't skip the step of freezing the mozzarella, as freezing prevents it from turning chewy when it comes in contact with the hot pasta.

¼ cup extra-virgin olive oil

2 teaspoons lemon juice, plus extra as needed

1 small shallot, minced

1 small garlic clove, minced

Salt and pepper

1½ pounds tomatoes, cored, seeded, and cut into ½-inch pieces

12 ounces fresh mozzarella cheese, cut into ½-inch pieces and patted dry with paper towels

1 pound penne, fusilli, or other short, tubular pasta

¼ cup chopped fresh basil

Sugar

1. Whisk oil, lemon juice, shallot, garlic, ½ teaspoon salt, and ¼ teaspoon pepper together in large bowl. Add tomatoes and gently toss to combine; set aside. (Do not marinate tomatoes for longer than 45 minutes.)

2. While tomatoes are marinating, place mozzarella on plate and freeze until slightly firm, about 10 minutes. Bring 4 quarts water to boil in large pot. Add pasta and 1 tablespoon salt and cook, stirring often, until al dente. Drain pasta well.

3. Add pasta and mozzarella to tomato mixture and gently toss to combine. Let sit for 5 minutes. Stir in basil, season with additional lemon juice, salt, pepper, and sugar to taste, and serve immediately.

RECIPE DETAILS

Timeline

• 1 hour to prepare and marinate tomatoes (boil water, freeze cheese, and cook pasta while tomatoes marinate)

• 5 minutes to let sauced pasta sit and cheese soften

Essential Tools

• Paring knife for coring tomatoes

• Large bowl for marinating tomatoes (Make sure the bowl is large enough to hold the pasta and let you toss together all the ingredients.)

• Plate for freezing mozzarella

Substitutions & Variations

• If handmade buffalo- or cow's-milk mozzarella is available (it's commonly found in gourmet and cheese shops packed in water), we highly recommend using it, but do not freeze it.

• There's something appealing about the utter simplicity of this recipe, but it does allow for some modest improvisation. Pitted chopped olives are a nice addition, and feel free to use another fresh herb along with (or instead of) the basil.

54 Potato Salad

A LIGHTER FRENCH TAKE ON AN AMERICAN CLASSIC

No picnic or summer cookout is complete without a big bowl of potato salad. Creamy and cool, it's the perfect side to barbecue, fried chicken, and almost anything from the grill. But when you taste this mayo-heavy salad on its own—that is, without a forkful of brisket or a bite of fried chicken—it doesn't have all that much personality. You mostly taste the rich dressing. The potatoes offer up their crumbly texture but not much in the way of actual flavor.

But potato salad doesn't have to be bland, right? It must be possible to prepare the potatoes so their flavor is more present in this dish. After all, potatoes are boiled for many other dishes (think mashed potatoes) and still retain their earthy, sweet flavor. The problem isn't the cooking method. It's the temperature (chilled foods often taste quite dull) and the flavor-deadening mayonnaise dressing.

To create a more versatile (and flavor-forward) potato salad, one that would work just as well with a grilled steak as a piece of fish, we looked to France. In Parisian bistros, potato salad is tossed with a lively herb and mustard vinaigrette. Not only is this approach so much lighter, but the bright vinaigrette also does a better job of flavoring the salad. It infuses the potatoes rather than coating them.

This style of potato salad is served warm or at room temperature so there's no flavor-dulling from a trip to the fridge. And no chilling means French potato salad can be ready in the time it takes to light the grill and cook dinner. We suspect that once you try the French approach to this American classic, you will be hooked.

WHY THIS RECIPE WORKS

Slice and Boil
Sliced red potatoes emerge from the cooking water with their skins intact. They have a clean (not starchy) taste, are evenly cooked, and hold together perfectly to make an attractive salad without torn skins or broken pieces.

Ramp Up the Vinegar
Classic vinaigrette recipes use a tame 1 part vinegar to 4 parts oil, but bland potatoes can handle extra acid, so it's best to go for 1 part vinegar to just 3 parts oil. Champagne vinegar adds sharp, bright flavor notes but white wine vinegar works well, too. Mustard helps emulsify the vinaigrette and adds a warm tang.

Save Some Cooking Water
Dressing potatoes with vinaigrette alone can yield a dry salad. Some recipes add chicken stock or wine. We take a cue from Julia Child and use some of the potato water from the pot. It's nicely seasoned and readily available.

Blanch Out the Bite
Raw garlic is too pungent a flavor for this delicate potato salad. Blanching the garlic clove before adding it to the dressing tones it down. And you can blanch the garlic right in the pot with the potatoes.

Spread and Dress
After the potatoes have been thoroughly drained, spread them out on a rimmed baking sheet and drizzle them with the vinaigrette. Spreading out the potatoes allows them to cool off a bit, preventing residual cooking and potential mushiness. It also allows us to get the warm potatoes to soak up the vinaigrette without damaging the slices by tossing them.

Shower with Herbs
Once the potato slices have absorbed the vinaigrette, transfer them to a wide, shallow serving bowl. Finish the potatoes with lots of chopped soft green herbs and a minced shallot and walk straight to the table instead of the fridge.

Poaching the garlic and then dressing the hot potatoes are two secrets to this bistro classic.

French Potato Salad with Mustard and Herbs

SERVES 6

For best flavor, serve the salad warm.

2 **pounds small red potatoes, unpeeled, cut into ¼-inch-thick slices**	¼ **cup olive oil**
2 **tablespoons salt**	½ **teaspoon pepper**
1 **garlic clove, peeled and threaded on skewer**	1 **small shallot, minced**
1½ **tablespoons champagne vinegar or white wine vinegar**	1 **tablespoon minced fresh chervil**
2 **teaspoons Dijon mustard**	1 **tablespoon minced fresh parsley**
	1 **tablespoon minced fresh chives**
	1 **teaspoon minced fresh tarragon**

1. Place potatoes and salt in large saucepan and add water to cover by 1 inch; bring to boil over high heat, then reduce heat to medium. Lower skewered garlic into simmering water and partially blanch, about 45 seconds. Immediately run garlic under cold running water to stop cooking; remove garlic from skewer and set aside. Continue to simmer potatoes, uncovered, until tender but still firm (thin-bladed paring knife can be slipped into and out of center of potato slice with no resistance), about 5 minutes. Reserve ¼ cup cooking water, then drain potatoes. Arrange hot potatoes close together in single layer on rimmed baking sheet.

2. Press garlic through garlic press or mince by hand. Whisk garlic, reserved potato cooking water, vinegar, mustard, oil, and pepper in small bowl until combined. Drizzle dressing evenly over warm potatoes; let stand 10 minutes. (Potatoes can be refrigerated for up to 2 days. Bring to room temperature before proceeding.)

3. Toss shallot and herbs in small bowl. Transfer potatoes to large serving bowl; add shallot-herb mixture and mix gently with rubber spatula to combine. Serve immediately.

FRENCH POTATO SALAD WITH ARUGULA, ROQUEFORT, AND WALNUTS

Omit herbs and toss dressed potatoes with ½ cup walnuts, toasted and chopped coarse, 1 cup crumbled Roquefort cheese, and 3 ounces baby arugula, torn into bite-size pieces (3 cups) along with shallot in step 3.

FRENCH POTATO SALAD WITH RADISHES, CORNICHONS, AND CAPERS

Omit herbs and substitute 2 tablespoons minced red onion for shallot. Toss dressed potatoes with 2 thinly sliced red radishes, ¼ cup rinsed and drained capers, and ¼ cup thinly sliced cornichons along with red onion in step 3.

RECIPE DETAILS

Timeline

- 10 minutes to prep potatoes and garlic
- 15 minutes to cook potatoes and blanch garlic (time will vary depending on how quickly water comes to a boil)
- 5 minutes to make dressing and drizzle over potatoes
- 10 minutes to let potatoes absorb dressing and cool
- 5 minutes to finish salad

Essential Tools

- Skewer for blanching garlic
- Paring knife for testing potatoes for doneness
- Rimmed baking sheet for cooling and dressing potatoes

Substitutions & Variations

- If fresh chervil isn't available, substitute an additional ½ tablespoon minced parsley and an additional ½ teaspoon minced tarragon.
- In addition to the variations listed, other possible additions to this salad include thinly sliced fennel, diced and seeded tomatoes, and chopped olives.

55 Composed Salad

ALICE WATERS WAS RIGHT ABOUT THIS DISH

A composed salad sounds like the perfect first course or lunch entrée. These fancy salads are a mainstay on restaurant menus because they are so much fun to eat. Each bite is a bit different from the last one.

Unfortunately, most composed salads don't work at home. There are just too many individual components to prepare. But there is an exception—a salad of tender greens topped with warm rounds of goat cheese that have been dusted with crisp crumbs.

The popularity of this combination can be traced to Alice Waters and her Berkeley restaurant Chez Panisse. Back in the early 1970s, Waters devised a menu of French-inspired dishes that showcased local Bay Area ingredients, including goat cheese. Many of the most important food trends of the past 40 years started in her restaurant kitchen.

With the help of legendary *New York Times* food editor Craig Claiborne, who wrote about this dish in 1983, baked goat cheese salad (also known as warm goat cheese salad) became a mainstay on restaurants menus across the country. And this dish has remained popular ever since for good reason. The crumb coating provides textural contrast to the soft cheese, while the acidity of vinaigrette keeps the richness in check. (This is a first course, after all.)

Goat cheese can be fairly pungent so this dish works best with salad greens that have some personality. A mix of greens (such as mesclun) provides some of the variety one expects from a composed salad. And for those with the time and inclination, the salad can be further embellished with fruit, nuts, or even a slice or two of prosciutto. This is California cuisine at its best.

WHY THIS RECIPE WORKS

The Answer Is the Oven
Restaurant cooks often pan-fry the goat cheese in this dish, which makes sense when you're cooking the cheese to order—and when you have multiple cooks on the line to handle the orders coming in. But at home, you're on your own, so turning multiple delicate disks of cheese in a skillet of hot oil without marring their browned crust becomes impractical. What works? Baking.

The Right Crumb
Baking the goat cheese rounds requires a durable breading to create a truly crisp crust. Melba toast, one of the sturdiest crackers around, is ideal once pulverized into sandy crumbs. You might think they'd be too dry, but brushing the crumb-coated rounds with olive oil gives the crumbs plenty of richness.

Build Flavor
The combination of herbs and goat cheese is a natural, so before coating the rounds in the crumb mixture, roll the cheese in chopped fresh thyme and chives. Dunking the herb-coated rounds in beaten egg helps the crumbs adhere, but eggs alone don't do much for flavor. Stirring a little mustard into the egg adds a pleasant bite.

Freeze, Please
Baking is easier than frying, but it does take a long time for the crust to brown. In fact, it takes so long that the cheese can melt into an unappealing puddle. In order to give the crust enough time to brown, freeze the cheese for 30 minutes before baking.

Cool and Serve
The baked goat cheese rounds will be too hot to serve right out of the oven. Let them cool for a few minutes while you toss together the salad. There's plenty of richness in this salad from the cheese, so when dressing the greens, remember that a little vinaigrette goes a long way.

Herbed goat cheese rounds are dipped in a mustardy wash and then rolled in Melba crumbs.

Salad with Herbed Baked Goat Cheese

SERVES 6

Hearty salad greens, such as a mix of arugula and frisée, work best here.

2	tablespoons red wine vinegar		Pepper
1	tablespoon Dijon mustard	14	ounces (14 cups) mixed hearty
1	teaspoon minced shallot		salad greens
¼	teaspoon salt	1	recipe Herbed Baked Goat Cheese
6	tablespoons extra-virgin olive oil		(recipe follows)

1. Combine vinegar, mustard, shallot, and salt in small bowl. Whisking constantly, drizzle in oil; season with pepper to taste.

2. Place greens in large bowl, drizzle vinaigrette over, and toss to coat. Divide greens among individual plates; place 2 rounds warm goat cheese on each salad. Serve immediately.

HERBED BAKED GOAT CHEESE MAKES 12 ROUNDS
The baked goat cheese should be served warm.

3	ounces white Melba toasts (2 cups)	1	tablespoon minced fresh thyme
1	teaspoon pepper	1	tablespoon minced fresh chives
3	large eggs	12	ounces firm goat cheese
2	tablespoons Dijon mustard		Extra-virgin olive oil

1. Process Melba toasts in a food processor to fine even crumbs, about 1½ minutes; transfer crumbs to medium bowl and stir in pepper. Whisk eggs and mustard in second medium bowl until combined. Combine thyme and chives in small bowl.

2. Using kitchen twine or dental floss, divide cheese into 12 even pieces. Roll each piece into ball; roll each ball in herbs to coat lightly. Transfer 6 pieces to egg mixture, turn each piece to coat; transfer to Melba crumbs and turn each piece to coat, pressing crumbs into cheese. Flatten each ball into disk about 1½ inches wide and 1 inch thick and set on baking sheet. Repeat process with remaining 6 pieces cheese. Freeze cheese until firm, about 30 minutes. (Cheese may be wrapped tightly in plastic wrap and frozen for 1 week.) Adjust oven rack to top position; heat oven to 475 degrees.

3. Remove cheese from freezer and brush tops and sides evenly with oil. Bake until crumbs are golden brown and cheese is slightly soft, 7 to 9 minutes (or 9 to 12 minutes if cheese is completely frozen). Using thin metal spatula, transfer cheese to paper towel–lined plate and let cool 3 minutes before serving.

RECIPE DETAILS

Timeline

• 15 minutes to coat goat cheese

• 30 minutes to freeze goat cheese (preheat oven and make dressing while cheese is chilling)

• 10 minutes to bake and cool goat cheese (dress salad greens while cheese is cooling)

Essential Tools

• Food processor to grind Melba toasts

• Kitchen twine or dental floss to cut goat cheese

Substitutions & Variations

• Here are two simple ideas for dressing up this salad:

• Dried Cherries, Walnuts, and Apples: Plump 1 cup dried cherries in ½ cup hot water for 10 minutes; drain. Divide cherries; 2 Granny Smith apples, sliced ⅛ inch thick, and ½ cup walnuts, toasted and chopped, among individual plates. Use cider vinegar in dressing.

• Grapes, Pine Nuts, and Prosciutto: Divide 1¼ cups red seedless grapes, halved, ½ cup toasted pine nuts, and 6 ounces thinly sliced prosciutto among individual plates. Use balsamic vinegar in dressing.

56 Cheese Soufflé

IT'S NEITHER FUSSY NOR FICKLE, AND IT'S SURPRISINGLY GOOD

A well-made cheese soufflé is a thing of beauty. Ethereally light eggs and nutty, tangy Gruyère cheese lifted to startlingly tall heights can't help but impress. And if you use good-quality cheese, the flavor of this dish will match its stunning looks. So why has the cheese soufflé almost disappeared from the modern table?

Classic cookbooks intimidate prospective cooks with pages upon pages filled with precise instructions for whipping egg whites, folding them into the soufflé base, and timing this dish perfectly. If you believe these experts, preparing a soufflé is a high-wire act likely to end in an embarrassing collapse if the slightest detail goes wrong. We respectfully disagree.

A soufflé won't fall because of loud noises or sudden movements, so go ahead and open that oven door to check on its progress and don't worry about the kids or the dog. The egg whites in a soufflé can withstand aggressive beating. There's no need to fret over gently folding the beaten whites into the base—in fact, we use a stand mixer for the job.

And soufflés certainly are not complicated. A cheese soufflé is nothing more than a sauce transformed into dinner through the addition of egg whites and air. The sauce itself is dead simple: Melt butter, stir in flour and seasonings, whisk in milk, and cook until thick and smooth. At this point, you add the cheese and egg yolks, followed by the whipped whites. That's it.

We think a cheese soufflé might just be the most impressive dish any cook—even someone with modest skills—can prepare. So put aside your fears (they are groundless) and rediscover the pleasures of a great cheese soufflé.

WHY THIS RECIPE WORKS

The Big Cheese
Most cheese soufflés start with a béchamel, essentially a butter and milk sauce thickened with flour—but that flour can dull the cheese flavor. Dialing down the flour and increasing the cheese—nutty Gruyère is classic—is a better strategy. Using all Gruyère results in a squat soufflé, but supplementing some of the Gruyère with feather-light but intensely flavored Parmesan works like a charm.

Whip It Good
Whipping egg whites to stiff peaks (until they're glossy, firm, and hold their shape) creates maximum volume, which you would think would be a good thing in soufflé. But it's also what gives it too much airiness. Whipping the egg whites to stiff peaks and then whipping in the cheese mixture breaks down some of the structure and brings the whites just where they need to be. As for the conventional step of folding the whites into the cheese base gradually and gently? Forget it. Folding in the whites all at once turns out a beautifully risen soufflé.

No Collars Needed
The theory with a parchment collar (securing a piece of parchment around the lip of the dish), is that it will create a tall soufflé, while preventing overflow as the soufflé rises. Save yourself some bother and simply leave at least 1 inch between the top of the batter and the dish—you'll get the same results.

Judging Doneness
When is it time to pull the soufflé from the oven? Please don't rely on the jiggle test. You might as well be looking at a crystal ball for signs of doneness. A soufflé is not a balloon—it's a matrix of very fine bubbles. No tool can pop enough of them to cause it to fall. So go ahead and use an instant-read thermometer when you really want to know when your soufflé is ready to be served.

Parmesan in the dish and two cheeses in the base create a soufflé packed with flavor.

Cheese Soufflé

SERVES 4 TO 6

Serve this soufflé with a green salad for a light dinner. To prevent the soufflé from overflowing the soufflé dish, leave at least 1 inch of space between the top of the batter and the rim of the dish; any excess batter should be discarded. The most foolproof way to test for doneness is with an instant-read thermometer. To judge doneness without an instant-read thermometer, use two large spoons to pry open the soufflé so that you can peer inside it; the center should appear thick and creamy but not soupy.

1 ounce Parmesan cheese, grated (½ cup)	4 tablespoons unsalted butter
¼ cup (1¼ ounces) all-purpose flour	1⅓ cups whole milk
¼ teaspoon paprika	6 ounces Gruyère cheese, shredded (1½ cups)
¼ teaspoon salt	6 large eggs, separated
⅛ teaspoon cayenne pepper	2 teaspoons minced fresh parsley
⅛ teaspoon white pepper	¼ teaspoon cream of tartar
Pinch ground nutmeg	

1. Adjust oven rack to middle position and heat oven to 350 degrees. Spray 8-inch round (2-quart) soufflé dish with vegetable oil spray, then sprinkle with 2 tablespoons Parmesan.

2. Combine flour, paprika, salt, cayenne, white pepper, and nutmeg in bowl. Melt butter in small saucepan over medium heat. Stir in flour mixture and cook for 1 minute. Slowly whisk in milk and bring to simmer. Cook, whisking constantly, until mixture is thickened and smooth, about 1 minute. Remove pan from heat and whisk in Gruyère and 5 tablespoons Parmesan until melted and smooth. Let cool for 10 minutes, then whisk in egg yolks and 1½ teaspoons parsley.

3. Using stand mixer fitted with whisk, whip egg whites and cream of tartar on medium-low speed until foamy, about 1 minute. Increase speed to medium-high and whip until stiff peaks form, 3 to 4 minutes. Add cheese mixture and continue to whip until fully combined, about 15 seconds.

4. Pour mixture into prepared dish and sprinkle with remaining 1 tablespoon Parmesan. Bake until risen above rim, top is deep golden brown, and interior registers 170 degrees, 30 to 35 minutes. Sprinkle with remaining ½ teaspoon parsley and serve immediately.

RECIPE DETAILS

Timeline

• 10 minutes to grate cheeses and separate eggs
• 15 minutes to make and cool soufflé base (whip egg whites while base cools)
• 35 minutes to fold in whites and bake soufflé

Essential Tools

• 8-inch round (2-quart) soufflé dish
• Stand mixer (A handheld electric mixer is fine too, as is a whisk, if you're willing to expend some elbow grease to whip the whites.)
• Instant-read thermometer (the most reliable way to judge doneness)

Substitutions & Variations

• Comté, sharp cheddar, or gouda cheese can be substituted for the Gruyère.

57 Cauliflower Soup

AN UNLIKELY METHOD REVEALS A SWEET SIDE TO THIS VEGGIE

If you judge cauliflower by the soups typically made with it, you might think this white vegetable is devoid not only of color but also of flavor. That's because most cauliflower soups go overboard on the cream, thicken with flour, or incorporate ingredients like bacon or curry powder, whose potent flavors smother this vegetable's more delicate ones.

But unlike potatoes (which are often used to similar effect in pureed soups), cauliflower actually has a wide range of flavors—from bright and cabbage-like to nutty and even sweet. The trick is to cook the cauliflower so these flavors come through in a soup.

The first step to repairing this recipe is omitting the cream. Most vegetables contain a lot of fiber that never breaks down, even after prolonged cooking. The cream is added to pureed soups to provide the illusion of silky smoothness. But cooked cauliflower purees more completely than other vegetables. It's creamy without the addition of cream.

And forget about using flour. This old-fashioned approach was designed to "stretch" a vegetable soup to serve more people. The modern cook should instead thicken pureed soups with more vegetables. It's also important to choose other ingredients that complement the flavor of the cauliflower. Leeks, onions, and a garnish of chives all play up the earthy, sweet notes in cauliflower.

But the real secret to this recipe is how the cauliflower is prepared. One head of cauliflower gets divided into three piles, each cooked differently, to create a soup that showcases the full range of flavors in this humble vegetable. This might just be the best soup you can make with so few ingredients.

WHY THIS RECIPE WORKS

Creamy Without the Cream
All vegetables have both soluble and insoluble fiber, but only the soluble kind fully breaks down during cooking, which contributes viscosity to soup. Insoluble fiber remains intact, and the best that the blades of a blender can do is break it down into smaller bits. But cauliflower has a leg up on other vegetables. It's very low in overall fiber—and only half of it is insoluble. This means that cauliflower is easily pureed into a silky-smooth soup with no cream at all.

Water, Not Broth
Chicken or vegetable broth might seem like they'd add flavor to this soup—and they will. But chicken broth is too dominant and vegetable broth muddies the cauliflower flavor. Sticking with water and reaching for onion and leek gives the soup a pleasant background sweetness and welcome grassiness. And when it comes to a cooking fat in this soup, the sweet, rich flavor of butter is best.

Coaxing Out Different Flavors
Cauliflower's flavor changes dramatically depending on how long you cook it. Shorter cooking times bring out its cabbage-like flavors, while longer cooking times turn it nuttier and sweet. Too much cooking time drives off all its flavor. To bring the full spectrum of possible flavors into this soup, add a portion of the cauliflower to the pot earlier in the cooking process and a portion a bit later.

A Cauliflower Garnish
Skip the usual crouton garnish and instead bring the intense nuttiness of roasted cauliflower to this soup by frying a handful of florets in lots of butter until golden brown. Tossed with sherry vinegar, the florets make an excellent complement when spooned onto the clean-tasting puree. And the browned butter left in the pan should not be forgotten; drizzling it over each bowl adds a complex richness as well as visual appeal.

To highlight the star ingredient, keep it simple—a sliced leek, butter, and lots of cauliflower.

Creamy Cauliflower Soup

SERVES 4 TO 6

Be sure to thoroughly trim the cauliflower's core of green leaves and leaf stems, which can be fibrous and contribute to a grainy texture in the soup.

1	head cauliflower (2 pounds)	1	small onion, halved and sliced thin
8	tablespoons unsalted butter, cut into 8 pieces		Salt and pepper
1	leek, white and light green parts only, halved lengthwise, sliced thin, and washed thoroughly	4½–5	cups water
		½	teaspoon sherry vinegar
		3	tablespoons minced fresh chives

1. Pull off outer leaves of cauliflower and trim stem. Using paring knife, cut around core to remove; slice core thin and reserve. Cut heaping 1 cup of ½-inch florets from head of cauliflower; set aside. Cut remaining cauliflower crosswise into ½-inch-thick slices.

2. Melt 3 tablespoons butter in large saucepan over medium-low heat. Add leek, onion, and 1½ teaspoons salt; cook, stirring frequently, until leek and onion are softened but not browned, about 7 minutes.

3. Increase heat to medium-high; add 4½ cups water, sliced core, and half of sliced cauliflower; and bring to simmer. Reduce heat to medium-low and simmer gently for 15 minutes. Add remaining sliced cauliflower, return to simmer, and continue to cook until cauliflower is tender and crumbles easily, 15 to 20 minutes longer.

4. While soup simmers, melt remaining 5 tablespoons butter in 8-inch skillet over medium heat. Add reserved florets and cook, stirring frequently, until florets are golden brown and butter is browned and imparts nutty aroma, 6 to 8 minutes. Remove skillet from heat and use slotted spoon to transfer florets to small bowl. Toss florets with vinegar and season with salt to taste. Pour browned butter in skillet into small bowl and reserve for garnishing.

5. Process soup in blender until smooth, about 45 seconds. Rinse out pan. Return pureed soup to pan and return to simmer over medium heat, adjusting consistency with remaining water as needed (soup should have thick, velvety texture but should be thin enough to settle with flat surface after being stirred) and seasoning with salt to taste. Serve, garnishing individual bowls with browned florets, drizzle of browned butter, and chives and seasoning with pepper to taste.

RECIPE DETAILS

Timeline

• 10 minutes to prepare cauliflower, leek, and onion

• 50 minutes to prepare soup (make garnish during this time)

• 5 minutes to puree, reheat, and season soup

Essential Tools

• Large saucepan for making soup

• 8-inch skillet for making garnish (Use a pan with a shiny or light surface so you can see when the butter has browned; don't use a nonstick pan.)

• Blender

Substitutions & Variations

• White wine vinegar may be substituted for the sherry vinegar.

58 Tomato Soup

REMOVE THE CREAM SO YOU CAN ACTUALLY TASTE THE TOMATOES

A warm bowl of tomato soup brings out the kid in all of us. But don't expect the familiar red-and-white striped can to provide as much satisfaction today as it did years ago. A grown-up palate will realize the contents are so sweet they are best described as "cream of ketchup soup." You can do better.

Tomato soup should have a bright taste balanced by the fruit's natural sweetness. And it must be velvety smooth. Many homemade versions get the texture right (add enough cream and any soup will be creamy), but the flavor is awfully dull. We find that adding any amount of cream to this recipe goes hand in hand with muting flavor.

But if you omit the cream, the tomatoes don't have sufficient body to make soup. And they taste very tart. Fixing the flavor is fairly easy. Sautéing an onion ramps up the sweet notes and balances the acidity of the tomatoes. Adding a spoonful of brown sugar (preferred over white sugar for its complexity) also helps.

The texture is a bigger challenge because cooked tomatoes are so watery. Soups that dial back the cream often rely on a starch to thicken the puree. Unfortunately, flour and cornstarch just make the tomatoes slimy, and adding a potato or handful of rice seems like a lot of work for a soup that should be simple. We took inspiration from a summer tomato soup. Gazpacho is often thickened with bread, a tradition that probably began for reasons of thrift. For our wintery soup, we blend the cooked tomatoes with a few slices of sandwich bread to create a velvety soup without a drop of cream. However unlikely, this Spanish innovation fixes an iconic American recipe.

WHY THIS RECIPE WORKS

Start with Canned Tomatoes

Canned tomatoes are almost always far better than "fresh" supermarket tomatoes; plus, they're already peeled. Whole tomatoes work better than diced, which often contain calcium chloride, an additive that prevents them from breaking down completely. And don't worry about needing to chop them up—the whole tomatoes will get crushed into small pieces with a potato masher right in the pot—and later whirred in a blender.

Oil, Not Butter

Butter lends a sweet, rich flavor to soups, but in this case the milk solids in the butter dull the flavor of the tomatoes. An easy fix is to swap in extra-virgin olive oil, which brightens the soup. To reinforce that fruity, peppery flavor, we drizzle the soup with more oil before pureeing it.

Sweet and Savory Seasoning

Tomato soup can be unbalanced or bland. Sautéed chopped onion and a little brown sugar coax out the sweetness of the tomatoes. Sautéing garlic with the onion and adding a pinch of red pepper flakes further boosts flavor. A splash of brandy edges the soup into sophisticated territory.

Use Bread for Body

Without some kind of thickener, tomato soup is thin and watery. A few slices of sandwich bread cooked right in the soup provide body and a velvety texture without obscuring the tomato flavor. To be sure the bread purees cleanly in the blender—no one wants pockets of soggy bread in their soup—we puree just the tomato mixture and bread and then whisk the chicken broth into the puree. A few grinds of pepper, fresh chives, and a drizzle of olive oil complete the soup.

Mash the tomatoes to thicken the soup and then add crustless sandwich bread to finish the job.

Creamless Creamy Tomato Soup

SERVES 6 TO 8

Make sure to purchase canned whole tomatoes in juice, not puree. If half of the soup fills your blender by more than two-thirds, process the soup in three batches.

¼ cup extra-virgin olive oil, plus extra for drizzling

1 onion, chopped

3 garlic cloves, minced

Pinch red pepper flakes (optional)

1 bay leaf

2 (28-ounce) cans whole tomatoes

3 slices hearty white sandwich bread, crusts removed, torn into 1-inch pieces

1 tablespoon packed brown sugar

2 cups chicken broth

2 tablespoons brandy (optional)

Salt and pepper

¼ cup chopped fresh chives

1 recipe Butter Croutons (recipe follows)

1. Heat 2 tablespoons oil in Dutch oven over medium-high heat until shimmering. Add onion, garlic, pepper flakes, if using, and bay leaf. Cook, stirring frequently, until onion is translucent, 3 to 5 minutes. Stir in tomatoes and their juice. Using potato masher, mash until no pieces bigger than 2 inches remain. Stir in bread and sugar. Bring soup to boil. Reduce heat to medium and cook, stirring occasionally, until bread is completely saturated and starts to break down, about 5 minutes. Discard bay leaf.

2. Transfer half of soup to blender. Add 1 tablespoon oil and process until soup is smooth and creamy, 2 to 3 minutes. Transfer to large bowl and repeat with remaining soup and remaining 1 tablespoon oil. Rinse out Dutch oven and return soup to pot. Stir in chicken broth and brandy, if using. Return soup to boil and season with salt and pepper to taste. Ladle soup into bowls, sprinkle with chives, and drizzle with olive oil. Serve with croutons.

BUTTER CROUTONS MAKES ABOUT 3 CUPS

Be sure to use regular or thick-sliced bread (do not use thin-sliced bread). Either fresh or stale bread can be used to make croutons, although stale bread is easier to cut and crisps more quickly in the oven. If using stale bread, reduce the baking time by about 2 minutes. Croutons made from stale bread will be more crisp than those made from fresh.

6 slices hearty white sandwich bread, crusts removed, cut into ½-inch cubes (about 3 cups)

Salt and pepper

3 tablespoons unsalted butter, melted

1. Adjust oven rack to upper-middle position and heat oven to 350 degrees. Combine bread cubes and salt and pepper to taste in medium bowl. Drizzle with butter and toss well with rubber spatula to combine.

2. Spread bread cubes in single layer on rimmed baking sheet or in shallow baking dish. Bake croutons until golden brown and crisp, 8 to 10 minutes, stirring halfway through baking. Let cool on baking sheet to room temperature. (Croutons can be stored at room temperature for up to 3 days.)

RECIPE DETAILS

Timeline

• 5 minutes to ready croutons for oven (bake them while working on soup)

• 20 minutes to prepare ingredients and cook soup

• 10 minutes to puree and finish soup

Essential Tools

• Rimmed baking sheet for making croutons

• Dutch oven for cooking soup

• Potato masher for breaking down tomatoes

• Blender (An immersion blender can be used to process the soup directly in the pot.)

Substitutions & Variations

• For a spicier soup, increase the amount of hot red pepper flakes or add some cayenne pepper.

• For an ultrasmooth soup, pass the pureed mixture through a fine-mesh strainer before stirring in the chicken broth in step 2.

59 Vegetable Soup

A HEARTY SOUP DOESN'T HAVE TO START WITH MEAT

Vegetable soups always sound so virtuous. The cook turns a crisper-full of cold-weather vegetables—carrots, potatoes, leeks, cabbage, and turnips—into a healthy, hearty meal. But virtue isn't reason enough to make a dish. It must taste good, and without meat in the mix vegetable soup is generally bland and watery.

Homemade stock is one way to solve this problem, but it's not terribly convenient. Is there a way to use commercial broth and still address the flavor and texture issues? In a word: yes. We begin with umami.

Umami is the fifth taste (along with sweet, sour, salty, and bitter); it describes a savory, almost meaty flavor in foods as diverse as Parmesan cheese and tomatoes. The development of umami is a key component in Asian cookery, but this same cooking principle can be applied to any recipe.

Soy sauce and dried porcini mushrooms are concentrated sources of umami, and together they transform vegetable soup into a flavor powerhouse. Soy sauce contains high levels of flavor-enhancing compounds called glutamates, a naturally occurring version of MSG. Mushrooms are rich in flavor-amplifying compounds known as nucleotides.

Soy sauce and dried mushrooms address the flavor deficit associated with the use of commercial, but they don't address the body issue. To give thin commercial broth more viscosity, we add a handful of barley. As the grains swell, they shed starch. Barley also adds a pleasantly chewy texture to a bowl of soup filled with tender vegetables. This isn't just healthy eating. This is delicious eating and that's the point of any recipe.

WHY THIS RECIPE WORKS

Aromatics on the Double
Sautéing aromatics (leeks, carrots, and celery) provides a savory base of flavor for vegetable soup. But to coax out the flavor of these aromatics even more, we use two ingredients: wine and soy sauce. Wine isn't surprising, as it's often used to give dishes a more complex character, but why soy sauce? Soy sauce contains high levels of naturally occurring flavor-enhancing compounds called glutamates.

Make Magic with Mushrooms
Like soy sauce, porcini mushrooms are also rich in flavor-enhancing compounds, but these are called nucleotides. No wonder these mushrooms taste so meaty and make a great addition to vegetable soup. Adding porcini is also a good move because when glutamates and nucleotides are used together, their combined effect strengthens, which has a profound impact on flavor. Porcini mushrooms vary in size, so to accurately measure them we grind the mushrooms to a powder first.

Build Body
Vegetables alone (even starchy potatoes) don't produce a soup with great body. Cream dulls the flavor of the vegetables but barley, a nutty grain that swells in liquid, adds just enough heft to the soup—and its appealing chew works well with the chunks of vegetables (potatoes, turnip, peas, and crisp cabbage). Barley takes longer to cook than the vegetables, so we give it a head start by adding it to the pot first. Peas are the outlier veggie in this soup—they cook so quickly, they should be stirred in off the heat, at the end of cooking.

Finish Bright
Finishing the soup with lemon juice and chopped parsley adds a burst of fresh brightness, but for another dimension of flavor, we like to serve the soup with butter flavored with thyme and more lemon—just a dollop adds a plush richness and even more brightness.

Dried porcini mushrooms ground to a powder supply flavor while barley provides heft.

Farmhouse Vegetable and Barley Soup

SERVES 6 TO 8

We prefer an acidic, unoaked white wine such as Sauvignon Blanc for this recipe.

⅛ ounce dried porcini mushrooms

8 sprigs fresh parsley plus 3 tablespoons minced

4 sprigs fresh thyme

1 bay leaf

2 tablespoons unsalted butter

1½ pounds leeks, white and light green parts only, halved lengthwise, sliced ½ inch thick, and washed thoroughly

2 carrots, peeled and cut into ½-inch pieces

2 celery ribs, cut into ¼-inch pieces

⅓ cup dry white wine

2 teaspoons soy sauce

Salt and pepper

6 cups water

4 cups chicken broth or vegetable broth

½ cup pearl barley

1 garlic clove, peeled and smashed

1½ pounds Yukon Gold potatoes, peeled and cut into ½-inch pieces

1 turnip, peeled and cut into ¾-inch pieces

1½ cups chopped green cabbage

1 cup frozen peas

1 teaspoon lemon juice

1. Grind porcini with spice grinder until they resemble fine meal, 10 to 30 seconds. Measure out 2 teaspoons porcini powder; reserve remainder for another use. Using kitchen twine, tie together parsley sprigs, thyme, and bay leaf.

2. Melt butter in Dutch oven over medium heat. Add leeks, carrots, celery, wine, soy sauce, and 2 teaspoons salt. Cook, stirring occasionally, until liquid has evaporated and celery is softened, about 10 minutes.

3. Add water, broth, barley, garlic, porcini powder, and herb bundle; increase heat to high and bring to boil. Reduce heat to medium-low and simmer, partially covered, for 25 minutes.

4. Add potatoes, turnip, and cabbage; return to simmer and cook until barley, potatoes, turnip, and cabbage are tender, 18 to 20 minutes.

5. Remove pot from heat and discard herb bundle. Stir in peas, lemon juice, and minced parsley; season with salt and pepper to taste. Serve

RECIPE DETAILS

Timeline

- 25 minutes to prepare vegetables and other ingredients
- 10 minutes to sauté vegetables
- 55 minutes to simmer soup (mostly hands-off)
- 5 minutes to finish soup

Essential Tools

- Dutch oven (at least 6 quarts)

Substitutions & Variations

- The soup can be garnished with crisp bacon, crumbled cheddar cheese, or herbed croutons. We especially love the richness added by a compound butter flavored with lemon and thyme.
- Lemon-Thyme Butter: Combine 6 tablespoons softened unsalted butter, 1 tablespoon minced fresh thyme, ¾ teaspoon finely grated lemon zest plus ¼ teaspoon juice, and pinch salt in bowl. Dollop butter into individual servings.
- Herbed Croutons: Melt 1 tablespoon unsalted butter in 10-inch skillet over medium heat. Add 1 teaspoon minced fresh parsley and ½ teaspoon minced fresh thyme and cook, stirring constantly, for 20 seconds. Add 4 slices hearty white sandwich bread, cut into ½-inch cubes, and cook, stirring frequently, until light golden brown, 5 to 10 minutes. Season with salt and pepper to taste.

60 Vegetarian Chili

IT SOUNDS SCARY BUT IT'S REALLY DELICIOUS (AND EVERYONE WILL EAT IT)

We love chili made with beef. We love it with pork. We even like this dish with turkey. But it's hard to get excited about vegetarian chili. The latter feels like something you make because you have to, not because you want to. Vegetarian chili usually relies on beans and chunky vegetables for heartiness—but in truth that heartiness is an illusion. Neither ingredient offers a real replacement for the flavor, texture, and unctuous richness of meat.

It doesn't help matters that vegetarian chili is typically made with canned beans and lackluster chili powder. Most recipe writers rush the process thinking that extra time isn't going to yield a better result. But does vegetarian chili have to be so bad? And wouldn't a bit more effort yield better results? Our goal was to build a version as savory and deeply satisfying as any meat chili—one that even meat lovers would make on its own merits, not just for vegetarian friends.

With that in mind, we started our recipe with dried beans. As beans cook, they shed flavor and starch that would no doubt help us build a better chili. Homemade chili powder was the next stop. We use this when making beef chili (see page 98), so why not do something similar here? Our real revelation, however, was to lose the chunky vegetables. No zucchini, potatoes, corn, or eggplant. This isn't vegetable stew. It's chili.

In the end, two unlikely ingredients—bulgur and walnuts—add the richness and chewy texture this dish needs to be great. Don't tell guests this is vegetarian chili. Just put out the usual accompaniments (lime wedges, sour cream, avocado, chopped onion, and cheese) and tell them this is your best chili. One taste and everyone will agree.

WHY THIS RECIPE WORKS

Brine the Beans
The combination of nutty cannellini and meaty pintos deliver complexity to this chili. And use dried, please. Rather than an overnight soak, we opt for a quick brine, bringing the beans to a boil in a pot of salted water and then letting them sit, covered, for an hour. The brine ensures soft, creamy well-seasoned beans.

DIY Chili Powder
Toast the chiles (we like mild, sweet ancho and earthy New Mexican) to bring out their flavor. When grinding the chiles, we include peppery oregano as well as dried shiitake mushrooms. The latter are rich in nucleotides, flavor-boosting compounds that impart a rich, meaty flavor to foods—in other words, umami.

Time the Tomatoes
Tomatoes are a given in this chili. We puree a can of diced tomatoes in a food processor with garlic and jalapeños to kick up the heat. To punch up the tomato flavor, we add umami-rich tomato paste and soy sauce.

The Power of Walnuts
For chili with savory depth, we turn to toasted and ground walnuts. They contain lots of flavor-boosting glutamates. In addition, the fat from the nuts offers richness and the tannins in the skins contribute a slightly bitter note that keeps the flavors in this chili in balance.

A Great Grain
Bulgur gives chili the same thick, rich texture as meat. When you pull the chili from the oven, you'll notice a slick of fat on top. No problem. Give the chili a vigorous stir and let it rest for 20 minutes. Stirring releases starches from the bulgur and beans, allowing the sauce to stabilize around the fat droplets and preventing them from separating out again. This chili is so thick you can stand a spoon in it.

Wait to add the tomatoes so the beans soften properly and finish with plenty of cilantro.

Best Vegetarian Chili

SERVES 6 TO 8

We recommend a mix of at least two types of beans, one creamy (such as cannellini or navy) and one earthy (such as pinto, black, or red kidney). For a spicier chili, use both jalapeños. Serve the chili with lime wedges, sour cream, diced avocado, chopped red onion, and shredded Monterey Jack or cheddar cheese, if desired.

1 pound (2½ cups) dried beans, picked over and rinsed

Salt

2 dried ancho chiles

2 dried New Mexican chiles

½ ounce dried shiitake mushrooms, chopped coarse

4 teaspoons dried oregano

½ cup walnuts, toasted

1 (28-ounce) can diced tomatoes, drained with juice reserved

3 tablespoons tomato paste

1-2 jalapeño chiles, stemmed and chopped coarse

3 tablespoons soy sauce

6 garlic cloves, minced

¼ cup vegetable oil

2 pounds onions, chopped fine

1 tablespoon ground cumin

⅔ cup medium-grind bulgur

¼ cup chopped fresh cilantro

1. Bring 4 quarts water, beans, and 3 tablespoons salt to boil in Dutch oven over high heat. Remove pot from heat, cover, and let stand for 1 hour. Drain beans and rinse well. Wipe out pot.

2. Adjust oven rack to middle position and heat oven to 300 degrees. Arrange anchos and New Mexican chiles on rimmed baking sheet and toast until fragrant and puffed, about 8 minutes. Transfer to plate and let cool, about 5 minutes. Stem and seed anchos and New Mexican chiles. Working in batches, grind mushrooms, oregano, and toasted chiles in spice grinder or with mortar and pestle until finely ground.

3. Process walnuts in food processor until finely ground, about 30 seconds. Transfer to bowl. Process drained tomatoes, tomato paste, jalapeño(s), soy sauce, and garlic in food processor until tomatoes are finely chopped, about 45 seconds, scraping down sides of bowl as needed.

4. Heat oil in now-empty Dutch oven over medium-high heat until shimmering. Add onions and 1¼ teaspoons salt; cook, stirring occasionally, until onions begin to brown, 8 to 10 minutes. Lower heat to medium and add cumin and ground chile mixture; cook, stirring constantly, until fragrant, about 1 minute. Add rinsed beans and 7 cups water and bring to boil. Cover pot, transfer to oven, and cook for 45 minutes.

5. Remove pot from oven. Stir in bulgur, ground walnuts, tomato mixture, and reserved tomato juice. Cover pot and return to oven. Cook until beans are fully tender, about 2 hours.

6. Remove pot from oven, stir chili well, and let stand, uncovered, for 20 minutes. Stir in cilantro and serve. (Chili can be refrigerated for up to 3 days.)

RECIPE DETAILS

Timeline

• 1¼ hours to brine beans (prepare chile powder, grind walnuts, and puree tomatoes with other ingredients while beans are brining)

• 10 minutes to sauté ingredients

• 3 hours to bring chili to boil and cook in oven (almost completely hands-off)

• 20 minutes to stir chili and let it thicken

Essential Tools

• Spice grinder for making homemade chile powder (or mortar and pestle)

• Food processor to grind walnuts and puree tomato mixture

• Dutch oven with lid to cook chili

Substitutions & Variations

• We prefer to make our own chile powder from whole dried chiles, but jarred chili powder can be substituted. If using jarred chili powder, grind the shiitakes and oregano and add them to the pot with ¼ cup of chili powder in step 4.

61 Braised Potatoes

A UNIQUE STOVETOP METHOD DELIVERS BOTH CREAMY AND CRISP TEXTURES

We love the versatility of waxy potatoes like Red Bliss. Steamed whole, they turn tender and creamy—perfect canvases for tossing with butter and fresh herbs. They also take well to halving and roasting, which browns their cut surfaces. Braising might seem like an unlikely method for cooking potatoes. (It's generally reserved for tough cuts of meat.) But it turns out that braising is the best—and possibly the only—way to produce creamy-on-the-inside, crispy-on-the-outside red potatoes.

The classic meat braise begins with a hard sear to impart color and flavor. Liquid is added to the pan, which is covered to trap the steam. After many hours, the meat becomes tender and the cooking liquid has been transformed into a lovely sauce.

Adapting this method to potatoes requires some changes if you want a crispy final result. Reversing the browning and steaming steps is a must. When it comes to potatoes, any initial browning gets washed away when liquid is added to the pan. We had far better results simmering the potatoes until tender, and then browning them.

It wasn't until we borrowed a trick from Chinese potstickers that we solved the biggest problem with cooking potatoes in a pan: sticking. Adding the fat at the outset glosses the potatoes and keeps them from fusing to the pan. Using butter, rather than oil, ensures that the potatoes really brown—the proteins in the milk solids amplify the browning process. Butter also makes the potatoes taste better. And it's easy to add other flavors like salt, pepper, garlic, and thyme. As unlikely as it sounds, braising might be our favorite way to cook red potatoes.

WHY THIS RECIPE WORKS

Simmer First

Braising following the conventional browning-and-simmering method is a bust for potatoes because the flavorful brown color that the potatoes develop during searing gets washed away by the time they cook through in the liquid. A better approach is to simmer, then brown, the potatoes, once the liquid has evaporated. To keep the potatoes from sticking to the pan (and scorching) once the liquid has evaporated, add butter to the cooking liquid at the start of cooking. Oil works too, but butter is much more flavorful.

The Benefits of Overcooking

It takes about 35 minutes for the liquid to cook off while simmering the potatoes. That seems like a long time to cook halved small red potatoes without their turning mushy and crumbled. But don't worry; low-starch potatoes like Red Bliss exude a fluid gel that keep the potato "glued" together and also gives the impression of extreme creaminess—the gel is called amylopectin. Don't try this method with starchy potatoes like russets—they contain a higher proportion of a second starch called amylose, which is less sticky, so the potatoes will fall apart during simmering in this recipe.

Add Complementary Flavors

Tossing a few sprigs of thyme into the skilletful of potatoes at the outset is an easy way to add herbal depth. Garlic is a natural partner with potatoes, but it will burn if tossed into the pan when the potatoes are browning. Simmering the whole cloves mellows the garlic bite, and the softened garlic is easy to mince into a paste and stir into finished spuds. A squirt of lemon juice adds brightness and minced chives add fresh oniony flavor.

Braise the halved potatoes cut side down until tender, then brown them until crisp.

Braised Red Potatoes with Lemon and Chives

SERVES 4 TO 6

Use small red potatoes measuring about 1½ inches in diameter.

1½	pounds small red potatoes, unpeeled, halved	3	sprigs fresh thyme
2	cups water	¾	teaspoon salt
3	tablespoons unsalted butter	1	teaspoon lemon juice
3	garlic cloves, peeled	¼	teaspoon pepper
		2	tablespoons minced fresh chives

1. Arrange potatoes in single layer, cut side down, in 12-inch nonstick skillet. Add water, butter, garlic, thyme, and salt and bring to simmer over medium-high heat. Reduce heat to medium, cover, and simmer until potatoes are just tender, about 15 minutes.

2. Remove lid and use slotted spoon to transfer garlic to cutting board; discard thyme. Increase heat to medium-high and vigorously simmer, swirling pan occasionally, until water evaporates and butter starts to sizzle, 15 to 20 minutes. When cool enough to handle, mince garlic to paste. Transfer paste to bowl and stir in lemon juice and pepper.

3. Continue to cook potatoes, swirling pan frequently, until butter browns and cut sides of potatoes turn spotty brown, 4 to 6 minutes longer. Off heat, add chives and garlic mixture and toss to thoroughly coat. Serve immediately.

BRAISED RED POTATOES WITH DIJON AND TARRAGON
Substitute 2 teaspoons Dijon mustard for lemon juice and 1 tablespoon minced fresh tarragon for chives.

BRAISED RED POTATOES WITH MISO AND SCALLIONS
Reduce salt to ½ teaspoon. Substitute 1 tablespoon red miso for lemon juice and 3 scallions, sliced thin, for chives.

RECIPE DETAILS

Timeline

- 10 minutes to prepare ingredients and bring potatoes to simmer
- 15 minutes to cook potatoes covered
- 15 to 20 minutes to cook potatoes uncovered (mince garlic while this is happening)
- 5 minutes to brown and finish potatoes

Essential Tools

- 12-inch nonstick skillet with lid (Don't try this recipe in a conventional pan; the potatoes will stick.)

Substitutions & Variations

- If you prefer, replace the lemon juice with vinegar and finish the potatoes with another fresh herb (parsley or cilantro are particularly good choices).
- Add a pinch of cayenne pepper to the garlic mixture for a bit of heat.

62 Sweet Potatoes

BRAISING AND THEN MASHING PRESERVES FLAVOR AND REDUCES THE MESS

We understand the nostalgic appeal of a sweet potato casserole topped with marshmallows. But this dish is simply too sweet to serve alongside turkey or ham. You wouldn't serve a slice of pie with the main course, so why serve a "casserole" that's even more sugary? Save the marshmallows for hot cocoa. Sweet potatoes should be mashed and seasoned like regular potatoes—just add cream and butter, plus salt and pepper.

But unlike regular potatoes, sweet potatoes don't fare well in a pot of boiling water. They contain a lot more moisture (and lot less starch) than potatoes. If you boil chunks of peeled sweet potatoes, they literally fall apart. The result is a tasteless, watery mash.

The key to great mashed sweet potatoes is to harness their natural moisture as the cooking medium. If cooked over low heat in a covered pot, sliced sweet potatoes will give up their liquid. To prevent scorching at the outset, add a few tablespoons of moisture. Rather than diluting their flavor with water, drizzle in a little cream and throw in a few pats of butter.

Other than preparing the sweet potatoes properly and using very low heat, there's not much to this recipe. And perhaps the best part comes at the end. There's no need to drain the sweet potatoes before mashing—so keep the colander at bay. Just lift off the lid, get out your masher, and work them right in the pot into a smooth, silky puree. It doesn't get sweeter than that.

WHY THIS RECIPE WORKS

All Sweet Potatoes Are Not Equal
Sweet potatoes come in several varieties. Our two favorites are the familiar, pleasantly sweet orange-fleshed Beauregard (usually sold as a conventional sweet potato) and the white-fleshed Japanese, which boasts a buttery chestnut flavor.

Slice Thin
Sweet potatoes should be sliced before braising so that they cook evenly. Try to keep the slices even and thin (about ¼ inch is just right); they'll release their moisture sooner and cook faster than thicker slices.

Keep a Tight Lid on Things
Reach for a heavy pan with a tight-fitting lid. The sweet potatoes will likely scorch in a lightweight pan and a loose-fitting lid will let steam escape, which will also encourage scorching. Keep the flame low—higher heat levels will cause the potatoes to cook unevenly and even burn.

Sweeten with Butter and Cream
Jump-starting the sweet potatoes with a little water buys the potatoes a little time before they give up their moisture—but water doesn't do much for flavor. To really make this mash stand out, replace the water with what you'd finish the potatoes with—butter and a little heavy cream. Although 2 tablespoons of cream doesn't seem like a lot for 2 pounds of sweet potatoes, it gives them a richer flavor and fuller body. And there can be too much of a good thing, so don't pour in any more, or the dairy will mute the sweet potatoes' flavor.

Go Bold—If You Like
Yes, you can go the sweet route (we offer a variation with maple and orange) but we think sweet potatoes also work well with savory ingredients—everything from garlic and garam masala to coconut milk and hot red pepper flakes.

Cook sweet potatoes with a little butter and cream, then mash them right in the pot until smooth and creamy.

Mashed Sweet Potatoes

SERVES 4

Cutting the sweet potatoes into slices of even thickness is important in getting them to cook at the same rate. A potato masher will yield slightly lumpy sweet potatoes; a food mill will make a perfectly smooth puree.

2 pounds sweet potatoes, peeled, quartered lengthwise, and cut crosswise into ¼-inch-thick slices

4 tablespoons unsalted butter, cut into 4 pieces

2 tablespoons heavy cream

1 teaspoon sugar

½ teaspoon salt

Pinch pepper

1. Combine sweet potatoes, butter, cream, sugar, and salt in large saucepan and cook, covered, over low heat, stirring occasionally, until potatoes fall apart when poked with fork, 35 to 45 minutes.

2. Off heat, mash sweet potatoes in saucepan with potato masher. (Alternatively, you can you use ricer or food mill to press or mill potatoes into warmed serving bowl.) Stir in pepper; serve immediately.

MAPLE-ORANGE MASHED SWEET POTATOES

Stir in 2 tablespoons maple syrup and ½ teaspoon grated orange zest along with pepper just before serving.

INDIAN-SPICED MASHED SWEET POTATOES WITH RAISINS AND CASHEWS

Substitute dark brown sugar for granulated sugar and add ¾ teaspoon garam masala to saucepan along with sweet potatoes in step 1. Stir ¼ cup golden raisins and ¼ cup roasted unsalted cashews, chopped coarse, into mashed sweet potatoes along with pepper just before serving.

GARLIC MASHED SWEET POTATOES WITH COCONUT

Substitute ½ cup coconut milk for butter and cream and add ¼ teaspoon red pepper flakes and 1 small minced garlic clove to saucepan along with sweet potatoes in step 1. Stir in 1 tablespoon minced fresh cilantro along with pepper just before serving.

RECIPE DETAILS

Timeline

• 10 minutes to peel and cut sweet potatoes
• 35 to 45 minutes to cook sweet potatoes (mostly hands-off)
• 5 minutes to mash and season sweet potatoes

Essential Tools

• Large saucepan with tight-fitting lid
• Potato masher (if you don't mind a few small lumps, and you shouldn't), ricer, or food mill

Substitutions & Variations

• This recipe can be doubled if you use a Dutch oven and increase the cooking time to about 1¼ hours.
• Sweet potatoes take well to potent seasonings, such as smoked paprika, grated fresh ginger, and chipotle chile in adobo sauce. For best results, add these ingredients to the pot at the outset.

63 Carrots

THE SECRET TO PERFECT TEXTURE IS TO COOK CARROTS VERY SLOWLY

Carrots are having a culinary moment at trendy farm-to-table restaurants, and if you haven't tried this dish you're in for a real treat. These new wave carrots have lost their sweet glaze (thank heavens) and taken on a decidedly savory profile. They are served whole, often with some greens attached.

Menus are cryptic about the cooking method, although the words "slow cooked" are common. The best examples of this dish are fork-tender without a hint of mushiness. The carrots have a dense, almost meaty quality and the flavor is super concentrated: sweet and pure, but still earthy.

To produce slow-cooked carrots, most chefs are braising or poaching them in water. And while replicating the clean, pure flavor of this restaurant dish is pretty straightforward (you do have water on hand!), figuring out the secret to achieving their unique texture is another matter. If the water is too abundant or boiling for too long, the carrots turn mushy. But if the water level is too low or the cooking time is too short, the carrots remain crunchy in spots.

It turns out that the solution is a dual cooking method. The carrots are first precooked at a relatively low temperature (in water between 120 and 160 degrees). We accomplish this by adding the carrots to simmering water, turning off the heat, and covering the pan for 20 minutes. This warm bath allows the carrots to withstand the second cooking—a gentle simmer that takes almost 50 minutes. Cooking carrots for over an hour on the stovetop might seem a bit crazy, but when you slice into these meaty carrots you will agree that this was time well spent.

WHY THIS RECIPE WORKS

Precook for Persistent Firmness

Precooking certain fruits or vegetables at a low temperature can help them retain a firm yet tender texture during a second cooking phase at a higher temperature. This phenomenon is called "persistent firmness." To initiate persistent firmness, we place carrots in a skillet filled with simmering water and let them steep off heat for 20 minutes. During this hot soak, an enzyme in the carrot called pectin methylesterase (PME) is activated. PME strengthens the pectin in the vegetable, making it resistant to breaking down when the carrots finish cooking at a higher temperature.

Water Is the Winner

When precooking the carrots, we use water because it allows the carrots to taste like carrots. We include a little butter for richness—it reduces to a light buttery glaze on the carrots as the water evaporates.

Pull Out the Parchment

After the 20-minute hot water bath, it's time to remove the lid and cook off the water. But simply removing the lid can result in unevenly cooked carrots on top. A trick from restaurant chefs, called a cartouche, is the solution. This is simply a piece of parchment paper that sits directly on the food as it cooks, regulating the reduction of moisture in cooking. In short, the paper allows for the perfect rate of evaporation as it keeps the carrots submerged, trapping more of the escaping steam and keeping it concentrated on top of the carrots, which ensures perfectly tender, evenly cooked results. Once most of the liquid evaporates (note that this will take a good 45 minutes), remove the paper and shake the pan a few times as the rest of the water cooks off and the carrots take on a buttery sheen.

Simmering carrots under a circle of parchment ensures even cooking without mushiness.

Slow-Cooked Whole Carrots

SERVES 4 TO 6

Use carrots that measure ¾ to 1¼ inches across at the thickest end. The carrots can be served plain, but we recommend topping them with one of our relishes (recipes follow).

3	cups water	½	teaspoon salt
1	tablespoon unsalted butter	12	carrots (1½ to 1¾ pounds), peeled

1. Fold 12-inch square of parchment paper into quarters to create 6-inch square. Fold bottom right corner of square to top left corner to create triangle. Fold triangle again, right side over left, to create narrow triangle. Cut off ¼ inch of tip of triangle to create small hole. Cut base of triangle straight across where it measures 5 inches from hole. Open paper round.

2. Bring water, butter, and salt to simmer in 12-inch skillet over high heat. Remove pan from heat, add carrots in single layer, and place parchment round on top of carrots. Cover skillet and let stand for 20 minutes.

3. Remove lid from skillet, leaving parchment round in place, and bring to simmer over high heat. Reduce heat to medium-low and simmer until almost all water has evaporated and carrots are very tender, about 45 minutes. Discard parchment round, increase heat to medium-high, and continue to cook carrots, shaking pan frequently, until they are lightly glazed and no water remains in skillet, 2 to 4 minutes longer. Transfer carrots to platter and serve.

GREEN OLIVE AND GOLDEN RAISIN RELISH MAKES ABOUT 1 CUP

⅓	cup golden raisins	2	tablespoons extra-virgin olive oil
1	tablespoon water	1	tablespoon red wine vinegar
⅔	cup pitted green olives, chopped	½	teaspoon ground fennel
1	shallot, minced	¼	teaspoon salt

Microwave raisins and water in bowl until steaming, about 1 minute. Cover and let stand until raisins are plump, about 5 minutes. Add olives, shallot, oil, vinegar, fennel, and salt to plumped raisins and stir to combine.

PINE NUT RELISH MAKES ABOUT ¾ CUP
Pine nuts burn easily, so be sure to shake the pan frequently while toasting them.

⅓	cup pine nuts, toasted	½	teaspoon minced fresh rosemary
1	shallot, minced	¼	teaspoon smoked paprika
1	tablespoon sherry vinegar	¼	teaspoon salt
1	tablespoon minced fresh parsley		Pinch cayenne pepper
1	teaspoon honey		

Combine all ingredients in bowl.

RECIPE DETAILS

Timeline

- 10 minutes to peel carrots and cut parchment
- 5 minutes to bring water to a simmer
- 20 minutes to warm carrots off heat
- 50 minutes to cook carrots

Essential Tools

- Parchment paper (to cover carrots and ensure even cooking)
- 12-inch skillet with lid

Substitutions & Variations

- The carrots can be served with other chunky relishes or potent sauces, anything from salsa verde and romesco sauce to pesto (page 25).

64 Quinoa

THIS SUPER FOOD DOESN'T HAVE TO BE BITTER AND MUSHY

In the span of a decade, quinoa has gone from obscurity to mass consumption in the United States. This seed with humble South American roots is even showing up at fast-food restaurants. Most of the hype has focused on the nutritional benefits—quinoa is a nearly complete protein that is rich in fiber.

But no one wants to eat something just because it's healthy. It has to taste good, too. And while quinoa fans talk up its crunchy texture and appealing nutty flavor, it's just as often a mushy mess with washed-out flavor and an underlying bitterness. In the rush to make quinoa an overnight sensation, misinformation from so-called experts has caused consumer confusion, which we intend to straighten out—right now.

First off: Quinoa is covered with a naturally occurring bitter-tasting compound called saponin. If you don't rinse quinoa before cooking, it will taste awful. You can buy prewashed quinoa, and we recommend doing so. If in doubt about the quinoa in your pantry, rinse it well.

Second, many recipe writers and package instructions direct you to boil quinoa. Don't do it—these tiny seeds are very delicate and will blow out if cooked this way. Gentle steaming via the absorption method is your best bet.

Finally, quinoa needs a lot less water than most recipes suggest. Unless you want soggy grains don't use 2 cups of water for every cup of quinoa. Our recipe calls for nearly equal amounts of water and quinoa. As long as you keep the lid on and the heat low, that's plenty of water. When prepared the right way (that is, our way), quinoa merits the hype, especially because it is so easy and quick—and best of all, great tasting.

WHY THIS RECIPE WORKS

Dry-Toasting Delivers

Cooking quinoa like rice pilaf—sautéing onion in butter, and then adding the quinoa to the pan so that it's coated with the fat before pouring in water—might be better than boiling, but not by much. The problem has to do with sautéing the quinoa in fat. While the majority of quinoa on the market has been prewashed, the bitter-tasting compound (called saponins) remains on the exterior—and the fat exacerbates this bitterness. Instead, toast the grains in a dry pan to bring out nutty flavors but keep bitterness at bay.

Build Flavor with Aromatics

Once the quinoa is toasted, remove it from the pan and sauté onion in butter until it's softened. Scallions can be swapped for onions and, for adding more layers of flavor, sautéing spices in the fat is a terrific option.

Stir Once

When cooking long-grain rice, it's important to avoid stirring the rice during cooking because it will turn into a starchy mess. Not so with quinoa, which should be stirred once halfway through cooking to encourage even cooking of the tiny seeds. Quinoa is starchy too, but it also contains twice as much protein as white rice. That protein is key, as it essentially traps the starch in place so you can stir it without causing it to turn gummy.

Steam Off the Heat

Finish cooking the quinoa gently, off the heat. This allows the grains to firm up, so that you're rewarded with light, fluffy grains. Skipping this step could result in clumpy quinoa, so avoid taking shortcuts. Once the quinoa has rested off heat, fluff it with a fork and finish with fresh herbs and a squeeze of lemon.

To eliminate bitterness, rinse the quinoa (unless prewashed) and then toast in a dry saucepan.

Quinoa Pilaf with Herbs and Lemon

SERVES 4 TO 6

Any soft herbs, such as cilantro, parsley, chives, mint, and tarragon, can be used.

1½	cups prewashed quinoa	¾	teaspoon salt
2	tablespoons unsalted butter, cut into 2 pieces	1¾	cups water
		3	tablespoons chopped fresh herbs
1	small onion, chopped fine	1	tablespoon lemon juice

1. Toast quinoa in medium saucepan over medium-high heat, stirring frequently, until quinoa is very fragrant and makes continuous popping sound, 5 to 7 minutes. Transfer quinoa to bowl and set aside.

2. Return now-empty pan to medium-low heat and melt butter. Add onion and salt; cook, stirring frequently, until onion is softened and light golden, 5 to 7 minutes.

3. Increase heat to medium-high, stir in water and quinoa, and bring to simmer. Cover, reduce heat to low, and simmer until grains are just tender and liquid is absorbed, 18 to 20 minutes, stirring once halfway through cooking. Remove pan from heat and let sit, covered, for 10 minutes. Fluff quinoa with fork, stir in herbs and lemon juice, and serve.

QUINOA PILAF WITH APRICOTS, AGED GOUDA, AND PISTACHIOS

Add ½ teaspoon grated lemon zest, ½ teaspoon ground coriander, ¼ teaspoon ground cumin, and ⅛ teaspoon pepper with onion and salt. Stir in ½ cup dried apricots, chopped coarse, before letting quinoa sit for 10 minutes in step 3. Substitute ½ cup shredded aged gouda; ½ cup shelled pistachios, toasted and chopped coarse; and 2 tablespoons chopped fresh mint for herbs.

QUINOA PILAF WITH CHIPOTLE, QUESO FRESCO, AND PEANUTS

Add 1 teaspoon chipotle chile powder and ¼ teaspoon ground cumin with onion and salt. Substitute ½ cup crumbled queso fresco; ½ cup roasted unsalted peanuts, chopped coarse; and 2 thinly sliced scallions for herbs. Substitute 4 teaspoons lime juice for lemon juice.

QUINOA PILAF WITH SHIITAKES, EDAMAME, AND GINGER

Substitute vegetable oil for butter and replace onion with 4 minced scallion whites; 4 ounces shiitake mushrooms, stemmed and sliced thin; and 2 teaspoons grated fresh ginger. Stir in ½ cup cooked shelled edamame before letting quinoa sit for 10 minutes in step 3. Substitute 4 scallion greens, sliced thin on bias; 4 teaspoons rice vinegar; and 1 tablespoon mirin for herbs and lemon juice.

QUINOA PILAF WITH OLIVES, RAISINS, AND CILANTRO

Add ¼ teaspoon ground cumin, ¼ teaspoon dried oregano, and ⅛ teaspoon ground cinnamon with onion. Stir in ¼ cup golden raisins halfway through cooking time in step 3. Substitute ⅓ cup pimento-stuffed green olives, chopped coarse; 3 tablespoons chopped fresh cilantro; and 4 teaspoons red wine vinegar for herbs and lemon juice.

Timeline

- 5 minutes to toast quinoa
- 5 minutes to cook onion
- 20 minutes to cook quinoa (stir just once)
- 10 minutes to let quinoa steam off heat

Essential Tools

- Saucepan with tight-fitting lid (A heavy-bottom pan with a capacity of roughly 3 quarts is ideal.)
- Fork for fluffing finished quinoa

Substitutions & Variations

- If you buy unwashed quinoa, rinse the grains in a fine-mesh strainer, drain them, and then spread them on a rimmed baking sheet lined with a dish towel and let them dry for 15 minutes before proceeding with the recipe.

65 Polenta

REPLACE STIRRING WITH SCIENCE TO SPEED UP THE COOK TIME

When it comes to peasant roots, it doesn't get much humbler than polenta. This simple, hearty dish of long-cooked cornmeal dates back to 16th-century Rome, where *polenta sulla tavola* was poured directly onto the table to soak up flavors from previous meals. These days, polenta passes for haute restaurant cuisine. Its nutty corn flavor and porridge-like texture make it an excellent foil for everything from a meat ragu to sautéed wild mushrooms.

The traditional recipe sounds easy enough: Boil water, whisk in cornmeal, and stir until the grains have swollen and softened. But the devil is in the details. Polenta can take up to an hour to cook, and if you don't stir almost constantly, it forms intractable clumps. Surely, after five centuries, it is time to find a better way.

So what's the problem with this recipe? When the starchy part of the corn kernels (the endosperm) comes in contact with hot water, it swells and bursts, releasing starch in a process known as gelatinization. At the same time, the grains soften and lose their gritty texture. But tough pieces of endosperm absorb liquid very slowly. Constant stirring is necessary to keep the cornmeal at the bottom of the pot from gelatinizing too quickly and sticking to itself (the source of the dreaded lumps) and to the pot (the source of much frustration for those who wash polenta pots).

Our recipe relies on an unconventional ingredient (baking soda) to change the pH of the water and thus speed up the softening process. And we found a low-tech solution that dramatically reduces the stirring. The end result is perfect polenta that requires little attention and even less fuss. Now that's progress.

WHY THIS RECIPE WORKS

Buy the Right Cornmeal
In the supermarket, cornmeal can be labeled anything from yellow grits to corn semolina. Forget the names. When shopping for the right product to make polenta, there are three things to consider: "Instant" or "quick-cooking" versus the traditional style; degerminated or full-grain meal; and grind size. Leave instant and quick-cooking cornmeals on the shelf. Though we love the full corn flavor of whole-grain cornmeal, it remains slightly gritty no matter how long you cook it. We prefer degerminated cornmeal (check the label), in which the hard hull and germ are removed from each kernel. As for grind, we found that coarser grains brought the most desirable and pillowy texture to polenta.

Flood the Grains with Water
Polenta typically requires a 4:1 ratio of water to cornmeal. But the coarse grains we prefer take a full hour to cook through, during which time the mixture turns extremely thick—not to mention the amount of stirring it requires. We found that a 5:1 ratio (or 7½ cups water for 1½ cups cornmeal) produces just the right loose, creamy consistency.

Add a Pinch of Baking Soda
Baking soda is sometimes added to dried beans to help break down the tough skins. Because corn, like beans, contains pectin, baking soda can work its magic in much the same way—in fact it cuts the cooking time of polenta in half. Be sure not to add too much—it can turn the polenta gluey and lend it an off, chemical flavor.

Use Your Lid
Use a low-tech solution to cut down on stirring—cover the pot and turn the flame to low. This low-heat, covered method cooks the polenta gently and evenly without any clumps—no vigorous stirring required. Just one stir right after the cornmeal goes in and another stir 5 minutes later are all you need.

Once the water comes to a boil, add the cornmeal in a slow, steady stream to prevent lumps.

Creamy Parmesan Polenta

SERVES 4

Coarse-ground degerminated cornmeal such as yellow grits (with grains the size of cous-cous) works best in this recipe. Avoid instant and quick-cooking products, as well as whole-grain, stone-ground, and regular cornmeal. Do not omit the baking soda—it reduces the cooking time and makes for a creamier polenta. If the polenta sputters even slightly after the first 10 minutes, the heat is too high. For a main course, serve the polenta with a topping (recipes follow) or with a wedge of rich cheese (like Gorgonzola) or a meat sauce.

7½	cups water	4	ounces Parmesan cheese, grated
1½	teaspoons salt		(2 cups), plus extra for serving
	Pinch baking soda	2	tablespoons unsalted butter
1½	cups coarse-ground cornmeal		Pepper

1. Bring water to boil in large saucepan over medium-high heat. Stir in salt and baking soda. Slowly pour cornmeal into water in steady stream, while stirring back and forth with wooden spoon or rubber spatula. Bring mixture to boil, stirring constantly, about 1 minute. Reduce heat to lowest possible setting and cover.

2. After 5 minutes, whisk polenta to smooth out any lumps that may have formed, about 15 seconds. (Make sure to scrape down sides and bottom of pan.) Cover and continue to cook, without stirring, until grains of polenta are tender but slightly al dente, about 25 minutes longer. (Polenta should be loose and barely hold its shape but will continue to thicken as it cools.)

3. Remove from heat, stir in Parmesan and butter, and season with pepper to taste. Let stand, covered, for 5 minutes. Serve, passing extra Parmesan separately.

WILD MUSHROOM AND ROSEMARY TOPPING

MAKES ENOUGH FOR 4 SERVINGS

If you use shiitake mushrooms, they should be stemmed.

2	tablespoons unsalted butter	1	pound wild mushrooms (such as
2	tablespoons olive oil		cremini, shiitake, or oyster), trimmed
1	small onion, chopped fine		and sliced
2	garlic cloves, minced	⅓	cup chicken broth
2	teaspoons minced fresh rosemary		Salt and pepper

1. Heat butter and oil in 12-inch nonstick skillet over medium-high heat until shimmering. Add onion and cook, stirring frequently, until onion softens and begins to brown, 5 to 7 minutes. Stir in garlic and rosemary and cook until fragrant, about 30 seconds longer.

2. Add mushrooms and cook, stirring occasionally, until juices release, about 6 minutes. Add broth and salt and pepper to taste; simmer briskly until sauce thickens, about 8 minutes. Spoon mushroom mixture over individual portions of polenta and serve.

RECIPE DETAILS

Timeline

- 10 minutes to bring water to a boil and whisk in cornmeal
- 30 minutes to cook polenta (whisk after 5 minutes to smooth out lumps)
- 5 minutes to finish polenta and let stand

Essential Tools

- Large saucepan (A 4-quart capacity is ideal; a pan with a heavy bottom is essential.)
- Wooden spoon for stirring
- Whisk for smoothing out lumps
- Rasp grater for preparing cheese

Substitutions & Variations

- This recipe depends on using the absolute lowest burner setting. If your cooktop runs hot, use a flame tamer or shape a sheet of heavy-duty foil into a 1-inch-thick ring that fits on the burner, making sure the ring is of even thickness.

SAUTÉED CHERRY TOMATO AND FRESH MOZZARELLA
TOPPING MAKES ENOUGH FOR 4 SERVINGS
Don't stir the cheese into the sautéed tomatoes or it will melt prematurely and turn rubbery.

3	tablespoons extra-virgin olive oil		Salt and pepper
2	garlic cloves, peeled and sliced thin	6	ounces fresh mozzarella cheese,
	Pinch red pepper flakes		cut into ½-inch cubes (1 cup)
	Pinch sugar	2	tablespoons shredded fresh basil
1½	pounds cherry tomatoes, halved		

Heat oil, garlic, pepper flakes, and sugar in 12-inch nonstick skillet over medium-high heat until fragrant and sizzling, about 1 minute. Stir in tomatoes and cook until they just begin to soften, about 1 minute. Season with salt and pepper to taste, and remove from heat. Spoon tomato mixture over individual portions of polenta, top with mozzarella, sprinkle with basil, and serve.

A Better Way to Grate Cheese
We prefer to grate cheeses by hand rather than in a food processor. (The shredding disk is fine for softer cheeses, but the metal blade doesn't grate hard cheese fine enough.) And we recommend two different graters, one for each type of cheese. For absolute accuracy, follow weight rather than volume measures in recipes. Grated cheese can fluff up (or pack down) quite considerably, making dry measuring cups far less precise than a good scale.

1. Use sharp rasp-style grater when handling hard cheeses like Parmesan and Pecorino Romano.

2. Use large holes of paddle-style or box grater for semisoft cheeses like mozzarella and fontina. To prevent grater from becoming clogged, coat holes with vegetable oil spray.

66 Rustic Bread

THE BEST ARTISAN LOAF YOU CAN MAKE AT HOME REQUIRES ALMOST NO KNEADING

In November 2006, *New York Times* writer Mark Bittman published a recipe developed by Jim Lahey of the Sullivan Street Bakery in Manhattan that promised to shake up the world of home baking. The recipe did the seemingly impossible: It allowed the average home cook to bake a loaf of bread that looked like it had been produced in a professional bakery.

The recipe's appeal was its simplicity and novelty. Mix a few cups of flour, a tiny amount of yeast, and a little salt together in a bowl; stir in a lot of water; and leave the dough to rise overnight. After 12 to 18 hours, the dough is turned a couple of times, shaped, risen, and baked in a Dutch oven (to mimic the steam-injected ovens used in bakeries.) An hour later, out comes the best loaf most people have ever baked at home—and all without kneading.

This bread succeeded in changing the conversation. Suddenly, everyone was making this recipe. But it had two significant flaws. The Dutch oven created an amazingly thick crust but the crumb didn't capture the complex yeasty, tangy flavor of a real artisanal loaf. And the recipe often yielded irregular blobs rather than a tidy round *boule*.

To fix these problems, we rethought the roles of water, time, and kneading and devised a more reliable method for shaping the dough and getting it into the Dutch oven. We also experimented with flavor boosters. In the end, we found two secret ingredients—already in your kitchen—that help produce a loaf that tastes as good as it looks. Our recipe (think of it as the 2.0 version) finally delivers on the promise of artisan-quality bread made easily at home.

WHY THIS RECIPE WORKS

Don't Knead—Much
The original no-knead bread has a hydration level of 85 percent. The high level of water, along with the long rest, helps to form the gluten strands and, in effect, takes the place of kneading. But handling this very wet dough is difficult, so we cut back on the water some. With the lower level of hydration, the gluten strands aren't arranged in the same way as the original recipe, so it is necessary to knead slightly—less than a minute.

Boost Flavor
Good rustic bread is made with a fermented starter, which takes days to develop flavor; a packet of yeast simply doesn't offer that complex flavor. But there is a solution—two, to be specific. Most bottled vinegars are 5 percent solutions of acetic acid, the same acid produced by bacteria during fermentation. Just a tablespoon adds tang. And for complexity, reach for a bottle of beer, specifically a lager for best flavor. During fermentation yeast produces alcohol, carbon dioxide, and sulfur compounds—which are all present together in beer.

Simplify Shape and Rise
Skip the complicated shaping techniques and follow our easy two-step process (see page 221). To help this wet dough hold its shape, let it rise right in the Dutch oven. And place the dough on a piece of greased parchment paper so that once the bread has finished baking you can use the edges of the paper to lift the bread out of the hot pot.

Hack a Bakers' Oven
Baking the bread in a Dutch oven essentially acts like a miniature version of a steam-injected oven used by professional bakers. Keep the lid on for part of the baking time and then remove it to allow the bread to finish baking and brown.

Spiking the water with beer and vinegar builds flavor in a flash. An instant-read thermometer is the best way to judge doneness.

Almost No-Knead Bread

MAKES 1 LOAF

Although an enameled cast-iron Dutch oven will yield the best results, the recipe also works in a regular cast-iron Dutch oven or heavy stockpot. Check the knob on your Dutch oven lid, as not all are ovensafe to 425 degrees; look for inexpensive replacement knobs from the manufacturer of your Dutch oven (or try using a metal drawer handle from a hardware store). This dough rises best in a warm kitchen that is at least 68 degrees.

3 cups (15 ounces) all-purpose flour	6 tablespoons mild-flavored lager, such as Budweiser, room temperature
1½ teaspoons salt	
¼ teaspoon instant or rapid-rise yeast	1 tablespoon distilled white vinegar
¾ cup water, room temperature	Vegetable oil spray

1. Whisk flour, salt, and yeast together in large bowl. Add water, beer, and vinegar. Using rubber spatula, fold mixture, scraping up dry flour from bottom of bowl, until shaggy ball forms. Cover bowl with plastic wrap and let sit at room temperature for at least 8 hours or up to 18 hours.

2. Lay 18 by 12-inch sheet of parchment paper on counter and coat lightly with oil spray. Transfer dough to lightly floured counter and knead by hand 10 to 15 times. Shape dough into ball by pulling edges into middle. Transfer loaf, seam side down, to center of greased parchment paper. Using parchment paper as sling, gently lower dough into heavy-bottomed Dutch oven. Mist dough lightly with oil spray, cover loosely with plastic, and let rise at room temperature until doubled in size, about 2 hours. (Dough should barely spring back when poked with your knuckle.)

3. Adjust oven rack to middle position. Lightly flour top of loaf. Using sharp serrated knife, cut ½-inch-deep X into top of loaf. Cover pot and place in oven. Heat oven to 425 degrees. Once oven reaches 425 degrees, bake 30 minutes.

4. Remove lid and continue to bake until crust is deep golden brown and loaf registers 210 degrees, 20 to 30 minutes longer. Carefully remove loaf from pot using parchment sling and transfer to wire rack, discarding parchment. Let cool to room temperature, about 2 hours, before serving. (Bread is best eaten on day it is baked but will keep wrapped in double layer of plastic and stored at room temperature for up to 2 days. To recrisp crust, place unwrapped bread in 450-degree oven for 6 to 8 minutes.)

ALMOST NO-KNEAD BREAD WITH OLIVES, ROSEMARY, AND PARMESAN

If you prefer black olives, substitute them for the green olives, or try a mix of green and black olives.

Add 2 cups finely grated Parmesan cheese and 1 tablespoon minced fresh rosemary to flour mixture in step 1. Add 1 cup pitted green olives, chopped, with water.

RECIPE DETAILS

Timeline

- 5 minutes to assemble dough
- 8 to 18 hours to let dough rise
- 5 minutes to knead and shape dough
- 2 hours to let dough proof
- 1 hour to slash and bake loaf
- 2 hours to cool loaf

Essential Tools

- Parchment paper for transporting dough
- Dutch oven (at least 6 quarts and preferably enameled cast iron) with tight-fitting lid for proofing and baking dough
- Bread knife (or single-edge razor blade) for slashing loaf
- Instant-read thermometer (the best tool for judging doneness in any bread)

Substitutions & Variations

- Add nuts, seeds, dried fruit, and herbs as desired, using the variations listed here as guidelines.

ALMOST NO-KNEAD SEEDED RYE BREAD

Replace 1⅜ cups all-purpose flour with 1⅛ cups rye flour. Add 2 tablespoons caraway seeds to flour mixture in step 1.

ALMOST NO-KNEAD WHOLE-WHEAT BREAD

Replace 1 cup all-purpose flour with 1 cup whole-wheat flour. Stir 2 tablespoons honey into water before adding it to dry ingredients in step 1.

ALMOST NO-KNEAD CRANBERRY-PECAN BREAD

Add ½ cup dried cranberries and ½ cup toasted pecans to flour mixture in step 1.

A Better Way to Shape Bread Dough

Most free-form loaves require complicated shaping techniques that novice bakers have trouble mastering. In addition to reducing kneading to a simple 30-second operation, this recipe simplifies the shaping process into two easy steps.

1. Shape dough into ball by pulling edges into middle. Make sure counter is lightly floured and roll dough back and forth between your hands to form neat ball.

2. Transfer dough to large sheet of greased parchment paper then transfer paper and dough to Dutch oven. Dutch oven is conveniently used for both proofing and baking dough.

67 Banana Bread

BELIEVE IT OR NOT, THE ULTIMATE VERSION STARTS IN A MICROWAVE

The tradition of banana bread-baking is more heavily steeped in parsimony than indulgence. When bananas get covered with brownish-black spots, the frugal alternative to pitching them in the trash has always been to mash them up, add them to a quick-bread batter, and bake.

We're all for thrift in the kitchen, but shouldn't banana bread be something you look forward to making? Any 10-year-old (sorry, kids) can make the typical dry, bland banana bread. But if you want to make a moist, tender loaf with over-the-top banana flavor, you need to think like a mad scientist.

To begin, you need to start with really ripe bananas. As bananas ripen, their starch converts to sugar at an exponential rate. In lab tests, we have found that heavily speckled bananas have three times the amount of fructose of less spotty bananas. First lesson: Wait until the bananas are heavily speckled. That said, there's no benefit to waiting further, until the bananas are black.

The second secret to great banana bread—with intense fruit flavor—is to use a lot of bananas. Most recipes rely on two or three bananas and taste mostly of sugar and spices. For full banana flavor, you need to cram in as many bananas as possible, without sinking the loaf's cake-like structure. Our recipe calls for six large bananas!

To prevent a soggy loaf, we devised an ingenious strategy for eliminating the excess moisture that causes so many recipes to skimp on the fruit. The key is using the microwave to "juice" the bananas. The final result is a tall, tender loaf with a velvety (but not wet) crumb. Now that's a proper way to celebrate America's best-selling fruit.

WHY THIS RECIPE WORKS

Squeeze in More Bananas
Packing more bananas into quick bread means packing in more moisture. To lighten the loaf, use your microwave to extract the moisture from the fruit—simply place the bananas (five, over the usual three) in a bowl, cover, and set the microwave for 5 minutes. Then strain the juice so the mashed banana pulp isn't as wet. But wait—don't throw away that flavorful liquid. Instead, reduce the liquid on the stovetop, then stir this superconcentrated banana juice into the batter to deliver potent banana flavor—without turning the loaf soggy.

Flavor and Enrich
The toasty flavor notes of light brown sugar are a better complement to bananas than white sugar. Vanilla rounds out the bananas' faintly boozy flavor and for rich, full flavor, melted butter is a better choice than vegetable oil—the typical fat used in quick breads.

Separate, Then Fold
Mixing this batter is easy. Mash the bananas and juice well and stir in the rest of the wet ingredients (including the sugar). Add them to the bowl of dry ingredients and fold together gently so that a few flour streaks remain. Further mixing (or the use of an electric mixer) will cause the bread to bake up tough, so go slow.

Top with More Bananas
Once the batter is mixed together, most recipes slide the loaf into the oven and set the timer—but there's one more opportunity to push this loaf into exceptional territory. Shingle a sliced banana over the top of the loaf. To ensure an even rise, place the slices along the sides of the pan. (If you arrange the bananas in the middle of the pan, the loaf will sink.) Sprinkle the top—including those shingled banana slices—with some granulated sugar so the top crust will bake into a caramelized crown for the ultimate loaf.

Extract juice from five bananas for intense flavor without sogginess, then shingle one on top.

Ultimate Banana Bread

MAKES 1 LOAF

Be sure to use very ripe, heavily speckled (or even black) bananas in this recipe. The texture is best when the loaf is eaten fresh, but once cooled completely, it can be covered tightly with plastic wrap and stored for up to three days.

1¾ cups (8¾ ounces) all-purpose flour	2 large eggs
1 teaspoon baking soda	¾ cup packed (5¼ ounces) light brown sugar
½ teaspoon salt	
6 large very ripe bananas (2¼ pounds), peeled	1 teaspoon vanilla extract
8 tablespoons unsalted butter, melted and cooled	½ cup walnuts, toasted and chopped coarse (optional)
	2 teaspoons granulated sugar

1. Adjust oven rack to middle position and heat oven to 350 degrees. Spray 8½ by 4½-inch loaf pan with vegetable oil spray. Whisk flour, baking soda, and salt together in large bowl.

2. Place 5 bananas in separate bowl, cover, and microwave until bananas are soft and have released liquid, about 5 minutes. Transfer bananas to fine-mesh strainer over medium bowl and allow to drain, stirring occasionally, for 15 minutes (you should have ½ to ¾ cup liquid).

3. Transfer liquid to medium saucepan and cook over medium-high heat until reduced to ¼ cup, about 5 minutes. Return drained bananas to bowl. Remove pan from heat, stir reduced liquid into bananas, and mash with potato masher until mostly smooth. Whisk in melted butter, eggs, brown sugar, and vanilla.

4. Pour banana mixture into dry ingredients and stir until just combined, with some streaks of flour remaining. Gently fold in walnuts, if using. Scrape batter into prepared pan. Slice remaining banana diagonally into ¼-inch-thick slices. Shingle banana slices on top of loaf in 2 rows, leaving 1½-inch-wide space down center to ensure even rise. Sprinkle granulated sugar evenly over loaf.

5. Bake until toothpick inserted in center of loaf comes out clean, 55 minutes to 1¼ hours, rotating pan halfway through baking. Let loaf cool in pan for 10 minutes, then turn out onto wire rack and let cool for 1 hour before serving.

RECIPE DETAILS

Timeline

- 20 minutes to microwave and drain bananas (prepare other ingredients while waiting for bananas to drain)
- 15 minutes to simmer banana liquid, assemble batter, and shingle sliced banana on top
- 1 hour to bake loaf
- 1 hour to cool loaf

Essential Tools

- 8½ by 4½-inch loaf pan (A 9 by 5-inch loaf pan will work, but start checking for doneness after 50 minutes.)
- Fine-mesh strainer

Substitutions & Variations

- This recipe can be made using five thawed frozen bananas; since they release a lot of liquid naturally, they can bypass the microwaving in step 2 and go directly into the fine-mesh strainer. Do not use a thawed frozen banana in step 4; it will be too soft to slice. Instead, simply sprinkle the top of the loaf with sugar.

68 Apple Pie

REIMAGINE PIE IN A SKILLET TO SIMPLIFY THE PROCESS

Can something be "all-American" if few Americans have the skills to make it well? As great as apple pie is, it's not a dish we make very often. Preparing a perfect filling, let alone a top and bottom crust, requires a few too many steps for everyday occasions. And the results are far from assured. Even experienced bakers know, firsthand, the possible pitfalls—a soggy bottom crust, overly dry or overly saucy apples, a top crust that gapes far above a shrunken filling.

But what if you could create something that eats like apple pie—that is, with juicy, tender, lightly spiced apples and a flaky crust—but isn't made like apple pie? In the spirit of American ingenuity that's exactly what we have done. And the solution has its roots in colonial America. Let us explain.

Among the panoply of old-fashioned American fruit desserts—which includes crisps, cobblers, buckles, grunts, slumps, and such—the pandowdy is surprisingly close to modern apple pie. Popular in colonial New England but now forgotten, a pandowdy is essentially an apple pie filling baked with a top crust. Traditionally, the filling was prepared in a cast-iron pan and then topped with a round of pastry. During or after baking, the baker would break the pastry and push it into the filling, a technique known as "dowdying" (and a reference, perhaps, to the dessert's resulting "dowdy" appearance).

Rustic looks aside, we love the simplicity of this no-frills recipe. With no fussy crimping, no filling that must be finessed to make it sliceable, and no bottom crust that could get soggy, this recipe is utterly reliable. We added some updates, as well as a new name, to create an apple pie every American can successfully make.

WHY THIS RECIPE WORKS

Caramelize the Apples
Simplifying apple pie starts with the apples. Use a mix of apples—sweet and tart for complex flavor. Slice the apples ½ inch thick, rather than the typical ¼ inch thick so that the apples don't disintegrate during the two-stage cooking process. Caramelize the apples first before adding the crust—it will intensify the apple flavor in the finished pie.

Enrich the Filling
Apples aren't as juicy as berries or stone fruits and benefit from extra moisture for a saucy filling. Adding cider to the apples does the job and delivers resonant apple flavor. Maple syrup instead of plain old sugar strikes the perfect balance on the sweetener front. Maple complements the natural sweetness of the apples without being cloying and it makes the filling even juicier. To give the juices body, add a little cornstarch.

The Upper Crust
The dough for the top crust is simple to prepare in a food processor. Butter adds flavor and shortening ensures a flaky outcome. Roll the dough into a round and simply drape it over the cooked apples in the skillet—no fluting necessary. Scoring the dough encourages a multitude of crisp edges that contrast nicely with the tender fruit and recalls (in a less dowdy way) the broken-up crusts of a traditional pandowdy. Brushing the dough with egg white and sprinkling it with sugar before baking gives it a golden brown sheen and sweet crunch.

Bake Quickly
The precooked apples need less time in the oven to become perfectly tender, so bake the skillet pie in a hot oven for just 20 minutes—less than half the time of a traditional apple pie. The top crust will be perfectly browned and flaky.

Cider keeps the sautéed apples moist while scoring the crust creates many crisp edges.

Skillet Apple Pie

SERVES 6 TO 8

Use a combination of sweet, crisp apples such as Golden Delicious and firm, tart apples such as Cortland or Empire. Serve warm or at room temperature with vanilla ice cream.

CRUST

- 1 cup (5 ounces) all-purpose flour
- 1 tablespoon sugar
- ½ teaspoon salt
- 2 tablespoons vegetable shortening, chilled
- 6 tablespoons unsalted butter, cut into ¼-inch pieces and chilled
- 3–4 tablespoons ice water

FILLING

- ½ cup apple cider
- ⅓ cup maple syrup
- 2 tablespoons lemon juice
- 2 teaspoons cornstarch
- ⅛ teaspoon ground cinnamon (optional)
- 2 tablespoons unsalted butter
- 2½ pounds apples, peeled, cored, and cut into ½-inch-thick wedges
- 1 large egg white, lightly beaten
- 2 teaspoons sugar

1. *For the Crust:* Pulse flour, sugar, and salt in food processor until combined, about 4 pulses. Add shortening and pulse until mixture resembles coarse sand, about 10 pulses. Sprinkle butter pieces over top and pulse until mixture is pale yellow and resembles coarse crumbs, with butter bits no larger than small peas, about 10 pulses. Transfer mixture to medium bowl.

2. Sprinkle 3 tablespoons ice water over mixture. With rubber spatula, use folding motion to mix, pressing down on dough until dough is slightly tacky and sticks together, adding up to 1 tablespoon more ice water if dough does not come together. Flatten dough into 4-inch disk, wrap in plastic wrap, and refrigerate for at least 1 hour or up to 2 days. Let sit at room temperature for 15 minutes before rolling.

3. *For the Filling:* Adjust oven rack to upper-middle position and heat oven to 500 degrees. Whisk cider, maple syrup, lemon juice, cornstarch, and cinnamon, if using, together in bowl until smooth. Melt butter in 12-inch ovensafe skillet over medium-high heat. Add apples and cook, stirring 2 or 3 times, until apples begin to caramelize, about 5 minutes. (Do not fully cook apples.) Off heat, add cider mixture and gently stir until apples are well coated. Set aside to cool slightly.

4. Roll dough out on lightly floured counter to 11-inch round. Roll dough loosely around rolling pin and unroll over apple filling. Brush dough with egg white and sprinkle with sugar. With sharp knife, gently cut dough into 6 pieces by making 1 vertical cut followed by 2 evenly spaced horizontal cuts (perpendicular to first cut). Bake until apples are tender and crust is deep golden brown, about 20 minutes, rotating skillet halfway through baking. Let cool about 15 minutes; serve warm.

RECIPE DETAILS

Timeline

- 10 minutes to make pie dough
- 1 hour to chill pie dough (prepare and cool apple filling at this point)
- 10 minutes to roll out dough and assemble pie
- 35 minutes to bake and cool pie

Essential Tools

- Food processor for making dough
- 12-inch ovensafe skillet (If your skillet is not ovensafe, transfer the cooked apples and cider mixture to a 13 by 9-inch baking dish, roll the dough a to 13 by 9-inch rectangle, then cut the crust and bake as instructed.)
- Rolling pin
- Pastry brush for applying egg wash

Substitutions & Variations

- If you do not have apple cider, reduced apple juice may be used as a substitute; simmer 1 cup apple juice in a small saucepan over medium heat until reduced to ½ cup, about 10 minutes.
- We like the simplicity of this filling, but other classic apple pie add-ins, such as chopped crystallized ginger or a handful of dried fruit, can be added along with the cider mixture.

69 Yellow Layer Cake

BECAUSE EVERYONE DESERVES A HOMEMADE BIRTHDAY CAKE

When it comes to celebrating a birthday, nothing says you care quite like a homemade cake. Of course, for many cooks "homemade" starts with a box mix. And that's a shame. These high-tech cakes certainly look great, but once the candles have been blown out things go downhill. All the additives that make the cake so tall and fluffy don't do much for the flavor.

Many bakers turn to box mixes because truly homemade recipes often yield dense, squat layers. Many from-scratch cakes taste buttery and delicious, but they don't have the necessary height to make a true showstopper. And their short stature means that the cake-to-frosting ratio is out of whack. (Yes, there is such a thing as too much frosting.)

We set out to rework the classic yellow cake recipe, taking what we like about the box mixes (height and texture) and combining that with real ingredients. Our goal was to produce fluffy cake layers that were sturdy enough to frost easily. An ingenious solution helped us achieve stunning results.

Chiffon cakes are especially weightless, springy, and moist, but they are too light to stand up to a serious slathering of frosting. So we adapted a chiffon technique (using a large quantity of whipped egg whites to get a light texture) with ingredients from our favorite butter cake recipe. This unorthodox method produces a light, porous cake that is sturdy enough to hold the frosting's weight.

As for the frosting, a hefty amount of cocoa powder combined with melted chocolate creates intense flavor, while corn syrup, along with the usual confectioners' sugar, makes it glossy. The food processor ensures a silky-smooth result in record time.

WHY THIS RECIPE WORKS

Fully Whip the Whites
The fluffy texture of the cake layers relies heavily on whipped egg whites. For maximum volume, whip the whites (and a pinch of cream of tartar for stabilization) until foamy and then gradually add some sugar to further stabilize them. Keep whipping until the whites reach stiff peaks (see page 15).

Flour First
In most cake recipes, the flour and other dry ingredients are the last items to go into the mixing bowl. In this recipe, once the whites are whipped and transferred to a clean bowl, you place the flour and dry ingredients (including most of the sugar) in the mixer bowl and begin mixing the batter by adding the egg yolk and melted butter mixture.

Fold Gently
Once the batter is smooth, it's time to fold in the whipped whites, by hand. (The mixer would knock out too much air.) The batter is quite thick so use one-third of the whipped whites to lighten it. You can stir in this first batch of whites quite thoroughly. However, the remaining whites must be gently folded into the lightened batter. Once you no longer see large streaks of whites, stop.

Don't Overbake
Many novice bakers worry that underbaked cake layers will stick to the pan. However, overbaked layers are just as problematic, becoming dry and even crumbly if they spend too long in the oven. Use a toothpick to tell when the cakes are done—it should come out clean when inserted into the center of the cakes.

Faster Frosting
Softened butter gives our frosting rich, old-fashioned flavor that trumps anything you can get from a can. Supplement some of the confectioners' sugar with corn syrup for a silky texture and mix it all in a food processor for ultimate ease.

For perfect results, prepare the pans as directed and whip the egg whites to stiff peaks.

Fluffy Yellow Layer Cake with Chocolate Frosting

SERVES 10 TO 12

Bring all the ingredients to room temperature before beginning this recipe. Cool the chocolate to between 85 and 100 degrees before adding it to the butter mixture.

CAKE

2½ cups (10 ounces) cake flour

1¾ cups (12¼ ounces) granulated sugar

1¼ teaspoons baking powder

¼ teaspoon baking soda

¾ teaspoon salt

1 cup buttermilk, room temperature

3 large eggs, separated, plus 3 large yolks, room temperature

10 tablespoons unsalted butter, melted and cooled

3 tablespoons vegetable oil

2 teaspoons vanilla extract

Pinch cream of tartar

FROSTING

20 tablespoons (2½ sticks) unsalted butter, softened

1 cup (4 ounces) confectioners' sugar

¾ cup (2¼ ounces) Dutch-processed cocoa powder

Pinch salt

¾ cup light corn syrup

1 teaspoon vanilla extract

8 ounces chocolate, melted and cooled

1. *For the Cake:* Adjust oven rack to middle position and heat oven to 350 degrees. Grease two 9-inch round cake pans, line with parchment paper, grease parchment, and flour pans. Whisk flour, 1½ cups sugar, baking powder, baking soda, and salt together in large bowl. In medium bowl, whisk together buttermilk, egg yolks, melted butter, oil, and vanilla.

2. Using stand mixer fitted with whisk, whip egg whites and cream of tartar on medium-low speed until foamy, about 1 minute. Increase speed to medium-high and whip whites to soft billowy mounds, about 1 minute. Gradually add remaining ¼ cup sugar and whip until glossy, stiff peaks form, 2 to 3 minutes; transfer to bowl.

3. Add flour mixture to now-empty bowl. With mixer on low speed, gradually pour in buttermilk mixture and mix until almost incorporated (a few streaks of dry flour will remain), about 15 seconds. Scrape down bowl, then beat on medium-low speed until smooth and fully incorporated, 10 to 15 seconds.

4. Using rubber spatula, stir one-third of whites into batter, then add remaining two-thirds whites and gently fold into batter until no white streaks remain. Divide batter evenly between prepared pans, smooth tops with rubber spatula, and gently tap pans on counter to release air bubbles.

5. Bake cakes until toothpick inserted in centers comes out clean, 20 to 22 minutes, switching and rotating pans halfway through baking. Let cakes cool in pans on wire rack for 10 minutes. Remove cakes from pans, discard parchment, and let cool completely, about 2 hours, before frosting. (Cooled cakes can be wrapped tightly in plastic wrap and kept at room temperature for up to 1 day. Cakes can also be wrapped tightly in plastic, then aluminum foil, and frozen for up to 1 month; defrost cakes at room temperature before unwrapping and frosting.)

RECIPE DETAILS

Timeline

• 30 minutes to prep ingredients (start by measuring buttermilk and separating eggs so these ingredients warm up to room temperature)

• 15 minutes to prepare cake batter

• 2½ hours to bake and cool cake layers (mostly hands-off)

• 15 minutes to make frosting (best done while cake layers are cooling)

• 10 minutes to frost cake

Essential Tools

• Two 9-inch round cake pans (at least 2 inches tall)

• Stand mixer

• Toothpick for testing cake layers (If you don't have a toothpick, gently press your fingertip into the top of a cake layer—yes, it will be hot, so be careful. If the top springs back when touched, the cake is done.)

• Food processor

• Large offset spatula for spreading the frosting

Substitutions & Variations

• Cake flour is a must here; all-purpose flour will make the layers tough, dry, and dense. In a pinch, you can use 2 cups plus 3 tablespoons all-purpose flour mixed with 5 tablespoons cornstarch.

• If you don't have buttermilk, mix 1 cup regular milk with 1 tablespoon lemon juice and use this "clabbered" milk instead.

• The frosting may be made with milk, semisweet, or bittersweet chocolate; we prefer milk chocolate for this recipe.

• The frosted cake can be refrigerated for up to one day; bring to room temperature before serving.

6. *For the Frosting:* Process butter, sugar, cocoa, and salt in food processor until smooth, about 30 seconds, scraping down bowl as needed. Add corn syrup and vanilla and process until just combined, 5 to 10 seconds. Scrape down bowl, then add chocolate and process until smooth and creamy, 10 to 15 seconds.

7. *To Assemble the Cake:* Line edges of cake platter with 4 strips of parchment paper to keep platter clean. Place 1 small dab of frosting in center of platter, then place cake layer on prepared platter. Place generous 1 cup frosting in center of cake layer and, using large offset spatula, spread in even layer right to edge of cake. Place second cake layer on top, making sure layers are aligned, then frost top in same manner as first layer, this time spreading frosting until slightly over edge. Gather more frosting on tip of spatula and gently spread frosting onto side of cake. Smooth frosting by gently running edge of spatula around cake and leveling ridge that forms around top edge, or create billows by pressing back of spoon into frosting and twirling spoon as you lift away. Carefully pull out pieces of parchment from beneath cake before serving.

A Better Way to Frost a Cake

Many cooks make a mess of the frosting process. They either try to move the cake to a serving platter after it's been frosted (a big mistake) or they frost the cake on the serving platter without protecting it. Before you start, make sure the cake layers are level. (Flat layers are essential for a well-constructed cake that doesn't lean.) If necessary, use a serrated knife to saw off the domed top.

1. Line flat platter or cake stand with 4 strips of parchment paper. Place small dab of frosting in center of platter, then set first cake layer on frosting to anchor it in place.

2. Place generous 1 cup frosting in center of cake layer and use large offset spatula to spread frosting up to edge of cake.

3. Align second cake layer on top. Frost top, this time spreading frosting until slightly over edge. Gather more frosting on tip of spatula and gently spread frosting onto side of cake, using gentle up and down motion.

4. Gently run edge of spatula around sides to smooth out bumps and tidy area where frosting on top and sides merge. Remove parchment strips and serve.

70 Chocolate Cupcakes

FINALLY, A CUPCAKE THAT MERITS SERIOUS ATTENTION

The trend took shape almost overnight: A pastel frosted cupcake lands a cameo on the HBO series *Sex and the City*, and before the owners of New York's Magnolia Bakery can blink, their single-serving sweet turns into a sugar-charged sensation. The cupcake concept—a dainty, portion-controlled, out-of-hand snack universally recognized from childhood birthday parties—was just waiting to take off, and it wasn't long before dedicated "cupcakeries" popped up across the country.

But if cupcake appeal is all about getting the best attributes of cake in a portable package, the irony is that most of these highly specialized bakeries can't deliver the goods—a moist, tender, pint-sized cake capped with just enough creamy, not-too-sweet frosting.

A chocolate cupcake is particularly hard to get right. If the cupcakes have decent chocolate flavor, their structure is too crumbly and you end up with more cupcake on your shirt than in your mouth. There's only so much chocolate you can cram into a cupcake before it literally falls apart. Or is there? What if you could make a sturdier cupcake?

Cakes are often made with low-protein cake flour to promote tenderness. Switching to all-purpose flour (which contains more protein) for cupcakes is an improvement. That's because more protein translates to more gluten, and more gluten means more structure. But we didn't really solve the problem until we tried bread flour, which contains still more protein.

And for the ultimate chocolate hit, we created a chocolate filling for our chocolate cupcakes. Cap them with chocolate frosting and you finally have something that deserves the hype.

WHY THIS RECIPE WORKS

Maximize Chocolate Flavor
To infuse the cupcakes with pure chocolate flavor through and through, team cocoa powder with bittersweet chocolate. Dairy dulls chocolate flavor—think about when you pour too much milk into your mug of cocoa. Instead, swap in coffee, which enhances and deepens chocolate flavor, especially when the chocolate is dissolved in hot coffee, a process called blooming.

Make an Oil Change
Kick butter to the curb too. Butter isn't bad in these cupcakes, but replacing dairy-rich butter with vegetable oil produces fuller, unadulterated chocolate flavor. Vegetable oil also makes the cupcakes extra moist (butter contains about 16 percent water, which can evaporate and leave the cake dry).

Centralize the Chocolate
Mimic the sweet filling of kid-centric packaged chocolate cupcakes with a decidedly grown-up replacement—a truffle-like ganache center. Top the batter of each cupcake with a spoonful of chocolate filling (a simple mixture of melted chocolate, cream, and confectioners' sugar). As the cupcakes bake, the filling will sink down into the middle for a sweet surprise.

Reconsider the Frosting
These refined cupcakes deserve a luxuriously rich frosting. Rather than the classic butter and confectioners' sugar frosting, turn to a cooked buttercream, the Swiss meringue variety, where egg whites and granulated sugar are heated over a double boiler, then whipped with knobs of softened butter, and finally melted bittersweet chocolate. The result? An utterly decadent frosting for a cupcake that's truly out of the ordinary.

For cupcakes worth the fuss, bloom cocoa and chopped bittersweet chocolate with hot coffee and then dollop fudgy ganache into the batter before baking.

Chocolate Cupcakes with Ganache Filling

MAKES 12 CUPCAKES

Use a high-quality bittersweet or semisweet chocolate for this recipe.

FILLING

- 2 ounces bittersweet chocolate, chopped fine
- ¼ cup heavy cream
- 1 tablespoon confectioners' sugar

CUPCAKES

- 3 ounces bittersweet chocolate, chopped fine
- ⅓ cup (1 ounce) Dutch-processed cocoa powder
- ¾ cup brewed coffee, hot
- ¾ cup (4⅛ ounces) bread flour
- ¾ cup (5¼ ounces) granulated sugar
- ½ teaspoon salt
- ½ teaspoon baking soda
- 6 tablespoons vegetable oil
- 2 large eggs
- 2 teaspoons distilled white vinegar
- 1 teaspoon vanilla extract

- 1 recipe Creamy Chocolate Frosting (recipe follows)

1. *For the Filling:* Microwave chocolate, cream, and sugar in medium bowl until mixture is warm to touch, about 30 seconds. Whisk until smooth, then transfer bowl to refrigerator and let sit until just chilled, no longer than 30 minutes.

2. *For the Cupcakes:* Adjust oven rack to middle position and heat oven to 350 degrees. Line 12-cup muffin tin with paper or foil liners. Place chocolate and cocoa in medium heatproof bowl. Pour hot coffee over mixture and let sit, covered, for 5 minutes. Whisk mixture gently until smooth, then transfer to refrigerator to cool completely, about 20 minutes.

3. Whisk flour, sugar, salt, and baking soda together in medium bowl. Whisk oil, eggs, vinegar, and vanilla into cooled chocolate mixture until smooth. Add flour mixture and whisk until smooth.

4. Using ice cream scoop or large spoon, divide batter evenly among prepared muffin cups. Place 1 slightly rounded teaspoon ganache filling on top of each portion of batter. Bake cupcakes until set and just firm to touch, 17 to 19 minutes, rotating muffin tin halfway through baking. Let cupcakes cool in muffin tin on wire rack until cool enough to handle, about 10 minutes. Lift each cupcake from tin, set on wire rack, and let cool completely, about 1 hour, before frosting. (Unfrosted cupcakes can be stored at room temperature for up to 1 day.)

5. Spread 2 to 3 tablespoons frosting over each cooled cupcake and serve.

RECIPE DETAILS

Timeline

- 35 minutes to make and chill ganache filling (melt and cool chocolate mixture for cupcakes while waiting)
- 10 minutes to make and portion out cupcake batter
- 30 minutes to bake and cool cupcakes in pan
- 1 hour to cool cupcakes out of pan
- 15 minutes to make frosting and finish cupcakes

Essential Tools

- Stand mixer for frosting
- Muffin tin
- Paper or foil cupcake liners (essential so cupcakes don't stick to pan)
- Small offset spatula for applying frosting

Substitutions & Variations

- You can omit the ganache filling for a more traditional cupcake.
- The frosting is easily varied as follows:
- Vanilla Frosting: Omit bittersweet chocolate and increase sugar to ½ cup. (If final frosting seems too thick, warm mixer bowl briefly over saucepan filled with 1 inch of barely simmering water and beat a second time until creamy).
- Peanut Butter Frosting: Omit bittersweet chocolate, increase sugar to ½ cup, and increase salt to ⅛ teaspoon. Add ⅔ cup creamy peanut butter with vanilla extract in step 2. Garnish cupcakes with ½ cup chopped peanuts.
- Butterscotch Frosting: Omit bittersweet chocolate, substitute ½ cup packed dark brown sugar for granulated sugar, and increase salt to ½ teaspoon.

CREAMY CHOCOLATE FROSTING MAKES ABOUT 2¼ CUPS

The melted chocolate should be cooled to between 85 and 100 degrees before being added to the frosting. If the frosting seems too soft after adding the chocolate, chill it briefly in the refrigerator and then rewhip it until creamy.

⅓ cup (2⅓ ounces) sugar

2 large egg whites

   Pinch salt

12 tablespoons unsalted butter,
    cut into 12 pieces and softened

6 ounces bittersweet chocolate,
   melted and cooled

½ teaspoon vanilla extract

1. Combine sugar, egg whites, and salt in bowl of stand mixer and set bowl over saucepan filled with 1 inch of barely simmering water. Whisking gently but constantly, heat mixture until it is slightly thickened, foamy, and registers 150 degrees, 2 to 3 minutes.

2. Fit stand mixer with whisk and whip mixture on medium speed until consistency of shaving cream and slightly cooled, 1 to 2 minutes. Add butter, 1 piece at a time, until smooth and creamy. (Frosting may look curdled after half of butter has been added; it will smooth with additional butter.) Once all butter is added, add cooled melted chocolate and vanilla; mix until combined. Increase speed to medium-high and beat until light, fluffy, and thoroughly combined, about 30 seconds, scraping down beater and sides of bowl with rubber spatula as necessary. (Frosting can be made up to 1 day in advance and refrigerated in airtight container. When ready to frost, warm frosting briefly in microwave until just slightly softened, 5 to 10 seconds. Once warmed, stir until creamy.)

A Better Way to Melt Chocolate

Many novice bakers rush this process and end up scorching the chocolate. Gentle heat is a must. We prefer the ease of the microwave, but either method works. Make sure to stir occasionally since that facilitates melting.

A. Place chopped chocolate in heatproof bowl set over saucepan of simmering water (water should not touch bottom of bowl). Adjust heat as necessary to maintain simmer, and stir occasionally until chocolate melts. For easy removal, choose bowl that hangs over pot.

B. Place chopped chocolate in microwave-safe bowl and heat in microwave at 50 percent power for 1 minute. Stir chocolate and continue heating until melted, stirring once every additional 30 seconds. Don't use full power or chocolate will scorch.

The Global Essentials

EXCITING RECIPES THAT BRING THE WORLD TO YOUR KITCHEN

71 Rice and Beans

COOKING RICE AND BEANS TOGETHER MAKES EACH BETTER

Rice and beans sustain many millions of people every day, from Brazil to Africa and from New Orleans to Delhi. The combination is satisfying and nutritious but rarely sexy—unless of course you're talking about the Cuban version.

Cuban black beans and rice is popular well beyond its island home because of the complex flavors contributed by sautéed vegetables, spices, and pork. The dried beans are traditionally simmered on their own, and then some of the inky bean liquid is used to cook the rice, adding still more depth to this one-dish meal.

While rice and beans should be hearty, it shouldn't be stodgy and, unfortunately, that's often the case. Likewise, getting the texture of the main elements just right is a challenge, especially if the rice and beans spend time cooking together. It seems that one element is either overdone or underdone.

Rinsing the rice and limiting the liquid in the pot with the rice are good first steps to eliminating the starch problem. And cooking the beans until they are completely tender (so that they are no longer soaking up liquid) makes it easier to determine the right amount of liquid for cooking the rice.

But the real secret is to reduce the number of burst beans—the main source of all that starch. Soaking dried beans helps, but brining the beans (that is, adding salt to the water) is transformative (see page 241 for more information). The salt weakens the pectin network in the skins, allowing them to soften and expand during the cooking process. Elastic skins are the key to beans that don't cook up starchy. They don't brine beans in Cuba—but maybe they should.

WHY THIS RECIPE WORKS

Flavor the Beans as They Cook

The traditional recipe has three parts—cook the beans, cook the sofrito, and then combine the sofrito and beans with the rice to finish cooking. Our version begins with brining the beans and then cooking them partway. A sofrito adds depth but we found we needed more. Our twofold solution: We add some vegetables to the pot of beans as they cook and we use a mixture of chicken broth and water. This gives flavor to the beans as well as to the cooking liquid (which is later used to cook the rice).

Make the Sofrito

The sofrito is commonly pureed before adding it to the beans and rice mixture, but this muddies the texture and eliminates the possibility of browning the vegetables for flavor. Instead, we chop the onion and peppers small (or pulse them in a food processor). Then we sauté them with some cumin and oregano in the

rendered fat from salt pork until they're golden brown and packed with flavor. A hit of minced garlic completes the sofrito, which is the backbone of this dish.

Prevent Scorched Rice

Many versions of this classic recipe suffer from rice that is scorched on the bottom of the pan and undercooked on top. What to do? First, we remove excess starch from the rice by rinsing it in water. This helps prevent the individual rice grains from clumping and becoming sticky. Then, we move the entire operation into the oven. The even heat from the oven cooks the rice perfectly from top to bottom.

Brighten the Flavors

When the pot (with the rice, beans, and liquid) goes into the oven, we add a splash of red wine vinegar for brightness. And we finish the dish with scallions and lime, which are important additions that really bring the other flavors to life.

Aromatic vegetables pull double duty, flavoring the beans as they simmer and creating a flavor base for the rice.

Cuban-Style Black Beans and Rice

SERVES 6 TO 8

It is important to use lean—not fatty—salt pork.

Salt

1 cup dried black beans, picked over and rinsed

2 cups chicken broth

2 large green bell peppers, halved, stemmed, and seeded

1 large onion, halved at equator and peeled, root end left intact

1 head garlic (5 cloves minced, rest of head halved at equator with skin left intact)

2 bay leaves

1½ cups long-grain white rice

2 tablespoons olive oil

6 ounces lean salt pork, cut into ¼-inch dice

4 teaspoons ground cumin

1 tablespoon minced fresh oregano

2 tablespoons red wine vinegar

2 scallions, sliced thin

Lime wedges

RECIPE DETAILS

Timeline

• 8 to 24 hours to brine beans
• 45 minutes to cook beans (rinse rice and prepare ingredients for sofrito while beans are cooking)
• 30 minutes to cook sofrito
• 40 minutes to cook rice and beans together (mostly hands-off)

Essential Tools

• Dutch oven with tight-fitting lid
• Colander for draining beans
• Fine-mesh strainer for rinsing rice

Substitutions & Variations

• If you can't find lean salt pork, substitute 6 slices of bacon. If using bacon, decrease the cooking time in step 4 to 8 minutes.
• For a vegetarian version, substitute water for chicken broth and omit salt pork. Add 1 tablespoon tomato paste with vegetables in step 4 and increase amount of salt in step 5 to 1½ teaspoons.

1. Dissolve 1½ tablespoons salt in 2 quarts cold water in large bowl or container. Add beans and soak at room temperature for at least 8 hours or up to 24 hours. Drain and rinse well.

2. In Dutch oven, stir together drained beans, broth, 2 cups water, 1 pepper half, 1 onion half (with root end), halved garlic head, bay leaves, and 1 teaspoon salt. Bring to simmer over medium-high heat, cover, and reduce heat to low. Cook until beans are just soft, 30 to 35 minutes. Using tongs, discard pepper, onion, garlic, and bay leaves. Drain beans in colander set over large bowl, reserving 2½ cups bean cooking liquid. (If you don't have enough bean cooking liquid, add water to equal 2½ cups.) Do not wash out Dutch oven.

3. Adjust oven rack to middle position and heat oven to 350 degrees. Place rice in large fine-mesh strainer and rinse under cold running water until water runs clear, about 1½ minutes. Shake strainer vigorously to remove all excess water; set rice aside. Cut remaining peppers and onion into 2-inch pieces and pulse in food processor until broken into rough ¼-inch pieces, about 8 pulses, scraping down bowl as necessary; set vegetables aside.

4. In now-empty Dutch oven, heat 1 tablespoon oil and salt pork over medium-low heat and cook, stirring frequently, until lightly browned and rendered, 15 to 20 minutes. Add remaining 1 tablespoon oil, chopped peppers and onion, cumin, and oregano. Increase heat to medium and continue to cook, stirring frequently, until vegetables are softened and beginning to brown, 10 to 15 minutes longer. Add minced garlic and cook, stirring constantly, until fragrant, about 1 minute. Add rice and stir to coat, about 30 seconds.

5. Stir in beans, reserved bean cooking liquid, vinegar, and ½ teaspoon salt. Increase heat to medium-high and bring to simmer. Cover and transfer to oven. Cook until liquid is absorbed and rice is tender, about 30 minutes. Fluff with fork and let rest, uncovered, 5 minutes. Serve, passing scallions and lime wedges separately.

A Better Way to Soak Dried Beans

Soaking dried beans shortens their cooking time and results in creamier beans with fewer burst or starchy samples. Adding salt to the soaking water—in effect, brining the beans—makes their skins more elastic and further reduces bursting. The amounts of salt and water listed here are for 1 pound of dried beans. Use half as much salt and water when soaking 1 cup of beans. To speed up the soaking process, bring the water and salt to a boil in a Dutch oven and then slide the pot off the heat. Add the beans and soak for 1 hour. Although less effective than an overnight soak, a quick soak is better than nothing.

1. Place dried beans on plate or cutting board and pick through them to remove any stones as well as beans that are broken or shriveled. (A plate or board with a contrasting color, or even a rimmed baking sheet, makes it especially easy to identify pebbles and other foreign matter.) Place beans in colander and rinse well.

2. Dissolve 3 tablespoons salt in 4 quarts cold water in large bowl or container. (Make sure to use table salt, not kosher salt; the former dissolves much more easily.)

3. Add beans and soak at room temperature for at least 8 hours or up to 24 hours.

4. Drain beans in colander and rinse well to flush out any traces of salt. Beans are now ready to cook.

72 Rice and Lentils

AN EASY METHOD FOR FRYING ONIONS TURNS RICE AND LENTILS INTO A MEAL

Essentially the rice and beans of the Middle East, *mujaddara* is an excellent example of how a few humble ingredients can add up to a dish that's satisfying, complex, and deeply savory. Unlike Cuban black beans and rice (see page 240), this dish is vegetarian and doesn't rely on a variety of sautéed aromatic vegetables for flavor. Lentils, rice, and spices, plus crispy onions—that's it.

Though the particulars differ, the basic approach is fairly consistent: Boil basmati rice and lentils together until each component is tender but intact and then work in warm spices such as coriander, cumin, cinnamon, allspice, and pepper, as well as a good measure of garlic. But the real showpiece of this dish is the onions— either fried or caramelized—which get stirred into and sprinkled over the pilaf just before serving. Their flavor is as deep as their mahogany color suggests. Finished with a bracing yogurt sauce, this pilaf is pure comfort food.

As with other rice and bean dishes, getting the rice and lentils both perfectly cooked is a challenge. Invariably, one element is either too firm or mushy. Cooking the lentils before they are combined with the rice is the best way to solve this problem. Tender lentils won't absorb any of the water needed to steam the rice so the two elements (cooked lentils and raw rice) can steam together without harming each other.

The onion garnish is the most important part of this recipe and the step that gives cooks the most trouble. The key is to drive off excess moisture in the onions so they can crisp quickly. A very modern tool—the microwave—turns out to be the ideal tool for the job.

WHY THIS RECIPE WORKS

Know Your Lentils
Many lentil dishes benefit from the firm, distinct texture of the French variety known as *lentilles du Puy*. But in this dish, the softer (but still intact) texture of green or brown lentils is best because it pairs well with the tender grains of rice.

Getting the Rice in Sync
Toasting the rice in oil brings out the grain's nutty flavor and is an opportunity to deepen the flavor of the spices and garlic by cooking them in the fat as well. But once the water and cooked lentils are added, it's a race to the finish—with the lentils still soaking up most of the liquid before the rice can cook through. Adding more liquid is a nonstarter. But soaking the raw rice in hot water (do this while the lentils simmer), softens the grains so that they can absorb water more easily. Plus, this step loosens and washes away some of the excess starches, helping the rice cook up fluffy, not sticky.

Remove Moisture in the Microwave
This dish calls for frying 2 pounds of onions, enough so that a portion can be stirred into the pilaf and the remaining sprinkled over the top as a garnish. That's a lot of onions, a lot of oil, and a lot of frying time (about an hour). Simply salting the onions removes some moisture, but salting and microwaving for just 5 minutes before rinsing and draining them does so much more effectively. The benefit is twofold: Removing much of the moisture shrinks the onions so they can all fit into the pan at once and the smaller volume of onions requires less oil.

Upcycle the Oil
Once you're finished frying the onions, don't discard the onion-infused oil. Use a few tablespoons when sautéing the rice and spices, where it will boost the savory flavor of the pilaf even further. So, yes, make the onion garnish first, before starting on the lentils and rice—the onions will stay crispy enough.

Soaking the rice removes excess starch and microwaving the onions helps them fry faster.

Rice and Lentils with Crispy Onions (Mujaddara)

SERVES 4 TO 6

Do not substitute smaller French lentils for the green or brown lentils. Make the Crispy Onions before starting this recipe. Serve with Yogurt Sauce (at right), if desired.

8½ ounces (1¼ cups) green or brown lentils, picked over and rinsed	1 teaspoon ground coriander
Salt and pepper	1 teaspoon ground cumin
1¼ cups basmati rice	½ teaspoon ground cinnamon
1 recipe Crispy Onions (recipe follows), plus 3 tablespoons reserved oil	½ teaspoon ground allspice
3 garlic cloves, minced	⅛ teaspoon cayenne pepper
	1 teaspoon sugar
	3 tablespoons minced fresh cilantro

1. Bring lentils, 4 cups water, and 1 teaspoon salt to boil in medium saucepan over high heat. Reduce heat to low and cook until lentils are tender, 15 to 17 minutes. Drain and set aside. While lentils cook, place rice in medium bowl and cover by 2 inches with hot tap water; let stand for 15 minutes.

2. Using your hands, gently swish rice grains to release excess starch. Carefully pour off water, leaving rice in bowl. Add cold tap water to rice and pour off water. Repeat adding and pouring off cold tap water 4 to 5 times, until water runs almost clear. Drain rice in fine-mesh strainer.

3. Heat reserved onion oil, garlic, coriander, cumin, cinnamon, allspice, ¼ teaspoon pepper, and cayenne in Dutch oven over medium heat until fragrant, about 2 minutes. Add rice and cook, stirring occasionally, until edges of rice begin to turn translucent, about 3 minutes. Add 2¼ cups water, sugar, and 1 teaspoon salt and bring to boil. Stir in lentils, reduce heat to low, cover, and cook until all liquid is absorbed, about 12 minutes.

4. Off heat, remove lid, fold dish towel in half, and place over pot; replace lid. Let stand for 10 minutes. Fluff rice and lentils with fork and stir in cilantro and half of crispy onions. Transfer to serving platter, top with remaining crispy onions, and serve.

CRISPY ONIONS MAKES 1½ CUPS

It is crucial to thoroughly dry the microwaved onions after rinsing. The best way to accomplish this is to use a salad spinner. Reserve frying oil for cooking rice.

2 pounds onions, halved and sliced crosswise into ¼-inch-thick pieces	2 teaspoons salt
	1½ cups vegetable oil

1. Toss onions and salt together in large bowl. Microwave for 5 minutes. Rinse thoroughly, transfer to paper towel–lined baking sheet, and dry well.

2. Heat onions and oil in Dutch oven over high heat, stirring frequently, until onions are golden brown, 25 to 30 minutes. Drain onions in colander set in large bowl. Transfer onions to paper towel–lined baking sheet to drain further.

RECIPE DETAILS

Timeline

- 5 minutes to make yogurt sauce
- 40 minutes to microwave, dry, and fry onions
- 20 minutes to simmer lentils and soak rice
- 30 minutes to cook rice and lentils (mostly hands-off)
- 5 minutes to finish dish

Essential Tools

- Microwave to precook onions
- Salad spinner for removing liquid from microwaved onions (otherwise you will need many, many paper towels)
- Dutch oven for frying onions and cooking rice
- Colander for draining fried onions and simmered lentils
- Fine-mesh strainer for draining soaked rice

Substitutions & Variations

- Leftover oil from frying the onions can be refrigerated in an airtight container for up to four weeks; use this oil to lend flavor to salad dressings, sautéed vegetables, eggs, and pasta sauces.
- A creamy, garlicky Yogurt Sauce makes this dish even better. Simply whisk together 1 cup plain whole-milk yogurt, 2 tablespoons lemon juice, ½ teaspoon minced garlic, and ½ teaspoon salt in a bowl and refrigerate the sauce while preparing the rice and lentils. Making the sauce first gives the garlic time to mellow and allows the flavors to blend.

73 Fried Rice

A UNIQUE PERSPECTIVE REVEALS COMPLEXITY IN THIS HUMBLE DISH

Fried rice is the frugal cook's template for using up leftovers: Take cold cooked rice, stir-fry it with whatever meat, vegetables, and aromatics are on hand, and toss it in a sauce that lightly coats the mixture and rehydrates the grains.

While this clean-out-the-fridge approach has its place, in Indonesia they take fried rice more seriously. The garden-variety brown sauce is replaced with a pungent chili paste called sambal, along with fermented shrimp paste and a syrupy-sweet soy sauce known as *kecap manis*. And instead of being loaded up with a hodgepodge of meats and vegetables, the rice is garnished with fried shallots, strips of tender omelet, and lime wedges. The final dish (called *nasi goreng*) boasts so much complexity in flavor and texture that it hardly seems like the typical afterthought.

To translate this dish for the American home kitchen we needed a workaround for some of the specialty ingredients as well as a plan for making this dish when leftover rice is not available. The latter proved far more challenging.

Leftover white rice that's been thoroughly chilled—essential to making any kind of fried rice—is a staple in Asian households but not something that most of us keep on hand. To condense the overnight chilling process, we came up with a three-pronged approach that produces comparably dry, firm rice in less than an hour. In addition to devising a hurry-up chilling method, we had to cook the rice differently—sautéing the grains in oil to create a greasy barrier and then reducing the amount of water. The end result is cooked rice firm enough to fry. Best of all, you don't have to wait for leftovers to enjoy this dish.

WHY THIS RECIPE WORKS

Create a Potent Paste
Sambal, or Indonesian chili paste, is essential for the heady heat in this fried rice. We coarsely puree garlic, shallots, and Thai chiles (found at most supermarkets) in the food processor before sautéing the mixture to deepen its flavor. Once the rice is added to the skillet, the paste will coat the rice with its complex, savory flavors.

Season with Sweet Soy Sauce
Along with heat, Indonesian fried rice is seasoned with salty-sweet kecap manis. Bottled versions contain soy sauce and palm sugar and have a caramelized flavor. To improvise your own, sweeten soy sauce with brown sugar and molasses.

Build a Briny Character
Shrimp paste imparts a briny essence to this fried rice. This ingredient can be hard to find outside of Asian markets, but a reasonable version can be replicated with sautéed chopped fresh shrimp and fish sauce.

Add a Simple Omelet
In addition to frizzled shallots, fresh-cut cucumber, and tomatoes, Indonesian fried rice is typically garnished with a fried egg or omelet for richness and contrasting texture. Making a rolled omelet ahead is much easier than frying eggs at the last minute. Simply pour the beaten eggs into the skillet and cook until just set, then slide out, roll up, and slice.

Fast-Forward Fresh Cooked Rice
Unlike freshly cooked rice, which forms soft, mushy clumps when stir-fried too soon, chilled rice undergoes a process called retrogradation, in which the starch molecules form crystalline structures that make the grains firm enough to withstand a second round of cooking—that's why fried rice is tailor-made for last night's leftover rice. But there's a way to condense the process: Sauté the rinsed rice in oil and then cook in less water for more rigid grains. You do need to chill the rice, but just for 20 minutes.

Spirals of tender omelet and chilled, fluffy rice are key components in this one-dish meal.

Indonesian-Style Fried Rice

SERVES 4 TO 6

This dish is traditionally served with sliced cucumbers and tomato wedges.

2 tablespoons plus ½ cup vegetable oil	2 tablespoons soy sauce
2 cups jasmine or long-grain white rice, rinsed	2 tablespoons fish sauce
	Salt
2⅔ cups water	4 large eggs
5 green or red Thai chiles, stemmed	12 ounces extra-large shrimp (21 to 25 per pound), peeled, deveined, and cut crosswise into thirds
7 large shallots, peeled	
4 large garlic cloves, peeled	
2 tablespoons packed dark brown sugar	4 large scallions, sliced thin
2 tablespoons molasses	Lime wedges

1. Heat 2 tablespoons oil in large saucepan over medium heat until shimmering. Add rice and stir to coat grains with oil, about 30 seconds. Add water, increase heat to high, and bring to boil. Reduce heat to low, cover, and simmer until all liquid is absorbed, about 18 minutes. Off heat, remove lid and place clean dish towel folded in half over saucepan; replace lid. Let stand until rice is just tender, about 8 minutes. Spread cooked rice onto rimmed baking sheet, set on wire rack, and let cool for 10 minutes. Transfer to refrigerator and chill for 20 minutes.

2. Meanwhile, pulse Thai chiles, 4 shallots, and garlic in food processor until coarse paste is formed, about 15 pulses, scraping down sides of bowl as necessary. Transfer mixture to small bowl and set aside. In second small bowl, stir together brown sugar, molasses, soy sauce, fish sauce, and 1¼ teaspoons salt. Whisk eggs and ¼ teaspoon salt together in medium bowl.

3. Thinly slice remaining 3 shallots (you should have about 1 cup sliced shallots) and place in 12-inch nonstick skillet with remaining ½ cup oil. Heat over medium heat, stirring constantly, until shallots are golden and crisp, 6 to 10 minutes. Using slotted spoon, transfer shallots to paper towel–lined plate and season with salt to taste. Pour off oil and reserve. Wipe out skillet with paper towels

4. Heat 1 teaspoon reserved oil in now-empty skillet over medium heat until shimmering. Add half of eggs to skillet, gently tilting pan to evenly coat bottom. Cover and cook until bottom of omelet is spotty golden brown and top is just set, about 1½ minutes. Slide omelet onto cutting board and gently roll up into tight log. Using sharp knife, cut log crosswise into 1-inch segments (leaving segments rolled). Repeat with 1 teaspoon reserved oil and remaining eggs.

5. Remove rice from refrigerator and break up any large clumps with your fingers. Heat 3 tablespoons reserved oil in now-empty skillet over medium heat until shimmering. Add chile mixture and cook until golden, 3 to 5 minutes. Add shrimp, increase heat to medium-high, and cook, stirring constantly, until exterior of shrimp is just opaque, about 2 minutes. Push shrimp to sides of skillet; stir molasses mixture to recombine and pour into center of skillet. When molasses mixture bubbles, add rice and cook, stirring and folding constantly, until shrimp is cooked, rice is heated through, and mixture is evenly coated, about 3 minutes. Stir in scallions and transfer to serving platter. Garnish with egg segments, fried shallots, and lime wedges and serve.

RECIPE DETAILS

Timeline

- 40 minutes to cook and cool rice (prep other ingredients during this time)
- 20 minutes to chill rice (fry shallots and cook eggs while rice chills)
- 10 minutes to cook shrimp and fry rice (don't start until rice is ready)

Essential Tools

- Large saucepan for cooking rice
- Rimmed baking sheet for cooling rice
- Food processor for pulsing chiles, shallots, and garlic
- 12-inch nonstick skillet for frying shallots, cooking eggs, and cooking shrimp and rice

Substitutions & Variations

- If fresh Thai chiles are unavailable, substitute 2 serranos or 1 medium jalapeño. Adjust the spiciness of this dish by removing the ribs and seeds from the chiles.

74 Paella

THIS PARTY IN A PAN DOESN'T HAVE TO BE A PROJECT

Paella wasn't always party food. Agricultural workers in the Valencia region of coastal Spain developed this method for cooking a large quantity of rice as a way to make lunch for everyone working in the fields. This utilitarian dish relied on whatever proteins and vegetables were on hand to turn saffron-infused rice into a hearty meal. And it was cooked in a flat-bottomed pan over an open wood fire—far from any ovens or formal kitchens.

Modern recipes have come a long way from these humble roots. But change doesn't always equate with progress. Most published recipes rely on a long list of ingredients and this approach complicates the prep—and the cooking. Just because paella is a one-dish meal doesn't mean you have to include two dozen ingredients.

There are five key steps to this recipe: browning the sturdier proteins, sautéing the aromatics, toasting the rice, adding liquid to steam the rice, and, last, cooking the seafood. When choosing proteins, we opt for availability and quick prep. That means yes to chorizo, chicken, shrimp, and mussels, and no to snails, rabbit, lobster, and squid. We follow the same approach with the vegetables—focusing on red bell pepper and peas (frozen are just fine). Sure, artichokes are a lovely addition, but who has the time?

Our final simplification is to ditch the skillet—the usual alternative to a paella pan. Even though they are the same shape, a 12-inch skillet can't take the place of a paella pan that measures 14 or 15 inches across. A high-sided Dutch oven has sufficient capacity to hold all the ingredients. And, believe it or not, this equipment swap makes the recipe easier for the cook.

WHY THIS RECIPE WORKS

Jump-Start Flavor from the Get-Go
Good paella starts with a sofrito, a mix of aromatics cooked in oil. By why cook the onions, garlic, and tomatoes in just oil, when you could cook them in oil and the flavorful fat left behind from browning the rich chicken thighs and spicy chorizo?

Choose the Right Rice
For best results, choose traditional Valencia rice, or Arborio. Sauté the rice in the flavorful sofrito until it becomes coated in the fat and toasts just slightly, before adding the cooking liquid.

Start on Stovetop, Move to Oven
We cook our paella in a Dutch oven because it can contain the pile of ingredients in this dish. To use a Dutch oven, you'll need to make a few easy adjustments. After starting the paella on the stovetop, move it to the oven to guarantee even cooking in this deep pot. And don't forget to put the lid on to contain the heat. This stovetop-to-oven method actually simplifies the recipe because it means you can walk away from the stove, rather than hovering over a simmering pot.

Finish with Seafood and Veggies
While mussels can simply be nestled into the pot, shrimp need a little boost in flavor, so first marinate them in olive oil, salt, pepper, and garlic. Likewise, red bell pepper can emerge washed out, so sauté strips of pepper first until browned. Peas cook quickly and should be scattered across the paella following the red pepper strips.

The Socarrat Solution
Socarrat is a crusty, flavorful brown layer of rice that develops on the bottom of a perfectly cooked batch of paella. To improvise in our Dutch oven version, move the pot out of the oven to the stovetop once it's cooked and remove the lid. Heat for just about 5 minutes and you'll be rewarded with a layer of toasty caramelized rice on the bottom of the pot.

Browned chicken and chorizo cook with the rice, but wait to add the seafood and veggies.

Paella

SERVES 6

Socarrat, a layer of crusty browned rice that forms on the bottom of the pan, is a traditional part of paella. In our version, socarrat does not develop because most of the cooking is done in the oven. We have provided instructions to develop socarrat in step 5; if you prefer, skip this step and go directly from step 4 to 6. To debeard the mussels, simply pull off the weedy black fibers.

1 pound extra-large shrimp (21 to 25 per pound), peeled and deveined	1 onion, chopped fine
8 garlic cloves, minced	1 (14.5-ounce) can diced tomatoes, drained, minced, and drained again
2 tablespoons olive oil, plus extra as needed	2 cups Valencia or Arborio rice
Salt and pepper	3 cups chicken broth
1 pound boneless, skinless chicken thighs, trimmed and halved crosswise	⅓ cup dry white wine
	½ teaspoon saffron threads, crumbled
1 red bell pepper, stemmed, seeded, and cut into ½-inch-wide strips	1 bay leaf
	12 mussels, scrubbed and debearded
8 ounces Spanish chorizo sausage, sliced ½ inch thick on bias	½ cup frozen peas, thawed
	2 teaspoons chopped fresh parsley
	Lemon wedges

1. Adjust oven rack to lower-middle position and heat oven to 350 degrees. Toss shrimp, 1 teaspoon garlic, 1 tablespoon oil, ¼ teaspoon salt, and ¼ teaspoon pepper, in medium bowl. Cover and refrigerate until needed. Season chicken thighs with salt and pepper and set aside.

2. Heat 2 teaspoons oil in Dutch oven over medium-high heat until shimmering. Add bell pepper and cook, stirring occasionally, until skin begins to blister and turn spotty black, 3 to 4 minutes. Transfer bell pepper to small plate and set aside.

3. Heat 1 teaspoon oil in now-empty pot until shimmering. Add chicken pieces in single layer and cook, without moving, until browned, about 3 minutes. Turn pieces and cook until browned on second side, about 3 minutes. Transfer chicken to medium bowl. Reduce heat to medium and add chorizo to pot. Cook, stirring frequently, until deeply browned and fat begins to render, 4 to 5 minutes. Transfer chorizo to bowl with chicken and set aside.

4. Add enough oil to fat in pot to equal 2 tablespoons and heat over medium heat until shimmering. Add onion and cook, stirring frequently, until softened, about 3 minutes. Stir in remaining garlic and cook until fragrant, about 1 minute. Stir in tomatoes and cook until mixture begins to darken and thicken slightly, about 3 minutes. Stir in rice and cook until grains are well coated with tomato mixture, 1 to 2 minutes. Stir in broth, wine, saffron, bay leaf, and ½ teaspoon salt. Return chicken and chorizo to pot, increase heat to medium-high, and bring to boil, stirring occasionally. Cover pot, transfer to oven, and cook until rice absorbs almost all liquid, about 15 minutes. Remove pot from oven. Uncover pot, scatter shrimp over rice, insert mussels, hinged side down, into rice (so they stand upright), arrange bell pepper strips in pinwheel pattern, and scatter peas over top. Cover, return to oven, and cook until shrimp are opaque and mussels have opened, 10 to 12 minutes.

RECIPE DETAILS

Timeline

- 30 minutes to prepare ingredients
- 5 minutes to blister bell pepper
- 10 minutes to brown chicken and chorizo
- 10 to 12 minutes to cook paella on stovetop
- 30 minutes to cook paella in oven (mostly hands-off)
- 5 minutes to create optional socarrat
- 5 minutes to let paella stand and garnish it

Essential Tools

- Dutch oven (11 to 12 inches in diameter and at least 6 quarts) with lid

Substitutions & Variations

- Dry-cured Spanish chorizo is the sausage of choice for paella, but fresh chorizo or linguiça is an acceptable substitute
- A paella pan makes for an attractive and impressive presentation. To make paella in a paella pan, use a pan that is 14 to 15 inches in diameter; the ingredients will not fit in a smaller pan. Increase chicken broth to 3¼ cups and wine to ½ cup. Before placing pan in oven, cover it tightly with aluminum foil. For socarrat, cook paella, uncovered, over medium-high heat for about 3 minutes, rotating pan 180 degrees after about 1½ minutes for even browning.

5. *For Socarrat:* If socarrat is desired, set pot, uncovered, over medium-high heat for about 5 minutes, rotating pot 180 degrees after about 2 minutes for even browning.

6. Let paella stand, covered, for 5 minutes. Discard any mussels that have not opened and bay leaf, if it can be easily removed. Sprinkle with parsley and serve, passing lemon wedges separately.

A Better Way to Peel Shrimp

Many cooks buy peeled shrimp and they are making a big mistake before they even get in the kitchen. The machines that peel shrimp rough up these delicate crustaceans and the end results are miserable. While peeled shrimp are a no-go, frozen shrimp are actually better than "fresh"—which are almost always thawed frozen shrimp that are past their prime. Better to buy individually quick frozen shrimp and defrost them at home.

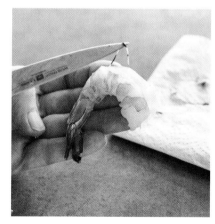

1. Thaw frozen shrimp in colander under cool running water. Depending on size, shrimp will be ready to cook in about 10 minutes. Thoroughly dry shrimp before proceeding.

2. Break shell on underside, under swimming legs. (The shell comes off the body of the shrimp very easily and the legs will come off as the shell is removed.) Leave tail end intact if desired, or tug tail end to remove shell.

3. Use paring knife to make shallow cut along back of shrimp to expose vein. (Although this vein doesn't affect flavor, we remove it to improve the appearance of cooked shrimp.)

4. Use tip of knife to lift vein out. Discard vein by wiping knife blade against paper towel.

75 Risotto

RISOTTO CAN BE EASY, IF YOU DON'T FOLLOW THE RULES

Cooking long-grain rice is simple: Bring your ingredients to a simmer, cover the pot, and wait. Cooking risotto is the exact opposite. Accepted culinary wisdom dictates near-constant stirring to achieve the perfect texture: tender grains with a slight bite in the center, bound together in a light, creamy sauce.

So why is the stirring such a big deal? As the rice cooks, it releases starch granules, which absorb liquid and expand, thickening the broth to a cream-like consistency. Constant stirring jostles the rice grains against one another, promoting the release of more starch granules from their exterior.

But frankly, most of us have neither the time nor the patience to stir anything for 30 minutes. Our goal was to rethink this recipe so the stirring was reduced to just 5 minutes. So how did we accomplish this? Rather than adding the broth in small increments (as tradition demands), we add most of the broth at the outset. And we ditch the usual open sauté pan or saucepan for a covered Dutch oven.

One thing you can't change is the rice. A short-grained rice like Arborio is a must. Long-grain rice doesn't have the right mix of starches to create the velvety sauce that is the hallmark of well-made risotto. In addition, the starches in Arborio don't break down as readily as the starches in other rice varieties, allowing the rice to maintain a firm, al dente center, even as the exterior becomes tender. Other Italian varieties, including carnaroli rice, make excellent risotto, but don't try to use other types of rice in this uniquely Italian recipe.

WHY THIS RECIPE WORKS

Don't Stir

To keep stirring to a minimum, flood the rice with most of the liquid at the outset and then use the lid to help the rice cook evenly. (But be sure to measure the liquid with care; success is dependent on the correct ratios and volumes.) Don't rinse the rice; you'll want that extra starch to help make the risotto creamy. Traditionally, it's the stirring that causes the rice to release its starch and create the creamy "sauce." Stirring also prevents sticking or scorching, but by flooding the rice and then bringing that liquid to a boil, you're letting the natural agitation of the rice take the place of stirring—the rice doesn't burn, and you'll get a great creamy sauce.

Use a Dutch Oven

Swap out the saucepan for a Dutch oven, which has a thick, heavy bottom, deep sides, and tight-fitting lid—perfect for trapping and distributing heat as evenly as possible. Also, its wider surface area means there's less differential in cooking rates between top and bottom; the rice is spread out in a thinner layer in the pot.

Cook with Residual Heat

Stir the rice twice in the first 16 to 19 minutes of cooking to help release some starch and build the sauce. After a second addition of broth, stir the pot constantly until the risotto is creamy, which will take just 3 minutes. Remove the pot from the heat, throw on the cover, and wait for 5 minutes. Without sitting over a direct flame, the heavy Dutch oven maintains enough residual heat to finish off the rice to a perfect al dente—thickened, velvety, and just barely chewy. Adding the Parmesan cheese before the off-heat "cooking" helps to build this creamy sauce.

Finish with Flavor

Just before serving, stir in extra butter to make the sauce velvety and add herbs and a squeeze of lemon for brightness.

Risotto can be cooked undisturbed as long as you finish with extra broth and gentle stirring.

Almost Hands-Free Risotto with Parmesan

SERVES 6

This more hands-off method requires precise timing, so we strongly recommend using a timer.

5 **cups chicken broth**	2 **cups Arborio rice**
1½ **cups water**	1 **cup dry white wine**
4 **tablespoons unsalted butter**	2 **ounces Parmesan cheese, grated**
1 **large onion, chopped fine**	**(1 cup)**
Salt and pepper	1 **teaspoon lemon juice**
1 **garlic clove, minced**	

1. Bring broth and water to boil in large saucepan over high heat. Reduce heat to medium-low to maintain gentle simmer.

2. Melt 2 tablespoons butter in Dutch oven over medium heat. Add onion and ¾ teaspoon salt and cook, stirring frequently, until onion is softened, 5 to 7 minutes. Add garlic and stir until fragrant, about 30 seconds. Add rice and cook, stirring frequently, until grains are translucent around edges, about 3 minutes.

3. Add wine and cook, stirring constantly, until fully absorbed, 2 to 3 minutes. Stir 5 cups hot broth mixture into rice; reduce heat to medium-low, cover, and simmer until almost all liquid has been absorbed and rice is just al dente, 16 to 19 minutes, stirring twice during cooking.

4. Add ¾ cup hot broth mixture and stir gently and constantly until risotto becomes creamy, about 3 minutes. Stir in Parmesan. Remove pot from heat, cover, and let stand for 5 minutes. Stir in remaining 2 tablespoons butter and lemon juice. To loosen texture of risotto, add remaining broth mixture as needed. Season with salt and pepper to taste, and serve immediately.

ALMOST HANDS-FREE RISOTTO WITH HERBS
Stir in 2 tablespoons minced fresh parsley and 2 tablespoons minced fresh chives before serving.

ALMOST HANDS-FREE RISOTTO WITH PORCINI
Add ¼ ounce rinsed and minced porcini mushrooms to pot with garlic. Substitute soy sauce for lemon juice.

ALMOST HANDS-FREE RISOTTO WITH FENNEL AND SAFFRON
Add 1 fennel bulb, cored and chopped fine, to pot with onion and cook until softened, about 12 minutes. Add ¼ teaspoon ground coriander and large pinch saffron threads to pot with garlic.

RECIPE DETAILS

Timeline

- 10 minutes to prepare ingredients (heat broth and water at same time)
- 10 minutes to start risotto (hands-on)
- 18 minutes to cook rice in broth (hands-off)
- 3 minutes to finish cooking rice (hands-on)
- 5 minutes to let risotto stand off heat (hands-off)

Essential Tools

- Dutch oven with tight-fitting lid
- Timer

Substitutions & Variations

- Use vegetable broth to make this recipe vegetarian. Adding some water to the broth reduces the chance that the final dish will be overly salty.
- This basic formula can be varied almost endlessly. Vegetables that can withstand a fair amount of cooking should be added to the pot at the outset, along with the onion. This includes leeks, radicchio, and squash. Very delicate vegetables (such as spinach or asparagus) as well as seafood should be added to the nearly finished risotto.

76 Potstickers

THE RIGHT WRAPPER MAKES CRISPY, CHEWY DUMPLINGS A SNAP

Some restaurant dishes are best left to professional kitchens. Anything that requires a great exhaust system falls into this category, as do multicomponent desserts. Other restaurant dishes might seem daunting for the home cook, but that's only because you have never seen the dish made. Potstickers are a perfect example of this second group.

Unlike other similar dishes (think ravioli or pierogi), you don't need to roll out the pasta. Asian dumpling wrappers are available in pretty much every American supermarket and they work beautifully. And the best fillings are simple combinations of raw ingredients. Yes, stuffing and sealing the wrappers takes some patience, but with just 20 minutes of work you can ready 24 dumplings for cooking.

The ideal potsticker is both crispy and chewy thanks to a unique cooking method. The filled dumplings are sautéed so that the part of the wrapper in contact with the hot pan becomes crisp. Next, water is added and the pan is covered to steam the rest of the wrapper to tenderness. The final step is to remove the lid, cook off any remaining water, and recrisp the bottom.

Potstickers can be shaped in various ways but we think half-moons are easiest to execute. As with all filled pasta, the seam is the trickiest part to cook right because it has two layers of dough. When the seam is on top of the dumpling, it takes a long time to soften. With two flat sides (rather than a wide flat bottom), a half moon ensures that the seam is closer to the pan so it cooks more quickly. The end result is a potsticker that is tender, crispy, and chewy, all in the same delicious bite.

WHY THIS RECIPE WORKS

Choose the Right Wrap
Two ready-made versions are widely available in supermarkets: wonton and gyoza wrappers. Wonton wrappers can be used but they are on the thin side. Gyoza-style wrappers are a better choice. Made without egg, they are sturdier and hold up better when pan-fried. Their substantial texture is also a better match for the flavorful filling.

Create a Potent, Juicy Filling
Cooked potsticker fillings will dry out in the dumpling wrappers. Instead we start fresh: We spike ground pork with ginger, garlic, scallions, and soy sauce. And we add cabbage (salted and drained first) for textural contrast and flavor.

Steal a Meatloaf Trick
To lighten the texture of the filling even further, we follow the lead of meatloaf cookery and add a lightly beaten egg to the pork and cabbage mixture.

Fold, Pinch, Flatten
After spooning the filling (be sure to measure it) onto the wrapper, moisten the edges with water and fold the wrapper over, pinching the edges closed to press out any air pockets. This is a critical step because air pockets can cause the potstickers to balloon during steaming, causing the wrapper to pull away from the meat and making for a messy first bite. Likewise, be sure to place the sealed potstickers on the counter to flatten the bottoms so that they can make full contact with the skillet for optimal browning and tender edges.

Start Cold, Finish Hot
For evenly cooked dumplings, oil a nonstick skillet, add the dumplings flat side down for maximum browning and tender edges, and then turn on the heat. Once they're browned, add water to the skillet, cover, and steam before removing the cover to let the water cook off for potstickers that are crispy, chewy, and tender.

An uncooked filling and three-step cooking method yield perfect potstickers.

Pork and Cabbage Potstickers

MAKES 24 DUMPLINGS

These dumplings are best served hot; we recommend serving the first batch immediately and then cooking the second batch. Serve with Scallion Dipping Sauce (at right), if desired.

FILLING

½	head napa cabbage, cored and chopped fine (6 cups)
¾	teaspoon salt
12	ounces ground pork
4	scallions, minced

1	large egg, lightly beaten
4	teaspoons soy sauce
1½	teaspoons grated fresh ginger
1	garlic clove, minced
⅛	teaspoon pepper

DUMPLINGS

24	round gyoza wrappers
4	teaspoons vegetable oil

1	cup water, plus extra for brushing

1. *For the Filling:* Toss cabbage with salt in colander set over bowl and let stand until cabbage begins to wilt, about 20 minutes. Press cabbage gently with rubber spatula to squeeze out any excess moisture, then transfer to medium bowl. Add pork, scallions, egg, soy sauce, ginger, garlic, and pepper and mix thoroughly to combine. Cover with plastic wrap and refrigerate until mixture is cold, at least 30 minutes or up to 24 hours.

2. *For the Dumplings:* Working with 4 wrappers at a time (keep remaining wrappers covered with plastic wrap), place wrappers flat on counter. Spoon 1 slightly rounded tablespoon filling in center of each wrapper. Using pastry brush or your fingertip, moisten edge of wrapper with water. Fold each wrapper in half; starting in center and working toward outside edges, pinch edges together firmly to seal, pressing out any air pockets. Position each dumpling on its side and gently flatten, pressing down on seam to make sure it lies flat against counter. Transfer dumplings to baking sheet and repeat with remaining wrappers and filling.

3. Line large plate with double layer of paper towels. Brush 2 teaspoons oil over bottom of 12-inch nonstick skillet and arrange half of dumplings in skillet, flat side down (overlapping just slightly if necessary). Place skillet over medium-high heat and cook dumplings, without moving them, until golden brown on bottom, about 5 minutes.

4. Reduce heat to low, add ½ cup water, and cover immediately. Continue to cook, covered, until most of water is absorbed and wrappers are slightly translucent, about 10 minutes. Uncover skillet, increase heat to medium-high, and continue to cook, without stirring, until dumpling bottoms are well browned and crisp, 3 to 4 minutes more. Slide dumplings onto paper towel–lined plate, browned side facing down, and let drain briefly. Transfer dumplings to serving platter and serve. Let skillet cool until just warm, then wipe out with paper towels and repeat from step 3 with remaining oil, dumplings, and water.

RECIPE DETAILS

Timeline

- 25 minutes to slice and salt cabbage (prep all other ingredients while cabbage is draining)
- 30 minutes to make and chill filling (prepare dipping sauce while filling chills)
- 15 minutes to assemble dumplings
- 40 minutes to cook dumplings in two batches

Essential Tools

- Colander or fine-mesh strainer for draining cabbage
- 12-inch nonstick skillet with lid

Substitutions & Variations

- We prefer the slightly chewier texture of gyoza-style wrappers to thinner wonton wrappers. However, wonton wrappers will work if you reduce the steaming time to about 6 minutes.
- To make shrimp dumplings, substitute 12 ounces peeled, deveined shrimp (any size), tails removed, pulsed 10 times in food processor, for pork.
- Uncooked dumplings can be placed on plate, wrapped tightly in plastic wrap, and refrigerated for up to 24 hours, or frozen for up to 1 month. Once frozen, dumplings can be transferred to zipper-lock bag; do not thaw before cooking.
- To make Scallion Dipping Sauce, combine ¼ cup soy sauce, 2 tablespoons rice vinegar, 2 tablespoons mirin, 2 tablespoons water, 1 teaspoon chili oil (optional), ½ teaspoon toasted sesame oil, and 1 minced scallion in bowl. (Sauce can be refrigerated for up to 24 hours.)

77 Fish Tacos

NO BREADING, NO FRYING, JUST FIERY, FRESH FLAVORS

Batter-fried, Baja-style fish tacos are a nearly perfect dish. The richness of the fried coating balances the mild flavor and flaky texture of the fish. And the soft corn tortillas ensure that every bite contains not just fish, but also some of the crunchy slaw and creamy sauce.

There's just one problem with this dish—and it's a big one. Frying at home is never easy and frying fish is particularly challenging. Water in food makes oil splatter and fish contains a lot of water. And then there's the smell that hangs in the kitchen for days. All in all, batter-fried fish tacos are best enjoyed outdoors, preferably on a boardwalk looking out over the Pacific.

To remake this recipe for the home kitchen, we look further south to the Yucatán. There, whole fish are often split lengthwise and bathed in an intense chile paste and grilled. Don't worry—we're not suggesting you grill a whole fish. It's the bold Yucatán approach to flavoring fish that we adapt to work with meaty strips of swordfish—no skin and no bones, thank you.

It takes just 10 minutes to ready a homemade chile paste. Orange juice cut with lime juice is a good approximation of the sour oranges used in Mexico and provides the citrus notes typical of Yucatan cooking. But this grilled fish needs even more acidity to balance all the spice. A salsa made with grilled pineapple is the right option. Sliced avocado adds the requisite creaminess while shredded iceberg lettuce takes care of the crunch. Serve with cold beer and you have the ideal summer meal, no beach required.

WHY THIS RECIPE WORKS

Stick with Sturdy Fish
Skip the delicate white fish used in fried fish tacos and go for fish with a meaty texture—swordfish is ideal. Slice the swordfish into strips (use 1-inch-thick steaks) before grilling so they can go from grill to taco without any further prep—and don't worry, this fish is firm enough that flipping the pieces on the grill will be easy.

A Paste from Your Pantry
The chile paste used to flavor the fish in the Yucatán is made from ingredients difficult to find outside of Mexico. Improvise with a mix of chile powders: fruity ancho and smoky chipotle, along with citrusy ground coriander and oregano. Bloom the mixture in oil with minced garlic and salt to round out their flavors. Add a couple tablespoons of tomato paste for a layer of savory sweet intensity and mimic the sour oranges with a mix of orange and lime juices. Combine the fish with the paste and let marinate so the salt in the paste can penetrate and season the fish.

No More Sticking
Fish is notorious for sticking to the grill. But we have a trick. Once the grill is heated, swab the cooking grate with a wad of well-oiled paper towels until the grate turns black and glossy—it will take several swipes but it means you won't need to pry the fish from the grate.

Grill the Salsa—and the Tortillas
For further flavor, skip the Baja-style creamy mayo-based sauce—it's out of place here. Instead, complement the chile-seasoned fish with heat, fruit, and crunch in the form of a grilled salsa. There's plenty of room on the cooking grate so simply grill sweet slices of pineapple and a fiery jalapeño opposite the fish. Once done, chop and toss with red bell pepper, cilantro, and a squeeze of lime juice. Grill the tortillas, too. They take just a few minutes to toast and soften—keep them warm wrapped in aluminum foil until they're ready for the table.

A citrusy chile paste flavors the fish, which grills alongside pineapple and a fresh jalapeño.

Grilled Fish Tacos

SERVES 6

3 tablespoons vegetable oil
1 tablespoon ancho chile powder
2 teaspoons chipotle chile powder
2 garlic cloves, minced
1 teaspoon dried oregano
1 teaspoon ground coriander
  Salt
2 tablespoons tomato paste
½ cup orange juice
6 tablespoons lime juice (3 limes)
2 pounds skinless swordfish steaks, 1 inch thick, cut lengthwise into 1-inch-wide strips

1 pineapple, peeled, quartered, cored, and each quarter halved lengthwise
1 jalapeño chile
18 (6-inch) corn tortillas
1 red bell pepper, stemmed, seeded, and cut into ¼-inch pieces
2 tablespoons minced fresh cilantro, plus extra for serving
½ head iceberg lettuce (4½ ounces), cored and thinly sliced
1 avocado, halved, pitted, and sliced thin
  Lime wedges

RECIPE DETAILS

Timeline

• 25 minutes to make and cool chile paste (prepare fish while paste cools)
• 30 minutes to marinate fish (prep all other ingredients and set up grill while fish is in the fridge)
• 10 minutes to grill fish, pineapple, chile, and tortillas
• 5 minutes to chop grilled pineapple and chile and combine with salsa ingredients

Essential Tools

• 8-inch skillet for preparing chile paste
• Grill brush for cleaning grill grate
• Paper towels and tongs for oiling grill grate (Don't skip this step; it's essential to the success of this recipe.)
• Thin spatula for turning fish on grill

Substitutions & Variations

• Mahi-mahi, tuna, and halibut fillets are all suitable substitutes for the swordfish, but to ensure the best results buy 1-inch-thick fillets and cut them in a similar fashion to the swordfish. Avoid flaky fish like grouper, hake, cod, or snapper, which are much more likely to stick to the grill and fall apart when you try to flip them.

1. Heat 2 tablespoons oil, ancho chile powder, and chipotle chile powder in 8-inch skillet over medium heat, stirring constantly, until fragrant, 2 to 3 minutes. Add garlic, oregano, coriander, and 1 teaspoon salt and continue to cook until fragrant, about 30 seconds longer. Add tomato paste and, using spatula, mash tomato paste with spice mixture until combined, about 20 seconds. Stir in orange juice and 2 tablespoons lime juice. Cook, stirring constantly, until thoroughly mixed and reduced slightly, about 2 minutes. Transfer chile mixture to large bowl and let cool for 15 minutes.

2. Add swordfish to bowl with chile mixture and stir gently with rubber spatula to coat fish. Cover and refrigerate for at least 30 minutes or up to 2 hours.

3A. *For a Charcoal Grill:* Open bottom vent completely. Light large chimney starter mounded with charcoal briquettes (7 quarts). When top coals are partially covered with ash, pour evenly over grill. Set cooking grate in place, cover, and open lid vent completely. Heat grill until hot, about 5 minutes.

3B. *For a Gas Grill:* Turn all burners to high, cover, and heat grill until hot, about 15 minutes. Turn all burners to medium-high.

4. Clean cooking grate, then repeatedly brush with well-oiled paper towels until grate is black and glossy, 5 to 10 times. Brush both sides of pineapple with remaining 1 tablespoon oil. Place fish on half of grill. Place pineapple and jalapeño on other half. Cover and cook until fish, pineapple, and jalapeño have begun to brown, 3 to 5 minutes. Using thin spatula, flip fish, pineapple, and jalapeño over. Cover and continue to cook until second sides of pineapple and jalapeño are browned and swordfish registers 140 degrees, 3 to 5 minutes. Transfer fish to large platter, flake into pieces, and tent with aluminum foil. Transfer pineapple and jalapeño to cutting board.

5. Clean cooking grate. Place half of tortillas on grill. Grill until softened and speckled with brown spots, 30 to 45 seconds per side. Wrap tortillas in dish towel or foil to keep warm. Repeat with remaining tortillas.

6. When cool enough to handle, finely chop pineapple and jalapeño. Transfer to medium bowl and stir in bell pepper, cilantro, and remaining ¼ cup lime juice. Season with salt to taste. Top tortillas with flaked fish, salsa, lettuce, and avocado. Serve with lime wedges and extra cilantro.

78 Corn on the Cob

THEY KNOW SOMETHING ABOUT COOKING CORN IN MEXICO

Along with hot dogs and burgers, nothing says "all-American summer" quite like corn on the cob. It's served at everything from fried chicken dinners to clambakes. Given how much we love corn on the cob, it's surprising that the rest of the world isn't on board. In much of Europe, fresh corn is something you feed farm animals, not people.

But Americans aren't totally alone in our fondness for corn on the cob. One of Mexico's most popular street foods is *elote asado*: corn on the cob grilled until it's intensely sweet, smoky, and charred, and then slathered with a cheesy sauce spiked with lime juice and chili powder.

If you're accustomed to boiling and buttering corn on the cob, Mexican street corn (as it is sometimes called) will be a revelation. Today's supersweet corn can seem like dessert. But on the grill those sugars brown and become more complex-tasting and the smoke balances out the sweetness. As you might expect, for maximum char the corn is stripped of its husks before grilling.

What happens after the ears come off the grill makes Mexican street corn even more appealing. A creamy, zesty sauce coats the kernels and restores some of the moisture lost during grilling. Best of all, that tangy sauce is the "glue" for the piquant cheese sprinkled over the ears. (Think of the cheese as taking the place of the salt Americans use at the table.) This is one messy dish to eat—invest in corn cob holders or be prepared to lick those fingers—but what a way to celebrate summer.

WHY THIS RECIPE WORKS

Lose the Husks
The goal with Mexican street corn is a cob with smoky, just charred kernels, so we remove the husks and oil the cooking grate well to prevent sticking. We oil the corn too, which also guards against excessive drying. To punch up its flavor, the oil is seasoned with chili powder and salt. We often pretoast spices like chili powder to deepen, or bloom, their flavors. No toasting is necessary here, as the chili powder will bloom right on the grill.

Concentrate the Fire
Grilling corn without the husk does put it at risk of drying out—sometimes well before the kernels char. The solution? Build a half fire, where all the coals in a full chimney are arranged over half the grill. This hotter side provides intense heat that will quickly char, but not dessicate, the corn. If you have a gas grill, simply turn all the burners to high and cook the corn with the lid down—you'll achieve the same results.

DIY Crema
The tangy sauce is paramount to this style of corn. Authentic recipes typically call for *crema* (soured Mexican cream) as the base, while some recipes call for easier-to-find mayonnaise. Mayonnaise adds an appealing richness but for the hallmark tang, we cut some of the mayo with regular sour cream. American sour cream is thicker than crema, which is a bonus because it helps create a sauce that clings more readily to the corn.

A Cheesy, Well-Seasoned Finish
Cheese is another important and flavorful component to the corn's coating. While you might be able to find the traditional *queso fresco* (a fresh, mild cheese) or Cotija (a drier, saltier more pungent aged cheese) in some markets, you can also substitute dry, tangy (and readily available) Pecorino Romano. Further season the sauce with cilantro, lime juice, and garlic, along with a little chili powder for lip-smacking heat.

Brush the corn with chili oil before grilling and toss with a creamy, cheesy sauce before serving.

Mexican-Style Grilled Corn

SERVES 6

If you prefer the corn spicy, add the optional cayenne pepper.

1½ ounces Pecorino Romano cheese, grated (¾ cup)	¾ teaspoon chili powder
¼ cup mayonnaise	¼ teaspoon pepper
3 tablespoons sour cream	¼ teaspoon cayenne pepper (optional)
3 tablespoons minced fresh cilantro	4 teaspoons vegetable oil
4 teaspoons lime juice	¼ teaspoon salt
1 garlic clove, minced	6 ears corn, husks and silk removed

1A. *For a Charcoal Grill:* Open bottom vent completely. Light large chimney starter filled with charcoal briquettes (6 quarts). When top coals are partially covered with ash, pour evenly over half of grill. Set cooking grate in place, cover, and open lid vent completely. Heat grill until hot, about 5 minutes.

1B. *For a Gas Grill:* Turn all burners to high, cover, and heat grill until hot, about 15 minutes.

2. Meanwhile, combine Pecorino, mayonnaise, sour cream, cilantro, lime juice, garlic, ¼ teaspoon chili powder, pepper, and cayenne, if using, in large bowl and set aside. In second large bowl, combine oil, salt, and remaining ½ teaspoon chili powder. Add corn to oil mixture and toss to coat evenly.

3. Clean and oil cooking grate. Place corn on grill (hotter side if using charcoal) and cook (covered if using gas) until lightly charred on all sides, 7 to 12 minutes, turning as needed. Place corn in bowl with cheese mixture, toss to coat evenly, and serve.

RECIPE DETAILS

Timeline

• 10 minutes to husk and silk corn (light grill before starting)
• 10 minutes to prepare cheese mixture
• 10 minutes to oil and grill corn
• 1 minute to toss grilled corn with cheese mixture

Essential Tools

• Grill brush and paper towels to ensure grill grate is clean and oiled
• Long-handled grill tongs for oiling grate and turning corn
• Sturdy rubber spatula for tossing grilled corn with cheese mixture

Substitutions & Variations

• The recipe is traditionally made with crumbled queso fresco (a mild fresh cheese) or Cotija (a drier, saltier, more pungent aged cheese). If you can find either cheese, feel free to use it in place of the Pecorino Romano. Finely crumbled feta is another decent substitute.

79 Vegetable Curry

EVEN SUPERMARKET STAPLES CAN MAKE GREAT CURRY

The term "curry" is derived from the Tamil word *kari*, which simply means "sauce" or "gravy." There are thousands of ways to make curry. When flavorful beef or lamb is the main ingredient, even a mediocre recipe yields a decent result. But vegetable curry is a different story. In the wrong hands, vegetables can be watery carriers for the sauce, offering little personality of their own.

To ensure that the vegetables add something beyond bulk to this dish, you must utilize techniques that develop flavor in the vegetables. Caramelizing the onions and browning the potatoes make a huge difference in this dish, as does sautéing the cauliflower in the aromatics (spices, garlic, ginger, chiles, and tomato paste) before the liquid goes into the pot.

If the vegetables contribute flavor, you can get away with using convenient ground spices (no grinding of whole spices needed). And rather than buying or measuring a dozen different ground spices, we recommend starting with two spice blends. Curry powder adds the familiar aromatic and floral notes as well as some color, while garam masala brings warm notes (from cinnamon and coriander) as well as a little heat (from black pepper and dried chiles). To maximize the flavor of the spice blends, take a minute to toast them together in a dry skillet and then bloom them in the fat in the curry pot.

As you will see, great vegetable curry doesn't require a long ingredient list. It doesn't require a lot of time either—our recipe is ready in less than 1 hour, including time to prep the vegetables. It's even possible to make curry on a busy weeknight. Who knew!

WHY THIS RECIPE WORKS

Toast and Bloom
We toast the curry powder and garam masala—which includes such warm spices as black pepper, cinnamon, coriander, and cardamom—in a dry skillet to intensify their flavors. Why is toasting in a dry skillet so beneficial? When added to a simmering sauce, the spices can be heated only to 212 degrees. In a dry skillet, temperatures can exceed 500 degrees, heightening flavors exponentially. (But be aware that you can overdo the toasting and burn the spices.) We add the toasted spices to the pot with the onions and aromatics so that the spices can bloom even further in the added oil.

Supercharge the Base
We caramelize the onions until fond (flavorful dark bits) develops in the bottom of the pan, and we add garlic, ginger, and a minced fresh chile for heat. A spoonful of tomato paste, though inauthentic, adds sweetness, helps browning, and boosts the sweet, savory flavors in the dish.

Coax Flavor Out of the Vegetables
Potatoes can be bland. To quickly boost their flavor, we cook them along with the onions until they're browned. We build more flavor with the cauliflower too by following an Indian cooking method called *bhuna*, which involves sautéing the spices and main ingredients together to enhance and meld flavors. This technique helps develop a richer, more complex flavor. Other sturdy vegetables, such as green beans and eggplant, work well with this technique.

Finish with Liquid and More Veggies
Toward the end of cooking, we pour a combination of water and chopped canned tomatoes into the pot and simmer until the vegetables are tender. No-prep vegetables like nutty chickpeas and sweet peas, added during the last few minutes, give the dish heft, as well as flavor. We finish with a small amount of cream or coconut milk—either adds richness without overpowering the delicate vegetables.

Hearty onions and potatoes get browned, while delicate cauliflower and peas are added later.

Indian Curry with Potatoes, Cauliflower, Peas, and Chickpeas

SERVES 4 TO 6

Gather and prepare all the ingredients before you begin cooking the curry. This recipe is moderately spicy when made with one chile. For more heat, use an additional half chile. For a mild curry, remove the chile's ribs and seeds before mincing. In addition to the suggested condiments, serve with Rice Pilaf (page 45), using basmati rice for the most authentic results.

2 tablespoons sweet or mild curry powder	2 onions, chopped fine
1½ teaspoons garam masala	12 ounces red potatoes, unpeeled, cut into ½-inch chunks
¼ cup vegetable oil	1¼ pounds cauliflower florets, cut into 1-inch pieces
3 garlic cloves, minced	1 (15-ounce) can chickpeas, rinsed
1 tablespoon grated fresh ginger	1¼ cups water
1 serrano chile, stemmed, seeds and ribs removed, and minced	Salt
1 tablespoon tomato paste	1½ cups frozen peas
1 (14.5-ounce) can diced tomatoes	¼ cup heavy cream or coconut milk

1. Toast curry powder and garam masala in 8-inch skillet over medium-high heat, stirring occasionally, until spices darken slightly and become fragrant, about 1 minute. Transfer spices to small bowl; set aside. In separate small bowl, stir 1 tablespoon oil, garlic, ginger, serrano, and tomato paste together; set aside. Pulse tomatoes and their juice in food processor until coarsely chopped, 3 to 4 pulses; set aside.

2. Heat remaining 3 tablespoons oil in Dutch oven over medium-high heat until shimmering. Add onions and potatoes and cook, stirring occasionally, until onions are caramelized and potatoes are golden brown around edges, about 10 minutes. (Reduce heat to medium if onions darken too quickly.)

3. Reduce heat to medium. Clear center of pot, add garlic mixture, and cook, mashing mixture into pan, until fragrant, 15 to 20 seconds. Stir garlic mixture into vegetables. Add toasted spices and cook, stirring constantly, for 1 minute longer. Add cauliflower and cook, stirring constantly, until spices coat florets, about 2 minutes longer.

4. Add tomatoes, chickpeas, water, and 1 teaspoon salt, scraping up any browned bits. Bring to boil over medium-high heat. Cover, reduce heat to medium, and cook, stirring occasionally, until vegetables are tender, 10 to 15 minutes. Stir in peas and cream and continue to cook until heated through, about 2 minutes longer. Season with salt to taste, and serve.

ONION RELISH MAKES ABOUT 1 CUP

If using a regular yellow onion, increase the sugar to 1 teaspoon.

1 Vidalia onion, chopped fine	½ teaspoon sugar
1 tablespoon lime juice	⅛ teaspoon salt
½ teaspoon paprika	Pinch cayenne pepper

Combine all ingredients in bowl. (Relish can be refrigerated for up to 24 hours.)

RECIPE DETAILS

Timeline

• 20 minutes to prepare ingredients and toast spices
• 15 minutes to sauté curry ingredients
• 10 to 15 minutes to simmer curry (mostly hands-off)
• 2 minutes to cook peas and season curry

Essential Tools

• 8-inch skillet for toasting spices
• Food processor for chopping tomatoes (can be done by hand if necessary)
• Dutch oven with heavy bottom to prevent scorching

Substitutions & Variations

• You can substitute 2 teaspoons ground coriander, ½ teaspoon ground black pepper, ¼ teaspoon ground cardamom, and ¼ teaspoon ground cinnamon for the garam masala.
• We strongly recommend making one or both accompaniments. But if you're absolutely pressed for time, serve with plain whole-milk yogurt—it's not as exciting as the relish or chutney but certainly better than nothing.
• If you want to use other vegetables, try this variation for Indian-Style Curry with Sweet Potatoes, Eggplant, Green Beans, and Chickpeas: Substitute 12 ounces sweet potatoes, peeled and cut into ½-inch dice, for red potatoes. Substitute 1½ cups green beans, trimmed and cut into 1-inch pieces, and 1 eggplant, cut into ½-inch pieces (3 cups), for cauliflower. Omit peas.

CILANTRO-MINT CHUTNEY MAKES ABOUT 1 CUP

2 cups fresh cilantro leaves	1 tablespoon lime juice
1 cup fresh mint leaves	1½ teaspoons sugar
⅓ cup plain whole-milk yogurt	½ teaspoon ground cumin
¼ cup finely chopped onion	¼ teaspoon salt

Process all ingredients in food processor until smooth, about 20 seconds, scraping down sides of bowl halfway through processing. (Chutney can be refrigerated for up to 24 hours.)

A Better Way to Chop an Onion

Many chefs lop off both the top and the root end before chopping an onion. However, for the average home cook, we find that leaving the root intact makes it easier to keep the layers together as you make each cut. The distance between the cuts made in steps 2 through 4 will determine the size of the final pieces. For chopped or diced onions, leave ¼ to ½ inch between each cut. For minced or finely chopped onions, leave ⅛ to ¼ inch between each cut.

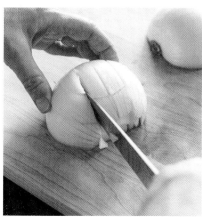

1. Halve onion pole to pole—that is, cutting through top and root end. Peel onion and trim top. (It's much easier to remove the skin once the onion has been cut.)

2. Lay peeled onion half flat side down on cutting board. With your hand on top of onion, make several horizontal cuts from 1 end to other but don't cut through root end.

3. Make several vertical cuts. (Be sure to cut up to but not through the root end.)

4. Rotate onion half so root end is in back. Slice onion thin across previous cuts. Use your knuckle as guide for knife while holding onion with your fingertips. Pull your fingertips in towards your palm, extending knuckles outward when cutting for more control.

80 Tuscan Bean Stew

THE BOWL THAT CAPTURES THE SOUL OF ITALIAN COOKING

We often think of Italy as the land of luxury goods from Prada and Maserati, but in the kitchen, simplicity and frugality rule. When it comes to turning modest ingredients into memorable dishes few cuisines can compete. Tuscan bean stew is the epitome of this thrifty tradition.

The people of Tuscany are known as *mangiafagioli*, or "bean eaters," for the prominent role beans play in their cuisine. Cannellini (white kidney beans) are the region's most famous legume, and Tuscan cooks take great care when preparing them. The traditional method calls for putting the dried beans and water in an empty wine bottle and slow-cooking them overnight in a fire's dying embers. Not only is this method energy- and cost-efficient, but it also yields beans that are especially creamy.

Cooking beans in a wine flask isn't practical but luckily a low-temperature oven works nearly as well. And using a Dutch oven means you can sauté vegetables and a little pancetta to build a strong flavor base for the stew.

But there's a part of the original Italian technique that's worth borrowing—the overnight time frame. We're not suggesting you cook the beans overnight. Even at the lowest setting, your oven runs too hot. However, to produce the creamiest beans possible, we recommend salt-soaking the beans for at least 8 hours. The salt tenderizes the skins so the beans can expand to accommodate the swelling starches inside without bursting.

And if you want a thicker stew, just use the back of a spoon to press some of the cooked beans against the side of the pot right before serving. This way you control the thickness of this Italian dish with humble roots and luxurious flavor.

WHY THIS RECIPE WORKS

Build a Rich Flavor Base
Sauté pancetta (salt-cured bacon) in olive oil, then add aromatics (onion, celery, carrots, and lots of garlic), all of which will lend the stew savory depth.

Cut the Water with Broth
While you could make this stew with all water (as Tuscans often do), we use a mix of chicken broth and water for a richer, more flavorful stew.

Go Slow and Steady
Brining the beans softens their skins so they take less time to cook (see "A Better Way to Soak Dried Beans" on page 241 for more information). Avoid cooking the beans on the stovetop—the agitation of the simmering water will result in beans that blow out. Instead, bring everything to a simmer, cover the pot, and slide it into a low oven (250 degrees) to cook gently for 1¼ to 1¾ hours—the beans will emerge creamy and intact. (Exact timing depends on the variety and age of the beans.)

Add Greens and Tomatoes Later
If added at the outset, the kale will become limp and gray. Add the greens later in the cooking process to preserve their color. And wait to add the tomatoes because their acidity will prevent the beans from softening.

Steep and Discard Rosemary
The flavor of rosemary can quickly become medicinal. Rather than mincing the rosemary and adding it with the aromatic vegetables, steep a sprig in the finished stew for 15 minutes—this infuses the broth with a delicate, not overpowering, herbal aroma.

Think Outside the Crouton
Another classic Italian bean soup, *ribollita*, is thickened with bread. You won't need to thicken this stew with bread, but consider ladling it on top of thick slices of toasted country bread to make a more substantial meal.

For optimal texture, soak the beans in salted water and wait to add the acidic tomatoes.

Hearty Tuscan Bean Stew

SERVES 8

We prefer the creamier texture of beans soaked overnight for this recipe. If you're short on time, use our quick-salt-soak method (see sidebar at right).

Salt and pepper	4 cups chicken broth
1 pound (2½ cups) dried cannellini beans, picked over and rinsed	2 bay leaves
1 tablespoon extra-virgin olive oil, plus extra for drizzling	1 pound kale or collard greens, stemmed and chopped into 1-inch pieces
6 ounces pancetta, cut into ¼-inch pieces	1 (14.5-ounce) can diced tomatoes, drained
1 large onion, chopped	1 sprig fresh rosemary
2 carrots, peeled and cut into ½-inch pieces	8 slices country white bread, 1¼ inch thick, broiled until golden brown on both sides and rubbed with garlic clove (optional)
2 celery ribs, cut into ½-inch pieces	
8 garlic cloves, peeled and smashed	

1. Dissolve 3 tablespoons salt in 4 quarts cold water in large bowl or container. Add beans and soak at room temperature for at least 8 hours or up to 24 hours. Drain and rinse well.

2. Adjust oven rack to lower-middle position and heat oven to 250 degrees. Heat oil and pancetta in Dutch oven over medium heat. Cook, stirring occasionally, until pancetta is lightly browned and fat has rendered, 6 to 10 minutes. Add onion, carrots, and celery and cook, stirring occasionally, until vegetables are softened and lightly browned, 10 to 16 minutes. Stir in garlic and cook until fragrant, about 1 minute. Stir in broth, 3 cups water, bay leaves, and soaked beans. Increase heat to high and bring to simmer. Cover pot, transfer to oven, and cook until beans are almost tender (very center of beans will still be firm), 45 minutes to 1 hour.

3. Remove pot from oven and stir in kale and tomatoes. Return pot to oven and continue to cook until beans and greens are fully tender, 30 to 40 minutes longer.

4. Remove pot from oven and submerge rosemary in stew. Cover and let stand 15 minutes. Discard bay leaves and rosemary and season stew with salt and pepper to taste. If desired, use back of spoon to press some beans against side of pot to thicken stew. Serve over toasted bread, if desired, and drizzle with olive oil.

VEGETARIAN HEARTY TUSCAN BEAN STEW

Omit pancetta, substitute 3 cups vegetable broth for chicken broth, and increase water to 4½ cups. Microwave ½ ounce dried porcini mushrooms with ½ cup water in covered bowl until steaming, about 1 minute. Let stand until mushrooms soften, about 5 minutes. Drain mushrooms in fine-mesh strainer lined with coffee filter, reserve liquid, and mince mushrooms. Stir mushrooms and reserved liquid into broth in step 2.

RECIPE DETAILS

Timeline

- 8 to 24 hours to salt-soak beans
- 20 minutes to prepare pancetta and vegetables
- 30 minutes to build stew base on stovetop
- 1½ hours to simmer stew in oven (add greens and tomatoes when beans are almost tender)
- 15 minutes to infuse stew with rosemary and season

Essential Tools

- Dutch oven with lid

Substitutions & Variations

- If pancetta is unavailable, substitute four slices of bacon.
- **Quick-Salt-Soak Method:** Place rinsed beans in large heatproof bowl. Bring 8 cups water and 3 tablespoons salt to boil. Pour water over beans and let them sit for 1 hour. Drain and rinse beans well before proceeding with step 2.
- **Hearty Tuscan Bean Stew with Sausage and Cabbage:** Substitute 1½ pounds sweet Italian sausage, casings removed, for pancetta; ½ head savoy cabbage, cut into 1-inch pieces, for kale; and 1 sprig fresh oregano for rosemary. Cook sausage in oil in step 2, breaking into small pieces with wooden spoon until no longer pink, about 8 minutes. Transfer sausage to paper towel–lined plate and place in refrigerator. Proceed with recipe as directed, stirring sausage and cabbage into stew along with tomatoes in step 3.

81 Peruvian Roast Chicken

A SPIT-ROASTED BIRD CAN BE REORIENTED FOR THE OVEN

Peruvian chicken joints have developed something of a cult following in the United States, and for good reason. The rotisserie bird that they serve is deeply bronzed from its slow rotation in a wood-fired oven and impressively seasoned with garlic, spices, lime juice, chiles, and a paste made with *huacatay*, or black mint. Off the spit, the chicken is carved and served with a garlicky, faintly spicy mayonnaise-like sauce.

There are two challenges in translating this dish for the American home kitchen. The first issue is about the technique. What's the best substitute for spit roasting—something that still yields a bird infused with smoky flavor and covered with bronzed skin? The second challenge is about ingredients. How do you replicate the hard-to-find black mint paste, along with the Peruvian aji peppers that give both the chicken and the dipping sauce their signature heat?

A vertical poultry roaster is the best tool for replacing the rotisserie. It allows the heat of a conventional electric (or gas) oven to sweep evenly over the bird, promoting far better browning than the usual V-rack. In addition, a vertical roaster encourages fat to drip freely out of the bird, resulting in rendered, crisp skin.

An interesting mix of smart substitutes addresses the flavor issue, but time and salt are equally important factors. In order for the seasonings to imbue the meat with the smoky, garlicky, and citrusy notes that are the hallmark of this dish, you must add a lot of salt to the herb paste. And you must rub that paste under the skin and then wait—at least 6 hours. The salt will eventually carry the flavors of the paste into the meat so that every bite is perfectly seasoned.

WHY THIS RECIPE WORKS

Build a Paste with Smart Substitutes
Start with a basic paste of salt, garlic, oil, lime juice, and cumin and add fresh mint (the best replacement for the earthy black mint paste), dried oregano, grated lime zest (for more citrus flavor without too much acidity), black pepper, sugar, and just a teaspoon of minced habanero chile.

Get Smoke from a Bottle of Paprika
The smoked version of this brick-red powder is a powerhouse of smoky flavor. Just a couple of teaspoons added to the paste approximates the subtle flavor of a wood-fire rotisserie.

Season Thoroughly
Apply the paste directly to the meat (underneath the skin) as well as to the exterior of the bird for chicken that is thoroughly seasoned from skin to bone. We recommend wearing gloves when working with the habanero—and wearing gloves while applying the paste to the bird will keep your hands clean. To further contain the mess, marinate the coated chicken in a zipper-lock bag.

Cook at Two Heat Levels
A vertical roaster takes the place of a rotisserie but you'll need to make some adjustments to the oven's heat to prevent the white meat from drying out. Start the chicken at 325 degrees and cook until partially done, let the chicken rest briefly at room temperature, and then crank up the heat to finish the bird at 500 degrees for a crisp, golden brown exterior.

Serve with a Sauce
The spicy sauce should be thinner than traditional mayo but still viscous enough to cling to the meat when dunked. To make the sauce, whip a whole egg and vegetable oil in a food processor with a little water, onion, lime juice, cilantro, yellow mustard, and garlic. Add jarred jalapeños to contribute the punch traditionally provided by the elusive aji chiles.

A potent puree and novel roasting method create a memorable roast chicken.

Peruvian Roast Chicken with Garlic and Lime

SERVES 3 TO 4

Wear gloves when working with the habanero. Serve with Spicy Mayonnaise (recipe follows).

¼ cup fresh mint leaves

3 tablespoons extra-virgin olive oil

6 garlic cloves, chopped coarse

1 tablespoon salt

1 tablespoon pepper

1 tablespoon ground cumin

1 tablespoon sugar

2 teaspoons smoked paprika

2 teaspoons dried oregano

2 teaspoons finely grated lime zest plus ¼ cup juice (2 limes)

1 teaspoon minced habanero chile

1 (3½- to 4-pound) whole chicken, giblets discarded

1. Process mint, oil, garlic, salt, pepper, cumin, sugar, paprika, oregano, lime zest and juice, and habanero in blender until smooth paste forms, 10 to 20 seconds. Use your fingers to gently loosen skin covering breast and thighs; place half of paste under skin, directly on meat of breast and thighs. Gently press on skin to distribute paste over meat. Spread entire exterior surface of chicken with remaining paste. Tuck wings behind back. Place chicken in 1-gallon zipper-lock bag and refrigerate for at least 6 hours or up to 24 hours.

2. Adjust oven rack to lowest position and heat oven to 325 degrees. Place vertical roaster on rimmed baking sheet. Slide chicken onto vertical roaster so drumsticks reach down to bottom of roaster, chicken stands upright, and breast is perpendicular to bottom of pan. Roast chicken until skin just begins to turn golden and breast registers 140 degrees, 45 to 55 minutes. Carefully remove chicken and pan from oven and increase oven temperature to 500 degrees.

3. Once oven has come to temperature, place 1 cup water in bottom of baking sheet and continue to roast until entire chicken skin is browned and crisp, breast registers 160 degrees, and thighs register 175 degrees, about 20 minutes, rotating sheet halfway through roasting. Check chicken halfway through roasting; if top is becoming too dark, place 7-inch square piece of aluminum foil over neck and wingtips of chicken and continue to roast. (If pan begins to smoke and sizzle, add additional water to pan.)

4. Carefully remove chicken from oven and let rest, still on vertical roaster, for 20 minutes. Using 2 large wads of paper towels, carefully lift chicken off roaster and onto carving board. Carve chicken and serve.

SPICY MAYONNAISE MAKES ABOUT 1 CUP

1 large egg

2 tablespoons water

1 tablespoon minced onion

1 tablespoon lime juice

1 tablespoon minced fresh cilantro

1 tablespoon minced jarred jalapeños

1 garlic clove, minced

1 teaspoon yellow mustard

¼ teaspoon salt

1 cup vegetable oil

Process all ingredients except oil in food processor until combined, about 5 seconds. With machine running, slowly drizzle in oil in steady stream until mayonnaise-like consistency is reached, scraping down bowl as necessary.

RECIPE DETAILS

Timeline

- 15 minutes to make marinade (paste)
- 6 to 24 hours to marinate chicken
- 45 to 55 minutes to roast chicken at 325 degrees (make Spicy Mayonnaise while chicken roasts)
- 10 minutes to increase heat in oven (remove chicken from oven while doing this)
- 20 minutes to roast chicken at 500 degrees
- 30 minutes to rest and carve chicken

Essential Tools

- Latex gloves for protecting hands while working with chile
- Blender for making marinade
- Vertical poultry roaster (If you don't have one, substitute a 12-ounce can of beer. Open the beer and pour out or drink about half of the liquid. Spray the can lightly with vegetable oil spray and proceed with the recipe.)
- Rimmed baking sheet for holding vertical roaster
- Food processor for making Spicy Mayonnaise

Substitutions & Variations

- If habanero chiles are unavailable, 1 tablespoon of minced serrano chile can be substituted.
- If you have concerns about consuming raw eggs, replace the egg in the Spicy Mayonnaise with ¼ cup of an egg substitute.

82 Chicken Tagine

WELL SPICED DOESN'T HAVE TO BE SPICY

When most people think of Morocco, they envision colorful souks, spindly minarets, and flowing djellabas. When most cooks think of Morocco, they think of tagines. These exotically spiced, assertively flavored stews are slow-cooked in earthenware vessels of the same name. Tagines can include all kinds of meat, vegetables, and fruit, although our favorite combines chicken with briny olives and tart lemon.

To make any tagine friendly for the American home kitchen, the first task is to figure out the cooking vessel. A lidded Dutch oven is the best choice. Not only does this heavy pot ensure even cooking but it also permits stovetop browning before the stewing begins. These cooking steps are key for developing flavor.

To start, browning the chicken pieces creates fond in the pot that will add flavor to the braising liquid. It also renders fat that can be used to cook the sliced onions and eventually the garlic. This dish is not spicy—there's just ¼ teaspoon of cayenne to provide a wisp of heat. But this dish is well spiced, with a mix of warm cinnamon, citrusy coriander, earthy paprika, and floral ginger.

To release the full flavor of convenient ground spices it is imperative to bloom them in the pot with the rendered chicken fat. That's because many of the essential flavor compounds in spices are fat-soluble. If the spices are added directly to the liquid, the final dish won't be nearly as flavorful. When blooming the spices, wait until their color darkens and they are very fragrant. At this point, it's safe to add the broth and simmer the chicken in this supercharged base.

WHY THIS RECIPE WORKS

Use the Skin and Then Lose the Skin
Brown the pieces of chicken skin-on to give the braising liquid deep flavor, but pull the skin off before simmering the stew. The skin will just turn rubbery once the lid goes on the pot.

Arrange the Meat Right
Thoughtful placement of the chicken and vegetables is important to the success of this dish. Place the thighs and drumsticks on the bottom of the pot and give them a head start with a 5-minute simmer. Then cover with the carrots and the breast pieces. Raising the white meat above the simmering liquid allows the delicate meat to cook gently. Simmering the dark meat directly in the liquid means all the chicken will be ready at the same time.

Be Selective About Spices
The spice blend for tagines can contain upward of 30 spices. You can build your own blend with spices you most likely already have in your pantry: cumin, ginger, cinnamon, cayenne (just a little), coriander, and finally paprika, which adds both sweetness and bright color.

Find the Right Olives
Big, meaty green Moroccan olives can be difficult to find so we swap in Greek "cracked" olives found in most supermarkets. Don't add the olives to the simmering stew because their flavor will leach out into the liquid and they'll emerge flavorless and mushy. Instead, add them just before serving so they retain their piquant flavor and firm texture.

Rethink the Preserved Lemon
The lemon flavor in authentic tagines comes from preserved lemon, a long-cured Moroccan condiment. Rather than try to source them, add a few broad ribbons of lemon zest and some juice—it will give the tagine a rich citrus back note. In addition, stir chopped zest mixed with raw garlic into the tagine just before serving for a welcome sharp finish.

Pantry spices create deep flavor, as do sautéed onions and strips of lemon zest.

Moroccan Chicken with Olives and Lemon

SERVES 4

If the olives are particularly salty, give them a rinse. Serve with couscous.

1¼ teaspoons paprika
½ teaspoon ground cumin
½ teaspoon ground ginger
¼ teaspoon cayenne pepper
¼ teaspoon ground coriander
¼ teaspoon ground cinnamon
3 (2-inch) strips lemon zest plus 3 tablespoons juice
5 garlic cloves, minced
1 (3½- to 4-pound) whole chicken, cut into 8 pieces (4 breast pieces, 2 thighs, 2 drumsticks), trimmed, wings and giblets discarded
Salt and pepper
1 tablespoon olive oil
1 large onion, halved and sliced ¼ inch thick
1¾ cups chicken broth
1 tablespoon honey
2 carrots, peeled and cut crosswise into ½-inch-thick rounds, very large pieces cut into half-moons
1 cup cracked green olives, pitted and halved
2 tablespoons chopped fresh cilantro

1. Combine paprika, cumin, ginger, cayenne, coriander, and cinnamon in small bowl and set aside. Mince 1 strip lemon zest, add 1 teaspoon minced garlic, and mince together until reduced to fine paste; set aside.

2. Season both sides of chicken pieces with salt and pepper. Heat oil in Dutch oven over medium-high heat until just beginning to smoke. Add chicken pieces, skin side down, and cook without moving until skin is deep golden, about 5 minutes. Using tongs, flip chicken pieces and brown on second side, about 4 minutes longer. Transfer chicken to large plate; when cool enough to handle, remove and discard skin. Pour off and discard all but 1 tablespoon fat from pot.

3. Add onion and remaining 2 lemon zest strips to pot and cook, stirring occasionally, until onion slices have browned at edges but still retain their shape, 5 to 7 minutes (add 1 tablespoon water if pan gets too dark). Add remaining garlic and cook until fragrant, about 30 seconds. Add spice mixture and cook, stirring constantly, until darkened and very fragrant, 45 to 60 seconds. Stir in broth and honey, scraping up any browned bits. Add thighs and drumsticks, reduce heat to medium, and simmer for 5 minutes.

4. Add carrots and breast pieces with any accumulated juices to pot, arranging breast pieces in single layer on top of carrots. Cover, reduce heat to medium-low, and simmer until breast pieces register 160 degrees, 10 to 15 minutes.

5. Transfer chicken to plate and tent with aluminum foil. Add olives to pot; increase heat to medium-high and simmer until liquid has thickened slightly and carrots are tender, 4 to 6 minutes. Return chicken to pot and stir in garlic mixture, lemon juice, and cilantro; season with salt and pepper to taste. Serve immediately.

MOROCCAN CHICKEN WITH CHICKPEAS AND APRICOTS

Replace 1 carrot with 1 cup dried apricots, halved, and replace olives with one 15-ounce can chickpeas, rinsed.

RECIPE DETAILS

Timeline

- 10 minutes to combine spices and make garlic-lemon paste
- 15 minutes to cut up chicken and prepare onion, carrots, and olives
- 10 minutes to brown chicken pieces (remove skin once chicken cools)
- 10 minutes to brown onion, garlic, and spices and add broth and honey
- 5 minutes to cook thighs and drumsticks
- 10 to 15 minutes to cook carrots and breast pieces
- 5 minutes to heat olives and thicken sauce (remove chicken from pot while doing this)
- 2 minutes to reheat chicken and finish dish

Essential Tools

- Vegetable peeler to remove wide strips of zest from lemon (Do this before juicing the lemon and make sure to trim any white pith from the zest, as it can impart a bitter flavor.)
- Chef's knife for cutting up whole chicken and preparing vegetables and aromatics
- Dutch oven with lid for cooking tagine

Substitutions & Variations

- Bone-in chicken parts can be substituted for the whole chicken. For best results, use four chicken thighs and two chicken breasts, each breast split in half; the dark meat contributes valuable flavor to the broth and should not be omitted.

83 Tandoori Chicken

A SPICY MARINADE AND QUICK CHAR MAKE CHICKEN EXCITING

Tandoori chicken is arguably India's best-known culinary export. Lightly charred pieces of juicy chicken are infused with smoke, garlic, ginger, and spices for a dish that manages to be both exotic and homey.

Authentic versions call for a 24-hour marinade and a tandoor, the traditional beehive-shaped clay oven that fires up to 900 degrees—requirements that keep this dish mainly in the realm of restaurants, even in India. But if we could develop a workaround for the tandoor, this recipe would be a welcome addition to the usual chicken rotation, especially if the 24-hour marinade was no longer essential.

The most obvious alternative might be the grill, but the yogurt-spice mixture that coats the chicken pieces burns very easily. Although a tandoor oven is very hot, the chicken is not exposed directly to the flames so there's little risk of a conflagration. As any novice griller knows, chicken parts and the grill don't always work well together. The oven is a more reliable tool for making tandoori chicken at home, especially if used in combination with the broiler.

As for the yogurt marinade, mixing the spices with salt and then rubbing the chicken with this mixture is the best way to get the spice flavor deep into the meat. Thirty minutes does the trick and there's no risk of the acid in the yogurt making the meat mushy. When it comes to the yogurt (which helps create a distinctive crust on the chicken pieces), it's best tossed with the chicken right before it goes into the oven. Adding more spices to the yogurt reinforces their flavor. Serve the chicken with *raita*, the bracing yogurt sauce, to create an Indian classic without the fuss.

WHY THIS RECIPE WORKS

Start with a Spice Rub
We trade a long soak in the traditional yogurt marinade for a spice rub—it flavors the chicken without turning the meat spongy. We use the same spices traditionally used in the marinade—garam masala, ground cumin, and a little chili powder—as well as some ginger, garlic, and lime. To intensify their flavors, we bloom the spices and garlic in oil. Two steps help the rub permeate the chicken with flavor: First we remove the skin (this also eliminates the risk of flare-ups under the broiler) and then we make shallow slashes into the meat so the rub can penetrate deep into the chicken pieces.

Don't Abandon the Yogurt Altogether
It will take about 30 minutes for the spice rub to penetrate the chicken. Afterward, give the chicken a quick dip in yogurt seasoned with the same spices in the rub—it will add an appealing tang to the exterior of the meat that is a hallmark of this dish.

Use Your Oven, Not a Tandoor
It's not possible to replicate the intense heat of a tandoor oven with your home oven—but that's OK. For nicely charred yet still juicy meat, start the chicken in a moderate oven (arrange the chicken on a wire rack set in a baking sheet so the chicken doesn't stew in its moisture) and then finish the chicken under the broiler.

Broil Carefully
The chicken finishes cooking under the broiler and emerges with a crisp crust (from the yogurt)—but only if you make sure the oven rack is positioned 6 inches from the heating element. If the rack is too close, the chicken will burn and if the rack isn't close enough, you'll be waiting (and waiting) for the exterior to crisp, risking dry meat. Don't leave the partially baked chicken in the oven while you heat the broiler—only a fully heated broiler will crisp the exterior and finish cooking the meat in sync.

A gentle oven method partially cooks the chicken without burning the yogurt crust. Only when the chicken is nearly done is it time to use the broiler.

Tandoori Chicken

SERVES 4

Serve with basmati rice pilaf (see page 45) and a few chutneys or relishes (see pages 266–267 for two options) as well as Raita (recipe follows). If using large chicken breasts (about 1 pound each), cut each breast into three pieces. If using smaller breasts (10 to 12 ounces each), cut each breast into two pieces.

2 tablespoons vegetable oil	¼ cup lime juice (2 limes), plus 1 lime, cut into wedges
6 garlic cloves, minced	
2 tablespoons grated fresh ginger	2 teaspoons salt
1 tablespoon garam masala	3 pounds bone-in chicken pieces (split breasts cut in half, drumsticks, and/or thighs), skin removed and trimmed
2 teaspoons ground cumin	
2 teaspoons chili powder	
1 cup plain whole-milk yogurt	

1. Heat oil in 10-inch skillet over medium heat until shimmering. Add garlic and ginger and cook until fragrant, about 30 seconds. Stir in garam masala, cumin, and chili powder and continue to cook until fragrant, 30 seconds longer. Transfer half of garlic mixture to medium bowl, stir in yogurt and 2 tablespoons lime juice, and set aside. In large bowl, combine remaining garlic mixture, remaining 2 tablespoons lime juice, and salt.

2. Using sharp knife, make 2 or 3 short slashes into skinned side of each piece of chicken. Transfer chicken to large bowl and gently rub with salt-spice mixture until all pieces are evenly coated. Let sit at room temperature for 30 minutes.

3. Adjust oven rack to upper-middle position and heat oven to 325 degrees. Set wire rack in aluminum foil–lined rimmed baking sheet. Pour yogurt mixture over chicken and toss until chicken is evenly coated with thick layer. Arrange chicken pieces, scored side down, on prepared wire rack. Discard excess yogurt mixture. Roast chicken until breast pieces register 125 degrees and thighs/drumsticks register 130 degrees, 15 to 25 minutes. (Smaller pieces may cook faster than larger pieces. Remove pieces from oven as they reach correct temperature.)

4. Adjust oven rack 6 inches from broiler element and heat broiler. Return chicken to prepared wire rack, scored side up, and broil until chicken is lightly charred in spots and breast pieces register 160 degrees and thighs/drumsticks register 175 degrees, 8 to 15 minutes. Transfer chicken to serving plate, tent loosely with foil, and let rest for 5 minutes. Serve with lime wedges.

RAITA MAKES ABOUT 1 CUP

1 cup plain whole-milk yogurt	Salt
2 tablespoons minced fresh cilantro	Cayenne pepper
1 garlic clove, minced	

Mix all ingredients together and season with salt and cayenne to taste. Cover and refrigerate until needed.

RECIPE DETAILS

Timeline

- 10 minutes to make yogurt basting mixture and salt-spice rub
- 10 minutes to slash chicken and rub with salt-spice mixture
- 30 minutes to let spices flavor chicken (make raita while waiting)
- 20 minutes to coat chicken with yogurt and bake
- 10 minutes to heat broiler (remove chicken from oven while doing this)
- 15 to 20 minutes to broil and rest chicken

Essential Tools

- 10-inch skillet for cooking spice paste
- Sharp paring knife for slashing chicken
- Rimmed baking sheet fitted with wire rack (line pan with foil to facilitate clean up)

Substitutions & Variations

- We prefer both the chicken and raita made with whole-milk yogurt, but low-fat yogurt can be substituted. Nonfat yogurt will make the raita taste hollow and bland and should not be used.

84 Chicken Adobo

A QUICK BRAISE WITH BOLD FLAVORS

Most braised chicken recipes rely on many ingredients and that means a lot of prep—mincing garlic, chopping onions, and slicing a myriad of vegetables. In chicken adobo, the national dish of the Philippines, the approach is quite different. The ingredient list is very short and nothing—other than the chicken—requires prep time. This formula works because the key ingredients that go into this braise—soy sauce, vinegar, garlic, bay leaves, and black pepper—are each so potent. The end result is a pantry-ready braise with bold, tangy flavors.

Adobo is reminiscent of teriyaki but instead of balancing the strong flavors of soy and garlic with a sweet element, adobo relies on something acidic. But a dish with a quarter cup or more of soy sauce and twice as much vinegar can be too pungent. Some recipes cut the braising liquid with water. While this approach tames the excessive tartness, it also makes the dish dull. A better approach is to add another Filipino staple—coconut milk. Just as oil balances the vinegar in a French vinaigrette, the fat in the coconut milk tempers (but doesn't dull) the acidity and salt in this sauce.

Another French technique—starting the chicken in a cold pan to render fat—ensures that the skin on the chicken thighs is well browned and rendered. You can't discard the skin (standard practice in most braises) because the chicken should be lacquered with sauce and the skin is key in helping the sauce to adhere. This cold pan method, which is typically used with fatty duck breasts, ensures that the skin will have some crackle, even after braising. Adobo might just be the simplest and best thing you can do with chicken.

WHY THIS RECIPE WORKS

Bone-In for Braising
Choose bone-in chicken thighs for adobo. They have more fat and collagen than chicken breasts, making them particularly well-suited to braising. They also have more meat on the bone than drumsticks. Keep the skin on so that you can crisp it into a craggy crust—it will give the sauce something to grab onto. But to prevent a greasy dish, trim the thighs and remove any knobby pockets of fat, which are difficult to render adequately.

Marinate in Soy Sauce
Start the chicken in a soy sauce–only marinade to help tenderize and flavor the meat—it takes just 30 minutes or up to 1 hour. The salt in the soy sauce will penetrate the meat without toughening it up or making it mushy.

Balance the Marinade
To even out the sharp saltiness of the traditional vinegar and soy sauce braising liquid, add a can of coconut milk, which is often done in a regional variation of adobo. The thick rich milk will mellow the harsh flavors while still allowing plenty of tanginess—and it will add welcome body to the sauce.

Start with a Cold Pan
To render the gummy fat layer in the chicken skin and crisp its surface, we take a cue from the French technique for preparing duck (a notoriously fatty bird). Start the meat in a room-temperature nonstick skillet and then turn up the heat. As the pan heats, the fat will have time to melt before the exterior burns. Be sure to remove the excess fat from the skillet to prevent the braise from being greasy.

Flip 'Em
Start the browned chicken pieces skin side down in the braising liquid and then to preserve as much crispness as possible in the finished dish, turn the chicken pieces skin side up—this will give the skin a chance to dry out a little before serving.

The chicken braises in a mix of supercharged ingredients, including coconut milk and garlic.

Filipino Chicken Adobo

SERVES 4

Serve this dish over rice.

8	(5- to 7-ounce) bone-in chicken thighs, trimmed	8	garlic cloves, peeled
⅓	cup soy sauce	4	bay leaves
1	(13.5-ounce) can coconut milk	2	teaspoons pepper
¾	cup cider vinegar	1	scallion, sliced thin

1. Toss chicken with soy sauce in large bowl. Refrigerate for at least 30 minutes or up to 1 hour.

2. Remove chicken from soy sauce, allowing excess to drip back into bowl. Transfer chicken, skin side down, to 12-inch nonstick skillet; set aside soy sauce.

3. Place skillet over medium-high heat and cook until chicken skin is browned, 7 to 10 minutes. While chicken is browning, whisk coconut milk, vinegar, garlic, bay leaves, and pepper into soy sauce.

4. Transfer chicken to plate and discard fat in skillet. Return chicken to skillet skin side down, add coconut milk mixture, and bring to boil. Reduce heat to medium-low and simmer, uncovered, for 20 minutes. Flip chicken skin side up and continue to cook, uncovered, until chicken registers 175 degrees, about 15 minutes. Transfer chicken to platter and tent loosely with aluminum foil.

5. Remove bay leaves and skim any fat off surface of sauce. Return skillet to medium-high heat and cook until sauce is thickened, 5 to 7 minutes. Pour sauce over chicken, sprinkle with scallion, and serve.

RECIPE DETAILS

Timeline

- 5 minutes to trim fat from chicken
- 30 minutes to 1 hour to marinate chicken in soy sauce
- 10 minutes to brown chicken (whisk coconut milk and other ingredients into reserved soy sauce)
- 2 minutes to transfer chicken to plate and discard fat from skillet
- 35 minutes to cook chicken in coconut mixture
- 5 minutes to reduce sauce (set chicken aside on platter)

Essential Tools

- 12-inch nonstick skillet (The nonstick coating reduces the risk of sticking.)
- Tongs for turning chicken thighs

Substitutions & Variations

- Light coconut milk can be substituted for the regular coconut milk.

85 Thai Basil Chicken

A GENTLE APPROACH TO STIR-FRYING PACKS A PUNCH

In China, the secret to a successful restaurant stir-fry lies not in what goes into the wok, but what's under it: a massive high-output burner with a flame the size of a jet engine's. The super-high heat rapidly sears the meat and vegetables, quickly cooking them through, while at the same time imparting intense flavor from all that browning. But that's not the only way to stir-fry.

In Thailand, street vendors use jury-rigged mobile kitchens to produce a variety of stir-fries, all over very modest flames. Chicken with basil is a classic example of this alternate style of stir-frying. Hand-chopped pieces of chicken are cooked with a big handful of hot basil (also known as Thai basil) as well as minced garlic and Thai chiles, sliced shallots, and splashes of fish sauce and oyster sauce. Even though the chicken is not browned, this dish is every bit as satisfying as any Chinese stir-fry.

The difference is the aromatics. In a high-heat stir-fry, the garlic and other aromatics are added at the end of the cooking process so they don't burn. In a Thai stir-fry, the aromatics go into the pan at the outset and they're cooked over low heat. The idea is that the flavor compounds in the garlic, chiles, and basil will infuse the oil they're cooked in, which in turn will coat the protein, giving the dish complexity.

This method of stir-frying is used in countless Thai dishes. And in this recipe a moderately cool pan has the added benefit of ensuring that the white meat chicken doesn't dry out. With its spicy, salty, floral, sweet, and tart notes, this basic stir-fry proves that less heat can, in fact, translate to more flavor.

WHY THIS RECIPE WORKS

Start with a Cold Skillet
For aromatics cooked to a perfect, even shade of golden brown, we start them in a cold skillet with a couple tablespoons of oil; this allows them to cook slowly and evenly, with no chance of burning.

Put the Food Processor to Work
Purchasing ground chicken might sound tempting. Don't do it. The grind is too fine and your dish will turn out mealy and mushy. Granted, the traditional method of hand chopping tender chicken breasts is a hassle, but you can use a food processor (you'll already have the food processor out to chop the garlic and chiles). Spoon a tablespoon of fish sauce into the food processor along with the chicken before chopping it, then transfer the chopped chicken to the refrigerator for 15 minutes. Due to its high concentration of salt, the fish sauce acts as a brine, seasoning the meat and helping it retain moisture as it cooks. The fish sauce won't make your chicken taste fishy, but it will add flavor.

Cook the Chicken in One Batch
In a Chinese stir-fry, the meat is seared in batches (for flavorful browning), but batch-cooking isn't necessary in the Thai approach. The chicken is cooked all at once toward the end of the process and the meat absorbs the fully developed flavors of the aromatic oil and sauce.

Brighten the Sauce
Thai oyster sauce is hard to come by, but you can swap in Chinese oyster sauce. It is thicker and heavier than Thai style, so add a little white vinegar—it does a remarkable job of balancing that heaviness.

Begin with Basil, End with Basil
Unlike hot basil, which has a robust texture that can withstand prolonged cooking, sweet Italian basil wilts under heat—but saving it for the end doesn't add nearly enough flavor. The solution? Chop a cup of basil to cook with the chiles and aromatics, then stir in an additional cup of whole leaves right before serving.

Fish sauce seasons the chicken at the outset, while a fistful of basil leaves finishes the job.

Thai-Style Chicken with Basil

SERVES 4

Since tolerance for spiciness can vary, we've kept our recipe relatively mild. Sweetness without sufficient heat can become cloying, so we also cut back the sugar. For a very mild version of the dish, remove the seeds and ribs from the chiles. In Thailand, crushed red pepper and sugar are passed at the table, along with extra fish sauce and white vinegar, so the dish can be adjusted to suit individual tastes. Serve with steamed rice and vegetables, if desired.

2 cups fresh basil leaves

3 garlic cloves, peeled

6 green or red Thai chiles, stemmed

2 tablespoons fish sauce, plus extra for serving

1 tablespoon oyster sauce

1 tablespoon sugar, plus extra for serving

1 teaspoon distilled white vinegar, plus extra for serving

1 pound boneless, skinless chicken breasts, trimmed and cut into 2-inch pieces

3 shallots, sliced thin

2 tablespoons vegetable oil

Red pepper flakes

1. Pulse 1 cup basil, garlic, and Thai chiles in food processor until finely chopped, 6 to 10 pulses, scraping down bowl once during processing. Transfer 1 tablespoon basil mixture to small bowl and stir in 1 tablespoon fish sauce, oyster sauce, sugar, and vinegar; set aside. Transfer remaining basil mixture to 12-inch nonstick skillet. Do not wash workbowl.

2. Pulse chicken and remaining 1 tablespoon fish sauce in food processor until meat is chopped into approximate ¼-inch pieces, 6 to 8 pulses. Transfer to medium bowl and refrigerate for 15 minutes.

3. Stir shallots and oil into basil mixture in skillet. Heat over medium-low heat (mixture should start to sizzle after about 1½ minutes; if it doesn't, adjust heat accordingly), stirring constantly, until garlic and shallots are golden brown, 5 to 8 minutes.

4. Add chicken, increase heat to medium, and cook, stirring and breaking up chicken with potato masher or rubber spatula, until only traces of pink remain, 2 to 4 minutes. Add reserved basil–fish sauce mixture and continue to cook, stirring constantly, until chicken is no longer pink, about 1 minute. Stir in remaining 1 cup basil and cook, stirring constantly, until basil is wilted, 30 to 60 seconds. Serve immediately, passing pepper flakes and extra fish sauce, sugar, and vinegar separately.

RECIPE DETAILS

Timeline

• 10 minutes to prepare aromatics

• 20 minutes to chop and chill chicken (slice shallots while chicken is in fridge)

• 10 to 15 minutes to cook stir-fry

Essential Tools

• Food processor for chopping aromatics and chicken

• 12-inch nonstick skillet for cooking stir-fry

• Potato masher for breaking up chopped chicken as it cooks (A rubber spatula can be used instead.)

Substitutions & Variations

• If fresh Thai chiles are unavailable, substitute 2 serranos or 1 medium jalapeño.

86 Chicken Souvlaki

THE BEST MEAL YOU CAN HOLD IN YOUR HANDS

Souvlaki is basically Greek for "meat grilled on a stick." Just about every meat-eating culture has a version, but when it comes to being documented masters (if not originators) of this technique, Greek credentials are hard to beat. Homer's *Iliad* and *Odyssey* are rich with detailed accounts of the heroes skewering meat and cooking it over fire, souvlaki-style.

In modern Greece, souvlaki is usually made with pork, but at Greek restaurants in the United States boneless, skinless chicken breast is most common. The chunks of white meat are marinated in a tangy mixture of lemon juice, olive oil, oregano, parsley, and sometimes garlic before being skewered and grilled until nicely charred. Souvlaki may be served with rice and cooked vegetables, but just as often the chicken is placed on a lightly grilled pita, slathered with a yogurt-based tzatziki sauce, and eaten out of hand.

This is among the most satisfying sandwiches on the planet. The creamy sauce, freshened with herbs and cucumber, complements the char of the chicken, and the soft pita offers more substance (and chew) than other wrappers. Tuck some grilled onions and peppers into the wrap and you have a meal.

The key to this dish is the lemony marinade. Rather than the usual 24 hours, which can dry out lean chicken and doesn't really get much flavor deep into the meat, we prefer a hurry-up approach that includes a 30-minute brine (to promote juiciness) and then a quick toss with the dressing right before skewering. The real secret is to reserve some dressing and use it to coat the grilled chicken and vegetables. This step rehydrates their dry exteriors and delivers a bright citrus and herb punch you can taste in every bite.

WHY THIS RECIPE WORKS

Marinade Matters

We trade in a long marinade for a quick brine but keep those traditional marinade flavors by giving the brined chicken a quick dip in an olive oil and lemon mixture seasoned with honey; the honey balances the flavors and promotes browning for a deeply flavorful charred crust. Be sure to reserve a portion of the olive oil–lemon mixture (before it's tossed with the raw chicken) so you can slide the grilled meat from the skewers right into the bowl of marinade to moisten the exteriors and add a fresh layer of flavor.

Create a Vegetable Shield

The pieces of chicken cooked on the ends of the skewers often cook faster than the pieces in the middle. To solve this problem, we string chunks of bell pepper and red onion onto the ends of each skewer. The vegetables function as shields, protecting the end pieces of chicken from the heat so they cook at the same rate as the middle pieces.

Get Saucy

Minced raw garlic is undeniably harsh, but there is a way to temper its pungency–briefly steep it in lemon juice. The acid converts the harsh-tasting garlic compound, allicin, into mellower compounds in the same way that cooking does. For perfect drizzling consistency, mix yogurt and cucumbers together and let the sauce rest, allowing the salt in the sauce to draw out the water from the cucumbers.

That's a Wrap

Moisten the tops and bottoms of pocketed pitas and wrap them in foil before grilling. The gently steamed pitas will turn out soft and warm. To fold souvlaki as tidily as a street cart master, place the warm pita at one corner of a 12-inch square piece of foil, then layer the sandwich ingredients on top of the pita, leaving a 1-inch border on all sides. Fold the sides of the pita over the filling, then fold one side of foil over the sandwich. Fold up the bottom of the foil. Finally, fold over the other side of foil.

There's a science to skewering the chicken, onion, and peppers and to assembling the wraps.

Grilled Chicken Souvlaki

SERVES 4

TZATZIKI SAUCE

1 tablespoon lemon juice	3 tablespoons minced fresh mint
1 small garlic clove, minced to paste	1 tablespoon minced fresh parsley
¾ cup plain Greek yogurt	⅜ teaspoon salt
½ cucumber, peeled, halved lengthwise, seeded, and diced fine (½ cup)	

CHICKEN

Salt and pepper	1 teaspoon dried oregano
1½ pounds boneless, skinless chicken breasts, trimmed, cut into 1-inch pieces	1 green bell pepper, quartered, stemmed, seeded, each quarter cut into 4 chunks
⅓ cup extra-virgin olive oil	
2 tablespoons minced fresh parsley	1 small red onion, ends trimmed, peeled, halved lengthwise, each half cut into 4 chunks
1 teaspoon finely grated lemon zest plus ¼ cup juice (2 lemons)	
1 teaspoon honey	4 (8-inch) pita breads

1. *For the Sauce:* Whisk lemon juice and garlic together in small bowl. Let stand for 10 minutes. Stir in yogurt, cucumber, mint, parsley, and salt. Cover and set aside.

2. *For the Chicken:* Dissolve 2 tablespoons salt in 1 quart cold water. Add chicken to brine, cover, and refrigerate for 30 minutes. While chicken is brining, combine oil, parsley, lemon zest and juice, honey, oregano, and ½ teaspoon pepper in medium bowl. Transfer ¼ cup oil mixture to large bowl; set aside to toss with cooked chicken.

3. Remove chicken from brine and pat dry with paper towels. Toss chicken with remaining oil mixture. Thread 4 pieces of bell pepper onto one 12-inch metal skewer. Thread one-quarter of chicken, then 2 chunks of onion onto skewer. Repeat skewering remaining chicken and vegetables on 3 more skewers. Lightly moisten 2 pita breads with water. Sandwich 2 unmoistened pita breads between moistened pita breads and wrap stack tightly in lightly greased heavy-duty aluminum foil.

4A. *For a Charcoal Grill:* Open bottom vent completely. Light large chimney starter mounded with charcoal briquettes (7 quarts). When top coals are partially covered with ash, pour evenly over half of grill. Set cooking grate in place, cover, and open lid vent completely. Heat grill until hot, about 5 minutes.

4B. *For a Gas Grill:* Turn all burners to high, cover, and heat grill until hot, about 15 minutes. Leave primary burner on high and turn off other burner(s).

5. Clean and oil cooking grate. Place skewers on hotter side of grill and cook, turning occasionally, until chicken and vegetables are well browned on all sides and chicken registers 160 degrees, 15 to 20 minutes. Using fork, push chicken and vegetables off skewers into bowl of reserved oil mixture. Stir gently, breaking up onion chunks; cover with foil and let sit for 5 minutes. Meanwhile, place packet of pitas on cooler side of grill. Flip occasionally to heat, about 5 minutes.

6. Lay each warm pita on 12-inch square of foil. Spread each pita with 2 tablespoons tzatziki. Place one-quarter of chicken and vegetables in middle of each pita. Roll into cylindrical shape and serve.

RECIPE DETAILS

Timeline

- 15 minutes to make tzatziki sauce
- 30 minutes to brine chicken (make oil mixture and light grill while chicken is in fridge)
- 15 minutes to toss chicken with oil mixture and thread chicken and vegetables on skewers
- 15 to 20 minutes to grill skewers
- 5 minutes to marinate grilled chicken and vegetables in reserved oil mixture (heat pitas on grill while waiting)
- 5 minutes to assemble wraps

Essential Tools

- Rasp grater for turning garlic into paste
- Four (12-inch) metal skewers
- Aluminum foil for protecting pitas on grill and for preparing wrap sandwiches

Substitutions & Variations

- We like the chicken as a wrap, but you may skip the pita and serve the chicken, vegetables, and tzatziki with rice.
- The tzatziki sauce is fairly mild; double the garlic if you like a more assertive flavor.

87 Tortilla Soup

CHICKEN SOUP, ONLY EASIER AND BOLDER

Tortilla soup is a meal in bowl. This spicy chicken-and-tomato soup is overflowing with garnishes—fried tortilla strips, crumbled cheese, diced avocado, lime wedges, fresh cilantro, and *crema*. It's a celebration of colors, flavors, and textures.

Because there's so much going on, the cook can take some shortcuts. We'd never make chicken noodle soup with commercial broth. But with tomatoes, onion, garlic, and chiles in the soup base, you won't miss homemade stock. Poaching the chicken parts in packaged broth ups the flavor in the broth, while onion, garlic, and fresh herb sprigs impart depth.

One place you can't compromise is the tortilla strips—they are the "noodles" in this soup. Store-bought tortilla chips will ruin the dish. But there's no need to fry sliced corn tortillas, as custom dictates. An easy oven method eliminates the fuss and yields terrific results.

The big flavor in this soup comes from the pureed tomato base. As is typical in many Mexican recipes, the process begins by cooking a mixture of pureed vegetables (in this case, tomatoes, onion, garlic, jalapeño, and chipotle chile) in hot oil to drive off excess moisture and concentrate flavors. You can see the transformation as the puree changes color from bright red to rust. And you can smell it as the potent aroma fills your kitchen. At this point, the fortified broth is returned to the pot to simmer with the tomato base for 15 minutes, and then the cooked shredded chicken is heated through. That's it.

Ladle the soup over the tortilla strips and then add the garnishes to create a vibrant soup that's spicy, creamy, crunchy, and herbaceous. In other words—a bowl of pure comfort, Mexican style.

WHY THIS RECIPE WORKS

Bake, Don't Fry
Tortilla strips add flavor, texture, and heft to the soup. Try our easy crisping method (no frying required), which bakes the tortilla strips tossed in a little oil on a baking sheet. The tortilla strips are much less trouble to prepare than their fried cousins and less greasy, too.

Build the Base
A deeply flavored tomato and chile base is the soul of this soup. Traditionally, fresh tomatoes, garlic, onion, and charred chiles form this base. The vegetables are cooked on a *comal*, or griddle, then pureed and fried to create a concentrated paste. It is a time-consuming process, but there is a way to speed things up. We swap in chipotle chile packed in adobo sauce for the charred tomatoes and dried chiles—chipotles boast a similar smoky flavor. Puree the vegetables first, then cook the mixture until the moisture evaporates and the paste becomes a flavor powerhouse.

Fortify the Broth
Homemade stock isn't necessary for this soup. Poach the chicken (bone-in chicken breasts have more flavor than boneless) in the broth with onion, garlic, and cilantro. Don't forget to remove the skin from the chicken or the broth will turn out greasy. While the chicken and vegetables cook in the broth, they'll infuse it with rich flavor. And likewise, the chicken will soak up flavor from the broth. Once the chicken is poached, remove it from the broth to prevent it from drying out. Shred the chicken and rewarm it in the soup.

Garnish Matters
The beauty of this soup isn't just in the richly flavored broth and meaty shreds of chicken, but in what the garnishes bring to the bowl. Serve this soup as thoughtfully as a well-known comfort soup from another culture, Vietnamese pho: Set the tortilla strips in the bottom of the bowl, ladle the soup over the strips, and add garnishes as you like.

Onions, garlic, tomatoes, and chipotle are pureed and fried to create a robust soup base.

Tortilla Soup

SERVES 6 TO 8

If you desire a soup with mild spiciness, trim the ribs and seeds from the jalapeño (or omit the jalapeño altogether) and use 1 teaspoon chipotle chile pureed with tomatoes in step 3. If you want a spicier soup, add up to 1 tablespoon more adobo sauce in step 4 before you add the shredded chicken.

TORTILLA STRIPS

8 (6-inch) corn tortillas, cut into ½-inch-wide strips	1 tablespoon vegetable oil
	Salt

SOUP

2 (12-ounce) bone-in split chicken breasts or 4 (5-ounce) bone-in chicken thighs, skin removed and trimmed	8–10 sprigs fresh cilantro plus 1 sprig fresh oregano or 2 sprigs fresh epazote
8 cups chicken broth	Salt
1 large white onion, trimmed of root end, quartered, and peeled	2 tomatoes, cored and quartered
	½ jalapeño chile
4 garlic cloves, peeled	1 tablespoon minced canned chipotle chile in adobo sauce
	1 tablespoon vegetable oil

GARNISHES

1 avocado, halved, pitted, and diced fine	Fresh cilantro
8 ounces Cotija cheese, crumbled	Minced jalapeño chile
Lime wedges	Mexican crema

1. *For the Tortilla Strips:* Adjust oven rack to middle position; heat oven to 425 degrees. Spread tortilla strips on rimmed baking sheet; drizzle with oil and toss until evenly coated. Bake until strips are deep golden brown and crisped, about 14 minutes, rotating baking sheet and shaking strips (to redistribute) halfway through baking. Season strips lightly with salt and transfer to paper towel–lined plate.

2. *For the Soup:* While tortilla strips bake, bring chicken, broth, 2 onion quarters, 2 garlic cloves, cilantro and oregano, and ½ teaspoon salt to boil over medium-high heat in large saucepan. Reduce heat to low, cover, and simmer gently until chicken registers 160 degrees, about 20 minutes. Using tongs, transfer chicken to large plate. Pour broth through fine-mesh strainer and discard solids. When cool enough to handle, shred chicken into bite-size pieces, discarding bones.

3. Puree tomatoes, remaining 2 onion quarters, remaining 2 garlic cloves, jalapeño, and chipotle in food processor until smooth. Heat oil in Dutch oven over high heat until shimmering. Add tomato-onion puree and ⅛ teaspoon salt and cook, stirring frequently, until mixture has darkened in color, about 10 minutes.

4. Stir strained broth into tomato mixture, bring to boil, then reduce heat to low and simmer to blend flavors, about 15 minutes. Add shredded chicken and simmer until heated through, about 5 minutes. Place portions of tortilla strips in bowls and ladle soup over. Serve, passing garnishes separately.

RECIPE DETAILS

Timeline

• 25 minutes to make tortilla strips (start on other ingredient prep while waiting for oven to preheat and strips to bake)
• 30 minutes to make fortified broth and cook chicken (shred chicken once it cools)
• 5 minutes to puree tomatoes, onions, garlic, and chiles
• 10 minutes to cook tomato base
• 20 minutes to simmer soup (prepare garnishes)
• 5 minutes to heat chicken and serve soup

Essential Tools

• Rimmed baking sheet for baking tortilla strips
• Large saucepan with lid for making fortified broth and cooking chicken
• Fine-mesh strainer for straining broth
• Food processor for pureeing tomato base
• Dutch oven for cooking soup

Substitutions & Variations

• Cotija is a sharp cheese with a crumbly texture. You can substitute an equal amount of crumbled queso fresco or shredded Monterey Jack.
• Mexican *crema* is a cultured cream with a thick but pourable texture. Sour cream, thinned with a little milk if you like, can be used in its place.
• The soup can be prepared up to adding the shredded chicken at the end of step 4; let cool and refrigerate for up to four days. Return the soup to a simmer over medium-high heat before proceeding. The tortilla strips and garnishes are best prepared the day of serving.

88 Enchiladas

AMERICA'S BEST CASSEROLE COMES FROM MEXICO

Americans love a good casserole. Tuna noodle, turkey tetrazzini, shepherd's pie... the list goes on. The appeal is clear: You get a meal from a single dish that bakes unattended. But the truth is most casseroles are stodgy affairs that require a ton of prep work or shortcuts from a can. No thanks.

For us, the ideal casserole would require no more than an hour to get a baking dish into the oven and the results would be remarkable. While we don't usually think of enchiladas as a casserole, this dish does meet the definition. (Corn tortillas are the "starch" that holds the saucy filling.)

Enchiladas with red sauce start with dried chiles, making them a project. But enchiladas verdes rely on fresh chiles so the prep is easier. The tomatillos and poblanos must be broiled, but otherwise the sauce requires no cooking—it comes together in a food processor. Sure, the chicken must be poached, but this is mostly hands-off work and some poaching liquid ends up flavoring the green chile sauce. Along with the chicken, the filling is simple—just shredded pepper Jack cheese (with flavor already built in) and minced cilantro.

One thing you can't finesse is the assembly process. The tortillas must be oiled, warmed, filled, and then placed in a baking dish already coated with green sauce. More green sauce goes on top to keep the tortillas from drying out. Covering the baking dish with foil ensures that the tortillas soften and everything heats up quickly. As with many Mexican dishes, the garnishes are not optional. Sliced radishes provide crunch, sliced scallions add allium flavor, and sour cream cools things down. No one will ever call this casserole stodgy.

WHY THIS RECIPE WORKS

Go Green
Broad, dark green poblano chiles have a mild to moderate heat and a deep herbal flavor that make them an ideal choice for this sauce; fresh tomatillos offer an unmistakable tangy flavor.

Broil Away
Traditional recipes dry-roast whole tomatillos and poblanos on the stovetop using a cast-iron griddle-like vessel known as a *comal*; dry roasting imparts smokiness and concentrates flavor, all the while wicking away excess moisture that makes for a watery sauce. We broil the vegetables for similar results.

Poach the Chicken
We poach the chicken in chicken broth spiked with sautéed onion, garlic, and cumin. The chicken becomes infused with flavor and the broth absorbs meaty flavor and richness from the chicken. When it's cool, we shred the chicken for the filling.

Puree and Sweeten Lightly
For a sauce with a coarse, rustic texture, we pulse the tomatillos and poblanos in a food processor; a little of the doctored chicken broth thins the sauce. A dash of sugar tempers the tartness of the sauce without making it taste overtly sweet.

Cheese, Please
The gooey richness of some cheese in the filling balances the bright tang of the sauce and let's face it—cheese does make this dish very appealing. We shred pepper Jack and add just enough to the chicken for a mildly spicy kick and then sprinkle a little more over the top of the casserole.

Oil, Warm, Then Roll
Traditionally, corn tortillas are dipped in hot oil to make them pliable. We recommend a less messy method: Spray the tortillas with vegetable oil spray and gently bake them for a few minutes. They'll turn soft and warm and won't tear or split once you add the filling and roll them up.

We rethink this classic recipe with new ways to char the vegetables and soften the tortillas.

Enchiladas Verdes

SERVES 4 TO 6

Halve large tomatillos (more than 2 inches in diameter) and place them skin side up for broiling in step 2 to ensure even cooking and charring. To increase the spiciness of the sauce, reserve some of the chiles' ribs and seeds and add them to the food processor in step 4. Be sure to cool the chicken filling before filling the tortillas; a hot filling will make the enchiladas soggy.

4 teaspoons vegetable oil	3 poblano chiles, stemmed, halved, and
1 onion, chopped	seeded
½ teaspoon ground cumin	1–2½ teaspoons sugar
3 garlic cloves, minced	Salt and pepper
1½ cups chicken broth	½ cup chopped fresh cilantro
1 pound boneless, skinless chicken breasts, trimmed	8 ounces pepper Jack or Monterey Jack cheese, shredded (2 cups)
1½ pounds tomatillos (16 to 20 medium), husks and stems removed, rinsed well and dried	12 (6-inch) corn tortillas
	Vegetable oil spray

GARNISHES

2 scallions, sliced thin
Thinly sliced radishes
Sour cream

1. Adjust 1 oven rack to middle position and second rack 6 inches from broiler element; heat broiler. Heat 2 teaspoons oil in medium saucepan over medium heat until shimmering. Add onion and cook, stirring often, until softened and lightly browned, 5 to 7 minutes. Stir in cumin and two-thirds of garlic and cook, stirring often, until fragrant, about 30 seconds. Decrease heat to low and stir in broth. Add chicken, cover, and simmer until it registers 160 degrees, 15 to 20 minutes, flipping chicken halfway through cooking. Transfer chicken to large bowl; place in refrigerator to cool, about 20 minutes. Measure out ¼ cup broth and set aside; discard remaining liquid.

2. Meanwhile, toss tomatillos and poblanos with remaining 2 teaspoons oil. Arrange tomatillos cut side down and poblanos skin side up on aluminum foil–lined rimmed baking sheet. Broil on upper rack until vegetables blacken and start to soften, 5 to 10 minutes, rotating sheet halfway through broiling.

3. Remove tomatillos and poblanos from oven, let cool slightly, then remove skins from poblanos (leave tomatillo skins intact). Decrease oven temperature to 350 degrees. Discard foil from sheet and set sheet aside for warming tortillas.

4. Transfer vegetables, along with any accumulated juices, to food processor. Add 1 teaspoon sugar, 1 teaspoon salt, remaining garlic, and reserved cooking liquid to food processor and pulse until sauce is somewhat chunky, about 8 pulses. Season with salt and pepper to taste, and adjust tartness by stirring in remaining sugar, ½ teaspoon at a time; set aside.

5. When chicken is cool, use 2 forks to shred into bite-size pieces. Combine chicken with cilantro and 1½ cups pepper Jack; season with salt to taste.

RECIPE DETAILS

Timeline

• 30 minutes to poach chicken (when done, reserve ¼ cup broth and refrigerate chicken)
• 20 minutes to broil tomatillos and poblanos and make green sauce (start this while chicken is poaching)
• 10 minutes to shred chicken and combine with cheese and cilantro
• 15 minutes to warm tortillas and assemble enchiladas
• 15 to 20 minutes to bake enchiladas

Essential Tools

• Medium saucepan with lid for cooking chicken
• Tongs for handling chicken
• Rimmed baking sheet for broiling tomatillos and chiles and warming tortillas
• Food processor for making green sauce
• Box grater for shredding cheese
• 13 by 9-inch baking dish
• Aluminum foil for covering baking dish and lining baking sheet

Substitutions & Variations

• You can substitute three 11-ounce cans tomatillos, drained and rinsed, for the fresh ones in this recipe.
• If you can't find poblanos, substitute four large jalapeño chiles (with seeds and ribs removed).

6. Spread ¾ cup tomatillo sauce evenly over bottom of 13 by 9-inch baking dish. Place tortillas in single layer on 2 baking sheets. Spray both sides of tortillas lightly with vegetable oil spray. Bake until tortillas are soft and pliable, 2 to 4 minutes. Increase oven temperature to 450 degrees. Place warm tortillas on counter and spread ⅓ cup chicken filling down center of each tortilla. Roll each tortilla tightly and place in baking dish, seam side down. Pour remaining tomatillo sauce over top of enchiladas and spread into even layer so that it coats top of each tortilla. Sprinkle with remaining ½ cup pepper Jack and cover tightly with foil.

7. Bake enchiladas on lower rack until heated through and cheese is melted, 15 to 20 minutes. Uncover, sprinkle with scallions, and serve immediately, passing radishes and sour cream separately.

A Better Way to Prepare Fresh Chiles

Many cooks don't realize that most of the heat resides in the seeds and white ribs that line the inside of every fresh chile. We find it best to separate the flavorful flesh from these spicy components. Once you've done this you can mince the flesh by simply cutting the chile into thin strips and then turning the knife 90 degrees to cut across the strips to yield a fine mince. Don't throw out the seeds and ribs. They can be minced and reserved. Taste the dish just before serving and add some of the minced seeds and ribs if desired. Finally, it's a good idea to wear gloves when working with very hot chiles. If you don't have gloves, avoid touching your eyes, nose, or mouth with your fingertips and make sure to wash well as soon as chile prep is completed.

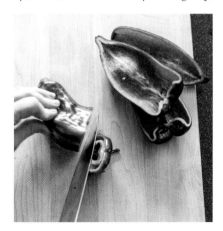

1. Using sharp knife, trim and discard stem end. Slice chile in half lengthwise.

2. Use small measuring spoon to scrape out seeds and white ribs along inside of chile. Reserve seeds and ribs if desired. Prepare seeded chile as directed in recipes.

89 Lo Mein

THEY REALLY DID INVENT NOODLES IN CHINA

The white boxes of greasy lo mein that show up at front doors every night in cities big and small don't do justice to the rich history of this recipe. One of the world's oldest (and greatest) dishes deserves a bit more respect. According to archaeologists, China is the birthplace of noodles. (Sorry, Italy.) The evidence is pretty convincing—an earthenware bowl found along the Yellow River that contained 4,000-year-old noodles.

Lo mein noodles (the "mein" part refers to the main ingredient, wheat) should have a chewy, almost firm texture so they can stand up to the sauce and bits of protein and vegetables. The most popular Chinese lo mein dish in the West contains bits of smoky barbecued pork (*char siu*) and still-crisp cabbage.

The noodles are the star ingredient and the curly fresh noodles labeled "lo mein" at many Asian markets are your best bet. Vacuum-packed fresh noodles from your typical supermarket (often labeled Chinese-style noodles) are pasty and gummy. If you can't find real Chinese lo mein, dried linguine (yes, the Italian stuff) is a better choice since it will provide chew similar to lo mein—a must for noodles that are so heavily sauced.

Of course, the sauce here is actually a stir-fry with meat and multiple vegetables in a lightly thickened soy-based liquid. This abundant approach to saucing works well with the American habit of serving pasta as a one-dish meal. Yes, to the cook used to preparing marinara and Bolognese, this method of sauce making will seem very novel. But that's the point.

WHY THIS RECIPE WORKS

Pin Down the Pork

For a facsimile of the slow-cooked pork shoulder used in restaurants for char siu, we swap in country-style pork ribs. These meaty ribs from the upper side of the rib cage have the same rich flavor of pork shoulder and they're naturally tender. Typical recipes use about one-quarter pound of pork. Bump it up to a full pound for a heartier stir-fry. (Do the same with the vegetables—it'll make for a fresher dish.)

Double-Duty Marinade

Marinate the thin strips of the pork in a classic Chinese mixture of hoisin sauce, oyster sauce, soy sauce, toasted sesame oil, and five-spice powder. If you like, add a few drops of liquid smoke to mimic the smoky flavor that's the hallmark of good char siu. Before adding the liquid smoke, reserve some marinade for the sauce—add chicken broth and a little cornstarch for body.

Stir-Fry in Batches

Use plenty of heat and cook the meat in small batches for best results. A cast-iron skillet will give you the best sear on the pork, but a nonstick skillet can also be used.

Cook the Noodles Last

Be sure to cook the noodles when the stir-fry is almost ready. If the noodles sit, they'll clump. And adding oil to them might prevent clumping, but this do-ahead trick will also prevent the sauce from clinging adequately to the noodles.

A Fresh Finish

There's no need to mess with tradition with the vegetables and seasoning in this stir-fry. For lots of flavor and texture, stir-fry shiitake mushrooms, scallions, and cabbage. Garlic and fresh ginger add assertive, aromatic flavor. Once the vegetables are done and tossed with the meat and noodles, spoon in a little Asian chili-garlic sauce for added kick.

Start the cooking by giving the pork a hard sear in a cast-iron pan; end by boiling the noodles.

Pork Lo Mein

SERVES 4

Use a cast-iron skillet for this recipe if you have one—it will help create the best sear on the pork. When shopping for Chinese rice wine, look for one that is amber in color. Liquid smoke provides a flavor reminiscent of traditional Chinese barbecued pork. It is important to cook the noodles at the last minute to avoid clumping.

3 tablespoons soy sauce

2 tablespoons oyster sauce

2 tablespoons hoisin sauce

1 tablespoon toasted sesame oil

¼ teaspoon five-spice powder

1 pound boneless country-style pork ribs, trimmed and sliced crosswise into ⅛-inch pieces

¼ teaspoon liquid smoke (optional)

½ cup chicken broth

1 teaspoon cornstarch

2 garlic cloves, minced

2 teaspoons grated fresh ginger

1½ tablespoons vegetable oil

¼ cup Chinese rice wine or dry sherry

8 ounces shiitake mushrooms, stemmed and halved if small or quartered if large

16 scallions, white parts sliced thin, green parts cut into 1-inch pieces

1 small head napa cabbage (1½ pounds), halved, cored, and sliced crosswise into ½-inch strips (4 cups)

12 ounces fresh Chinese egg noodles or 8 ounces dried linguine

1 tablespoon Asian chili-garlic sauce

1. Bring 4 quarts water to boil in Dutch oven over high heat.

2. Whisk soy sauce, oyster sauce, hoisin, sesame oil, and five-spice powder together in medium bowl. Place 3 tablespoons soy sauce mixture in 1-gallon zipper-lock bag; add pork and, if using, liquid smoke. Press out as much air as possible and seal bag, making sure that all pieces are coated with marinade. Refrigerate for at least 15 minutes or up to 1 hour. Whisk broth and cornstarch into remaining soy sauce mixture in medium bowl. In small bowl, mix garlic and ginger with ½ teaspoon vegetable oil; set aside.

3. Heat 1 teaspoon vegetable oil in 12-inch cast-iron or nonstick skillet over high heat until just smoking. Add half of pork in single layer, breaking up clumps with wooden spoon. Cook, without stirring, for 1 minute. Continue to cook, stirring occasionally, until browned, 2 to 3 minutes. Add 2 tablespoons wine to skillet; cook, stirring constantly, until liquid is reduced and pork is well coated, 30 to 60 seconds. Transfer pork to medium bowl and repeat with 1 teaspoon vegetable oil, remaining pork, and remaining 2 tablespoons wine. Wipe skillet clean with paper towels.

4. Return now-empty skillet to high heat, add 1 teaspoon vegetable oil, and heat until just smoking. Add mushrooms and cook, stirring occasionally, until light golden brown, 4 to 6 minutes. Add scallions and continue to cook, stirring occasionally, until scallions are wilted, 2 to 3 minutes longer; transfer vegetables to bowl with pork.

RECIPE DETAILS

Timeline

• 20 minutes to slice and marinate pork (pork can marinate for up to 1 hour; make sure to bring water to boil)

• 25 minutes to prepare aromatics and vegetables (do this while pork is marinating)

• 25 minutes to stir-fry pork and vegetables (boil pasta while cabbage is cooking)

• 2 minutes to drain noodles and toss with stir-fry mixture and chili-garlic sauce

Essential Tools

• Rasp grater for grating ginger

• 12-inch skillet, preferably cast iron (or nonstick if cast iron is not available)

• Tongs for stir-frying meat and vegetables and tossing noodles

• Dutch oven for boiling noodles

• Colander for draining noodles

Substitutions & Variations

• If no hoisin sauce is available, substitute 1 tablespoon of sugar.

• If boneless pork ribs are unavailable, substitute 1½ pounds of bone-in country-style ribs, followed by the next best option, pork tenderloin.

5. Add remaining 1 teaspoon vegetable oil and cabbage to now-empty skillet; cook, stirring occasionally, until spotty brown, 3 to 5 minutes. Clear center of skillet; add garlic mixture and cook, mashing mixture with spoon, until fragrant, about 30 seconds. Stir garlic mixture into cabbage; return pork-vegetable mixture and broth-soy mixture to skillet; simmer until thickened and ingredients are well incorporated, 1 to 2 minutes. Remove skillet from heat.

6. While cabbage is cooking, stir noodles into boiling water. Cook, stirring occasionally, until noodles are tender, 3 to 4 minutes for fresh Chinese noodles or 10 minutes for dried linguine. Drain noodles and transfer back to Dutch oven; add cooked stir-fry mixture and chili-garlic sauce, tossing noodles constantly, until sauce coats noodles. Serve immediately.

A Better Way to Prepare Ginger

Mincing doesn't work well with fibrous ginger, especially in sauces, dressings, glazes, and other dishes where smoothness is key. That's why we often use a grater—rather than a knife—when preparing ginger. Note that freezing the peeled ginger for 30 minutes firms it up, making it easier to grate.

1. Use rounded edge of small spoon, vegetable peeler, or small knife to remove skin from portion of gingerroot. (Leaving the skin on the remaining portion gives you a "handle" that keeps your fingers away from the grater in the next step.)

2. Holding unpeeled end, run ginger along fine teeth of rasp-style grater to yield smooth puree. (The fine holes on a box grater will also work nicely.)

90 Thai Beef Salad

FIVE THAI TASTES BUILD FLAVOR FAST

American salads can be awfully bland. Key ingredients (iceberg lettuce and out-of-season tomatoes) add bulk but not much flavor. That's the role of the dressing, which often seems designed to make all that roughage more palatable.

In Thailand, food is rarely bland and that certainly applies to the country's most famous salad made with grilled beef. Served warm or at room temperature, this preparation features slices of deeply charred steak tossed with thinly sliced shallots and handfuls of mint and cilantro leaves in a bright, bracing dressing. Every ingredient in this dish is bold—even brash—yet they work together. In the best versions, the cuisine's five signature flavor elements—hot, sour, salty, sweet, and bitter—come into balance, making for a light but satisfying dish.

So how do you build flavors in this Thai classic? A fresh Thai chile creates bright, fruity heat in the dressing, while a generous 3 tablespoons of fresh lime juice adds sharp acidity. Pungent fish sauce amps up the salty, umami notes. A half-teaspoon of sugar tames the salty-sour flavors without becoming cloying, or noticeable. And thoroughly charred steak supplies both a pleasing textural contrasts and a subtle bitter edge.

At the table, the dish is sprinkled with two condiments. Toasted rice powder adds sweet notes and mild crunch. Toasted chile powder provides earthy flavors but not much heat. Rather than toasting a single dried chile for this dish, we found that a mix of cayenne and sweet paprika (to tame the heat) did the job. Toasting the jarred spices in a dry pan for just 1 minute unlocks their flavor and makes an unusually flavorful table condiment for an unusually flavorful salad.

WHY THIS RECIPE WORKS

High-Steaks Decisions
You don't need to break the bank with this salad—flank steak boasts good beefy flavor and decent tenderness at a moderate price. Its uniform shape also makes it easier to grill evenly and slice neatly.

Old Grill, New Tricks
Start the meat over high heat to sear the crust. When beads of moisture appear on the surface of the meat, it's ready to flip to finish cooking. This Thai technique of gauging cook progress relates to the name of the dish, *nam tak*, which translates to "water falling." It sounds romantic, but there's actually a scientific explanation. As the steak's interior gets hotter, its tightly packed fibers contract and release moisture, which the fire's heat pushes to the meat's surface. When flipped at this point and cooked for an equal amount of time on the second side, the steak emerges deeply charred on the outside and medium-rare within.

Balancing Act
The dressing should have a good balance between hot, sour, salty, and sweet to provide a counterpoint to the subtle bitter char of the meat. Fish sauce, lime juice, and sugar will provide three of these elements. For the hot element, a fresh Thai chile fits the bill, but traditional recipes also use a powder made from dried Thai chile pods to give the heat a deep, earthy flavor. You can skip this latter step and add a little toasted cayenne and sweet paprika, which impart similar character.

Don't Skip the Toasted Rice
You might think a tablespoon of rice powder wouldn't make much difference in this salad and be tempted to omit it—don't. It adds extra body to the dressing and offers a pleasant toasty crunch when passed at the table. If you can't find a commercially made version, you can easily make your own. No excuses. Simply toast white rice in a dry skillet and grind to a fine meal in a spice grinder.

Toasted rice powder adds body and crunch to this salad that features perfectly grilled steak.

Grilled Thai Beef Salad

SERVES 4 TO 6

Don't skip the toasted rice; it's integral to the texture and flavor of the dish. Any variety of white rice can be used. Toasted rice powder (kao kua) can also be found in many Asian markets; substitute 1 tablespoon rice powder for the white rice. Serve with rice, if desired.

1 teaspoon paprika	Salt and coarsely ground white pepper
1 teaspoon cayenne pepper	1 seedless English cucumber, sliced
1 tablespoon white rice	¼ inch thick on bias
3 tablespoons lime juice (2 limes)	4 shallots, sliced thin
2 tablespoons fish sauce	1½ cups fresh mint leaves, torn
2 tablespoons water	1½ cups fresh cilantro leaves
½ teaspoon sugar	1 Thai chile, stemmed, seeded,
1 (1½-pound) flank steak, trimmed	and sliced thin into rounds

1. Heat paprika and cayenne in 8-inch skillet over medium heat; cook, shaking pan, until fragrant, about 1 minute. Transfer to small bowl. Return skillet to medium-high heat, add rice and toast, stirring constantly, until deep golden brown, about 5 minutes. Transfer to small bowl and let cool for 5 minutes. Grind rice with spice grinder, mini food processor, or mortar and pestle until it resembles fine meal, 10 to 30 seconds (you should have about 1 tablespoon rice powder).

2. Whisk lime juice, fish sauce, water, sugar, and ¼ teaspoon toasted paprika mixture in large bowl and set aside.

3A. *For a Charcoal Grill:* Open bottom vent completely. Light large chimney starter filled with charcoal briquettes (6 quarts). When top coals are partially covered with ash, pour in even layer over half of grill. Set cooking grate in place, cover, and open lid vent completely. Heat grill until hot, about 5 minutes.

3B. *For a Gas Grill:* Turn all burners to high, cover, and heat grill until hot, about 15 minutes. Leave primary burner on high and turn off other burner(s).

4. Clean and oil cooking grate. Season steak with salt and pepper. Place steak on hotter side of grill and cook until beginning to char and beads of moisture appear on outer edges of meat, 5 to 6 minutes. Flip steak and continue to cook on second side until meat registers 125 degrees, about 5 minutes longer. Transfer to carving board, tent loosely with aluminum foil, and let rest for 10 minutes (or let cool to room temperature, about 1 hour).

5. Line large platter with cucumber slices. Slice steak ¼ inch thick against grain on bias. Transfer sliced steak to bowl with fish sauce mixture; add shallots, mint, cilantro, Thai chile, and half of rice powder; and toss to combine. Arrange steak over cucumber-lined platter. Serve, passing remaining rice powder and toasted paprika mixture separately.

RECIPE DETAILS

Timeline

- 12 minutes to toast spices and make toasted rice powder (light grill while waiting for rice to cool)
- 15 minutes to make dressing and prepare other ingredients
- 10 minutes to grill steak
- 10 minutes to rest steak
- 5 minutes to slice and dress steak and assemble salad

Essential Tools

- 8-inch skillet for toasting spices and rice
- Spice grinder for grinding toasted rice (A mini food processor or mortar and pestle can be used instead.)
- Slicing knife for carving grilled steak (A chef's knife will also work but a slicing knife will make it easier to get thin slices.)

Substitutions & Variations

- If a fresh Thai chile is unavailable, substitute ½ serrano chile.
- We like the cool crispness of the sliced cucumbers along with the beef salad but shredded cabbage, watercress, and salad greens are also traditional.

91 Pho

THE SOUP THAT BREAKS ALL THE RULES

Most soups follow the same pattern: Start by sautéing aromatic vegetables to build a flavor base. Next, simmer the broth and the main ingredients. Season with fresh herbs, citrus juice, or olive oil and then ladle the finished soup into bowls. Pho, Vietnam's famed beef and noodle soup, doesn't read like other recipes.

The biggest selling point of this soup is its killer broth—a beefy, fragrant, faintly sweet concoction produced by simmering beef bones and water, along with ginger, onions, cinnamon, and star anise, for hours. Notably, those bones are often the only form of meat added to the "soup." Actual pieces of beef aren't introduced until serving time, when the broth is strained and ladled directly into large soup bowls filled with very thin slices of raw steak (typically sirloin) and cooked rice noodles. Onion slices, herbs, and scallions are often waiting in the bowls, too; the only "cooking" they receive happens on the way to the table. Condiments such as salty-sweet hoisin sauce, chili sauce, fish sauce, and lime wedges allow for individual flavor tinkering so no two bowls of pho are alike.

Getting the broth right is the key to this recipe. Homemade bone broth is an all-day affair. To turn store-bought beef broth into something worthy of this recipe, you need think outside the box. It turns out that ground meat releases its flavor into liquid remarkably fast. The grinding process breaks up muscle fibers so a single pound of ground beef can transform 3 quarts of packaged broth in just 45 minutes. Ladle this cheater broth over tender noodles and steak shaved ever so thin and you have made perfect bowls of pho.

WHY THIS RECIPE WORKS

Blanch and Then Simmer Beef
A brief (2-minute) blanch thoroughly agitates the ground beef so that its proteins and fat slough off but the meat doesn't cook long enough to wash away much flavor. The quick rinse rids the surface of any stubborn clingy bits. In short, blanching and rinsing the meat yields a clearer, cleaner-tasting broth.

More Than Meaty
Once the ground beef is blanched, it's ready for a 45-minute simmer in a mix of store-bought broth and water, where it will release its beefy flavor. This also is the opportunity to build out the fragrant dimension of the broth with onion, fresh ginger, and fish sauce, and warm spices such as cinnamon, star anise, and clove.

Strain Twice for Clarity
Start by pouring the broth through a colander to discard the solids like the quartered onions and pieces of ground meat. Then strain the broth again through a cheesecloth-lined fine-mesh strainer to get rid of the smaller bits.

The Skinny on the Beef
To cut thin slices against the grain, freeze the meat until it's very firm (chilling also helps prevent the meat from overcooking in the hot broth). Then, stand the meat on its cut end and using the sharpest, thinnest blade you have, slice the meat.

Soak and Then Boil the Noodles
Simply soak strands of thin dried rice noodles in warm water and then briefly boil them. Soaking helps the noodles shed excess starch and makes them soften evenly and quickly in the boiling water.

A Balanced Finish
We've pared down the usual list of tableside garnishes and condiments to the essentials: bean sprouts for crunch, basil, lime wedges, hoisin and chile sauces, and additional fish sauce to balance the broth with heat, acidity, and freshness.

You can almost see the bold flavors in this pot of dark broth and bowl of brightly colored soup.

Vietnamese Beef Pho

SERVES 4 TO 6

One 14- or 16-ounce package of rice noodles will serve four to six. Look for noodles that are about ⅛ inch wide; these are often labeled "small." Don't use Thai Kitchen Stir-Fry Rice Noodles since they are too thick and don't adequately soak up the broth.

1	pound 85 percent lean ground beef		Salt
2	onions, quartered through root end	1	teaspoon black peppercorns
12	cups beef broth	1	(1-pound) boneless strip steak,
¼	cup fish sauce, plus extra for		trimmed and halved
	seasoning	14–16	ounces (⅛-inch-wide) rice noodles
1	(4-inch) piece ginger, sliced into	⅓	cup chopped fresh cilantro
	thin rounds	3	scallions, sliced thin (optional)
1	cinnamon stick		Bean sprouts
2	tablespoons sugar, plus extra for		Sprigs fresh Thai or Italian basil
	seasoning		Lime wedges
6	star anise pods		Hoisin sauce
6	whole cloves		Sriracha sauce

1. Break ground beef into rough 1-inch chunks and drop in Dutch oven. Add water to cover by 1 inch. Bring mixture to boil over high heat. Boil for 2 minutes, stirring once or twice. Drain ground beef in colander and rinse well under running water. Wash out pot and return ground beef to pot.

2. Place 6 onion quarters in pot with ground beef. Slice remaining 2 onion quarters as thin as possible and set aside for garnish. Add broth, 2 cups water, fish sauce, ginger, cinnamon, sugar, star anise, cloves, 2 teaspoons salt, and peppercorns to pot and bring to boil over high heat. Reduce heat to medium-low and simmer, partially covered, for 45 minutes.

3. Pour broth through colander set in large bowl. Discard solids. Strain broth through fine-mesh strainer lined with triple thickness of cheesecloth; add water as needed to equal 11 cups. Return broth to pot and season with extra sugar and salt (broth should taste overseasoned). Cover and keep warm over low heat.

4. While broth simmers, place steak on large plate and freeze until very firm, 35 to 45 minutes. Once firm, cut against grain into ⅛-inch-thick slices. Return steak to plate and refrigerate until needed.

5. Place noodles in large container and cover with hot tap water. Soak until noodles are pliable, 10 to 15 minutes; drain noodles. Meanwhile, bring 4 quarts water to boil in large pot. Add drained noodles and cook until almost tender, 30 to 60 seconds. Drain immediately and divide noodles among individual bowls.

6. Bring broth to rolling boil over high heat. Divide steak among individual bowls, shingling slices on top of noodles. Pile reserved onion slices on top of steak slices and sprinkle with cilantro and scallions, if using. Ladle hot broth into each bowl. Serve immediately, passing bean sprouts, basil sprigs, lime wedges, hoisin, Sriracha, and extra fish sauce separately.

RECIPE DETAILS

Timeline

- 10 minutes to blanch and rinse ground beef
- 1 hour to make fortified beef broth (freeze and slice steak while broth simmers)
- 15 minutes to soak and cook rice noodles
- 5 minutes to reheat broth and assemble soup in bowls

Essential Tools

- Dutch oven (at least 6 quarts) with lid
- Colander for rinsing beef, straining broth, and draining noodles
- Fine-mesh strainer for clarifying broth
- Cheesecloth for clarifying broth
- Second Dutch oven or pot for cooking noodles

Substitutions & Variations

- An equal weight of tri-tip steak or blade steak can be substituted for the strip steak; make sure to trim all connective tissue and excess fat.

92 Spanish Beef Stew

HOW TO BUILD FLAVOR WITHOUT THE HASSLE OF BROWNING THE MEAT

Few cuisines can rival the complexity of Spanish food, with its influences from ancient Greece and Rome, North Africa, and even the Americas. The multilayering of flavors and textures is particularly apparent in meat stews from the country's easternmost region of Catalonia. Almost all begin with a slow-cooked jam of onions and tomatoes known as *sofrito* and end with a dollop of *picada*, a pesto-like paste of fried bread, herbs, and ground nuts that gives the stew body and dimension. Warm spices such as cinnamon and smoked paprika add another level of depth.

With so much going on, you can skip the stew-making step most cooks dread— the browning of the meat, which takes half an hour of constant attention and leaves your stovetop a mess. Short ribs work best in this recipe because of their beefy flavor. And boneless short ribs have far less fat than the bone-in option so you don't have to worry about degreasing the stew. But just because we skip the stovetop sear doesn't mean we don't want browning.

We have discovered that browning of the meat can occur during the long stewing process if you follow these steps: First, move the operation to the oven and keep the lid off. Second, don't flood the pot with too much liquid. If the meat is poking above the liquid, it will brown during the 3-hour stewing time. Speaking of liquid, there's so much flavor in short ribs that we don't bother with beef broth. A modest amount of water and white wine (a better complement to the flavors in this stew than red wine) is sufficient. If you think beef stew requires a lot of work, you've been making the wrong recipe.

WHY THIS RECIPE WORKS

Streamline the Sofrito
A good sofrito, the flavor base for this stew, takes time, but there are some shortcuts. We add a sprinkle of salt and sugar to the onions to draw out moisture, which in turn, hastens and deepens caramelization. A can of tomatoes might seem like an obvious shortcut, but it's a bad one. Go for the brightness and acidity of fresh tomatoes. Skip the tedious step of blanching and peeling the tomatoes and grate the pulpy flesh with a box grater to rid them of their leathery skins. Perk up the flavor of the sofrito further with a bay leaf and the powerful character of smoked paprika.

Swap Out the Sherry
Sherry is a traditional addition to Spanish beef stew but it can become cloying. Red wine, a common pairing with beef, is too dominating here. Instead, reach for a dry white, such as a Spanish Albariño; thyme and cinnamon are also welcome additions.

Enrich with Mushrooms
We dispense with chunks of starchy vegetables like potatoes and carrots in favor of oyster mushrooms, a Catalan ingredient. Resist the urge to cook the mushrooms in the stew, which will only spoil their delicate flavor and texture. Sauté the mushrooms separately, and stir them into the stew just before serving.

Brighten It Up
For the stew's final flourish, the picada, pull out a food processor and whiz together fried blanched almonds, toasted bread crumbs, and raw garlic (better than sautéed as it gives the picada an appealing pungency). Adding the traditional parsley to the food processor ruins its grassy flavor, so chop it by hand before combining it with the rest of the ingredients. Splash in a little sherry vinegar at the end for an extra-bright finish that complements the warm spices of the stew.

Boneless short ribs are incredibly beefy and require no browning because of the sautéed sofrito.

Catalan-Style Beef Stew with Mushrooms

SERVES 4 TO 6

Remove the woody base of the oyster mushroom stems before cooking. Serve the stew with boiled or mashed potatoes or rice.

STEW

- 2 tablespoons olive oil
- 2 large onions, chopped fine
- ½ teaspoon sugar
- Kosher salt and pepper
- 2 plum tomatoes, halved lengthwise, pulp grated on large holes of box grater, and skins discarded
- 1 teaspoon smoked paprika
- 1 bay leaf
- 1½ cups dry white wine
- 1½ cups water
- 1 large sprig fresh thyme
- ¼ teaspoon ground cinnamon
- 2½ pounds boneless beef short ribs, trimmed and cut into 2-inch cubes

PICADA

- ¼ cup whole blanched almonds
- 2 tablespoons olive oil
- 1 slice hearty white sandwich bread, crust removed, torn into 1-inch pieces
- 2 garlic cloves, peeled
- 3 tablespoons minced fresh parsley

- 8 ounces oyster mushrooms, trimmed
- 1 teaspoon sherry vinegar

1. *For the Stew:* Adjust oven rack to middle position and heat oven to 300 degrees. Heat oil in Dutch oven over medium-low heat until shimmering. Add onions, sugar, and ½ teaspoon salt; cook, stirring often, until onions are deeply caramelized, 30 to 40 minutes. Add tomato pulp, paprika, and bay leaf; cook, stirring often, until darkened and thick, 5 to 10 minutes.

2. Add wine, water, thyme sprig, and cinnamon to pot, scraping up any browned bits. Season short ribs with 1½ teaspoons salt and ½ teaspoon pepper and add to pot. Increase heat to high and bring to simmer. Transfer to oven and cook, uncovered. After 1 hour stir stew to redistribute meat, return to oven, and continue to cook until meat is tender, 1½ to 2 hours longer.

3. *For the Picada:* While stew is in oven, heat almonds and 1 tablespoon oil in 10-inch skillet over medium heat; cook, stirring often, until almonds are golden brown, 3 to 6 minutes. Using slotted spoon, transfer almonds to food processor. Return now-empty skillet to medium heat, add bread, and cook, stirring often, until toasted, 2 to 4 minutes; transfer to food processor with almonds. Add garlic to almonds and bread and process until mixture is finely ground, about 20 seconds, scraping down bowl as needed. Transfer mixture to separate bowl, stir in parsley, and set aside.

4. Return now-empty skillet to medium heat. Heat remaining 1 tablespoon oil until shimmering. Add mushrooms and ½ teaspoon salt; cook, stirring often, until tender, 5 to 7 minutes. Transfer to bowl and set aside.

5. Discard bay leaf. Stir picada, mushrooms, and vinegar into stew. Season with salt and pepper to taste, and serve.

RECIPE DETAILS

Timeline

- 50 minutes to prepare onion-tomato base (mostly hands-off)
- 2½ hours to 3 hours to simmer beef in oven (make picada and prepare mushroom garnish while stew simmers)
- 5 minutes to finish and season stew

Essential Tools

- Dutch oven
- 10-inch skillet for frying almonds and bread and sautéing mushrooms
- Food processor for grinding picada ingredients

Substitutions & Variations

- An equal amount of quartered white mushrooms may be substituted for the oyster mushrooms.
- To make the stew ahead, follow the recipe through step 2 and refrigerate for up to three days. To serve, add 1 cup water and reheat over medium heat. Proceed with step 3.

93 Argentinian Steaks

GREAT GRILLED STEAK STARTS IN THE FREEZER

In Argentina, where cattle farming is a major industry and per capita beef consumption is the highest in the world (roughly 150 pounds annually—twice the U.S. consumption), grilling steaks over burning embers is not just a means of getting dinner on the table, but a nationwide ritual. This obsession has a name: *churrasco*, which refers both to the technique and to the huge slabs of meat cooked this way.

There are two immediate challenges to making this dish in your backyard. In Argentina, the steaks are huge—literally weighing in at 2 pounds each—which means they have plenty of time to pick up smoke flavor. And then there's the fire. The traditional method calls for slowly grilling steaks over hardwood logs, which imbues them with smoke flavor.

To adapt this recipe for 1-pound steaks (the biggest size regularly available in our markets) and an American grill, you must employ some unusual strategies. Freezing the steaks is the key to developing the mahogany-hued crust that is the hallmark of this dish. Supercold steaks can spend more time on the grill without overcooking. But it's the dehydrating effect of the freezer, along with an unusual rub, that creates a superb crust.

Finally, in Argentina, steak is served with bracing *chimichurri*—a mix of herbs, garlic, red wine vinegar, and olive oil that balances the richness of the beef. We found that hot water not only blooms the flavor of dried oregano (a standard addition to this sauce) but also tames the acidity so you can really taste the other ingredients.

WHY THIS RECIPE WORKS

Make a Really Dry Rub
Great churrasco boasts a charred crust. To drive off exterior moisture so that that deep crust can form, rub the steaks with cornstarch and salt. The salt also helps to season the meat. The starches in the cornstarch also enhance browning by adding more "fuel" for the Maillard reaction—when the meat browns, hundreds of new flavor compounds develop.

Use the Freezer as Dehydrator
The freezer is a harsh environment for meat. Even when well wrapped, steaks can lose moisture and become covered with freezer burn. But you can use this effect to your advantage. Freeze the rubbed steaks for a half-hour and they'll emerge firmer and drier thanks to the evaporation of surface moisture. The chilled meat will also be less prone to overcooking.

Get Smoking
You need to use a lot of wood to produce sufficient smoke to flavor the steaks during the quick cooking time. Oak is the traditional choice for this recipe, but any wood will do. Place the lid on the grill for the first few minutes of cooking time to trap the smoke and help jump-start the flavoring process. A charcoal grill does a much better job of producing smoke, although you can use a gas grill by placing the packets with the wood chips directly on the cooking grate.

Create a Big But Balanced Sauce
Steaks in Argentina are traditionally served with a tart herb-based sauce called chimichurri. The sharp, grassy flavors of the sauce are the perfect complement to the fatty, smoky beef. It's easy to make, especially if you have a food processor. Pulse the parsley, cilantro, oregano mixture, garlic, red wine vinegar, and red pepper flakes and emulsify with a fruity extra-virgin olive oil. Rest the sauce for an hour to allow the big flavors to mellow slightly and pass it at the table with the sliced steak.

For the ultimate steak experience, rub, freeze, grill, rest, slice, and then sauce.

Grilled Argentine Steaks with Chimichurri Sauce

SERVES 6 TO 8

Flipping the steaks three times as they cook ensures even cooking and limits flare-ups.

SAUCE

¼ cup hot water

2 teaspoons dried oregano

1 teaspoon salt

1⅓ cups fresh parsley leaves

⅔ cup fresh cilantro leaves

6 garlic cloves, minced

½ teaspoon red pepper flakes

¼ cup red wine vinegar

½ cup extra-virgin olive oil

STEAKS

1 tablespoon cornstarch

Salt and pepper

4 (1-pound) boneless strip steaks, 1½ inches thick, trimmed

4 cups wood chips

1. *For the Sauce:* Combine hot water, oregano, and salt in small bowl and let sit until oregano is softened, about 15 minutes. Pulse parsley, cilantro, garlic, and pepper flakes in food processor until coarsely chopped, about 10 pulses. Add water mixture and vinegar and pulse to combine. Transfer mixture to bowl and slowly whisk in oil until emulsified. Cover with plastic wrap and let sit at room temperature for 1 hour.

2. *For the Steaks:* Combine cornstarch and 1½ teaspoons salt in bowl. Pat steaks dry with paper towels and place on wire rack set in rimmed baking sheet. Rub entire surface of steaks with cornstarch mixture and place steaks, uncovered, in freezer until very firm, about 30 minutes.

3. Just before grilling, soak wood chips in water for 15 minutes, then drain. Using 2 large pieces of heavy-duty aluminum foil, wrap soaked chips in 2 foil packets and cut several vent holes in top.

4A. *For a Charcoal Grill:* Open bottom vent halfway. Light large chimney starter filled with charcoal briquettes (6 quarts). When top coals are partially covered with ash, pour evenly over grill. Place wood chip packets on coals. Set cooking grate in place, cover, and open lid vent halfway. Heat grill until hot and wood chips are smoking, about 5 minutes.

4B. *For a Gas Grill:* Place wood chip packets on cooking grate. Turn all burners to high, cover, and heat grill until hot, about 15 minutes. Leave all burners on high.

5. Clean and oil cooking grate. Season steaks with pepper. Place steaks on grill, cover, and cook until beginning to brown on both sides, 4 to 6 minutes, flipping halfway through cooking.

6. Flip steaks again and cook, uncovered, until well browned on first side, 2 to 4 minutes. Flip steaks once more and continue to cook until meat registers 115 degrees (for rare) or 120 degrees (for medium-rare), 2 to 6 minutes longer.

7. Transfer steaks to carving board, tent loosely with aluminum foil, and let rest for 10 minutes. Cut each steak crosswise into ¼-inch-thick slices. Transfer to serving platter and serve, passing sauce separately.

RECIPE DETAILS

Timeline

• 10 minutes to make chimichurri sauce (let stand for at least 1 hour to blend flavors)
• 35 minutes to rub steaks and freeze (soak and wrap chips and light grill while steaks are in freezer)
• 8 to 12 minutes to grill steaks with lid on (to trap smoke)
• 4 to 10 minutes to finish grilling steaks with lid off
• 15 minutes to rest and slice steaks

Essential Tools

• Food processor for making herb sauce
• Wire rack set in rimmed baking sheet for freezing steaks
• Wood chips (We like oak or hickory best.)
• Heavy-duty aluminum foil for protecting soaked wood chips
• Tongs for flipping steaks

Substitutions & Variations

• Strip steaks offer the best balance of beefy flavor and pleasantly chewy texture. If you'd rather try a less expensive cut, boneless shell sirloin (also called New York sirloin steak) is a good option.
• Chimichurri sauce (which can be prepared three days in advance and kept in the refrigerator) is the classic accompaniment here. If you prefer, you can omit the cilantro and just use more parsley.

94 Schnitzel

A GOOD BREADING MAKES ANY CUTLET MEMORABLE

Wiener schnitzel (considered the national dish of Austria) features thin, tender veal cutlets coated in ultrafine bread crumbs and then fried until puffy and golden brown. What separates schnitzel from ordinary breaded cutlets is the coating's rumpled appearance. When properly cooked, the thin coating will puff up, leaving enough space to slide a knife between the meat and the crisp exterior. This wrinkled coating gives schnitzel an air of refinement and makes the pan-fried meat seem lighter than it really is.

Given the price of veal, many restaurants have switched to pork cutlets. Though the meat is cheaper, it's no easier to get the breading right. At worst, the coating is soggy and greasy. Even if you avoid this pitfall, the breading invariably fuses with the meat and you lose the light quality the puffed coating should provide.

Don't bother with packaged pork cutlets—they are sinewy and fatty. It takes 5 minutes to turn a tenderloin into cutlets. And this cut of pork is very tender and very mild—just like veal. As for the breading, the secret is to dry fresh sandwich bread quickly in a microwave (that's right, a microwave) so that it can be ground into a fine powder.

There's no mystery to applying the crumbs—the usual process of dusting the cutlets with flour and then dipping them in an egg wash works best. However, adding a little oil to the wash is essential. The oil keeps the breading from fusing to the meat so it can puff when the pot is shaken (and produce that wrinkled coating) during cooking. Yes, it turns out that some wrist action produces the wrinkled coating that defines this Old World classic.

WHY THIS RECIPE WORKS

Choice Cuts

Most pork schnitzel recipes call for boneless pork chops, pounded thin. However pork chops have very compact muscle fibers, which means that pounding thin cutlets is a chore. It also means that once cooked, the pork has a dry, mealy texture. Use pork tenderloin instead. Pounded thin and fried, cutlets from the tenderloin are remarkably tender with a mild flavor similar to veal.

Slice on the Bias

The only aspect of the tenderloin that isn't ideal is its long, cylindrical shape, but that's easily fixed. Cut the tenderloin in half at a 20-degree angle. Using the same angle, cut each half in half again, cutting the tapered tail pieces slightly thicker than the middle medallions. The pieces are now ready to pound into thin cutlets.

Precook the Crumbs

Using raw homemade bread crumbs can result in a pork cutlet that is overcooked before the crumbs are crisp. Additionally, the crust will have an overly coarse texture. We have an easy fix: Crisp the crumbs before you coat the cutlets. To do so, simply microwave cubes of bread on high power, then medium, and transfer to a food processor and grind. You'll be rewarded with superfine, dry bread crumbs that will fry up extra-crisp.

Up the Oil and Use Arm Power

Most recipes for pan-frying typically call for ½ to 1 cup of oil. You will need 2 cups for this recipe, so put away your skillet and grab a Dutch oven. Shake the pan as the cutlets cook in the hot oil. The shaking sends the hot oil over the top of the cutlets, speeding up the setting process and enhancing the puff for perfect pork schnitzel. As the egg in the coating solidifies, it forms a barrier, which traps moisture on the surface of the pork, creating that puffed crust. You'll know you're on the right track when the crust resembles a rumpled shar-pei.

An unusual frying method creates a puffy, well-browned exterior on these oversized cutlets.

Pork Schnitzel

SERVES 4

The 2 cups of oil called for in this recipe may seem like a lot, but this amount is necessary to achieve a wrinkled texture on the finished cutlets. When properly cooked, the cutlets absorb very little oil. Cutting the pork tenderloin at about a 20-degree angle will yield pounded cutlets that fit easily into the pan.

7 slices hearty white sandwich bread, crusts removed, bread cut into ¾-inch cubes	1 tablespoon plus 2 cups vegetable oil
½ cup all-purpose flour	1 (1¼-pound) pork tenderloin, trimmed and cut on angle into 4 equal pieces
2 large eggs, plus 1 large hard-cooked egg, yolk and white separated and passed separately through fine-mesh strainer (optional)	Salt and pepper
	Lemon wedges
	2 tablespoons chopped fresh parsley
	2 tablespoons capers, rinsed

1. Place bread cubes on large plate. Microwave on high power for 4 minutes, stirring well halfway through microwaving. Microwave on medium power until bread is dry and few pieces start to lightly brown, 3 to 5 minutes, stirring every minute. Process dry bread in food processor to very fine crumbs, about 45 seconds. Transfer bread crumbs to shallow dish (you should have about 1¼ cups crumbs). Spread flour in second shallow dish. Beat eggs with 1 tablespoon oil in third shallow dish.

2. Set wire rack in rimmed baking sheet and line plate with triple layer of paper towels. Working with 1 piece at a time, place pork, with 1 cut side down, between 2 sheets of parchment paper or plastic wrap and pound to even thickness between ⅛ and ¼ inch. Pat cutlets dry with paper towels and season with salt and pepper. Working with 1 cutlet at a time, dredge cutlets thoroughly in flour, shaking off excess; coat with egg mixture, allowing excess to drip back into dish to ensure very thin coating; and coat evenly with bread crumbs, pressing on crumbs to adhere. Place breaded cutlets in single layer on prepared wire rack; let coating dry for 5 minutes.

3. Heat remaining 2 cups oil in large Dutch oven over medium-high heat to 375 degrees. Lay 2 cutlets, without overlapping, in pot and cook, shaking pot continuously and gently, until cutlets are wrinkled and light golden brown on both sides, 1 to 2 minutes per side. Transfer cutlets to paper towel–lined plate and flip cutlets several times to blot excess oil. Repeat with remaining cutlets. Serve with lemon wedges, parsley, capers, and, if desired, hard-cooked egg.

RECIPE DETAILS

Timeline

- 20 minutes to prepare hard-cooked egg (prepare other garnishes at same time)
- 10 minutes to prepare bread crumbs
- 15 minutes to cut, pound, and bread cutlets
- 5 minutes to let breaded cutlets rest before frying (heat oil while waiting)
- 5 to 10 minutes to fry cutlets in two batches

Essential Tools

- Microwave for drying bread
- Food processor for grinding bread into crumbs
- Tongs for handling cutlets during breading process
- Wire rack set in rimmed baking sheet for holding breaded cutlets
- Dutch oven (at least 6 quarts) for frying schnitzel
- Instant-read thermometer for gauging temperature of oil (A clip-on candy/deep-fry thermometer can also be used.)
- Paper towels for draining fried cutlets

Substitutions & Variations

- In lieu of a thermometer to gauge the oil's temperature, place a fresh (not dry) bread cube in the oil and start heating; when the bread is deep golden brown, the oil is ready.
- This recipe calls for one large (1¼-pound) tenderloin to yield four cutlets. Pork tenderloins vary considerably in size, with some weighing in at just ¾ pound. If that's the case, cut just three cutlets per tenderloin. The key is to make sure the cutlets—no matter the starting point—are between ⅛ and ¼ inch when pounded.

FOOLPROOF HARD-COOKED EGGS MAKES 6 EGGS

You may double or even triple this recipe as long as you use a pot large enough to hold the eggs in a single layer, covered by an inch of water, while they cook. You can also cook fewer eggs if you like—the timing remains the same.

6 large eggs

Place eggs in medium saucepan, cover with 1 inch of water, and bring to boil over high heat. Remove pan from heat, cover, and let sit for 10 minutes. Meanwhile, fill medium bowl with 1 quart water and 1 tray of ice cubes (or equivalent). Transfer eggs to ice water bath with slotted spoon; let sit for 5 minutes. Peel and use as desired. (Hard-cooked eggs can be refrigerated for up to 1 week.)

A Better Way to Peel Hard-Cooked Eggs

Because our method for hard-cooking eggs relies on residual heat to gently cook the eggs there's no risk of overcooking. Just set the timer when the water comes to a boil and move the pot off the heat and you can banish all worries about greenish yolks. However, even if the eggs are perfectly cooked, you still need a method for peeling them. Here's how to accomplish this task easily. Note that the ice bath is crucial to the success of this method. Not only does the ice water stop the cooking process (and thus prevent overcooking), but the water seeps under the cracked shells and helps to loosen them.

1. When timer goes off, immediately pour water from saucepan and gently shake back and forth to crack egg shells. Use slotted spoon to transfer eggs to ice bath and let sit for 5 minutes.

2. Remove eggs from ice bath. Starting at wider end of each egg, peel away shell in one strip. (The wider end has an air pocket, which makes it the best place to tear the shell without cutting into the white.) When done, dunk peeled egg back into ice bath to remove any stray bits of shell (if necessary).

95 Tinga

SPICY, PORKY, CRUNCHY, AND FRESH—ALL IN ONE BITE

True Mexican shredded pork—or *tinga*—is a far cry from the bland burrito-joint version often found languishing in steam tables in this country. As with good barbecued pulled pork, tinga's moist, tender shreds possess an intense, almost sweet, meatiness. To make this dish, pork is typically braised until tender and then sautéed until it acquires deeply browned edges that stay crisp even after a quick simmer in a chipotle-infused tomato sauce.

To play off its supple texture, tinga is served on crunchy tostada shells (toasted or deep-fried corn tortillas) and then garnished with avocado, sour cream, *queso fresco*, cilantro, and lime wedges. Every bite of this messy dish (use a fork and knife, please!) includes a mix of complementary flavors and textures. This is Mexican cooking at its best.

As might be expected, this recipe starts with the same cut used for barbecued pulled pork—the shoulder. The cooking takes place in two phases. The meat is traditionally simmered in salted water until tender, drained, and then shredded. This requires several hours but little attention from the cook. For the next phase, the shredded pork is sautéed with onion and then simmered in tomato sauce. The key here is to really brown the meat and finely chopped onion, both of which should be almost crisp by the time you add the liquid ingredients—the reserved simmering liquid (rich with porky flavor) and canned tomato sauce.

At this point, everything comes together in a mad rush. As the tinga simmers, you're frying corn tortillas (or using our easier oven method), so make sure all those garnishes are ready for the table.

WHY THIS RECIPE WORKS

Cube and Simmer
Boneless pork butt is well marbled and suited to tinga's cooking method. Cut it into 1-inch pieces and simmer it in water with onion, garlic, and thyme for a subtle vegetal flavor.

Shred and Crisp the Meat
Once the pork is tender, drain it (reserving some of the braising liquid) and shred the pork using a potato masher, which maximizes the surface area for optimal browning. Sauté the meat in olive oil, along with some chopped onion and oregano, until the pork is browned and crisp. Add more garlic toward the end of cooking.

Finish in Sauce
Finish the pork with a simmer in a smoky tomato sauce until most of the liquid has evaporated. Canned tomato sauce works best; it contributes a smooth texture and bright tomato flavor. Canned chipotles might seem like an obvious addition, but in this application, we found that they varied too much from brand to brand—some were more salty, sweet, and vinegary than spicy, while others offered searing heat and not much else. Instead, reach for ground chipotle powder, which may be harder to track down, but it delivers a consistent, deep, and complex smokiness. As for the pork liquid you reserved earlier—pour that into the pan, too, where it will enrich the sauce with its meaty flavor.

Creating Crispy Tostadas
Traditionally, the tinga is served on top of crisp tostada shells (flat fried corn tortillas). To fry the shells, cook them one at a time in hot oil in a skillet. Use a fork to poke the center of each shell before frying—this will prevent puffing and allow for even cooking. Wash off the potato masher you used for the pork and use it to submerge the tortilla in the hot oil so that the top and bottom cook simultaneously, eliminating the need for flipping.

Braised pork shoulder is browned until crisp and then braised in a spicy tomato sauce.

Spicy Mexican Shredded Pork (Tinga) Tostadas

SERVES 4 TO 6

Boneless pork butt roast is often labeled Boston butt in the supermarket. The trimmed pork should weigh about 1½ pounds. Make sure to buy tortillas made only with corn, lime, and salt—preservatives will compromise quality.

TINGA

2	pounds boneless pork butt roast, trimmed and cut into 1-inch pieces
2	onions (1 quartered, 1 chopped fine)
5	garlic cloves (3 peeled and smashed, 2 minced)
4	sprigs fresh thyme
	Salt

2	tablespoons olive oil
½	teaspoon dried oregano
1	(14.5-ounce) can tomato sauce
1	tablespoon ground chipotle chile powder
2	bay leaves

TOSTADAS

¾	cup vegetable oil
12	(6-inch) corn tortillas

	Salt

GARNISHES

Queso fresco or feta cheese	Diced avocado
Fresh cilantro leaves	Lime wedges
Sour cream	

1. *For the Tinga:* Bring pork, quartered onion, smashed garlic, thyme sprigs, 1 teaspoon salt, and 6 cups water to simmer in large saucepan over medium-high heat, skimming off any foam that rises to surface. Reduce heat to medium-low, partially cover, and cook until pork is tender, 1¼ to 1½ hours. Reserve 1 cup cooking liquid and drain pork. Discard onion, garlic, and thyme sprigs. Return pork to saucepan and, using potato masher, mash until shredded into rough ½-inch pieces; set aside. (Pork can be prepared through step 1 and refrigerated for up to 2 days.)

2. Heat oil in 12-inch nonstick skillet over medium-high heat until shimmering. Add oregano, shredded pork, and chopped onion; cook, stirring often, until pork is well browned and crisp, 7 to 10 minutes. Add minced garlic and cook until fragrant, about 30 seconds.

3. Stir in tomato sauce, chipotle powder, bay leaves, and reserved pork cooking liquid; simmer until almost all liquid has evaporated, 5 to 7 minutes. Discard bay leaves and season with salt to taste.

4. *For the Tostadas:* Heat oil in 8-inch skillet over medium heat to 350 degrees. Using fork, poke center of each tortilla 3 or 4 times. Fry one at a time, holding metal potato masher in upright position on top of tortilla to keep it submerged, until crisp and lightly browned, 45 to 60 seconds (no flipping is necessary). Drain on paper towel–lined plate and season with salt to taste. (Tostadas can be made up to 1 day in advance and stored at room temperature.)

5. *To Serve:* Spoon small amount of shredded pork onto center of each tostada and serve, passing garnishes separately.

RECIPE DETAILS

Timeline

- 2 hours to trim, simmer, and shred pork (mostly hands-off; prepare garnishes)
- 20 minutes to make tinga (if you like, start to fry tostadas while tinga cooks)
- 15 minutes to fry tostadas

Essential Tools

- Large saucepan with lid for simmering pork
- Fine-mesh strainer for draining pork
- Potato masher for shredding pork
- 12-inch nonstick skillet for preparing tinga
- 8-inch skillet for frying tostadas
- Paper towels for draining tostadas

Substitutions & Variations

- We prefer the complex flavor of chipotle chile powder, but two minced canned chipotle chiles can be used in its place.
- Tinga is traditionally served on tostadas (crisp fried corn tortillas), but you can also use the meat in tacos and burritos or simply serve it over rice.
- The cheese, cilantro, sour cream, avocado and lime wedges are excellent garnishes but other classic Mexican table accompaniments are appropriate, too, including pickled radishes and/or onions and a tangy cabbage slaw. And feel free to replace the diced avocado with guacamole.
- If you prefer not to fry the tostadas, use this oven method: Arrange tortillas in single layer on 2 rimmed baking sheets. Brush both sides of each tortilla with vegetable oil (about ¼ cup total). Bake on upper-middle and lower-middle racks in 450-degree oven until lightly browned and crisp about 10 minutes, switching and rotating sheets halfway through baking.

96 Scones

FORGET AMERICAN "ROCK CAKES"—A REAL SCONE IS LIKE CAKE

In the past decade or two, Americans have embraced scones. Fueled by the proliferation of coffee houses (thank you, Starbucks), the scone is now as popular as the muffin. And in typical American fashion, our bakers add almost anything to scones—chocolate chips, chiles, cheese—you name it.

Real scones, the kind made in Britain, are rather different. Like two cousins who have grown up in dissimilar environments, American and British scones share the same name and a lot of the same DNA, but they are, as the Brits might say, as different as chalk and cheese.

Proper British scones are round and tall (not wedges or amorphous blobs), with a light, cake-like crumb and a soft, tender crust. They're not as sweet or as rich as American scones, but that's because they're usually split in half, lavishly spread with butter or clotted cream, and piled high with jam at teatime. While American scones work well as an on-the-go snack, British scones are ideally suited for the home baker, on both sides of the Atlantic, who can enjoy a scone while sitting down. (Salted butter mandatory; tea optional.)

Since the typical American scone can have two or three times as much butter, the finished product is often much heavier and denser. (Brits visiting America often describe our scones as "rock cakes.") To achieve a fluffy texture, Brits use less butter, and they soften that butter so that it can be fully incorporated into the flour. (American scones usually call for chilled butter). To taste the difference, try our recipe. It's amazing how the same familiar ingredients—handled differently—can yield something so novel. To Yanks, anyway.

WHY THIS RECIPE WORKS

Soft (Not Chilled) Butter

American scones (and biscuits) are typically made with chilled butter that is cut into the flour mixture until the pieces have been reduced to broad flakes, which give the scone a flaky, biscuit-like texture. British scones, however, are fine-textured and cakey. To achieve this type of crumb, use soft butter and pulse it into the dry ingredients until the pieces are no longer visible. Because more of the flour particles are coated with fat, and thus protected from the wet ingredients, a lot of the protein in the flour is prevented from linking to form gluten. While it's traditional to use your fingers to combine the butter and flour mixture, we recommend a food processor for ease.

Milk and Eggs

Once the butter and dry ingredients are combined, it's time to add whole milk, beaten with two eggs. Reserve a couple of tablespoons of the beaten egg and milk to use as a wash to brush over the rolled and stamped scones. The wash encourages browning and yields a soft, tender crust.

You Need to Knead

The dough for American scones must be handled as little as possible. But in this recipe kneading is actually beneficial, since it offers those proteins still available from any uncoated flour a chance to link together, giving the scones more structure to support the lift. Likewise, don't be reluctant to roll and stamp more scones from the scraps—this sturdy dough can be worked quite a bit.

Oven Spring

Breads often start in an extremely hot oven to maximize oven spring, the rise that happens when water vaporizes into steam and the air in the dough heats up and expands. Then the heat is lowered to ensure that the crust doesn't burn before the interior is cooked through. Follow suit here and you'll be rewarded with the lightest, fluffiest scones ever.

Softened butter is fully incorporated into the flour; slather on more butter at serving time.

British-Style Currant Scones

MAKES 12 SCONES

The dough will be quite soft and wet; dust your work surface and your hands liberally with flour. For a tall, even rise, use a sharp-edged biscuit cutter and push straight down; do not twist the cutter. Serve these scones with jam as well as salted butter or clotted cream.

3 cups (15 ounces) all-purpose flour
⅓ cup (2⅓ ounces) sugar
2 tablespoons baking powder
½ teaspoon salt
8 tablespoons unsalted butter, cut into ½-inch pieces and softened

¾ cup dried currants
1 cup whole milk
2 large eggs

1. Adjust oven rack to upper-middle position and heat oven to 500 degrees. Line rimmed baking sheet with parchment paper. Pulse flour, sugar, baking powder, and salt in food processor until combined, about 5 pulses. Add butter and pulse until fully incorporated and mixture looks like very fine crumbs with no visible butter, about 20 pulses. Transfer mixture to large bowl and stir in currants.

2. Whisk milk and eggs together in second bowl. Set aside 2 tablespoons milk mixture. Add remaining milk mixture to flour mixture and, using rubber spatula, fold together until almost no dry bits of flour remain.

3. Transfer dough to well-floured counter and gather into ball. With floured hands, knead until surface is smooth and free of cracks, 25 to 30 times. Press gently to form disk. Using floured rolling pin, roll disk into 9-inch round, about 1 inch thick. Using floured 2½-inch round cutter, stamp out 8 rounds, recoating cutter with flour if it begins to stick. Arrange scones on prepared sheet. Gather dough scraps, form into ball, and knead gently until surface is smooth. Roll dough to 1-inch thickness and stamp out 4 rounds. Discard remaining dough.

4. Brush tops of scones with reserved milk mixture. Reduce oven temperature to 425 degrees and bake scones until risen and golden brown, 10 to 12 minutes, rotating sheet halfway through baking. Transfer scones to wire rack and let cool for at least 10 minutes. Serve scones warm or at room temperature.

RECIPE DETAILS

Timeline

- 30 minutes to cut and soften butter at room temperature (heat oven and gather ingredients while waiting)
- 15 minutes to make dough and stamp out scones
- 10 to 12 minutes to bake scones
- 10 minutes to cool scones

Essential Tools

- **Rimmed baking sheet**
- **Parchment paper**
- **Food processor for cutting butter into dry ingredients**
- **Rolling pin**
- **2½-inch round biscuit cutter with sharp edges**
- **Pastry brush for brushing scones with milk mixture**

Substitutions & Variations

- We prefer whole milk in this recipe, but low-fat milk can be used.
- The currants are classic but other add-ins can be used in their place, including chopped crystallized ginger, toasted nuts, or other dried fruits.
- These scones are best served fresh, but leftover scones may be stored in the freezer and reheated in a 300-degree oven for 15 minutes before serving.

97 Focaccia

DON'T FORGET THE ITALIAN ROOTS OF THIS MODERN AMERICAN CLASSIC

In the pantheon of artisan breads, focaccia has a looser history than most. Centuries ago, it began as a byproduct: When Italian bakers needed to gauge the heat of a wood-fired oven—the word "focaccia" stems from *focolare*, meaning "fireplace"—they would tear off a swatch of dough, drizzle it with olive oil, and pop it into the hearth to bake as an edible oven thermometer.

Because this technique was handy with just about any bread, there evolved countless variations on the theme. That said, it's the deep-dish Genovese interpretations that most Americans recognize: dimpled, chewy, and thick, with a smattering of herbs. This bread should be flavorful enough to eat on its own but not so greasy that it can't be split to make sandwiches.

Most focaccia sold in this country misses the mark: It's too oily and too densely textured. The problem is that American recipes add olive oil to the dough to ramp up the flavor. However, all this oil gives the bread a leaden texture. The ideal focaccia has a lighter, airier crumb marked with plenty of bubbles. The original technique—simply oiling the exterior of the dough to create a crisp crust—has been lost in translation.

Patience is the key to making great focaccia. In fact, our recipe requires a two-day (but mostly hands-off) process. During this long fermentation, flavor compounds can multiply so the dough is flavorful on its own—no olive oil required. Slow fermentation also develops structure in the dough so that it rises really well and the crumb is light and open. And by baking focaccia in oiled cake pans, we ensure plenty of oil where we want it—and none where we don't.

WHY THIS RECIPE WORKS

Begin with a Biga
A brush of fruity olive oil and heady seasonings give focaccia an addictive savory edge, but that doesn't mean a thing if the dough itself lacks flavor. The biggest key here is fermentation—the process by which long chains of carbohydrates with little taste convert to sugars, alcohol, acids, and carbon dioxide. To get the benefits of long fermentation with minimal effort, we use a "pre-ferment" (also known as a sponge, or *biga* in Italian): a mixture of flour, water, and a small amount of yeast that rests overnight before being incorporated into a dough along with more yeast.

Use a Lot of Water
Dough with a higher level of hydration is more capable of expanding without tearing, promoting the formation of larger bubbles and open crumb structure. A high proportion of water to flour and a long resting process also help the natural enzymes in the wheat replicate the effect of kneading.

Rest and Fold
Don't knead the dough; fold it. Folding and resting the dough between sets of folds brings the wheat proteins into closer proximity with one another; it aerates the dough, replenishing the oxygen that the yeasts consume during fermentation; and it elongates and redistributes the bubbles. Folding will give you well-risen focaccia with a tender, moist crumb.

Keep the Oil in the Pan
You want the oil in direct contact with the dough for a crackly crisp crust, so bake the focaccia in cake pans. (If the focaccia were baked on a baking sheet, much of the oil would seep out and burn.)

Poke and Sprinkle
Poke the surface of the dough 25 to 30 times with a dinner fork. This will pop large bubbles of air and allow any extra gas to escape. Sprinkle the dough with a healthy dose of minced fresh rosemary before sliding it into a hot oven.

The key flavors—the olive oil and the rosemary—aren't actually incorporated into the dough.

Rosemary Focaccia

MAKES TWO 9-INCH ROUND LOAVES

Fresh, not dried, rosemary is a must with this bread.

SPONGE

½ cup (2½ ounces) all-purpose flour

⅓ cup warm water (110 degrees)

¼ teaspoon instant or rapid-rise yeast

DOUGH

2½ cups (12½ ounces) all-purpose flour

1¼ cups warm water (110 degrees)

1 teaspoon instant or rapid-rise yeast

Kosher salt

¼ cup extra-virgin olive oil

2 tablespoons minced fresh rosemary

1. *For the Sponge:* Combine flour, water, and yeast in large bowl and stir with wooden spoon until uniform mass forms and no dry flour remains, about 1 minute. Cover bowl tightly with plastic wrap and let stand at room temperature for at least 8 hours or up to 24 hours. Use immediately or store in refrigerator for up to 3 days (let stand at room temperature for 30 minutes before proceeding with recipe).

2. *For the Dough:* Stir flour, water, and yeast into sponge with wooden spoon until uniform mass forms and no dry flour remains, about 1 minute. Cover with plastic and let rise at room temperature for 15 minutes.

3. Sprinkle 2 teaspoons salt over dough; stir into dough until thoroughly incorporated, about 1 minute. Cover with plastic and let rise at room temperature for 30 minutes. Spray rubber spatula or bowl scraper with vegetable oil spray. Fold partially risen dough over itself by gently lifting and folding edge of dough toward middle. Turn bowl 90 degrees; fold again. Turn bowl and fold dough 6 more times (for total of 8 folds). Cover with plastic and let rise for 30 minutes. Repeat folding, turning, and rising 2 more times, for total of three 30-minute rises.

4. One hour before baking, adjust oven rack to upper-middle position, place baking stone on rack, and heat oven to 500 degrees. Gently transfer dough to lightly floured counter. Lightly dust top of dough with flour and divide it in half. Shape each piece of dough into 5-inch round by gently tucking under edges. Coat two 9-inch round cake pans with 2 tablespoons oil each. Sprinkle each pan with ½ teaspoon salt. Place round of dough in 1 pan, top side down; slide dough around pan to coat bottom and sides with oil, then flip dough over. Repeat with second piece of dough. Cover pans with plastic and let rest for 5 minutes.

5. Using your fingertips, press dough out toward edges of pan, taking care not to tear it. (If dough resists stretching, let it relax for 5 to 10 minutes before trying to stretch it again.) Using dinner fork, poke entire surface of dough 25 to 30 times, popping any large bubbles. Sprinkle rosemary evenly over top of dough. Let dough rest in pans until slightly bubbly, 5 to 10 minutes.

6. Place pans on baking stone and lower oven temperature to 450 degrees. Bake until tops are golden brown, 25 to 28 minutes, rotating pans halfway through baking. Transfer pans to wire rack and let cool for 5 minutes. Remove loaves from pans and

RECIPE DETAILS

Timeline

- 5 minutes to make sponge
- 8 to 24 hours to let sponge develop (totally hands-off)
- 5 minutes to make dough
- 1¾ hours to let dough rise (add salt after 15 minutes and fold dough 3 times; start preheating oven halfway through rising time)
- 20 minutes to shape dough and sprinkle with rosemary
- 30 minutes to bake focaccia and cool in pans
- 30 minutes to cool focaccia on rack

Essential Tools

- Wooden spoon for mixing dough
- Plastic wrap for covering bowl as dough rises
- Rubber spatula or bowl scraper for folding dough as it rises (make sure to grease spatula)
- Baking stone (If you don't have a baking stone, bake the bread on an overturned, preheated baking sheet set on the upper-middle oven rack.)
- Two 9-inch round cake pans
- Fork for poking surface of dough right before baking
- Wire rack for cooling focaccia

Substitutions & Variations

- Other hardy fresh herbs can be used in place of the rosemary, including thyme or oregano.
- Sun-dried tomatoes or roasted red peppers (both patted dried and chopped) also make good toppings.
- Grated Parmesan can be sprinkled over the just-baked focaccia.

return to rack. Brush tops with any oil remaining in pans. Let cool for 30 minutes before serving. (Leftover bread can be wrapped in double layer of plastic and stored at room temperature for up to 2 days. Wrapped with additional layer of aluminum foil, bread can be frozen for up to 1 month.)

FOCACCIA WITH KALAMATA OLIVES AND ANCHOVIES

Omit salt from pans in step 4. Substitute 1 cup kalamata olives, pitted, rinsed, and chopped coarse, 4 rinsed and minced anchovy fillets, and 1 teaspoon red pepper flakes for rosemary. Sprinkle each focaccia with ¼ cup finely grated Pecorino Romano as soon as it is removed from oven.

FOCACCIA WITH CARAMELIZED RED ONION, PANCETTA, AND OREGANO

Cook 4 ounces finely chopped pancetta in 12-inch skillet over medium heat, stirring occasionally, until most of fat has been rendered, about 10 minutes. Remove pancetta with slotted spoon and transfer to paper towel–lined plate. Add 1 chopped red onion and 2 tablespoons water to fat left in skillet and cook over medium heat, stirring often, until onion is soft and beginning to brown, about 12 minutes. Remove skillet from heat and set aside. Omit rosemary. After poking surface of dough rounds in step 5, sprinkle with pancetta, onion, and 2 teaspoons minced fresh oregano. Continue with recipe as directed.

A Better Way to Knead Bread Dough

In most recipes, dough is kneaded, left alone to rise, and then shaped. However, when making many rustic breads as well as pizzas and focaccia, we often interrupt the process by turning and folding the dough. In many respects, this step is a continuation of kneading since it is designed to build structure. In fact, turning and folding the dough lets you reduce kneading time. And since kneading can be excessively rough (mixers cause dough to warm up and can actually rob the dough of flavor), turning and folding is an easy and gentle way to produce better bread. Use a plastic bowl scraper or rubber spatula that has been coated with vegetable oil spray. The exact number of turns and folds will vary from recipe to recipe but the process is the same.

1. Slide bowl scraper or rubber spatula under 1 side of dough. Gently lift and fold about one-third of dough toward center.

2. Turn bowl as directed (often 90 degrees) and repeat folding motion, making sure to fold dough toward center each time. Continue turning bowl and folding until you have worked your way around circumference of bowl.

98 Italian Almond Cake

ELEGANCE + SIMPLICITY = LA DOLCE VITA

The scariest part about throwing a dinner party is dessert. Many good cooks don't have the confidence to roll out pastry or frost a cake, so they just buy something. We think anyone who entertains needs a go-to dessert—something that looks impressive but requires little effort. It should allow you to end your dinner party on a high note. We have the answer—Italian almond cake.

We know what you're thinking: A cake isn't easy. Trust us, this one is. Not only will this recipe change your mind about baking, but it will also change your mind about cake.

All too often we view cake as a vehicle for frosting. It has to be sturdy and tall so we care mostly about texture, not flavor. But it is possible to make a cake that tastes great on its own. The first step is to replace some of the flour (the main ingredient) with something flavorful that can provide structure. That's where the almonds come in—they are ground to a fine powder and act like flour in this recipe. Lemon zest adds depth and brightness, and more sliced almonds—this time left as is—provide crunch on top.

Italian almond cake is rich enough that a small piece satisfies—no frosting required. No mixer is needed either, just a food processor. And there are no fussy techniques like creaming (the butter is melted). If you can make pancakes or muffins, you can make this cake. And best of all, all those nuts produce a very moist cake that can be prepared up to three days in advance so you can relax and enjoy the party.

WHY THIS RECIPE WORKS

All Almonds

Almond paste (a mix of ground almonds in sugar along with a binding agent such as glucose syrup) gives traditional Italian almond cake an almost fudgy texture. For cake with a lighter crumb that's not so candy-like, we use toasted ground almonds. A splash of almond extract adds concentrated nut flavor. Blanched almonds are best since the skins on almonds can make the cake bitter.

Finesse the Flour

When butter and sugar are creamed, the airy pockets can help give a cake lift—but only if the batter contains enough gluten to support it. Most recipes use a modest amount of flour, but if you use a little more the cake will rise higher. Baking powder is important too. Just ¼ teaspoon will help inflate the air pockets, resulting in a higher rise and lighter crumb. (And we add a second leavener, baking soda, not so much for lift, but to encourage browning.)

A Whipped Egg Process

Whip the eggs and sugar in a food processor. While you might think the stand mixer is a better tool for the job, it actually produces a foam with a too-strong protein network that holds onto air and results in a fluffy, domed cake, which is the opposite of what this cake should be—a flat-topped cake with a rustic crumb. And besides, there's no need to haul out a second appliance since you've already used the food processor to grind the almonds. Grab a couple lemons and grate a little zest. Whir it in the food processor with the eggs and sugar—it imparts a subtle citrus perfume to the cake that accents the almonds.

Two Fats Are Better Than One

Using all butter will produce a cake on the dry side. But don't count it out altogether—it's got great flavor. Team it up with vegetable oil. Unlike butter, which contains water that evaporates during baking, vegetable oil is 100 percent fat, which makes for cake with a moister crumb.

Toasted sliced almonds are ground to a flour and also used whole on top of the cake for crunch.

Italian Almond Cake

SERVES 8 TO 10

Serve plain, dusted with confectioners' sugar, or with Orange Crème Fraîche (recipe follows).

1½ cups plus ⅓ cup blanched sliced almonds, toasted

¾ cup (3¾ ounces) all-purpose flour

¾ teaspoon salt

¼ teaspoon baking powder

⅛ teaspoon baking soda

4 large eggs

1¼ cups (8¾ ounces) plus 2 tablespoons sugar

1 tablespoon plus ½ teaspoon grated lemon zest (2 lemons)

¾ teaspoon almond extract

5 tablespoons unsalted butter, melted

⅓ cup vegetable oil

1. Adjust oven rack to middle position and heat oven to 300 degrees. Grease 9-inch round cake pan and line with parchment paper. Pulse 1½ cups almonds, flour, salt, baking powder, and baking soda in food processor until almonds are finely ground, 5 to 10 pulses. Transfer almond mixture to bowl.

2. Process eggs, 1¼ cups sugar, 1 tablespoon lemon zest, and almond extract in now-empty processor until very pale yellow, about 2 minutes. With processor running, add melted butter and oil in steady stream, until incorporated. Add almond mixture and pulse to combine, 4 or 5 pulses. Transfer batter to prepared pan.

3. Using your fingers, combine remaining 2 tablespoons sugar and remaining ½ teaspoon lemon zest in small bowl until fragrant, 5 to 10 seconds. Sprinkle top of cake evenly with remaining ⅓ cup almonds followed by sugar-zest mixture.

4. Bake until center of cake is set and bounces back when gently pressed and toothpick inserted in center comes out clean, 55 minutes to 1 hour 5 minutes, rotating pan after 40 minutes. Let cake cool in pan on wire rack for 15 minutes. Run paring knife around sides of pan. Invert cake onto greased wire rack, discard parchment, and reinvert cake onto second wire rack. Let cake cool, about 2 hours. Cut into wedges and serve. (Cake can be stored at room temperature for up to 3 days.)

ORANGE CRÈME FRAÎCHE MAKES ABOUT 2 CUPS

2 oranges

1 cup crème fraîche

2 tablespoons sugar

⅛ teaspoon salt

Remove 1 teaspoon zest from 1 orange. Cut away peel and pith from oranges. Slice between membranes to release segments and cut segments into ¼-inch pieces. Combine orange pieces and zest, crème fraîche, sugar, and salt in bowl and mix well. Refrigerate for at least 1 hour before serving.

RECIPE DETAILS

Timeline

- 10 minutes to heat oven and prepare cake pan (gather and prepare ingredients)
- 10 minutes to toast almonds and finish preparing ingredients
- 10 minutes to make cake batter and top with toasted almonds and lemon sugar
- 55 minutes to 1 hour 5 minutes to bake cake (rotate pan after 40 minutes)
- 15 minutes to cool cake in pan
- 2 hours to cool cake on rack (make orange crème fraîche, if using, and refrigerate for at least 1 hour)

Essential Tools

- 9-inch round cake pan
- Parchment paper for lining cake pan
- Rimmed baking sheet for toasting almonds in oven
- Food processor for grinding nuts and making cake batter
- Rasp grater for zesting lemons
- Wire rack for cooling cake

Substitutions & Variations

- If you can't find blanched sliced almonds, grind slivered almonds for the batter and use unblanched sliced almonds for the topping.

99 Latin American Flan

THE WORLD'S MOST POPULAR DESSERT—SERIOUSLY

Spanish is the primary language spoken in nearly two dozen countries with a total population of 500 million people. And in the Spanish-speaking world, no dessert is as popular as flan. This humble baked custard with caramel is known across the globe, appearing regularly on menus from Madrid to Lima and Havana to Manila.

As you might expect with a recipe that has spread wide and far, there are regional variations. Spain is known for flan that is creamy and lightly set—almost indistinguishable from French crème caramel. (Same recipe, different name.) In most of Latin America, flan isn't light and quivering like its European counterparts. The custard is far richer and densely creamy, with a texture somewhere between pudding and cheesecake. It also boasts a more deeply caramelized, toffee-like flavor.

The main difference is the milk. In Spain (and neighboring France), fresh milk is the default choice. However, in Latin America, canned milk—evaporated as well as condensed—is more typical. (This change is most likely due to the historical challenges of keeping milk fresh in warm climates before the advent of refrigeration.) So why does this matter? Canned milk is richer than fresh milk because much of the water has been removed. In addition, the cooking process that concentrates canned milks causes the natural sugars and proteins in the milk to brown, which accounts for the light tan color and toffee flavor they lend this style of flan.

But no matter where flan is made, producing a thick layer of fluid caramel that doesn't harden into a candy-like shell can be tricky. The key to perfect caramel is as simple as turning on the tap.

WHY THIS RECIPE WORKS

Loosen the Caramel
The rich layer of caramel on top of the flan is the best part of the dessert—except when most of it sticks to the pan like glue. We add a couple of tablespoons of warm water to the syrup after it's caramelized to dissolve some of the sugar and keep it runny.

Mix Up the Milks
Evaporated and sweetened condensed milks give flan a distinctively thick, luxurious texture and caramelized notes, but they have twice as much protein as fresh dairy, which can create an overly tight structure. To loosen the texture, we add ½ cup of fresh milk.

Cut Back on the Whites
We loosen the texture further by addressing the protein in the eggs. In short, we eliminate most of the whites. Using two whole eggs and five egg yolks yields a creamy, thick flan. Fewer whites means better flavor, too—the flan tastes less overtly eggy and more rich and creamy.

Think Outside of the Pan
For a family-style flan, you might think a cake pan is ideal, but a wide, shallow flan is inclined to crack. Pull out another pan you probably have on hand—a loaf pan. The deeper walls and narrower surface area produce a sturdier, taller flan—one that is statuesque and will definitely earn you presentation points at the table.

Cook Under Cover and in Water
Custards are often baked in a water bath (the pan is placed in a larger pan and hot water is added) to prevent overcooking. Follow suit here, and to prevent a skin from forming on the top of the custard cover the loaf pan tightly in aluminum foil.

Chill It
Rest the flan overnight to allow the moisture from the custard to dissolve more of the sugar in the caramel, ensuring that once you turn out the flan it will be covered in a substantial layer of runny caramel.

A loaf pan and specific combination of three milks gives this flan its distinct look and flavor.

Perfect Latin Flan

SERVES 8 TO 10

This recipe should be made at least one day before serving. Serve the flan on a platter with a raised rim to contain the liquid caramel.

⅔ cup (4⅔ ounces) sugar	1 (12-ounce) can evaporated milk
2 large eggs plus 5 large yolks	½ cup whole milk
1 (14-ounce) can sweetened	1½ tablespoons vanilla extract
condensed milk	½ teaspoon salt

1. Stir together sugar and ¼ cup water in medium heavy saucepan until sugar is completely moistened. Bring to boil over medium-high heat, 3 to 5 minutes, and cook, without stirring, until mixture begins to turn golden, another 1 to 2 minutes. Gently swirling pan, continue to cook until sugar is color of peanut butter, 1 to 2 minutes. Remove from heat and swirl pan until sugar is reddish-amber and fragrant, 15 to 20 seconds. Carefully swirl in 2 tablespoons warm tap water until incorporated; mixture will bubble and steam. Pour caramel into 8½ by 4½-inch loaf pan; do not scrape out saucepan. Set loaf pan aside.

2. Adjust oven rack to middle position and heat oven to 300 degrees. Line bottom of 13 by 9-inch baking pan with dish towel, folding towel to fit smoothly, and set aside. Bring 2 quarts water to boil.

3. Whisk eggs and yolks in large bowl until combined. Add sweetened condensed milk, evaporated milk, whole milk, vanilla, and salt and whisk until incorporated. Strain mixture through fine-mesh strainer into prepared loaf pan.

4. Cover loaf pan tightly with aluminum foil and place in prepared baking pan. Place baking pan in oven and carefully pour all of boiling water into pan. Bake until center of custard jiggles slightly when shaken and custard registers 180 degrees, 1¼ to 1½ hours. Remove foil and leave custard in water bath until loaf pan has cooled completely. Remove loaf pan from water bath, wrap tightly with plastic wrap, and chill overnight or up to 4 days.

5. To unmold, slide paring knife around edges of pan. Invert serving platter on top of pan and turn pan and platter over. When flan is released, remove loaf pan. Using rubber spatula, scrape residual caramel onto flan. Slice and serve. (Leftover flan may be refrigerated for up to 4 days.)

ALMOND LATIN FLAN
Reduce vanilla to 1 tablespoon and whisk 1 teaspoon almond extract into egg-milk mixture.

ORANGE-CARDAMOM LATIN FLAN
Whisk 2 tablespoons orange zest and ¼ teaspoon ground cardamom into egg-milk mixture before straining.

COFFEE LATIN FLAN
Whisk 4 teaspoons instant espresso powder into egg-milk mixture until dissolved.

RECIPE DETAILS

Timeline

- 10 minutes to make caramel
- 10 minutes to make custard (preheat oven and bring water to boil at same time)
- 1¼ to 1½ hours to bake flan (hands-off)
- 12 hours (minimum) to chill flan
- 5 minutes to unmold flan

Essential Tools

- Medium saucepan (Something with a heavy bottom and light color like stainless steel is best; avoid nonstick since you won't be able to judge the progress of the caramel.)
- 8½ by 4½-inch loaf pan for flan (If the only loaf pan in your kitchen measures 9 by 5 inches, begin checking for doneness at 1 hour. The finished flan will be a bit squat.)
- 13 by 9-inch baking pan for water bath that holds loaf pan
- Dish towel for lining baking pan (This prevents the bottom of the flan from overheating.)
- Fine-mesh strainer for removing any clumps of egg
- Aluminum foil for covering loaf pan
- Instant-read thermometer for judging doneness
- Paring knife for loosening flan from pan
- Platter with raised edges for holding flan and caramel

Substitutions & Variations

- You may substitute 2 percent milk for the whole milk, but do not use skim milk.

100 Chocolate Pots de Crème

FRENCH REFINEMENT MINUS THE USUAL HASSLE

The French really do make simple things better. Take chocolate pots de crème. To call this "chocolate pudding" doesn't do this custard justice. A better description might be "crème brûlée minus the caramelized crust but enriched with dark chocolate." Pots de crème are incredibly silky and pack an intense hit of chocolate. Classically, this dessert is made in petite lidded pots, but ramekins work just as well. These rich custards are served in small portions because more would be too much.

As the comparison to crème brûlée suggests, recipes can be quite fussy because they require a water bath—a large roasting pan filled with hot water that accommodates all the ramekins and prevents overcooking. Besides being cumbersome, this setup can lead to mistakes. Water splashes every time you move the roasting pan and can ruin individual custards if you're not careful. And the water bath doesn't guarantee uniform cooking, so you end up gauging doneness in each vessel and then plucking hot ramekins out of near-simmering water. There has to be a simpler way.

This is where the comparison to American-style chocolate pudding can be helpful. Can't you just cook the custard on the stovetop and then chill the pots de crème? In fact, you can if you make a stirred custard (aka crème anglaise). The egg yolks, sugar, and dairy are heated on the stovetop, the resulting custard is poured over the chopped chocolate, and then the mixture is gently whisked until smooth. That sounds easy because it is. The whole process takes half an hour and no special equipment is required. This might just be the simplest French dessert anyone can make at home.

WHY THIS RECIPE WORKS

Rich, But Not Too Rich
Which dairy should you reach for when making the crème anglaise, which forms the base of the pots de crème? Most recipes use one or a combination of milk, half-and-half, and heavy cream. For just the right amount of richness and body, we pair half-and-half with heavy cream.

Yolks Only, and Less of Them
Using just egg yolks is the norm for the crème anglaise, but unless your goal is a rubbery custard, knock off a few yolks. Because you'll want to pack in the chocolate, which will help solidify the pudding, those extra yolks are unnecessary.

Judging When the Anglaise Is Ready
There are two ways to gauge doneness of the custard. An instant-read thermometer is the most reliable—the custard is done when it reaches 175 to 180 degrees. But you can also judge the progress of the custard by its thickness. Dip a wooden spoon into the custard and run your finger across the back.

Ramp Up the Chocolate
Pots de crème should possess intense chocolate flavor. We skip over the milk chocolate and semisweet (they're too mild) and reach for bittersweet chocolate—and a lot of it. We use 50 percent more chocolate than most recipes. Add instant espresso powder dissolved in water to enhance the chocolate flavor—just ½ teaspoon will do the job without calling attention to itself. Vanilla extract is important, too. Vanilla is a powerful "flavor potentiator," meaning it enhances our ability to taste other foods including chocolate, so pour in a full tablespoon.

The Big Chill
Once you pour the custards into the ramekins, your hands-on work is done. Cover the ramekins with plastic wrap and move them to the refrigerator so the pots de crème can chill and firm up.

Pour the hot custard over the chopped chocolate, stir until smooth, chill, and then serve.

Chocolate Pots de Crème

SERVES 8

We prefer pots de crème made with 60 percent bittersweet chocolate. Our favorite brands are Ghirardelli 60 Percent Cacao Bittersweet Chocolate Premium Baking Bar and Callebaut Intense Dark Chocolate, L-60–40NV.

POTS DE CRÈME

10 ounces bittersweet chocolate, chopped fine	1½ cups heavy cream
5 large egg yolks	¾ cup half-and-half
5 tablespoons (2¼ ounces) sugar	1 tablespoon water
¼ teaspoon salt	½ teaspoon instant espresso powder
	1 tablespoon vanilla extract

WHIPPED CREAM AND GARNISH

½ cup heavy cream, chilled	Unsweetened cocoa powder (optional)
2 teaspoons sugar	Chocolate shavings (optional)
½ teaspoon vanilla extract	

1. *For the Pots de Crème:* Place chocolate in medium bowl; set fine-mesh strainer over bowl and set aside.

2. Whisk egg yolks, sugar, and salt in bowl until combined. Whisk in cream and half-and-half. Transfer mixture to medium saucepan and cook over medium-low heat, stirring constantly and scraping bottom of pot with wooden spoon, until thickened and silky and registers 175 to 180 degrees, 8 to 12 minutes. (Do not let custard overcook or simmer.)

3. Immediately pour custard through fine-mesh strainer over chocolate. Let mixture stand to melt chocolate, about 5 minutes; whisk gently until smooth. Combine water and espresso powder and stir to dissolve, then whisk dissolved espresso powder and vanilla into chocolate mixture. Divide mixture evenly among eight 5-ounce ramekins. Gently tap ramekins against counter to remove air bubbles.

4. Let pots de crème cool to room temperature, then cover with plastic wrap and refrigerate until chilled, at least 4 hours. Before serving, let pots de crème stand at room temperature for 20 to 30 minutes. (Pots de crème can be refrigerated for up to 3 days.)

5. *For the Whipped Cream and Garnish:* Using handheld mixer or stand mixer fitted with whisk, whip cream, sugar, and vanilla on medium-low speed until foamy, about 1 minute. Increase speed to high and whip until soft peaks form, 1 to 3 minutes. Dollop each pot de crème with about 2 tablespoons whipped cream and garnish with cocoa and/or chocolate shavings, if using. Serve.

RECIPE DETAILS

Timeline

- 10 minutes to chop chocolate, separate egg yolks, and gather ingredients
- 10 minutes to cook custard
- 5 minutes to strain custard over chopped chocolate and set mixture aside
- 5 minutes to finish flavoring pots de crème and divide among ramekins
- 30 minutes to cool pots de crème to room temperature
- 4 hours (minimum) to chill pots de crème thoroughly
- 20 minutes to take chill off pots de crème (whip cream and make chocolate shavings)

Essential Tools

- Whisk for combining ingredients
- Wooden spoon for stirring custard as it cooks
- Medium saucepan with heavy bottom for cooking the custard
- Fine-mesh strainer for straining custard
- Eight (5-ounce) ramekins (Pudding cups or small parfait glasses can be used if you prefer.)
- Handheld or stand mixer for whipping cream

Substitutions & Variations

- If using a chocolate with 70 percent cacao, use just 8 ounces to keep the custards from becoming overly stiff.
- A tablespoon of strong brewed coffee can be used in place of the instant espresso powder and water.
- Sweetened whipped cream and a few chocolate shavings are the perfect garnish for this simple dessert. If you like, flavor the whipped cream with a splash of cognac or bourbon and try white or milk chocolate shavings.

MILK CHOCOLATE POTS DE CRÈME

Milk chocolate behaves differently in this recipe than bittersweet chocolate, and more of it must be used to ensure that the custard sets. And because of the increased amount of chocolate, it's necessary to cut back on the amount of sugar so that the custard is not overly sweet.

Substitute 12 ounces milk chocolate, chopped fine, for bittersweet chocolate and reduce sugar in pots de crème to 2 tablespoons.

A Better Way to Whip Cream

Many experts make it sound like whipping cream is tricky. It's not. In the old days, you needed to worry about chilling the bowl and the beaters. But the ultrapasteurized cream sold in most supermarkets contains additives that ensure good results. Even organic brands that don't contain additives and are merely pasteurized will whip up nicely as long as the cream is cold. There are, however, a few other tricks to whipping cream like a pro. At the outset, use a relatively low speed to minimize the splattering. As the cream becomes foamy, you can increase the speed of the mixer. As for the sugar, we prefer granulated sugar (confectioners' sugar contains a little cornstarch which can impart a starchy texture), but you must add the sugar before mixing commences so that it has time to dissolve.

1. Using handheld mixer or stand mixer fitted with whisk, whip cream, sugar, and vanilla on medium-low speed until foamy, about 1 minute. (While you can omit the sugar if you like, don't skip the vanilla—it makes the cream more flavorful.)

2. Increase speed to high and whip until soft or stiff peaks form, 1 to 3 minutes. (Soft peaks are fine for dolloping but stiff peaks are a must for recipes where whipped cream is used for coverage—like cakes or cream pies.)

Conversions and Equivalents

Some say cooking is a science and an art. We would say that geography has a hand in it, too. Flour milled in the United Kingdom and elsewhere will feel and taste different from flour milled in the United States. So we cannot promise that the loaf of bread you bake in Canada or England will taste the same as a loaf baked in the States, but we can offer guidelines for converting weights and measures. We also recommend that you rely on your instincts when making our recipes. Refer to the visual cues provided. If the bread dough hasn't "come together in a ball," as described, you may need to add more flour—even if the recipe doesn't tell you to. You be the judge.

The recipes in this book were developed using standard U.S. measures following U.S. government guidelines. The charts below offer equivalents for U.S., metric, and imperial (U.K.) measures. All conversions are approximate and have been rounded up or down to the nearest whole number.

EXAMPLE:

1 teaspoon = 4.9292 milliliters, rounded up to 5 milliliters

1 ounce = 28.3495 grams, rounded down to 28 grams

VOLUME CONVERSIONS

U.S.	METRIC
1 teaspoon	5 milliliters
2 teaspoons	10 milliliters
1 tablespoon	15 milliliters
2 tablespoons	30 milliliters
¼ cup	59 milliliters
⅓ cup	79 milliliters
½ cup	118 milliliters
¾ cup	177 milliliters
1 cup	237 milliliters
1¼ cups	296 milliliters
1½ cups	355 milliliters
2 cups (1 pint)	473 milliliters
2½ cups	591 milliliters
3 cups	710 milliliters
4 cups (1 quart)	0.946 liter
1.06 quarts	1 liter
4 quarts (1 gallon)	3.8 liters

WEIGHT CONVERSIONS

OUNCES	GRAMS
½	14
¾	21
1	28
1½	43
2	57
2½	71
3	85
3½	99
4	113
4½	128
5	142
6	170
7	198
8	227
9	255
10	283
12	340
16 (1 pound)	454

CONVERSIONS FOR COMMON BAKING INGREDIENTS

Baking is an exacting science. Because measuring by weight is far more accurate than measuring by volume, and thus more likely to achieve reliable results, in our recipes we provide ounce measures in addition to cup measures for many ingredients. Refer to the chart below to convert these measures into grams.

INGREDIENT	OUNCES	GRAMS
1 cup all-purpose flour*	5	142
1 cup cake flour	4	113
1 cup whole-wheat flour	5½	156
1 cup granulated (white) sugar	7	198
1 cup packed brown sugar (light or dark)	7	198
1 cup confectioners' sugar	4	113
1 cup cocoa powder	3	85
4 tablespoons butter† (½ stick, or ¼ cup)	2	57
8 tablespoons butter† (1 stick, or ½ cup)	4	113

* U.S. all-purpose flour, the most frequently used flour in this book, does not contain leaveners, as some European flours do. These leavened flours are called self-rising or self-raising. If you are using self-rising flour, take this into consideration before adding leavening to a recipe.

† In the United States, butter is sold both salted and unsalted. We generally recommend unsalted butter. If you are using salted butter, take this into consideration before adding salt to a recipe.

CONVERTING OVEN TEMPERATURES

FAHRENHEIT	CELSIUS	GAS MARK (IMPERIAL)
225	105	¼
250	120	½
275	135	1
300	150	2
325	165	3
350	180	4
375	190	5
400	200	6
425	220	7
450	230	8
475	245	9

CONVERTING FAHRENHEIT TO CELSIUS

We include doneness temperatures in a few of the recipes in this book. We recommend an instant-read thermometer for the job. Refer to the above table to convert Fahrenheit degrees to Celsius. Or, for temperatures not represented in the chart, use this simple formula:

Subtract 32 degrees from the Fahrenheit reading, then divide the result by 1.8 to find the Celsius reading.

EXAMPLE:

"Bake until soufflé has risen above rim, top is deep golden brown, and interior registers 170 degrees, 30 to 35 minutes." To convert:

170°F − 32 = 138°

138° ÷ 1.8 = 76.67°C, rounded up to 77°C

Index

Note: Page references in *italics* indicate recipe photographs.

Butter (continued)

Garlic-Lemon, Pan-Seared Shrimp with, 82

Lemon Thyme, 198

Shallot and Parsley, 66

Thai Chili, 71

Whipped Honey, 114

Butterscotch Frosting, 234

C

Cabbage

Farmhouse Vegetable and Barley Soup, *196,* 197–98

Pork Lo Mein, 296–99, *297*

and Pork Potstickers, 255–56, *257*

and Sausage, Hearty Tuscan Bean Stew with, 270

Cakes

Almond, Italian, *326,* 327–28

Chocolate Cupcakes with Ganache Filling, *232,* 233–35

Fluffy Yellow Layer, with Chocolate Frosting, 228–31, *229*

frosting, tips for, 231

Caper(s)

and Cornichons, Parsley Sauce with, 132

and Herb Vinaigrette, Poached Salmon with, 143–45, *144*

Radishes, and Cornichons, French Potato Salad with, 183

Zesty Quick Tomato Sauce, 28

Cardamom-Orange Latin Flan, 330

Carrots

Best Chicken Stew, 140–42, *141*

Classic Pot Roast with Root Vegetables, 87

Whole, Slow-Cooked, *208,* 209–10

Cashews and Raisins, Indian-Spiced Mashed Sweet Potatoes with, 206

Catalan-Style Beef Stew with Mushrooms, *306,* 307–8

Cauliflower

Potatoes, Peas, and Chickpeas, Indian Curry with, *264,* 265–66

Soup, *190,* 191–92

Cheddar Drop Biscuits, 111

Cheese

Almost Hands-Free Risotto with Parmesan, *252,* 253–54

Almost No-Knead Bread with Olives, Rosemary, and Parmesan, 220

Arugula and Ricotta Pesto, 25

Cheese (continued)

Baked Manicotti, *172,* 173–74

Basil-Parmesan Drop Biscuits, 111

Blue, and Crispy Shallots, Juicy Pub-Style Burgers with, *101,* 102

Cheddar Drop Biscuits, 111

Creamy Parmesan Polenta, *214,* 215–16

Enchiladas Verdes, *292,* 293–95

Fluffy Omelet, *12,* 12–15

French Potato Salad with Arugula, Roquefort, and Walnuts, 183

Goat, Herbed Baked, Salad with, *184,* 185–86

grating, by hand, 217

Grilled, Sandwiches, Grown-Up, with Asiago and Dates, *50,* 51

Grilled, Sandwiches, Grown-Up, with Cheddar and Shallot, 49–51, *50*

Grilled, Sandwiches, Grown-Up, with Comté and Cornichon, *50,* 51

Grilled, Sandwiches, Grown-Up, with Gruyère and Chives, *50,* 51

Grilled, Sandwiches, Grown-Up, with Robiola and Chipotle, *50,* 51

Macaroni and, Classic, *34,* 35–36

Macaroni and, Classic, with Ham and Peas, 36

Macaroni and, Classic, with Kielbasa and Mustard, 36

Mexican-Style Grilled Corn, 261–62, *263*

Pasta Caprese, *178,* 179–80

Quinoa Pilaf with Apricots, Aged Gouda, and Pistachios, 212

Quinoa Pilaf with Chipotle, Queso Fresco, and Peanuts, 212

Roasted Broccoli with Shallots, Fennel Seeds, and Parmesan, 48

Sautéed Cherry Tomato and Fresh Mozzarella Topping for Polenta, 217

Skillet Lasagna with Sausage and Red Bell Pepper, 176

Skillet Meaty Lasagna, 175–76, *177*

Soufflé, 187–88, *189*

Spaghetti with Pecorino Romano and Pepper, *166,* 167–68

Spicy Jalapeño-Cheddar Cornbread, 114

E

Eggplant, Sweet Potatoes, Green Beans, and Chickpeas, Indian-Style Curry with, 266

Eggs

Cheese Soufflé, 187–88, *189*

Fluffy Omelet, *12,* 12–15

Fried, and Bread Crumbs, Spaghetti with, 11

Fried, Perfect, 9–11, *10*

Hard-Cooked, Foolproof, 315

hard-cooked, peeling, 315

Indonesian-Style Fried Rice, 245–47

Scrambled, Perfect, 6–8, *7*

Scrambled, Perfect, for One, 8

Scrambled, Perfect, for Two, 8

Scrambled, Smoked Salmon, with Chive Butter, 8

separating yolks and whites, 15

whipping whites of, 15

Enchiladas Verdes, *292,* 293–95

F

Farmhouse Vegetable and Barley Soup, *196,* 197–98

Fennel and Saffron, Almost Hands-Free Risotto with, 254

Fennel Seeds, Shallots, and Parmesan, Roasted Broccoli with, 48

Filipino Chicken Adobo, 280–82, *281*

Fish

Crunchy Oven-Fried, *78,* 79–80

Grilled, Tacos, *258,* 259–60

Grilled Blackened Red Snapper, *146,* 147–48

Poached Salmon with Dill and Sour Cream Sauce, 145

Poached Salmon with Herb and Caper Vinaigrette, 143–45, *144*

Smoked Salmon and Asparagus Filling for Omelets, 14

Smoked Salmon Scrambled Eggs with Chive Butter, 8

see also Anchovies

Flan, Latin

Almond, 330

Coffee, 330

Orange-Cardamom, 330

Perfect, 329–30, *331*

Fluffy Omelet, *12,* 12–15

Fluffy Yellow Layer Cake with Chocolate Frosting, 228–31, *229*

Focaccia

with Caramelized Red Onion, Pancetta, and Oregano, 325

with Kalamata Olives and Anchovies, 325

Rosemary, 322–25, *323*

Foolproof Double-Crust Pie Dough, 127

Foolproof Hard-Cooked Eggs, 315

Foolproof Vinaigrette, *16,* 17–18

French Chicken in a Pot, 133–35, *134*

French Potato Salad

with Arugula, Roquefort, and Walnuts, 183

with Mustard and Herbs, 181–83, *182*

with Radishes, Cornichons, and Capers, 183

Frostings

applying to cakes, 231

Butterscotch, 234

Chocolate, Creamy, 235

Chocolate, Fluffy Yellow Layer Cake with, 228–31, *229*

Peanut Butter, 234

Vanilla, 234

Fruit. *See specific fruits*

G

Garlic

Chimichurri Sauce, 310, *311*

and Chipotle Butter with Lime and Cilantro, 66

-Lemon Butter, Pan-Seared Shrimp with, 82

and Lime, Peruvian Roast Chicken with, 271–73, *272*

Mashed Sweet Potatoes with Coconut, 206

mincing, 33

and Oil, Pasta with (Aglio e Olio), 20–22, *21*

Olive Oil, and Artichokes, Spaghetti with, 22

Olives, Oregano, and Lemon, Roasted Broccoli with, 48

Picada, 308

Roasted Broccoli with, 48

-Rosemary Smashed Potatoes, 38

Ginger

-Apple Glaze, 108

-Hoisin Glaze, Pan-Seared Shrimp with, 82

preparing, 299

Shiitakes, and Edamame, Quinoa Pilaf with, 212

-Tomato Vinaigrette, Warm, 132

AMERICA'S TEST KITCHEN

17 Station Street, Brookline, MA 02445

Library of Congress Cataloging-in-Publication Data
100 recipes : the absolute best ways to make the true essentials / the editors at America's Test Kitchen ; photography, Carl Tremblay ; food styling, Marie Piraino.
    pages cm
ISBN 978-1-940352-01-5 (hardback)
1. Cooking. I. America's Test Kitchen (Firm) II. Title: One hundred recipes.
TX714.A1825 2015
641.5--dc23

2015018863

Hardcover: US $40.00 / $51.00 CAN

Manufactured in the United States of America
10 9 8 7 6 5 4 3 2 1

DISTRIBUTED BY
Penguin Random House Publisher Services
Tel. 800.733.3000

EDITORIAL DIRECTOR: Jack Bishop
EDITORIAL DIRECTOR, BOOKS: Elizabeth Carduff
EXECUTIVE FOOD EDITOR: Julia Collin Davison
EXECUTIVE EDITOR: Lori Galvin
SENIOR EDITOR: Debra Hudak
ASSISTANT EDITOR: Rachel Greenhaus
EDITORIAL ASSISTANT: Samantha Ronan
BOOK DESIGN: Amy Klee
DESIGN DIRECTOR: Greg Galvan
ART DIRECTOR: Carole Goodman
DEPUTY ART DIRECTOR: Taylor Argenzio
GRAPHIC DESIGNER: Jen Kanavos Hoffman
PHOTOGRAPHY DIRECTOR: Julie Cote
ASSOCIATE ART DIRECTOR, PHOTOGRAPHY: Steve Klise
PHOTOGRAPHER: Carl Tremblay
STAFF PHOTOGRAPHER: Daniel J. van Ackere
CAST PHOTOGRAPH: Christopher Churchill
FOOD STYLING: Marie Piraino
PHOTOSHOOT KITCHEN TEAM:
    ASSOCIATE EDITOR: Chris O'Connor
    TEST COOK: Daniel Cellucci
    ASSISTANT TEST COOKS: Allison Berkey and Matthew Fairman
PRODUCTION DIRECTOR: Guy Rochford
SENIOR PRODUCTION MANAGER: Jessica Quirk
PRODUCTION MANAGER: Christine Walsh
IMAGING MANAGER: Lauren Robbins
PRODUCTION AND IMAGING SPECIALISTS: Heather Dube, Sean MacDonald, Dennis Noble, and Jessica Voas
PROJECT MANAGER: Britt Dresser
COPY EDITOR: Cheryl Redmond
PROOFREADER: Elizabeth Wray Emery
INDEXER: Elizabeth Parson

PICTURED OPPOSITE HALF TITLE PAGE: Tortilla Soup (page 291)
PICTURED OPPOSITE TITLE PAGE: French Chicken in a Pot (page 135)
PICTURED ON CONTENTS PAGE: Chocolate Cupcakes with Ganache Filling (page 234)

AMERICA'S
TEST KITCHEN
RECIPES THAT WORK®

Master twenty recipes in this book
and you will have earned the right to
call yourself a great cook.